A Question
of Survival

A Question of Survival

Quakers in Australia in the Nineteenth Century

William Nicolle Oats

University of Queensland Press

ST LUCIA • LONDON • NEW YORK

First published 1985 by University of Queensland Press
Box 42, St Lucia, Queensland, Australia

© W.N. Oats 1985

This book is copyright. Apart from any fair dealing for the
purposes of private study, research, criticism or review, as
permitted under the Copyright Act, no part may be reproduced
by any process without written permission. Enquiries should
be made to the publisher.

Typeset by University of Queensland Press
Designed by Paul Rendle
Printed in Australia by Dominion Press—Hedges & Bell, Melbourne

Distributed in the USA and Canada by University of Queensland Press,
5 South Union Street, Lawrence, Mass. 01843 USA

Cataloguing in Publication Data

National Library of Australia

Oats, William Nicolle, 1912—
   A question of survival.

   Bibliography.
   Includes index.

   1. Society of Friends — Australia — History
   2. Quakers — Australia — History. I. Title

289.6'94

Library of Congress

Oats, William Nicolle, 1912—
   A question of survival.

   Bibliography: p.
   Includes index.
   1. Society of Friends—Australia—History—19th
century. 2. Quakers—Australia—History—19th century.
3. Australia—Church history. I. Title.
BX7725.018   1985   289.6'94   84-2351

ISBN 0 7022 1708 5

Contents

List of Illustrations   *vii*
List of Tables   *ix*
Acknowledgments   *x*
Introduction   *xiii*

Part One: Quaker Migration to Australia

1   The Background of English Quakerism   *3*
2   The First Thousand Quaker Migrants to Australia   *26*
3   Quaker Attitudes to Migration   *50*
    Personal Motivation   *50*
    Corporate Concern   *61*

Part Two: Quakers in Australia: 1770–1861

Introductory Note   *75*
4   Backhouse and Walker   *78*
    The Gospel of Christian Love   *83*
    Prisons and Penal Reform   *87*
    Australian Aborigines   *102*
    The Temperance Cause   *115*
    A Place in History   *117*
5   Quakers in Van Diemen's Land   *127*
    Australia's First Quaker Meeting   *127*
    The Convicted   *138*
    The Disowned   *153*
    The Convinced   *160*
    George Washington Walker   *164*
6   Quakers in New South Wales   *170*
    John Tawell   *173*
    The Sydney Meeting   *188*

7   Quakers in South Australia   195
       John Barton Hack   196
       Adelaide's Quaker Meeting House   206
       A Quaker Community of Families   213
       Early Difficulties   216
8   Quakers in Victoria   232
       The Lure of Gold   232
       The Irish Connection   240
       Lindsey and Mackie   245
       The Melbourne Meeting   248

Part Three: Quakers in Australia: 1862–1901

Introductory Note   257
9   The Years 1862–1875   260
       Quakers in Ballarat   262
       Quakers in South Australia — and India   264
       Quakers in Hobart   269
       Quakers in Sydney   269
       Quakers in Queensland   278
       The Australian Deputation — 1875   285
10 Towards an Australian Quakerism:
       1875–1901   291
       The Role of English Friends   291
       Growing Points for the Development
          of an Australian Identity   305
       Towards an Australian General Meeting   324
11 Retrospect: 1832–1901   331
       Quaker Migrations to America   331
       Migration of Quakers to Australia   335
       A Question of Survival   338

Appendix 1   Biographical Index of Quakers in Australia
                 before 1862   350
Appendix 2   Visiting Friends from Overseas,
                 1832–1901   360
Abbreviations   362
Notes to Text   363
Bibliography   387
Index   401

Illustrations

1. Entrances to Port Davey   xii
2. Sydney Parkinson   76
3. James Backhouse   80
4. George Washington Walker   80
5. David Stead   130
6. Friends' Meeting House, Hobart   133
7. Elinor Clifton   135
8. Friends' Meeting House, Australind   135
9. Francis Cotton   154
10. "Kelvedon", East Coast of Tasmania   154
11. G.W. Walker's drapery shop and savings bank   167
12. First Friends' Meeting House, Sydney   179
13. Second Friends' Meeting House, Sydney   180
14. John Barton Hack   198
15. Jacob Hagen   198
16. Friends' Meeting House, Adelaide   206
17. Joseph May   217
18. "Fairfield", Mount Barker   217
19. Frederick Mackie   221
20. Friends' Meeting House, Melbourne   251
21. Joseph James Neave   273
22. Friends' Meeting House, Brisbane   280
23. Friends' Meeting House, Rockhampton   281
24. Francis and Felicia Hopkins   282
25. William Hopkins   282
26. Edwin Ransome   294
27. Joseph Francis Mather   295
28. First committee of the Friends' School, Hobart   307
29. "Hobartville"   309
30. Samuel Clemes   310

Tables

1. Quakers in Australia 1852—54   27
2. Quaker migration to Australia before 1862   31
3. Loss of membership before 1862   33
4. Analysis of disownments of Quaker migrants   36
5. Disownments in English Meetings 1800—51   36
6. Analysis of reasons for resignations   38
7. Arrivals of Quaker migrants in the colonies before 1852   39
8. Meetings of origin   40
9. Pattern of occupations of Quaker migrants to Australia   42
10. Attendance of migrants at Quaker schools   46
11. Membership records of Adelaide Monthly Meeting   265

Acknowledgments

I have enjoyed writing this book. There was so much of interest and inspiration in the lives of those whose footsteps I followed into the past. The tracking itself was the easier, not only because of the care which Quakers took in recording faithfully details of births, marriages, and deaths and the Minutes of their corporate decisions, but also because they added the flesh and blood of lively letter-writing and daily diary commentary to this skeletal information.

I have enjoyed too discovering the part played by Quakers in the early white settlement of Australia. They are part of the history which our Bicentennial will celebrate in 1988. Sections of chapter four of this book have already appeared in a volume, *Backhouse and Walker,* published in 1982 to mark the sesqui-centenary of the arrival in Van Diemen's Land of these two English Quakers.

Many people have helped me. The granting of a fellowship at Woodbrooke College, Birmingham, and support from the Paul Cadbury and Geraldine S. Cadbury Trusts made it possible for the basic research to be undertaken in England. My personal thanks are due to Paul Cadbury, to John Punshon at Woodbrooke, to Ted Milligan and Malcolm Thomas at Friends' House Library, London, who tenderly guided my research into the wealth of Australian Quaker material held there, to the members of the Friends' Historical Society at Eustace Street, Dublin, and to the Clerks and archivists of at least fifty English Quaker Monthly Meetings, who shepherded my wanderings in search of the Quaker origins of over a thousand Quaker-connected settlers in Australia before 1862.

In Australia also there are too many to thank individually, but I gratefully acknowledge the assistance of the

Australia Yearly Meeting of the Religious Society of Friends, the continuing help of Dan Sprod, the publisher of my two other books on Australian Quaker history, and of Professor Michael Roe, the eminent Australian historian, who gave me invaluable detailed comments as each chapter was written.

I acknowledge gratefully permission received from the Oxford University Press to use information on Quaker occupations in Elizabeth Isichei's *Victorian Quakers*; from the Mitchell Library, Sydney; and from Peter Benson Walker, Hobart, for access to the Journals of Backhouse and Walker; from the State Library of Victoria to quote an extract from the manuscript *Foster Fyans, Reminiscences*; and from the National Library of Australia, the State Library of South Australia, and the University of Tasmania to reprint illustrations.

Many Friends have supplied me with historical material. Four of these, Charles Stevenson, Vaughn Evans, Nancie Hewitt, and Arthur Clarke, have already contributed much to the writing of Australian Quaker history.

My wife, Marjorie, has given me unwavering support and encouragement. Without her this book would have been neither attempted nor completed.

Entrances to Port Davey, Van Diemen's Land from a sketch by James Backhouse, engraved in England by his cousin, Edward Backhouse. In James Backhouse, *A Narrative of a Visit to the Australian Colonies* (London: Hamilton, Adams, 1843).

Introduction

From James Backhouse, A Narrative of a Visit to the Australian Colonies (pp. 44-45).

On the morning of the 4th of 6th month, land was descried through the hazy atmosphere, and all sail was made with a varying but generally favourable wind, till we came distinctly in view of Cape Sorell, at the entrance of Macquarie Harbour. On approaching nearer we were thrown into much perplexity, no signal being made from the pilot's station for an hour and a half, either to approach nearer or to stand off. During this time we stood backward and forward outside the dangerous bar, which is of wide extent, while the sea was again getting up. At length, when about to run back for shelter to Port Davey, we were descried, and a signal to enter was hoisted.

We immediately stood in, and in a few minutes the opportunity to return was past. The pilot put off, knowing better than ourselves, our danger: his boat could only be seen now and then above the billows; but he was soon alongside, and ordered all the sails to be squared, that we might go right before the wind.

On coming on board, he commanded the women and children below, and then came to me, and advised me to go below also. I replied that if we were lost I should like to see the last of it, for the sight was awfully grand.

Laying hold of a rope at the stern, he said, "Then put your arm round this rope and don't speak a word." To my companion he gave similar instructions, placing him at the opposite quarter. A man was sent into the chains on each side, with the sounding lead. The pilot went to the bows, and nothing was now to be heard through the roar of the wind and the waves, but his voice calling to the helmsman, the helmsman's answer, and the voices of men in the chains, counting off the fathoms as the water became shallower.

The vessel was cast alternately from one side to the other, to prevent her sticking on the sand, in which case the billows would have run over her, and have driven her upon a sandbank a mile from the shore, on which they were breaking with fury.

The fathoms decreased, and the men counted off the feet, of which we drew 7½, and there were but seven in the hollow of the sea, until they called out eleven feet. At this moment a huge billow carried us forward on its raging head into deep water.

The pilot's countenance relaxed: he looked like a man reprieved from the gallows, and coming aft, shook hands with each individual, congratulating them on a safe arrival in Macquarie Harbour.

James Backhouse's pen-sketch of his entry into Port Davey and his word-picture of the dangerous passage through Hell's Gates into Tasmania's West Coast Macquarie Harbour provide, as it were, a background for this story of another kind of venture.

In the first half of the nineteenth century Quakers were amongst the many migrants who left England to face the anxieties and perils of entry into a new and strange land. They brought with them their Quaker testimonies and practices. The difficulties they faced are the subject of this book.

Not only were there the problems which faced every settler of coming to terms with a harsh and threatening environment, with loneliness and isolation. Their Quakerism also was on trial and their way of life was being tested. In Van Diemen's Land a significant proportion of the first members consisted of convicts. In Sydney the early history of the Quaker Meeting was bound up more than members wished to admit with one who was later hanged for murder. In South Australia early promise of "a new Pennsylvania of the South" was blighted by financial depression and a crisis of confidence. In Victoria the lure of gold presented the threat of materialism in a new guise.

The English Quakerism they knew and brought with them was itself going through a period of questioning and change, which led to its being labelled by some Quaker historians as "the darkest period of Quakerism".

How then did Quakerism stand the test? For Quakerism, the institution, it came to be a question of survival. There were times when Quakerism could easily have gone under and left only jetsam on the waters of history. That the institution survived to enter with hope upon the twentieth century was due to the quality of life of individual Quakers, whose story is the purpose of this book.

The answer to "A Question of Survival" lies in a remarkable series of Quakers, a veritable "Quaker apostolic succession". Without them there would be no story to tell.

PART ONE

Quaker Migration to Australia

One
The Background of English Quakerism

To understand the history of Quakers in Australia in the nineteenth century it is necessary to see that history against the background of Quakerism in Great Britain and Ireland, for Australian Quakers were conditioned by their upbringing in British and Irish Quaker homes and by their membership of their home Quaker Meetings. They would have had an image of what it meant for them to "be" "Quakers" and of what would be expected of them if they bore that name.

The original name by which the followers of George Fox were known as early as 1652 was "Friends in the Truth". They did not look upon themselves as a separate sect. The term "Quaker" was a nickname, coined as the result of a courtroom rejoinder by Fox to the judge, Gervase Bennett, who was examining him on a charge of blasphemy. Fox said that Justice Bennett "first called us Quakers because we bid them tremble at the word of God, and this was in the year 1650".[1]

The term "Society of Friends" began to be used towards the end of the eighteenth century.[2] Until the end of the eighteenth century the term "People called Quakers" was in general use. The full descriptive term used now is "The Religious Society of Friends (Quakers)". "Quaker" tends to be the more popular usage, the more distinctive, whereas "The Society of Friends" carries an institutional flavour.

A brief survey of the origins and development of the Society of Friends will help to explain why Quakers acted as they did when they attempted to practise their Quakerism in the strange environment of the Colonies.

Quakerism had its beginnings in the middle of the seventeenth century. England was then in a state of political and religious turmoil that left many feeling that they no longer knew where they might find the truth by which to live. They had come to trust the outward authority of neither state nor church. Ritual had lost its meaning and creeds their relevance. A gap had opened up between profession and practice.

The appearance of George Fox had a catalytic effect upon those who were called "Seekers". Under this name were grouped those who were dissatisfied with the religious sects of their day and who were awaiting expectantly new light and guidance. George Fox crystallized for them what many had felt but could not formulate. Seekers became finders. For George Fox himself the revelation came when he discovered that the answer to his searching lay, not in priests or "professors", but in the discovery of an inward voice which said, "There is one, even Christ Jesus, that can speak to thy condition".[3] For George Fox this was a rediscovery of what he felt had happened to the first Christians, who went out filled with the Holy Spirit. He used the metaphor-words of the "seed" and the "light" to communicate his experience. The light of Christ was within the heart of every human being: it was universal. On Pendle Hill in Yorkshire Fox had a vision of "a great people to be gathered".[4] "He saw people", said William Penn, "as thick as motes in the sun, that should in time be brought to the Lord, that there might be but one shepherd and one sheepfold in all the earth."[5] The vision, it has been said, caught on like a brushfire. Indeed, fired by Fox's assurance, the early Quakers made a profound impression on many thousands of people as they spread their message through the villages and towns of England with something of a revolutionary ecstasy.

Puritan and Anglican alike, seeing their authority threatened, reacted with persecution and imprisonment. Thousands of Quakers, men and women, were imprisoned and many died in dungeons. The violence of the reaction of church and civil authorities was largely the result of the Quakers' determination to translate their vision into practice in their daily lives. They were nothing if not thorough in their attempt to make practice cohere with principle. The core of that vision was that God was present in every human being, that thereby direct communion between God and man was possible without the intervention of a priest, that the knowledge of this presence and a turning to this light of Christ in the heart could transform one's life and indeed could so transform a community. In the context of the religious outlook of the seventeenth century, George Fox's proclamation that "Christ has come to teach his people himself" was seen as blasphemy.

To the onlooker the Quaker presented a negative and therefore a threatening image — no priest, no liturgy, no sacrament (and therefore no baptism), no creed. To the Quaker each of these negatives was the result of a positive affirmation: no priest, because all believers were priests and could commune direct in the heart with the Holy Spirit; no liturgy, because to worship was to listen in silence to the voice of God within — a spontaneous, not a predetermined, prepared, other-person-directed activity; no sacrament, because the whole of life was sacramental, and therefore no day, nor act, nor moment should be separated from its potential for revealing the presence of God; no baptism with water but baptism with the Holy Spirit, for all were birthright children of God; no creed, because truth cannot be confined within the limits of any fixed man-made form of words.

John Wilhelm Rowntree summed up the positive basis of the Quaker reliance on the reality of the inward experience and not on the outward form or symbol.

> To the soul that feeds upon the bread of life the outward conventions of religion are no longer needful. Hid with Christ in God, there is for him small place for outward rites, for all experience is a holy baptism, a perpetual supper with the Lord, and all life a sacrifice, holy and acceptable unto God. This hidden life, this inward vision, this immediate and intimate union between the soul and God, this, as revealed in Jesus Christ, is the basis of the Quaker faith.[6]

The "Inward Light of Christ in the heart" led Quakers to affirm in their personal living the need for speaking the truth in their relations with others, for honesty in business dealings, for recognition of the equality of all in the sight of God, and for simplicity in personal and family life.

Speaking the truth in all circumstances led to the refusal to swear an oath. By Act of Parliament in 1749 (22 George II)

Quakers were granted the concession of affirmation except in criminal cases, or service on juries, or for bearing any office or place of profit in government. By the time Quakers needed to claim this right in Australia, these exceptions had been removed in English law by an Act of 3 and 4 of William IV in 1833 which declared that "every person of the persuasion of the people called Quakers be permitted to make his or her solemn oath, in all places and for all purposes whatsoever where an oath is or shall be required". Quakers quoted scriptural justification for this testimony, for, they said, did not Jesus command, "I say unto you: swear not at all"[7] and "Let your yea be yea, your nay, nay."[8] This had particular repercussions in courts of law.

The application of honesty to business dealings gained for Quakers not only a reputation for trustworthiness and a recognition that a Quaker's "fair price" did not admit of bargaining, but also notable success in trading. As they prospered and as honesty proved to make very good business sense, they became very jealous of this reputation for straight and honourable dealing. For this reason they maintained in their Meetings a watchful eye over the financial health of their members and reacted very sternly to any evidence of malpractice or failure to pay just debts.

Members kept watch over each other in things temporal as well as eternal and if any member was said to be in financial difficulties, visitors were appointed to enquire into the state of his affairs. If it could be shown that the reasons for failure might have been beyond his control, and if he showed unmistakable intention of repaying creditors to the limit of his ability, no disownment would be pursued by the Meeting. If, however, the Meeting was not satisfied on these two points, the minute of disownment made it clear that the offender had damaged not only his own reputation but also that of the Society in the eyes of the community.

Ignatieff's comments on the disownment of Friends for dishonesty in business and in certain cases for insolvency are relevant here. "By expelling any Friend found guilty of dishonest business practice," he said, "they gained a reputation of probity that served them well as bankers."[9] It was no accident, therefore, that some of the pioneers of banking such as the Barclays and Lloyds were Quakers. The more successful Quakers became in business, the more jealously did they guard this reputation for honesty, for this reputation was part of the image of the nineteenth-century Quaker. Failure to live up to this image had a stigmatic effect on the defaulter, even if he had failed through the operation of market forces beyond his immediate control. It is understandable therefore that not a few Quakers, faced with the social effect of disownment by their Meetings, sought escape from alienation by migration.

Belief in the equality of all found expression, for example, in the recognition given to the role of women in the Society of Friends. Women were to share in the active life of the Meetings as elders, overseers, and ministers, but men and women still continued to hold separate sessions at London Yearly Meeting until 1896. Additional Meetings were held after 1896 until 1908, which was the first year when separate Women's Meetings ceased to be held.

The outward expression of the testimony to simplicity led to what were later regarded as Quaker "peculiarities". Yet at first the outward expression was a relevant response to a contemporary situation and stemmed from an inward conviction that practice should cohere with principle. Simplicity called for plainness of dress, for men the collarless coat and broad-brimmed hat, for women the Quaker bonnet and dress of sober grey. This was a response to the lavish spending in the Restoration period on dress and adornment. Retention of the Quaker dress was, in a sense, a protest against the unwarranted demands of changing fashion.[10] The testimony to simplicity also led to a number of peculiarities of speech, or what Quakers called "Address". A testimony to equality as well as to simplicity lay in the use of the singular "thou" in place of the plural "you" when speaking to individuals. "You" had originated in the practice of addressing so-called "superiors" by the use of the plural form, a mark of flattery.[11] Similarly the addresses of Mr, Mrs and Miss and all acknowledgment of complimentary titles or decorations were avoided. Plainness of speech therefore led to the use of the simple "Mary Smith" in place of Mrs or Lady Smith. Days of the week were to be labelled simply "first day", instead of the pagan name "Sunday"; months of the year by "first month", instead of names derived from what were considered pagan deities. A refusal to doff the hat, except in the presence of God in solemn acts of worship, led, like the use of "thou" to a superior, to many confrontations with authority in court, church, or public life. George Fox was amazed at the virulence of the reaction.

> Oh, the rage and scorn, the heat and fury that arose! Oh, the blows, punchings, beatings, and imprisonments that we underwent for not putting off our hats to men! For that soon tried all men's patience and sobriety, what it was. Some had their hats violently plucked off and thrown away so that they quite lost them. . . . And though it was but a small thing in the eye of man, yet a wonderful confusion it brought among all professors and priests. But, blessed be the Lord, many came to see the vanity of that custom of putting off the hat to men, and felt the weight of Truth's testimony against it.[12]

Thomas Clarkson, who in 1807 wrote a lengthy three-volume *Portraiture of Quakerism*, gave a particularly perceptive image of a Quaker of this period. He was writing as an Anglican clergyman and not as a Quaker, but he was a sympathetic friend of Quakers, for he had worked closely with them in the anti-slavery movement and had come to respect them in spite of some of their "peculiar" customs, such as those of "Dress and Address". What he wrote is relevant to an understanding of the image conjured up by the term "Quaker" at the time Quakers were migrating to the colonies. He said that he found the differences suggested by this image "entertaining", for they tended to draw attention to many things that had ceased to be considered important by the nineteenth century — a sort of vestigial Quakerism. Some Quaker practices had persisted when the reasons for their particular relevance had ceased to exist. Clarkson had in mind those practices mentioned above, the use of "thou", the adoption of simple Quaker dress, and the replacement of what Quakers held to be "pagan" names for days of the week and months. Yet Clarkson appreciated the moral reasons behind those odd survivals of earlier practice and, behind the moral reasons, the basic Quaker belief in the Inward Light, which was both teacher and guide, and universal.

Confrontation with authority, either of state or church, was not sought deliberately, but was the inevitable result of Quakers' upholding the supremacy of the individual conscience where the laws of God and man were in tension. This tension sharpened into confrontation on two particular issues, refusal to pay tithes and refusal to bear arms.

Refusal to pay tithes had its roots in opposition to the payment of priests.[13] They therefore refused to pay taxes to support the clergy and the established church. For this they suffered severely, their property being confiscated, or "distrained". It was alleged in 1834 by what was held to be a competent authority that the total loss up to that year to members of the Society of Friends through distraints of property amounted to £1,143,000.[14] Though tithes were not to be an issue in the Australian context, they had some bearing on Quaker migration. No relaxation in payment of tithes was conceded until 1837, when tithes were changed to rent charges on land payable to the State and not direct to the Church. Nevertheless some Quaker farmers, threatened with distraints if they refused to pay tithes and with disownment by their Monthly Meeting if they did, gave up the struggle and left their farms and migrated. Tithes also affected the small trader, probably more seriously than the small farmer, for not only did he have to face distraint of property, but the possibility that this meant loss of stock and eventual insolvency. Quakers complained bitterly that the amount of goods distrained far exceeded in value the amount of the tithes refused. This niggling and persistent oppression was but one more inducement to consider migration.

The refusal to bear arms came from a positive declaration by George Fox of the power of love. The Quaker Peace Testimony, for which perhaps the Society of Friends has come to be most widely known, stemmed from George Fox's declaration to the Commonwealth Commissioners when he refused the offer of a commission in Cromwell's army. "I told [them]", he said, "I lived in virtue of that life and power that took away the occasion of all wars."[15] Though individual Friends have interpreted this testimony in varied ways, the Society of Friends, as a religious body, has maintained a clear record of faithful adherence to George Fox's declaration.

Quaker social concerns, like their testimonies, sprang from the common root of their belief in the presence of God within everyone. Education had been a concern of Friends as early as 1668, when George Fox urged the foundation of schools for girls as well as boys. "Then I came to Waltham and established a school there (for teaching of boys) and ordered a women's school to be set up at Shacklewell to instruct young lasses and maidens in whatsoever things were civil and useful in creation."[16] By 1840, at the time of the main flow of migrants to Australia, there were at least sixty-seven Friends' schools operating in England, for this was the number listed by a Friend, Edwin Tregelles, for visiting in that year.[17] Many of these were private schools run by individuals who were members of the Society of Friends and only eight were schools which could be classified as Friends' Schools attached to Meetings of the Society of Friends. Most of those emigrating by the mid-nineteenth century could be expected to have had a Friends' School education and therefore to have regarded Friends' schooling as an integral part of their Quaker tradition. Other social concerns which were to have echoes in the colonies were prison reform, protection of native races from exploitation by white settlers, and the cause of Temperance.

Quakers had known the inside of gaols from personal experience. Thousands of seventeenth-century Quakers had been imprisoned for their steadfast adherence to their faith. Charges levelled against them were blasphemy, because of their insistence on the Indwelling Spirit of God, refusal to pay tithes, or to swear oaths, or to perform military service. By the time persecution finally eased with the proclaiming of a Royal Pardon in March 1686, thousands had been in gaol, many for long periods. Over 400 are said to have died in prison. Immediately after the Royal Pardon a Royal Warrant released over 1400 Quakers imprisoned for non-attendance at church. Their belief that there was "that of God" even in the abandoned and depraved made them ready supporters of nineteenth-century prison reformers such as Howard. "When Howard set out to harmonize the imperatives of discipline and humanity," said Ignatieff, "Quakers were among the first in his support."[18] Leading Quakers were prominent in such organizations as the Prison Discipline Society, founded in 1817, and the Prison Reform Society. It was Stephen Grellet who is said to have introduced Elizabeth Fry to Newgate Gaol,[19] and Elizabeth Fry who turned James Backhouse's thoughts to visiting penal settlements in the Australian colonies.

The Aborigines Protection Society was founded in 1837 "to promote the interests of native races, especially those under British control, by providing correct information, by appealing to the Government and to Parliament when appeal is needed, and by bringing public opinion to exert its proper influence in advancing the cause of justice".[20] This Society attempted to stir the British conscience to feel a sense of concern for the native peoples wherever these were subject to exploitation by white settlers. One hundred and fifty years earlier William Penn had set the pattern for Quaker action by his sympathetic treatment of the Indians in America. Publications of the Society of Friends, under the stimulus of the Aborigines Protection Society, carried reports of exploitation from the colonies and it was not long before the Australian Aborigines found prominence in these journals.

Until the eighteen-thirties temperance was the subject of advice to Friends rather than a distinct concern. Prominent Quaker names had been connected with the business of brewing, but it was the social effects of the excessive drinking of what were called "ardent spirits" which aroused many Friends in the nineteenth century to take Temperance as a social cause and to give Temperance a capital T.[21]

The deplorable effects of rum-drinking were reported by Friends such as Backhouse visiting the Australian colonies and these reports were not without influence in effecting this capital transformation.

Thus by the mid-nineteenth century there were certain practices and attitudes which were expected of those called "Quakers". Quakers were recognizable not only by the externals of dress and speech and by their non-conformity in matters of worship, oath-swearing, army service, and deference to "superiors", but also by the causes they espoused and by their testimonies to simplicity of living, honourable practice in business, and truth-speaking.

To "be" a "Quaker" also implied membership of a Quaker Meeting. A Quaker belonged to a cohesive group and was subject to a well-defined discipline. Membership could be obtained in two ways. If both parents were members, it was likely that registration of the child had taken place from birth, with no further decision on membership being required of such "birthright" members. Membership could also be by application through "convincement". In this case members would have been appointed by the Monthly Meeting to visit the applicant and determine whether the responsibilities of membership were understood and accepted.

Membership involved participation in the corporate meetings of the Society, both in the Meeting for Worship and the Meeting for Church Affairs. The Meeting for Worship was regarded as the fount from which came inspiration and guidance for the individual and for the Society. Meetings for Church Affairs were held regularly and were intended to be conducted in a spirit of worship. One of the queries Quakers addressed to themselves emphasized this view of the Meeting for Church Affairs as an extension of the Meeting for Worship. "Are your Meetings for Church Affairs held in loving dependence upon the Spirit of God?"[22]

The Monthly Meeting was the decision-making body, admitting applicants to membership and, where it was felt necessary, terminating membership. It had organizational and disciplinary functions: organizational because it required accurate and faithful maintenance of records and proper attention to the business affairs of the Meeting; disciplinary because, through its overseers, it watched over its members, giving pastoral care and, where necessary, admonition if there was any evidence of departure from what was held to be accepted Quaker practice.

Quakers who emigrated to Australia remained until 1861 members of their original Monthly Meetings in England or Ireland, even though they were thousands of miles distant. This separation was to present unexpected problems of communication and discipline for both the Monthly Meetings and their distant members.

The Monthly Meeting itself was a cluster of local Meetings, called "Preparative", which were recognized as having the duty to "prepare" and bring up matters for consideration at Monthly Meetings. Monthly Meetings in turn were grouped in districts as Quarterly Meetings. These acted as Meetings of Appeal against decisions of Monthly Meetings and exercised a disciplinary role over the constituent Monthly Meetings by requiring them to submit answers periodically to a series of set queries designed to remind these Meetings of their own disciplinary duties. Hours were spent religiously — and laboriously — recording the results of such periodic self-examination. The Quarterly Meeting was also a clearing-house for matters which eventually found their way to the Yearly Meeting in London, the decision-making body for Friends in Great Britain. Ireland had its own independent Yearly Meeting.

The word "concern" has had a particularly Quaker usage and connotation. It denotes not simply a "concern about" or a "concern for" but carries the implied meaning of what has been called[23] "a gift from God, a leading of His Spirit which may not be denied". This "concern" is shared by the member with his Monthly Meeting, which often expresses its support or otherwise for the genuineness of the "leading" and for the practicality of what the member proposes to do about the concern to which he is willing to commit himself. Corporate action by the Society may well be the ultimate result of one member's 'concern" and of commitment to that "concern".

The sieve-like processing of concerns, beginning from the Preparative Meeting through successively the Monthly Meeting and Quarterly Meeting to the Yearly Meeting, meant that when a decision was finally taken, there was some guarantee that it had been given weighty prior consideration. This is seen, for example, in the way decisions were reached about "travelling in the ministry". The term "minister" had a specific meaning. When a Meeting felt that a member had shown special gifts for "ministering" or speaking in Meetings for Worship, such a member, man or woman, would be "recognized" and recorded as a "minister".[24] Only such members were given authority by the Meeting to "travel in the ministry", expenses for such travel being accepted by the appropriate Monthly, Quarterly, or Yearly Meeting. During the early years of the Meetings in the Australian colonies, travelling ministers going out with the full backing of London Yearly Meeting were to play a significant role in the development of Quakerism in Australia. Those who felt a special concern to make the long voyage to the colonies had first to take their concern through the testing progression of Meetings to a special Yearly Meeting of Ministers and Overseers, held at the time of London Yearly Meeting.

The Monthly Meetings however had social as well as organizational and disciplinary functions. Their records, dating in some cases back to 1669, provided a register of births, marriages, and deaths of members. The necessity to know which Monthly Meeting the poor had claims on for assistance had led in 1737 to inordinately complex rules on removals and settlement by London Yearly Meeting: these lasted until 1861. The Monthly Meeting had to accept responsibility for its poor. The question was to arise later whether this responsibility extended twelve thousand miles away to migrant members who had fallen on bad times in the colonies.

Monthly Meetings also accepted responsibility for the vocational training of their younger members. Friends not only looked after their young apprentices during their training, but they also endeavoured to place them with Quaker employers who could be expected to exercise on them a Quaker influence.

A typical example is that of George Armfield, a member of Southwark Monthly Meeting, London. Minutes of this Meeting recorded his apprenticeship to a coach-builder.

10 i 1832 Southwark Monthly Meeting accepts responsibility to find apprenticeship for George Armfield (age 14).

9 xi 1832 A five-pound apprenticeship fee is paid by Southwark M.M. for George Armfield's apprenticeship with a Friend, Arthur Nainby.
A twenty-pound gratuity is available "under William Howard's legacy to young men bound apprentice with their Meeting."

In 1853 George Armfield emigrated to South Australia and

applied his coach-building skill to the less glamorous but allied trade of a wheelwright.

A Quaker migrant was likely to miss this closeness of association with his Meeting and to feel a sense of social deprivation. He no longer had the companionship of other members of the Meeting, nor the social contacts on the days of Monthly Meetings. Membership at a distance did not bring much comfort in times of loneliness and need. It was understandable therefore that the isolated member might be tempted to turn to other religious communities to satisfy his social and religious needs.

It was also likely that members who had experienced the disciplinary powers of their Meetings in England and Ireland would not be unwilling to put some distance between themselves and those who had pronounced sentence of disownment upon them. The figures given in chapter two[25] indicate that a significant proportion of Quakers migrating had at the time of their departure already been disowned by their Meetings.

The most common ground for disownment was for "marrying out", that is, for marrying one who was not a member of the Society of Friends. At first sight this appears to represent a harsh and even bigoted attitude to those outside the membership of the Society. This judgment however must be tempered in the light of the historical background. Quakers had struggled to gain recognition of the right to marry in their own meeting-houses without priest or civil registrar. George Fox had opposed the idea of priestly interference or of making marriage merely a civil contract. "Marriage", he said, "was God's joining, not man's." Man was but a witness, the declaration of marriage being made by each, the man and the woman, in the presence of God. He laid down however such clear-cut procedures for the marriage of Friends that he won the right for Friends to have marriages conducted according to these procedures which were recognized as legal. The procedures included the giving of ample notice of intended marriage, public announcement of such intention, prior investigation by Friends of the "clearness" of both parties to enter into marriage, and celebration of the marriage in a place open to the public. All present signed the certificate, which was then available to the magistrate as evidence of the marriage. Recognition of Quaker marriages was given as early as 1661 in civil law judgments, and children of such marriages were regarded as legitimate. Quakers were said to have made it abundantly clear to the authorities that, rather than accept the intolerable alternatives offered to them, they would live together as man and wife without any legal ceremony at all.[26] In 1753 Quakers were the only sect, apart from Jews, legally able to celebrate marriages in their Meeting-houses, provided both parties were members of the Society of Friends.[27] In 1837 specific conditions were laid down by Act of Parliament "that the Society of Friends, commonly called Quakers, may continue to contract and solemnize marriage, according to the usages of the said Society; and every such marriage is hereby declared and confirmed good in law, provided that both parties to the said marriage be both of the said Society: provided also that notice to the superintendent registrar shall have been given and the said registrar's certificate shall have been issued in the provided."[28]

From the wording of both the Acts of 1753 and 1837 it will be seen that Friends had to insist on both partners being members of the Society for the marriage to be recognized in law. It was not until after the London Yearly Meeting of 1859 that disownment for marrying out was discontinued and that Friends' marriage usage was made available to those "in profession with Friends" as well as those who were members.[29] The Yearly Meeting hastened to make it clear that "in extending the liberty of allowing marriages to be solemnized in our Meetings, beyond the line of membership, it is not intended by such marriages to confer on the contracting parties, or on their offspring, any right of membership, or any claims of maintenance".[30]

The unfortunate result of disownment for "marrying out" was that the minute of disownment often read almost as if it were the sentencing of a criminal in the dock. What was technically unlawful was made to appear immoral and sinful. Further, disownment meant separation from the fellowship of a closely knit group. Barclay Fox[31] confessed in his journal that disownment sounded so "like loss of caste. I cannot believe", he added, "that a religious body has any right to alienate one of its body who concurs with them in faith and practice and commits no breach either of the human, moral or religious law." A sentence of disownment for the Quaker could have had much the same impact as a sentence of excommunication upon the faithful Catholic. This may well have been for some of the disowned the added incentive to seek in migration escape from what Barclay Fox called "loss of caste".

One indication of the Society's recognition of the serious effects of disownment on members was their decision in 1832 to set up a school, Rawdon, for the children of those who had been disowned. This had been the result of a conference at the London Yearly Meeting of 1827 to consider "providing for the education of children, descendants of those who have forfeited their membership in the Society of Friends, or such as profess with Friends and are not in membership".[32] Three more schools were set up in quick succession — Penketh in 1834, Ayton in 1841 and Sibford in 1842. Nevertheless the sting of disownment must still have rankled.

Two particular features of English Quakerism were dominant in the period 1835–55, the main period of Quaker migration to Australia.

The first was the strength of the Evangelical influence upon the Society of Friends, and the second was the increasing emphasis placed by the Society on outward and formal discipline, which led Rufus Jones to label this period "the darkest and saddest in the history of Quakerism".[33]

By 1835, a serious rift had developed between two extremes of religious thought in London Yearly Meeting. During the period of what was called "Quietism" Quakers tended to become more concerned with the development of the inner life than with the state of the world about them. Relying on "the pure spirit of God's guidance", as they put it, they waited in silence in expectation of God's intervention. Anything in the nature of preparation, or of "creaturely activity", such as the reading of the Scriptures in Meeting for Worship, was frowned upon. True, this direct experience of the inward authority, the light of Christ within, had been the core of the message of George Fox, for he had rejected reliance upon the external authority of priest, book, ritual, or creed. The Quietists, in rejecting any external assistance whatever, had created another imbalance by total reliance upon inward authority. The steady growth of the influence of the Evangelicals in Quaker Meetings in the nineteenth century can be seen as a reaction against the extreme of Quietism and a move to correct the imbalance.

The social activism of the Evangelicals, expressed in such movements as the anti-slavery crusade, made a powerful impact on Quakers. The Quietist period had left many Quakers feeling spiritually destitute and therefore ready to respond to Evangelical fervour. The Evangelical espousal of social causes both awoke the dormant social conscience of Quakers and provided a means of satisfying any qualms of conscience provoked by the unlooked-for acquisition of worldly wealth. This view is supported by Ignatieff. "The evangelicals' call for social activism had a powerful effect on Quakers, partly because it appealed to their long-standing philanthropic tradition, but also because its attack on materialism called them back from worldly success to the rigors of their own past."[34]

A growing interest in philanthropy at the turn of the nineteenth century provided a common meeting ground for Quakers and Evangelicals. Quakers took a very active part in the anti-slavery movement and worked closely with Evangelicals from other churches. T. Fowell Buxton, one of the leaders of the anti-slavery campaign, was closely linked with Friends. His mother was a member of the Society and he married Hannah Gurney, a sister of Elizabeth Fry. What is not generally known is that Buxton applied for and was granted membership by Devonshire House Monthly Meeting in 1807, shortly before he married Hannah Gurney at Earlham on 13 May 1807. Hannah Buxton was disowned by Devonshire House M.M. in 1816 for non-attendance, and T. Fowell Buxton for the same reason in 1817. Wilberforce was a great friend of the Quaker family of Gurneys and of Clarkson who has already been noted as the author of what Rufus Jones called "one of the most important expositions of Quakerism that has ever been written by an outsider — *A Portraiture of Quakerism.*[35]

Friends like William Allen in his opposition to the slave trade and Peter Bedford in his work for the depressed Spitalfield weavers were prominent in the great humanitarian movements of the early nineteenth century. Others, like William Forster and Elizabeth Fry, aroused the public conscience about conditions in prisons. All these brought a revived sense of social concern into Friends' Meetings, but with this came also a growing Evangelical influence. The extent of this influence can be seen in the Epistle of London Yearly Meeting in 1836.

> In conformity with these principles it has ever been, and still is, the belief of the Society of Friends, that the Holy Scriptures of the Old and New Testament were given by the inspiration of God; that therefore the declarations contained in them rest on the authority of God himself, and there can be no appeal from them to any other authority whatsoever.[36]

The doctrines of the infallibility of the Scriptures, of the Atonement and Salvation almost became accepted as the basis of a credal statement by London Yearly Meeting. This tension between the Evangelicals, upholding the centrality of these doctrines, and those Friends who maintained the traditional insistence on the authority of the Light Within, developed into an open split in American Meetings. In England there was tension, but only a relatively small schism, affecting particularly the Meeting of Hardshaw East in Lancashire, where Isaac Crewdson had gathered around him a number of Friends who held that the Inner Light was unreliable as an authority, the only sound guide being the infallible Scriptures.

The image of the Evangelical Quaker was certainly that which the Quaker migrant took with him to the colonies. This was also the image which the travelling ministers of the thirties, fifties, and seventies presented when they came out "under concern" from London Yearly Meeting to visit the scattered membership. James Backhouse and George Washington Walker, Robert Lindsey and Frederick Mackie, Isaac Sharp and Joseph James Neave, who figured so prominently in the history of Australian Quakerism, were all deeply evangelical in outlook and expression, but they did not erect into a dogma their beliefs in the Atonement,

Salvation, and the authority of the Scriptures. They were representative of Evangelicals such as Joseph John Gurney, of whom Rufus Jones said, "All that was finest, purest and most lovely in the evangelical movement came to flower in him".[37]

The Evangelical influence acted positively by reawakening the dormant Quaker social conscience and negatively by leading many Quakers to insist that doctrines of the infallibility of the Scriptures, the Atonement, and Salvation should be accepted as a credal basis by the Society of Friends.

The drift of the Society towards greater rigidity of discipline was however much more serious. Disquiet within the membership about the consequent "state of the Society" mounted steadily. Elizabeth Fry expressed on several occasions her misgivings at the way in which the Society of Friends was moving towards increasing formalism and rigidity. She felt humiliated by seeing one after another of her children brought to trial before her Meeting for marrying out. There was even a rule that Friends should not be permitted to attend such a marrying ceremony and Friends who were parents could be disowned for attending the marriage of their own children. "Bitter experience", Elizabeth Fry said, "has proved to me that Friends do rest too much on externals . . ." and has "led me earnestly to desire that we might dwell less on externals."[38]

A further example of this disquiet can be seen in the Howitt family, some of whom became well known migrants to Victoria.[39] William Howitt won wide recognition as a writer and journalist. He was a friend of Wordsworth, an admirer of Byron, and a radical — or so he was judged by some of the more conservative members of London Yearly Meeting. His wife, Mary, came from a staunch Quaker family and was also a well-known writer. Her autobiography, edited by her daughter, Margaret, reveals the reasons which prompted William and herself to resign from the Society of Friends in 1847. There is one particularly telling passage, describing the visits by Friends of Kingston Monthly Meeting on the occasion of the arrival of the Howitt family to settle in Kingston in 1837.

> Nothing has given me a more unpleasant confirmation of my opinion

of Friends' contracted and sectarian feeling than our experience in this neighbourhood, including the town of Kingston. Some Friends came from that Meeting to announce to us the receipt of our certificate, with the utmost solemnity and shut-up-ness. They never said they were glad to have an addition to their Meeting, that they hoped our residence had proved so far agreeable, or that it might be so, or even that we might have our health. They had no congratulations, no good wishes. Perhaps they felt none. But if so, it was not according to my notions of Christian charity, that wishes good to all men. They warned us against literature and politics and when William inadvertently used the word "Radical", the man-Friend asked if he thought that word a desirable one for Friends to use. Everything with these Kingston Friends was warning and prohibition. They would not read books. They would not go into society. They would not look at a newspaper, nay, even would not admit a newspaper into their houses. Now, is not this a miserable state to be in: yet these are among the approved and most orthodox members.[40]

Mary Howitt was also upset by what she felt to be the uncharitable attitude of the well-known Quakeress, Sarah Lynes Grubb, in the Yearly Meeting of 1837. "It was such a sermon as Christ would not have preached."[41] It is not surprising therefore that both William and Mary had resigned in 1847. Mary added to her report of her resignation: "And yet I do love them all with an ingrained sentiment, which makes me feel as if somehow they were kindred to me".[42]

That this unease was widespread in England and not an isolated disenchantment is shown by an advertisement which led to the publication in 1859 of *Quakerism, past and present* by John Stephenson Rowntree, an essay which was to have a profound effect on the outlook of members of the Society of Friends. The advertisement was inserted in a number of papers by a non-Friend, who wished to probe the reasons for the decline of the Society. "A gentleman who laments that, notwithstanding the population of the United Kingdom has doubled itself in the last fifty years, the Society of Friends is less in number than at the beginning of the century . . . offers a prize of one hundred guineas for the best essay that shall be written on the subject and a prize of fifty guineas for the next in merit."[43]

A significant pointer to the widespread nature of the concern about the state of the Society of Friends was the unexpected spate of entries. One hundred and fifty were submitted and wide publicity was given to the leading entries. Rowntree's *Quakerism, past and present* won the first prize. His research revealed the extent of the decline. Using membership figures in relation to the total population of the British Isles, he gave the following comparison:

> In 1680 there were 66,000 members, 1 : 130 of total population
> In 1800 there were 33,000 members, 1 : 470 of total population
> In 1840 there were 26,000 members, 1 : 1,100 of total population

Allowance for emigration to America would account for some of the drop in the figures for 1800, but Rowntree saw cause for real alarm in the 1840 figures. He further noted that in the period 1800-1859 there had been 8,400 resignations and disownments. His analysis of the reasons for decline focussed the attention of the Society on the increasing tendency to formalism of practice and rigidity of outlook.

> The increased attention to the discipline, valuable and important as it was, was too often associated with too rigid an adherence to forms and a tendency to multiply rules and to make the exact carrying of them out, in degree at least, a substitute for that patient and discriminating wisdom tempered with love which should ever characterize Christian discipline.[44]

Other reasons given for the decline included the unwillingness of Friends to accept any external aids, such as readings from the Bible, in their Meetings for Worship; the unnecessary Quaker distrust of the arts — an accident of time, and not a basic feature of Quakerism; the deadening effect of increasingly silent Meetings for Worship; the practice of acknowledging "ministers", a practice which led to the assumption that only those so acknowledged should speak in Meeting; and birthright membership, which came by accident of birth and not by conviction.

The London Yearly Meeting which followed the publication of this analysis of the decline of the Society accepted that it was time for change and modified its stand on disownment for marrying out. It also abandoned its insistence on Quaker "Dress and Address".

A fresh spirit of enquiry and a tempering of discipline with charity was evident. The Society of Friends, by the very freedom which its method of holding Meetings for Discipline implied bore within its own structure the means of self-regeneration. From 1860 until the end of the century the Society steadily and progressively fitted itself to meet the challenges which Science and the new Higher Criticism of the Bible were raising.

Another reason for decline also surfaced at this time of review. This was the increasing concern expressed by a growing number of members about the effects of wealth upon individual Quakers. J. J. Fox, who had won third prize to Rowntree's first, traced the changes that had taken place in the class structure of the Society during the two centuries of its history. He recalled that among the early Friends only a few could have been considered wealthy, the mass springing from the humbler and relatively uneducated classes. He pointed out that with the growth in membership and the emphasis on education, sobriety, and honesty of practice in business, there was a steady upgrading of the membership from the lower to the middle class. Then, with entry to professions denied to dissenters, the energies of Quakers tended to be channelled into manufacturing and commercial enterprises. "The reaction of wealth", he observed, "and social position — and the consequent worship of the crowd — on the high concerns of vital religion are too self-evident to be portrayed. We have here, if not a cause, a concomitant of religious democracy."[45]

Some Quakers prospered and accumulated wealth, but, regarding such wealth as given in trust and therefore to be spent for the betterment of their fellows, used it with a sense of stewardship and remained within the Society. Others, succumbing to the temptations of wealth, moved away from simple, unostentatious life styles and also away from the Society of Friends into the Established Church.

London Yearly Meeting of 1837, when it was considering, as it did in great detail each year, the "State of the Society", expressed alarm at the evidence of falling membership. One of the major reasons for this was put strongly by one member in the form of a question: "May not the deficiencies arise from our leading and most active members being men of the world, absorbed in the accumulation of wealth, and of a carnal mind, which is spiritual death?"

The upward mobility of Quakers at the time of the migrations to Australia had several observed effects on the Society itself. There was an increasing tendency for the affluent Quakers to find their social, if not their spiritual, needs met in affiliation with the Established Church rather than with their Quaker Meeting. Though there was a renewed dedication to philanthropic good works, the cynics might claim that some Quakers regarded this as a "quid pro quo" for the privilege of being entrusted with rather more than their share of worldly wealth. There was also a third result — a deepening fear of radicalism in politics.

E. P. Thompson suggests that prosperity had muted the radical element which had been strong in the tradition of first generation Quakers such as Fox and Penn. "They had prospered too much: had lost some of their most energetic spirits in successive emigrations to America: their hostility to State and authority had diminished to formal symbols — the refusal to swear oath or to bare the head."[46]

Thompson goes on to allege that Quakers were regarded as so "safe" politically, that one of the editors of a radical paper, wanting to escape the notice of constables trying to arrest him, eluded them by donning the garb of a Quaker.[47]

Few Quakers of the early nineteenth century wanted to be reminded that the radical Tom Paine, the author of *The Age of Reason* and *The Rights of Man*, had Quaker origins. His father and grandfather were Quakers, his mother not. An article in *Quakeriana*,[48] a publication begun in March 1894 to collect items of Quaker history, said that Tom Paine owed his sturdy independence to his father and claimed that he was not, as he was often portrayed, an "infidel". This was also corroborated by the memoirs of the Quaker, Stephen Grellet, who, towards the end of his life, lived in Greenwich Village near the so-called "notorious" Tom Paine. Grellet recorded an account of Tom Paine's last days. His impression was that Tom Paine found comfort in Quaker companionship in his dying moments. Paine asked to be buried in a Quaker cemetery, but Quakers refused his request because they said they thought Paine's friends might want to raise a memorial over his grave and this was, they pointed out, contrary to the Quaker practice of marking a grave with a simple tombstone.

It is perhaps more likely that the real reason was that these Quakers desired to distance themselves from any link with the radical Paine. Evidence of this rejection continued to appear years after his death. The English Quaker, Walter Robson, recorded in his diary for 16 February 1868 that in his meeting that night in Melbourne there was "a nephew of the late celebrated Thomas Paine and holding the same atheistical notions".[49] One of Tom Paine's best known sayings, "The world is my country, my religion to do good", may owe something of its inspiration to Quaker faith in the universality of the Inward Light. *Quakeriana* quoted these words as evidence of his humanitarian spirit, "from which all narrowness is excluded".

While internal factors operating within the Society itself, such as the decline in Quaker morale, the rash of disownments and resignations, or the effects of wealth, cannot be directly claimed as major reasons for Quaker migration, it would appear that a considerable number of Quakers who migrated had had what might be called a disillusioning experience within the Society, resulting in resignation or disownment. Others who had been birthright members and who therefore had not been required to make a deliberate commitment to active membership did not necessarily feel a due sense of loyalty to it once they had moved outside the orbit of their own familiar Meeting. Others again may have shared some of the doubts which culminated in Rowntree's penetrating analysis and therefore arrived in the colonies without any impelling enthusiasm for the work of the Society or for its propagation in the colonies.

Before analyzing in more detail the reasons which prompted Quakers to migrate to Australia, it is important to find out the extent and nature of Quaker migration.

Two
The First Thousand Quaker Migrants to Australia

The history of Quakerism in Australia can be approached not simply as a record of the reactions of Quaker migrants to a new and strange environment, but as an interpretation of their actions in the light of information about the origins of the migrants themselves. The question should be asked, "How did Quakers, nurtured in the supportive atmosphere of English and Irish Quaker Meetings, apply their Quaker testimonies and practices when they were separated by twelve thousand miles of ocean from others of the same Quaker background?"

The answer may lie as much in the origins and personal Quaker backgrounds of those who had to face the challenge of living in a frontier-type society as in a descriptive account of the specific issues thus encountered. An analysis of the identity, geographical origin, Quaker affiliation, occupation, and schooling of Quakers who migrated to Australia may help to explain the subsequent history of Quakerism in Australia. This can be understood only in the light of information about the Quakers themselves who were part of that history, about their backgrounds, and the motives which led them to migrate. This was the reason for undertaking a survey of the first thousand who migrated to the Australian colonies.

The investigation was set within the limits of the years from the earliest settlement in the Colonies to the end of 1861, when the regulations adopted by London Yearly Meeting for the recognition of Monthly Meetings in Melbourne, Adelaide, and Hobart were received in these three Meetings. Though a few settlers and convicts with Quaker connections had arrived in the Australian colonies before 1832, the major influx occurred in the years following the arrival of the two English Quakers, James Backhouse and George Washington Walker, in Van Diemen's Land in 1832.

Though Backhouse and Walker during their visit to the Australian Colonies in the years 1832-37 recorded in their daily journals the names of any they met who had connection with Friends, the first systematic list was that commissioned by London Yearly Meeting in preparation for the visit of Robert Lindsey and Frederick Mackie to the colonies in the years 1852-54. Quarterly Meetings had been requested to supply the names of all those members and attenders who were known to have migrated to Australia. A similar request was made by Ireland Yearly Meeting. From this information Lindsey and Mackie compiled a "List of Friends and those connected with them in the Colonies, Van Diemen's Land, New Zealand and South Africa, 1854". This list, together with additions and emendations made on the spot by Lindsey and Mackie, has been used as the starting-point of the search for the "first thousand" Quaker migrants to Australia before 1862. Mackie identified those known to be members of English or Irish Meetings or accepted as members of the as yet unrecognized Australian Meetings. The Meetings of origin and colonial addresses were also given. On one of these lists Mackie recorded a numerical summary of members and of those "connected with Friends". This list (table 1) may be taken as a reliable estimate of those members and non-members known officially to be in Australian colonies by 1854.

Table 1. Quakers in Australia 1852-54 (according to Lindsey and Mackie)

	Members	Not-members
In V.D.L. connected with Fds.	59	21
heard of, but not seen		2
In N.S.W. connected with Fds.	34	68
heard of, but not seen	3	
In Victoria, connected with Fds.	120	110
heard of, but not seen	12	20
In S. Aus. connected with Fds.	83	79
heard of, but not seen	2	3
In W. Aus. connected with Fds.	1	14
	314	317
Total		631

These statistics reveal the thoroughness of Lindsey's and Mackie's search and the extent of an identifiable Quaker community, based on information received from Quaker Meetings and emended during their visit to the colonies. It would have been tempting to have accepted these figures and gone no further in search of possible additional Quaker migrants. Other sources, however, revealed some unsuspected omissions. When John Stephenson Rowntree was writing his essay, *Quakerism, past and present*, in which he analyzed the reasons for what he saw to be a decline in numbers and in effectiveness of the Society of Friends in Great Britain, his father supplied some research data compiled from answers to a questionnaire which had been sent out to all Quarterly Meetings in England to gather information on the location of Ackworth scholars who had left school before 1840. Rowntree found that out of 1550 scholars of the years 1800-1840 a total of 171 had emigrated.[1] The answers to the original questionnaire had been retained at Ackworth School and these gave name, home address, year of entry and of exit, trade, membership of the Society, reason for disownment, and location. From this list it was clear that some had emigrated who were not on Mackie's list and who perhaps were content not to be included. Old scholar records of other Friends' Schools produced additional names.

Obituary notices in Friend periodicals or in the collection of obituaries, known as the *Annual Monitor*, also furnished names, the clue being the place of death. On at least three occasions, lists of migrant members were supplied from London, the first being in 1847 by the Continental Committee, which was responsible for communications with overseas Friends on the Continent of Europe and in the colonies. Ireland Yearly Meeting sent out a list of Irish emigrant Quakers to Melbourne in 1853. In Hobart, Melbourne, and Adelaide, lists of members were compiled periodically from information supplied in the above overseas lists, or in letters from individual Meetings in England, or from evidence gleaned in the colonies.

To find out whether the names gathered from a variety of sources were those of Friends who were committed members, or ones who had lost interest and lapsed, it seemed necessary to trace as many as possible back to their home Meetings and find out how active they had been as members in those Meetings. In this search one came to appreciate the accuracy and consistency of Quaker records.[2] The founder of the Society of Friends, George Fox, had impressed upon his followers the need for careful registering of births, marriages, and deaths. The cessation of christening ceremonies made it all the more important for Friends to keep careful records themselves. The exigencies of Poor Relief and the difficulties of deciding who were eligible to receive poor relief from the Society of Friends led to a minute of 1 April 1737 which declared "that all Friends shall be deemed members of the Quarterly Meeting or Two Weeks Meeting within the compass of which they inhabited or dwelt, the first day of the 4th month 1737".[3] A hundred years later, under the Registration Act of 1836 and the Non-Parochial Act (3 and 4 Victoria c 92), commissioners were appointed to acquire all non-parochial registers in England and Wales. Meetings were asked to hand in registers to London for inspection. Digests of all the Quarterly Meeting and Monthly Meeting records of births, deaths, and marriages to 1837 are now centred in Friends' House Library, Euston Road, London.[4] From these records it was possible to check the members listed as migrants against the Meeting records. The records of births gave not only place of birth, parents' names, and residence, but the father's occupation at the time of birth. The Irish Quaker records were not so explicit. They did not normally give details of parents' occupations.

The consistency of organization and presentation of records facilitated the search. There were two basic sources of information — the Monthly Meeting registers and the Monthly Meeting minutes, sometimes indexed. Membership registers usually gave particulars of entry to Meeting, whether by birth, convincement, or transfer. Exits were also given — by death, resignation, disownment, or transfer. Minutes of Monthly Meetings were usually brief, non-descriptive, simply recording Meeting decisions, but in cases of disownment the records gave detailed reports of committees of investigation into such disownable actions as marrying out of the Society, insolvency, or delinquency. As there proved to be a significant number of disownments of members before and after migration, minutes of disownment were welcomed by the researcher as particularly revealing. The handing down of Christian first names from generation to generation sometimes led to confusion of identity. One was therefore thankful to come upon the unmistakable identity of a Gabriel Unthank, or a Rolles Biddle, or a Sir Benjamin Smart, whose father was so determined to protest against worldly titles that he prefixed each successive Benjamin with a Sir, or Master, or Prince.

Although Friends were meticulous in recording transfers from one Meeting to another, the trail of a particular Friend was sometimes lost, as some of the Quaker migrants had already indulged their migratory whims by frequent moves in their own country before seeking the ultimate answer by distancing themselves as far away from home as possible. The recording of members and non-members up to 1837, sometimes without clear distinction, particularly with respect to the registering of children as members, led to occasional difficulties of deciding whether individuals were members or attenders.

From the information gathered from a variety of sources[5] on individual migrants linked with the Society of Friends, it was possible to estimate the total number of the Quaker "connection" to the end of 1861 and to compare this with Mackie's estimate of 631 in the year 1854, a total made up of 314 members and 317 non-members. For Mackie "non-members" covered both those who continued links with the Society, even after disownment, by attendance at Meetings for Worship and also those who were connected in some way with members, but who may have given no evidence of active attendance or interest when they went to Australia.

In Table 2 the non-member group has been subdivided into "attenders" and "connected with Friends" — by family, school or burial. Under "connected by family" would be included some for whom severance of formal membership by parents in the past did not necessarily imply severance of all ties with the Society of Friends. The strength of such connections is difficult to determine, but the inclusion of this group in the survey seemed necessary if some indication was to be given of the extent of a Quaker potential in the colonies.

"Connection by school" implies that there was some formal connection with Friends' Meetings, either as members or attenders, for an enrolment to be accepted at a Friends' school. Further, it might be expected that the student during three or four years of attendance at a Friends' school was at least exposed to some Quaker influence. That this was no guarantee of continuing Quaker involvement was often the lament of those who remained faithful and who seemed unable to awaken in some ex-Friends' school students any corresponding glimmer of interest in Quakerism.

"Connection by burial" indicated a retrospective rather than a contemporary interest. On entry into new territory, such as a recently settled colony, Friends endeavoured to seek land for a Meeting House and for a burial ground, the latter generally being acquired before the first, because burial by a priest was considered unthinkable. Records were faithfully kept of all interments and frequently in the record of burials names appeared which had not been in evidence elsewhere in membership lists or in Monthly Meeting records. Again, an assumption was made that the relatives of any person for whom a Friends' burial was requested had some valid reason for the request and the Meeting a valid reason for according a right to burial "after the manner of Friends", that

Table 2. Quaker migration to Australia before 1862
(based on an analysis of the biographical survey)

Members (at any time before 1862)	M.	F.	Totals	
Adults from the U.K.	526	181	707	
joined in Australia	30	18	48	(755)
Children from the U.K.			102	
joined in Australia			7	(109)
				864
Attenders — Adults from the U.K.	61	31	92	
Children			9	101
Connected with Friends				
Adults by family	98	74		
by school	3	1		
by burial	7	3		
by other	7		193	
Children			55	248
	732M	308F	173 ch.	1213

is, a burial conducted by Friends as a Meeting for Worship.

The total number of those listed in the survey covers, therefore, members, attenders, and those connected with Friends. There is one further difference between tables 1 and 2. Mackie did not give separate statistics for adults and children.

There is clearly a marked difference between Mackie's total of 631 in 1854 and the total of 1213 in table 2. Mackie's list was basically compiled from information received by London Yearly Meeting before 1852, though emendations made by Lindsey and Mackie during their travels in Australia would have brought the list up-to-date to include known arrivals in 1852-53. Table 2 is compiled from a much wider range of sources, unofficial as well as official. It reveals, for example, that many more Quakers migrated to the colonies than were officially listed by their Meetings as having emigrated. Mackie, indeed, realized this soon after his arrival with his official list and he regretfully concluded that some who had been members of the Society of Friends in England had deliberately concealed their membership on arrival in the colonies, nor had they given any notice of removal to their Meetings. The reasons for this might have been attributable to their previous history as Friends in England or to what Mackie called the "entanglements" of frontier living in a new land.

William Howitt, who had resigned his membership in the Society of Friends before coming to Australia to seek adventure on the goldfields, recalled in his memoirs of the goldfields meeting with a shepherd, an educated person, but a wanderer, mentally as well as territorially. "I had a strange feeling," he said, "that I had seen him somewhere before in England: a feeling much strengthened by his use of 'thee' and 'thou' in conversation. From this and other circumstances I had a very strong impression that in early life he had been a member of the Society of Friends."[6]

The total in table 2 also includes a significant addition of Quaker migrants for the years 1852-61.[7] It includes all those dead or alive, who had been in Australia before 1862, whereas table 1 lists only those who were thought to be living in Australia in the years 1852-53.

To get a more fruitful comparison, particularly with respect to the number of members thought to be in Australia, an analysis of the loss of membership before 1862 is necessary (see table 3).

Table 3. Loss of membership *before* 1862

	M.	F.	Total	As % of adult membership (755) from Table 2
By disownment				
before embarkation	82.	16	98	
after arrival	42	13	55	
			153	20.3
By resignation				
before embarkation	17	3	20	
after arrival	25	7	32	
			52	6.9
By death	71	24	95	12.6
By return to England	65	5	70	
to Ireland	19	1	20	
			90	11.9
By transfer to N.Z.	7			
to Canada	2			
to S. Africa	1			
to U.S.A.	1		11	1.4
			401	53.1

For comparative purposes the total of 864 members, 755 adults, and 109 children, must be reduced by the total of losses, 401, given in table 3. The remainder in 1861 of 463 represents an increase of 47 per cent on Mackie's total of 314. At first sight this would appear to be a pointer to an encouraging future, but any optimism must be tempered by further analysis of the subsequent history of the group of 755 adult members in table 3. In the years immediately following 1861 a further thirty of these were disowned, twenty-two disassociated (a milder term of censure), and twenty-four resigned. These losses bring the percentage of losses through disownment, disassociation, and resignation to about thirty-three per cent of the adult membership of 755.

Disownment was not an Australian phenomenon. The loss of twenty-seven per cent of adult members[8] was not atypical when compared with the statistics of loss through disownment in English Meetings of the same period. Thus Brighouse Monthly Meeting, with 820 members in 1851, had a loss through disownments of 33.5 per cent for the period 1800-1854; Pontefract, with 430 members, a loss of 34 per cent for 1800-1854; York with an average membership of 302 for 1837-45, a loss of 19.8 per cent; and Frenchay, with an average membership of 123 for 1801-1851, 32.5 per cent.[9]

Resignations were closely related to both disownments and disassociations. It was often a question of which party took the initiative in breaking the link between members and Meeting. Some resigned membership because of their intention to marry a non-Friend, knowing that breach of the strict rules which governed this "offence" would probably mean disownment. Members, who, through isolation or lapse of interest or desire to associate with another church, felt that they no longer wished to retain their membership, would either take the initiative and submit their resignation or run the risk of unwelcome disownment later by their Meetings. In table 3 it will be seen that 40 per cent of the resignations took place before embarkation and therefore were not related to factors operating in Australia.

The percentage of return to England and Ireland was 11.9 per cent. A high proportion of these consisted of single males, returning home after an adventurous fling on the gold fields. A few continued on the gold-digging circuit, hoping to retrieve their fortunes in New Zealand or on the American continent. Most of the immigrants however were prepared to remain and battle against whatever odds their choice of occupation and settlement presented to them. The costs of return, particularly for a family, were in any case likely to be prohibitive, except for those who prospered quickly.

The death-rate of 12.6 per cent was not high, considering the span of years covered by table 3. The major influx of migrants occurred in the forties and fifties and the average age of the migrants was young. The deaths that occurred were due to a variety of causes, not only longevity. Ten died on the voyage out, six of these being in one family lost off the Irish coast only two days out from Liverpool, the other four from the ill-health which was possibly the reason for their migration. Eight met with violent deaths — one killed by Aborigines, one by execution for an offence committed on his return to England, one by explosion on a River Murray steamer, one by a falling tree in the bush, one in an overturned buggy, one by a fall from a horse, and two by drowning. Fevers of various kinds carried off at least eight. Three daughters of the one family were victims of what was called "colonial fever" in Melbourne, two dying on the one day and the third a few days later. Alcoholism was responsible for several deaths. For these alcoholics the migration to Australia, which had been thought of as offering hope of a cure, became a curse. The Australian colonies with their harsh conditions of living and habits of hard drinking were not suited as rehabilitation centres for alcoholics.

If this loss had been counter-balanced by the entry of new members, the picture would not perhaps be considered so depressing. The forty-eight who were accepted as members in Australia were mostly those who were attracted to the Society during the six years of the visit of James Backhouse and George Washington Walker in the eighteen-thirties. This rate of recruitment was not however maintained and the members thus added were subject to the same rate of loss as those who came from English and Irish Meetings.

The other areas from which the membership might have been expected to be replenished were the children, the attenders and those "connected with Friends". Of the children registered as members in 1861 thirty per cent were subsequently lost through disownment, disassociation, and resignation. Very few of the remainder appear to have retained any active interest as adults in the Society of Friends. Evidence could be found for only eleven of the 101 attenders being admitted to membership and only four of the 248 considered as "connected with Friends".

The statistical evidence therefore does not present Quakers in the colonies in 1861 as a promising and viable religious group. Some of the internal problems facing this group, in common with Meetings in the parent Society in England, appear more specifically in table 4.

If one adds to the disownments for "marrying out" eleven resignations for the reason given as anticipation of disownment,[10] it will be seen that "marrying out" was by far the greatest single cause of loss of membership in the Society. The reason for the hard line taken by the Society and the changes made in 1860 by London Yearly Meeting have been explained.[11]

Table 4. Analysis of Disownments of Quaker migrants (both before and after migration)

Total of disownments:
Adults before 1862 (from table 3)   153
after 1861   52
Children as adults
after 1861   16
    221

Reason: disownment for	M.	F.	Total	As % of 221
"marrying out"	71	24		
probably "m.o."	6		101	45.6
"reproachful conduct"	26	3	29	13.1
joining other churches	10	14	24	10.8
non-attendance at Meetings	13	8	21	9.5
insolvency	17		17	7.6
loss of contact	17		17	7.6
uncertain reasons	6	2	8	3.6
non-payment of debts	5		5	2.2

Comparative percentages from a sample of English Meetings indicate that the above pattern of disownments for Quaker migrants to Australia was similar to the pattern in English Meetings for the same period.

Table 5. Disownments in English Meetings 1800–1851[12]

English Meeting	Total Disowned for	m.o. %	non-att. %	insolvency %	immorality %	misc. %
Brighouse	279	not available				
Pontefract	147	46.2	—	8.2	34.0	11.6
York	60	43	6.7	21.7	21.7	6.7
Frenchay	40	not available				
Bristol	293	33.1	—	26.6	11.9	27.6
Devonshire House, London	253	47.4	19	12.2	21.3	—

Table 5 shows that "marrying out" was the most common cause of disownment in English as well as in Australian Meetings. The supply and proximity of daughters of marriageable age in membership with Friends was a much greater problem, however, in the young colonies with so few in membership and with these scattered and separated by great distances. There were sixteen marriages out of the Society in Australia before 1860 which did not result in disownment. This was an indication that some Meetings recognized the intolerable difficulties which strict application of the marriage regulations placed upon members of the Society in the colonies. Walter Robson, an English Friend, who visited the colonies in 1868, saw the effects very clearly. "This old rule of our Society", he wrote in his diary, "seemed particularly cruel to those young men who have settled in the colonies, from the fact that there were no young lady Friends for them to have. We have already visited many who were disowned in this way."[13]

Insolvency was another common cause of loss of membership. When insolvency occurred some twelve thousand miles away, it was more difficult for the Meeting to determine the extent to which circumstances beyond the insolvent's control had contributed to the failure, particularly because economic fluctuations made business enterprises precarious in the colonies. The English Meetings had to rely upon reports from Australian members on which to base their judgment of insolvency.

Terms such as "reproachful conduct" and "immorality" covered a whole spectrum of "sins", including offences punishable by law and leading to imprisonment or transportation. But these terms were also used to describe conduct which showed disregard for accepted Quaker codes of behaviour, such as the frequenting of public houses, indulging in gaming, sex before marriage, enrolment in the militia.

Disownment for joining other churches was not common. Usually a member attracted to another church resigned rather than invite disownment. The disownment percentage for this cause in table 4 can be attributed mainly to one family of seven who had been baptized into the Church of England and who therefore merited the stern reproof of their Meeting.

The main expressed reason for resignation was the wish to link up with another church, particularly where isolation meant that a member felt the need for religious fellowship which the Society of Friends with its scattered and numeric-

Table 6. Analysis of reasons for Resignations by Quaker migrants to Australia, both before and after migration.

```
              Totals of resignations:
     Adults before 1862 (from table 3)    52
                           after 1861     24
          Children as adults after 1861   14
                                          90
```

Reason for resignation	Total	As % of total (90)
Undefined (loss of interest)	28	31.1
Joining another church	27	30.0
Non-attendance	16	17.8
Marrying Out	11	12.2
Doctrinal disagreement	8	8.9

ally small membership could not satisfy. Letters from London Yearly Meeting or from individual Monthly Meetings, urging faithfulness and reminding members of the presence of God, even "where two or three are gathered together", were judged by wavering members to be no substitute for the satisfaction of worshipping with more than two or three.

Disinclination to continue in membership, leading to non-attendance, was not necessarily motivated by a decision to seek membership with another religious denomination. For some, the cares of earning a living crowded out thoughts of spiritual matters, particularly where the nearest Meeting for Worship was miles away. For others the reasons lay in the country of origin rather than the country of adoption. Disenchantment may have already led to lapse of interest and, though contact may again have been sought in Australia, the strength of the Society of Friends in the colonies was not sufficient to restore interest or promote active participation.

Friends, with their reluctance to formulate creeds, did not usually resort to theological disputations. However, there were some echoes of two schisms from Ireland and England. An Irish couple living in Melbourne belonged, it is thought, to the so-called "White Quakers", a dissenting Quaker group in Dublin.[14] There were several adherents of the Beaconites, followers of Isaac Crewdson of Hardshaw East Monthly Meeting in Manchester, who found their way to Melbourne, but it is not clear whether theology or economics was the primary motive for their migration. In any case, they appear to have been exhausted by the controversy, for they showed little interest in Crewdson or Quakerism on their arrival. There were at least two examples in Victoria of resignations made on the grounds of inability to accept what Quakers at that time were prone to regard as essentials of Quaker faith. Another went further and claimed that he could not accept the Biblical account of the fall of man and the consequent belief in the necessity of an atoning sacrifice. Quaker statements of belief, often strongly evangelical in tone and language, had apparently provoked this reaction.

Table 7. Arrivals of Quaker migrants in the colonies before 1862

		before 1820	20–29	30–36	37–43	44–50	51–56	57–61	Totals	
N.S.W.										
	Adults	12	16	33	51	11	32	18	173	
	ch.u	16		4	14	12	4	12	10	56	229
V.D.L.	ad.	2	8	39	23	7	10	5	94	
	ch.		9	7	13	3	10	3	45	139
Vict.	ad.				20	19	225	67	331	
	ch.				8	2	67	2	79	410
S. Aust.	ad.				74	16	33	7	130	
	ch.				46		4		50	180
Qu.	ad.				2			5	7	
	ch.				2				2	9
W.Aust.	ad.			2	4	2			8	
	ch.				12				12	20
TOTALS		14	37	95	267	64	393	117	987[15]	

The States with the peaks of Quaker migration were Victoria and South Australia, Victoria's coinciding with the gold-rush of the fifties and South Australia's in the early years of its settlement. There was a secondary influx in South Australia, and in New South Wales, during the Victorian gold-rush years. The early fifties also saw the arrival of a number of young Irish Quakers.

The figures for New South Wales and Van Diemen's Land show a steady flow of migrants. Before 1830 the migrants were largely the unwilling, transported to the penal settlements. A trickle of free settlers began in the twenties and strengthened in the thirties. Quaker migration to Queensland did not become significant until the sixties. In Western Australia, after an initial burst of interest in the early years of settlement, economic disaster caused the exodus to the

Eastern states. The only Quaker contingent was a family of fourteen, of whom the only one in full membership was the mother, Elinor Clifton. Her husband, Marshall Clifton, was the Chief Commissioner of the Western Australian settlement at Australind.[16]

Table 8 shows the distribution of members migrating to Australia who could be traced to their Monthly and Quarterly Meetings in England, Scotland, and Ireland. Totals are

Table 8. Meetings of origin

	Quarterly Meetings		Monthly Meetings (with significant nos. of migrants)	
England	London & Middlesex	101	Devonshire House	38
			Southwark	32
	Lancashire & Cheshire	78	Hardshaw East	36
			Hardshaw West	25
	Yorkshire	67	Brighouse	37
	Essex & Suffolk	40	Witham	21
	Berks. & Oxon.	33	Witney	17
	Bristol & Somerset	27	Bristol & Frenchay	25
	Devon & Cornwall	25	Devon, W. Division	15
	Warwickshire, Leicester & Stafford	25	Warwickshire North	15
	Bedfordshire	22	Hertford & Hitchin	13
	Durham	20	Newcastle	13
	Sussex & Surrey	18	Lewes & Chichester	16
	Derbyshire, Lincs. & Notts.	18	Nottingham	8
	Hampshire, I. of Wight & Channel Is.	8	Poole & Southampton	8
	Norfolk, Cambridge & Huntingdon	4		
	Westmoreland	4		
	Cumberland	3		
	Kent	3		
	Western Gen. Meeting	2		
		498		
Scotland		3		
Ireland	Leinster	55	Dublin	40
			Mountmellick	13
	Munster	33	Cork	11
			Waterford	7
	Ulster	26	Lisburn	17
			Grange & Richhill	8
	Uncertain	7		
		121		
	Total	622		

given for all the Quarterly Meetings, but figures for constituent Monthly Meetings are restricted to those from which significant migration took place. The total of 622 represents those who had at any time been members and includes those who resigned or were disowned.

The major sources of Quaker migration were London and Middlesex, the manufacturing areas of Lancashire and Yorkshire, the farming counties of Bedfordshire, Essex, Suffolk, Berkshire, and Oxfordshire, and the seaport of Bristol. Some of these were the most densely populated areas in England. It is important therefore to look at the distribution in table 8 against the background of distribution of Quaker population. A map of England,[17] showing the distribution of Friends in 1851 proportionate to the general population, reveals that the heaviest concentration of Friends (with a population density of 1 in 800 or over) was in London and Middlesex, Essex, Gloucestershire including Bristol, Oxfordshire, Warwickshire, Yorkshire, Cumberland, and Westmoreland, with the next highest concentration being in Lancashire. It will be seen therefore that, in the distribution of Quaker migrants given in table 8, there is no significant difference from the contemporary pattern of the distribution of Quaker membership throughout England. Quaker migrants came from the areas where Quakers were most numerous.

An occupational survey of the Quaker migrant group (table 9) was undertaken to see to what extent socio-economic factors influenced the decision to migrate.

To give a basis for comparison with the general occupational pattern of English Quakers a control group has been used. The statistics in column 1 are taken from an occupational survey made by Isichei[18] of Quakers who died in 1841. Of the 364 deaths in that year occupations were specified in the records of interment for 224, giving a sample of 60 per cent.

Though attenders and those "connected with Friends" were included in the occupational survey, it is reasonable to assume that the information concerning the occupations of parents of migrants in column 2 was confined almost entirely to parents of those who were or who had been members, for the only reliable source of information about parents'

Table 9. Pattern of occupations of Quaker migrants to Australia

	Column 1 Control group- Eng. Q. 1841		Column 2 Parents of migrants		Column 3 Occupns. before migration		Column 4 Occupns. in Australia	
	Nos.	%	Nos.	%	Nos.	%	Nos.	%
Class One								
a) gentleman	27	12	2	0.7	—		2	0.5
b) manufacturer	8	3.6	27	10.1	5	4.8	4	1.0
c) banker	6	2.7	8	3.0	—		6	1.6
d) professional	16	7.1	7	2.6	9	8.6	30	7.9
e) merchant	16	7.1	49	18.4	10	9.5	20	5.2
f) land-owner	28	12.5	20	7.5	5	4.8	97	25.4
g) agent	4	1.8	4	1.5	—		13	3.4
h) brewer	6	2.7	11	4.1	3	2.9	6	1.6
i) managerial	1	0.4	2	0.7	3	2.6	6	1.6
	112	49.9	130	48.6	35	33.2	184	48.2
Class Two								
j) retailer	39	17.4	66	24.8	30	28.6	76	19.9
k) commerc. trav.	1	0.4	—		—		2	0.5
l) ind. craftman	13	5.8	42	15.8	17	16.2	40	10.5
m) teacher	4	1.8	8	3.0	5	4.8	28	7.3
n) clerk	1	0.4	2	0.8	2	1.9	3	0.8
o) innkeeper	1	0.4	4	1.5	5	4.8	9	2.6
	59	26.2	122	45.9	59	56.3	158	41.6
Class Three								
p) shop assistant	1	0.4	1	0.4	4	3.8	2	0.5
q) skilled or semi-skilled	34	15.1	12	4.5	4	3.8	19	5.0
	35	15.5	13	4.9	8	7.6	21	5.5
Class Four								
r) unskilled	7	3.1	1	0.4	1	1.0	10	2.6
s) agric. lab.	6	2.7	—		1	1.0	3	0.8
t) sailor	3	1.3	—		1	1.0	6	1.6
u) unspecified	2	1.0						
	18	8.1	1	0.4	3	3.0	19	5.0
Totals on which percentages were based:	224		266		105		382	

occupations came from English Quaker records of births, marriages, and deaths and from Friends' schools' records of enrolment. The Irish Quaker records did not contain such information. The total of 266 in column 2 represents a sample of approximately 47 per cent.[19] No claim of any kind can be made about the significance of the figures in column 3 for the occupations of migrants before departure, as information about these was very scanty. The column is included, however, for interest.

In column 4 twenty females are included (eleven teachers, five in matron or house-keeping positions, two as shop assistants, two as domestic servants), but the sample is mainly of the male membership, though where information was available about attenders or those connected with Friends, these were included. It is probable therefore that the total of 362 occupations (male) in column 4 represents approximately a 50 per cent sampling of the total of 732 male adults from table 2. Mackie was the main source of information about occupations in Australia.

Another reason for reference to Isichei's table of occupations is the classification adopted. The class scale used is a four-point rather than a five-point. (The class of titled, land-owning aristocracy is missing from Isichei's four-point "Quaker" scale.) This would appear to be based on the value accorded to such factors as degree of independence, social standing, wealth, mobility, and managerial responsibility. In Quaker circles independence and mobility were two important marks of a "weighty" Quaker, for participation in the Monthly, Quarterly, and Yearly Meetings of Friends required not only some financial resources, but also a certain independence of action and willingness to travel. The relatively large number of Quaker "gentlemen" in class one clearly did not belong to the titled land-owning class. The figures reflect rather the higher mortality rate amongst those who had retired and who therefore were regarded as "gentlemen" because they no longer had an occupation. By the middle of the nineteenth century, however, there was already a group of wealthy Quaker families linked by business interests in manufacture, banking and trade, and often by marriage. These families, by birth, power and influence, had the characteristics of a Quaker "aristocracy".

Amongst these families there are some well-known names such as the Pease family in railways, coal and iron; Lloyd and Barclay in banking; Rowntree, Fry and Cadbury in chocolate; Bryant and May in matches; Huntley and Palmer in biscuits; and the Darbys of Ironbridge, to whose leadership in iron manufacturing is often attributed Britain's head start in the Industrial Revolution.

The term "gentleman" in class one was taken to apply to a person of independent means, who either had no occupation or had retired from active work and was not attached to any specific occupation. This use of the term was evidently understood by some Quakers in Australia, for a Melbourne Quaker, successful in business and with leisure to return for an extended trip to England, listed himself as "gentleman". So too did a disowned Quaker from Hobart who conferred upon himself in later retirement the same distinction.

The merchant in class one apparently rated a class above the retailer in class two on the assumption that the merchant, dealing in wholesale trade, had a greater freedom of movement than the retailer whose living depended on his being constantly available to customers. It was often difficult to determine where precisely to locate some occupations. Was the "grocer", for example, to be grouped with the wholesale merchant in class one or with the retailer in class two? "Grocer" originally meant a "grosser", a wholesaler, but by the middle of the nineteenth century it is likely that the grocer was more often simply a storekeeper, a retailer of foodstuffs, for this is the connotation of the term in an Australian context. The grocer therefore has been placed in class two.

The distinction between yeoman, husbandman, and farmer had also been blurred by the mid-nineteenth century. Even in the seventeenth century, John Camm, one of the early Quakers, though a landowner of some substance, was referred to as a husbandman.[20] Farmers, therefore, whether labelled yeomen, husbandmen, large or small land-owners, were grouped in class one.

The independent craftsman was placed in class two, the skilled worker in class three. It was often, however, impossible to determine from the meagre evidence available the degree of craftsmanship, skill, or independence on which to base a distinction. It was also difficult to know, for example, whether a woolcomber should be regarded as a member of the industrial work force in class three, or whether he enjoyed some degree of independence and of skill to warrant his being placed in class two. Vann, having examined the value of estates left by some Quaker woolcombers in the eighteenth century, concluded, "It is thus impossible to relegate all the woolcombers and worsted weavers to the independent proletariat".[21] Harrison commented, "The skilled woolcomber did not drink in the same pubs with the more lowly members of the textile fraternity."[22]

A comparison of the occupational status of the migrants (and their parents) with that of the general body of Quakers in England in the mid-nineteenth century shows that the great majority came from classes one and two, with fewer from classes three and four. It might be said therefore that the migrants, and their parents, were drawn from upper middle and middle classes. Few had the leisure — until perhaps late in their colonial history — of the English gentleman Quaker, but there were also very few in labourer groups.

While migrants and their parents maintained a strong representation in retailing and crafts, there were some significant shifts of interest. Among the parents merchants predominated[23] but the next generation turned in Australia to farming.[24] The prospect of owning land was a strong incentive to migration, even though this meant an abrupt change in occupation.

Another interesting shift of occupation was the marked increase in the number of migrants who took up so-called "professional" occupations, though only a few of their parents were thus classified. One suspects that professional qualifications for some of the professions were not yet established or controlled in the colonies. There was, too, an element of opportunism evident in some migrants' assumptions of professional status. One, for example, trained as a teacher, came out to New South Wales, but switched to farming in New Zealand until the Maori wars led him to seek his future in sugar-growing near Port Macquarie. When the weather in this region proved to be too cold for sugar-growing, he turned to making his living as a doctor.

The inclusion of teachers in class two and not with the professional group in class one reflects the mid-nineteenth century attitude to teaching. Isichei comments:

> School teaching was regarded with relative disfavour — Friends repeatedly claimed at Yearly Meetings that Quaker schools were inadequately staffed, and recognized it was because teachers were

poorly paid. In the early Victorian period Quaker men became teachers out of a rare sense of vocation, or because they lacked the talents or opportunities for business.[25]

It should be pointed out that two significant "occupations" have not been included in this survey — gold-diggers and convicts. Seventy-five gold-diggers have been identified, together with an additional fourteen who were engaged in storekeeping or carting at the diggings. Many of these returned to England or Ireland after trying their luck and are therefore not included in the occupational survey. Those who remained in Australia either returned to the occupations they had temporarily deserted, or switched to some other activity. Where these more permanent occupations have been known, they have been included. Similarly those who came initially as convicts have been included in the survey only when subsequent occupations have been known.

Table 10. Attendance of migrants at Quaker schools

Ackworth	111 b.	19 g.	130	Great Ayton	4 b.	1 g.	5
Croydon	41	17	58	Penketh	4	1	5
Sidcot	18	1	19	Wigton	6		6
Newtown, Ireland	18		18	Grove House	2		2
				Sibford	1		1
Mountmellick, Ireland	15	3	18	York Girls		1	1
				Rawden	3	1	4
Lisburn, N. Ireland	9	5	14				
Bootham	9		9				
	Totals				241 b.	49 g.	290

A significant proportion of the migrants had attended a Friends' school. The first column of table 10 shows which schools provided a majority of the migrants.[26]

Within the Society of Friends there was an accepted class ranking of these Quaker schools. The first to be established, Ackworth, was founded in 1779 by London Yearly Meeting to meet the needs of Friends "not in affluence". It was assumed that wealthy Quakers would continue to send their sons to private schools or to engage private tutors for their children. This view of Ackworth persisted well into the twentieth century, for a correspondent to the Friends' Education Quarterly (1935, p. 142) complained that people of means were sending their children to Ackworth. "It is unjust," he wrote, "because it keeps some of the poor out, and unfair to the private schools which are never full." In 1859 Rowntree[27] commented that Ackworth raised boys in the social scale and this led to movement from rural occupations into commerce and hence to a drift of Quakers into the towns.

Sidcot and Wigton schools were established by Quarterly Meetings on the Ackworth model. Bootham and York Girls' School, however, served a more wealthy Quaker clientele which wanted an education leading to the professions rather than to manual, rural, and commercial occupations. Croydon School[28] developed a trade emphasis with a combination of manual labour and school work. There was a well-developed link between Croydon and Monthly Meetings in London to encourage the training of apprentices. Of the forty-one boys who had been at Croydon and who later migrated to Australia, a number had been supported by Meetings and had had apprenticeships arranged for them with Quaker masters through Croydon.

The four schools, Rawdon, 1832, Penketh, 1834, Ayton, 1841, and Sibford, 1842, set up specifically for the children of disowned Friends, had an explicit vocational emphasis. "The view of Friends is to embrace what may be termed the labouring classes of those in any way connected with our Society, combining labour with learning to perhaps a greater extent than any of our schools, Brookfield, Ireland, excepted."[29] Rawdon, by stressing manual labour, aimed to cater for children of the trade and labouring classes. Penketh, serving the Lancashire Meetings of Hardshaw East and Hardshaw West, was designed to serve the needs of Friends "in limited circumstances". Penketh undertook to find suitable employment for its students.[30]

A class view of Quaker schools appeared without apology in *The Friend* of 1846[31] where Friends had questioned where they were to get qualified teachers of mathematics and classics. Some suggested that any promising students at "lower class" schools, such as Ackworth and Croydon, established for children of poorer Friends "likely to go into trade or commerce", should be transferred to "higher class" schools.

The significant number of Ackworth and Croydon scholars who emigrated suggests that it was particularly in the trade and commerce areas that economic pressure to emigrate was most felt. Rowntree[32] said that 171 out of 1550 scholars emigrated in the years 1800–1840 and that in some of the rural Quaker Meetings, where economic depression drove people to seek alternative means of livelihood, as many as a quarter of Ackworth scholars in those Meetings emigrated.

Over a hundred Ackworth scholars emigrated to Australia. It is likely that associations formed at school led to small groups of Ackworth old scholars going out together for mutual support, to the gold-diggings, for example.[33]

This analysis of the identity of the Quaker migrants, their Meetings of origin, social background, Quaker membership, occupations, and education, provides a basis for an examination of the reasons which led them to migrate.

The survey showed that the Quaker community in the colonies was larger, at least in potential, than Mackie and Lindsey had suspected or London Yearly Meeting had fully realized. The Quaker migrants shared a similar background of upbringing and education and a tradition of practising in their daily living the religious principles they espoused. This tradition of disestablished, dogma-free, practical religion might have been expected to nurture a plant of sturdy growth in the colonies.

For a significant proportion of the Quaker migrants, however, links with their Quaker Meetings had been broken either by disownment or resignation. Others were often members in name only, registered at birth, but lacking conviction or commitment. The prognosis for the continuing association of many of the migrants with any Quaker Meetings set up in Australia was not encouraging, particularly when the factors of isolation and difficulties of communication aggravated disinterest and disaffection.

Most of the Quaker migrants came from Meetings in areas which were badly affected by the fluctuations of booms and depressions — the manufacturing towns of Lancashire and Yorkshire and metropolitan London — and their occupations as tradesmen, small businessmen, craftsmen, and farmers were those which were most vulnerable to these fluctuations.

Migration therefore held out hopes of a new beginning and a new opportunity.

The survey of occupations and schooling indicated that the great majority of migrants came from the middle classes. Few of these came with adequate financial resources. In fact a considerable number came because of straitened financial circumstances. Lacking in most cases independent means and probably spending what small reserves they may have gathered on passage money, equipment and goods to make a start on arrival, most of them had to struggle to make their way in a frontier society.

What the survey did not reveal explicitly were the reasons which led the "first thousand" to migrate. Some of these reasons can be inferred from the information contained in these first two chapters. Others need to be sought from a review of the social and economic conditions operative in England and Ireland in the first half of the nineteenth century.

Three
Quaker Attitudes to Migration

It is important to set the Quaker migrations of the first half of the nineteenth century to the Australian colonies in the context of the economic and social conditions operative in England and Ireland in this period. Then, using the factual information provided by the survey in chapter two, it should be possible to determine whether economic and social pressures were the major factors motivating migration.

Personal Motivation

The years following the Napoleonic Wars were characterized by considerable political and social turbulence and unprecedented growth not only in national wealth but in population. Figures for population trends in England and Wales for the nineteenth century indicate a doubling of the population in the first fifty years, 1801–1851, and a trebling in the first eighty to 1881. There is still no agreement on the reasons for this phenomenon.

    1801 :   8,872,980 (excluding 469,188 seamen and 1,410 convicts)
    1851 : 17,927,609
    1871 : 22,712,261
    1881 : 25,974,439.[1]

With this came what E. P. Thomson[2] called a half-century of chronic under-employment. With changes in technology, the skilled tradesmen felt themselves threatened by cheap unskilled labour which was in demand for the steadily increasing number of factories. The rapid out-dating of skills added to the general sense of employment insecurity. Many tradesmen, proud of their skill, had to face the "dishonouring" of their trades by what they saw as the trend to produce shoddy goods for the growing mass markets.[3] Displaced skilled tradesmen were therefore potential migrants.

The unplanned growth of towns in the great industrial areas of Lancashire, the Midlands, and Yorkshire, with all the consequent problems of disease, poor food, and inadequate housing, had a damaging effect on family life and provided a motive for people to see in migration a key to the future of their children.

For those engaged in trade and commerce the relatively new phenomenon of economic booms and depressions introduced a new hazard of uncertainty. Asa Briggs[4] traced the pattern and showed how in the period 1825-50 booms and depressions followed each other in quick succession. J. F. C. Harrison[5] called the six years 1837-42 "the grimmest period in the history of the nineteenth century". Industry was at a standstill, unemployment was high, food prices increased sharply, and relief measures were totally inadequate. This period coincides with one of the two periods of maximum migration to the colonies of South Australia and Victoria.[6]

Table 9 of the survey indicates that the major proportion of occupations of Quaker migrants before leaving England was in the merchant, trades, and shopkeeping groups. These were particularly vulnerable to unpredictable booms and depressions. A marked shift of Quakers from agricultural, craft, and artisan occupations had been noted in a survey made by William Beck and T. F. Hall.[7]

	1690	1780
Group 1 — professions, wholesale dealers	27	46
Group 2 — shopkeepers, small dealers	58	141
Group 3 — smaller craftsmen, labourers	147	30

Not only was there this upward class shift, but two other factors affecting Quakers motivated a drift away from the country to the towns and particularly to certain Midland towns. The first factor has already been commented on — the effect of tithes on Quaker landowners and particularly on small farmers. If they refused to pay tithes, distraints were put on their household goods. If they paid tithes, they were in danger of disownment by their Meetings. Hence to break this tension many left the land. The second factor was the effect of the Corporation Act of 1661, by which all members of corporations had to take, in addition to the oath of allegiance, the sacraments according to the rites of the Established Church. The sacrament-taking section was repealed in 1828, the Test Act in 1863, but the Corporation Act not until 1871. In many corporate towns it was impossible to carry on a trade except as a freeman, and this involved taking an oath. Therefore Quakers tended to be attracted to non-corporate towns like Birmingham. Table 8 reflects the high concentration of Quakers in the industrial areas of Lancashire and Yorkshire and lends weight to the view that one of the main reasons for migration was the effect of recurring economic depressions on trade and industry.

Another pointer to the effects of economic depression on migration is seen in the significant number of Quakers disowned for insolvency, who subsequently — and often forthwith — sought in migration an opportunity to make a new start. The case of Edward Tatham, a member of Brighouse (Leeds) Monthly Meeting illustrates this point. Tatham had incurred debts amounting to £25,000, but could pay only nine shillings in the pound. The Meeting committee of investigation learnt that Tatham had invested in machinery to manufacture goods for export to France, but that a change of tariffs in that country had disrupted the market. The Meeting recognized that Tatham was to some extent a victim of the unpredictability of markets and as he had expressed his intention, if not his guarantee, to repay his debts and reduce his own personal expenditure, did not disown him. When Tatham's second insolvency, however, was reported to Leeds from Southwark, where Tatham had apparently moved to set up a new business of hat-making, the Meeting found Tatham less than candid in facing up to his responsibilities and, "in consideration of his not having learnt by his previous bankruptcy", disowned him. It was further recorded that Tatham "declined to receive the minute".[8] Disowned in 1849, Tatham migrated with his family to Victoria in 1850. To failure in business was added a rupture of relationships with his Meeting — a double reason for seeking his fortune twelve thousand miles away. The relationship of a Quaker to his Meeting may not have been the main reason, but it may have had the effect of tipping the scale in favour of migration.

The Society of Friends also began to take note of the serious effects of economic depression on its members. In 1843 a Friends' Relief Committee was established to raise funds for the relief of distress in manufacturing districts of the north. The depression was due, it was claimed, to the fall in demand for cotton goods from Leeds in America and China.[9] The Society was equally alert to the effect of economic "booms" upon the business world, for in April 1845, the year of the railway "boom", *The Friend* issued a caution to members against speculation. The timeliness of such caution was evident when the "boom" just as suddenly became a "bust" in October of the same year.[10] The same paper, two years later, directly related the increase in migration to the sudden reappearance of economic depression. "Great numbers of people, many of them the more thrifty among the small farmers, have sought to escape from the general uncertainty by means of migration."[11] Eight months later the writer, warning again about the dangers of unwise speculation, made a pointed reference to the effect of this on members of the Society of Friends. "The severity of the crisis is such as had hardly before been experienced; and not a few members of our society have been involved in losses and sufferings with which it has been accompanied."[12]

Unemployment, which has been noted as a feature of the post-Napoleonic War period, had a direct relation to migration, which was seen as a way for the unemployed to escape "the recurrent depressions and misery occasioned by the new industrial society".[13] From 1820 onwards there was a determined effort to promote emigration as a positive way to meet the problems of over-population and under-employment. Societies were formed for the promotion of colonization.

The year 1847 saw the onset of the potato famine in Ireland. *The Friend* during the years 1847–50 carried reports of the devastating nature of the famine and of the measures being taken by Irish and British Friends to organize relief.[14] To thousands emigration held out the only hope of escape and in 1847 the exodus began. *The Friend* reported that in December the number of Irish flocking across the Irish Sea to Liverpool was 13,471, compared with 897 in December

1845. The story of the trans-Atlantic exodus is told in such books as Cecil Woodham-Smith's *The Great Hunger*.[15] Here the estimate of emigrants to the Americas during the famine years was given as more than a million, apart from a similar number to Liverpool and the ports of Scotland and Wales. Woodham-Smith claims that Irish emigration in this famine period to Australia was negligible because of the length and cost of passage, and because of the lack of an Irish community in Australia encouraging friends and relations to join them. The survey, in chapter two, however, showed that there was a significant number, over a hundred, of Irish Quakers who came to Australia in the years during and immediately following the famine.[16] By contrast with the general mass of poor, unskilled, illiterate Irish who crowded the notorious emigrant ships freighting Irish famine refugees to America, the Irish Quakers who came to Australia were from upper middle class families. Joseph Beale was a typical example. He was a leading merchant and miller in Mountmellick, Queen's County, Ireland, with extensive properties and business interests, particularly in wool. When the Irish famine struck in 1847, Beale turned his mill to grinding corn for the starving. His woollen trade collapsed because of the disastrous effect the famine had on the whole of Ireland's economic structure. Many, like Joseph Beale, found their prosperous businesses in ruins. Four of his family of ten children died.

It is a sad commentary on the rigidity of the Quaker attitude to insolvency that Joseph was disowned by his Meeting. Faced with this alienation, with threats to the health of his family, and with bleak prospects of any immediate revival of the Irish economy, he at last decided to emigrate. The address which his fellow Mountmellick citizens presented to him on the eve of his departure in 1852 shows that the community of Mountmellick was more understanding of his achievements and his difficulties than was his Monthly Meeting. It also sums up both the cause of migration and the expectations which led him to choose the formidable long voyage to Australia rather than the shorter crossing to America.

To Joseph Beale.
Esteemed friend,
We feel it is a pleasing duty which we owe you, to express on your removal from amongst us to settle in Australia our recollection of the benefits conferred on the locality from the extensive employment given by you: 'Whose family have been residing here nearly two centuries' more particularly in the Woollen and Cotton manufacture which owing to your own enterprise and exertions was brought to near perfection. We regret that the great depression in those branches of trade a few years ago forced you to relinquish a business which altho' unprofitable to yourself diffused the benefit of extensive employment to others and which period of depression has been succeeded by years of famine and consequent destitution of a large proportion of the population.

Under those circumstances we consider the decision you have come to of removing to Australia is judicious, offering as it does so wide a field of success to those possesed (sic) of industry and perseverance — You carry with you our best wishes for the welfare of yourself and family and we earnestly hope that your new settlement may realize for you, those advantages which at present appear unattainable in this land. Your character, education, habits of business and perfect knowledge of the Wool trade, and its manufacture qualifies you beyond most others to succeed in that part of the world. And whilst we regret the loss of a useful member of Society we feel assured that the change will be for your advantage.[17]

Joseph Beale was over fifty years of age when he landed with his two older sons at Port Phillip in 1852 to prepare the way for the arrival of his wife, Margaret, and the rest of their family two years later. A blend of desperation and optimism must have prompted this Irishman to attempt to start a new life for himself and his family at this late stage of his life.

Most of the Irish migrants were young men of educated middle-class families with bleak prospects of employment and therefore easily persuaded that the answer to all their problems lay in the goldfields of this new Eldorado of the South. The clearest picture of a young Irish Quaker's reason for leaving Ireland is given in the unpublished autobiographical notes of Alfred Webb.[18] He came from a comfortable upper middle-class family, his father owning a printing business in North Brunswick Street, Dublin. His uncle, "an unpractical man, always in difficulties", according to Webb, had tried America first, returned with difficulties still unresolved, and then gone to Victoria. Webb's friend, Thomas Walpole, had already left for Australia. Webb had the impression that his family was on the verge of bankruptcy, and, his own health being poor, emigration was seen as a possible solution to both difficulties — economic and personal. "Doubtless father thought", he wrote, "I might carve out a future abroad and do better than I could at home." This was perhaps a hope that other fathers had, particularly for younger sons without an assured future in the family business. Webb had other reasons, which were not typical of young Quakers of his generation. He confessed that he had been disillusioned by the failure of the Chartist movement of reform and by what he saw as the brazen indifference of the English who had allowed corn to be exported from Ireland while masses of the Irish were starving. He claimed that the press in England took an "almost fiendish pleasure at the reduction of our population". Disillusioned by the collapse of the Chartist movement he looked forward to the possibility of a simpler and higher state of society beyond the seas "with purer manners, better laws". He found his mood matched in a verse of a song sung by Henry Russell, a popular entertainer in his day.

> Here we have toil, and little to reward us.
> There shall plenty smile upon our pain.
> Ours shall be the prairie and the forest
> And boundless meadows ripe with golding grain.
> Hope points before and shows a bright tomorrow.
> Let us forget all the badness of today.[19]

So far as one can judge, Webb was the only Quaker migrant to express anything akin to a political reason for migration. He shared with fellow migrants however the urge to "forget the badness of today" in the hope of "a bright tomorrow" and "boundless meadows ripe with golding grain". A combination of ill-health, political disillusion, the pressure of famine on family fortunes and the example of migrating friends and relatives led him to set sail in May 1853 for Victoria.

Alfred Webb was in Australia from 1853 to 1855. He resigned his membership of Dublin Monthly Meeting in 1858 to join the Church of England. It was a stirring of the radical in him and his feeling that Friends had lost their radical role in society that seemed to be the main reason for his resignation. He considered that Friends had lost their original independence of thought and action and had increasingly conformed to established society. His experience in Australia apparently did nothing to change this view. "They were more directly philanthropic than now. Now that they have come under the influence of 'the good society' they are less inclined to act independently or do anything that is not good form."[20]

He took an active interest in Irish Republican politics, was treasurer of the Parnell Party and three times member of Parliament for Waterford. He wrote for various papers, including *The Manchester Guardian*. In 1894 he was invited to be president of the Indian National Congress in Madras. Quakers, particularly John Bright, had given strong support to the launching of this national movement in 1885. It was probably on his way home from the Madras Conference that he chose to pay a return visit to Australia with his wife. There is a report in *The Australian Friend* of January 1896 that Mr Alfred Webb, member for West Waterford, had visited Tasmania, where "he had some social intercourse with Friends. He gave an interesting address on 'Home Rule' in one of the school rooms in Hobart". Webb died in 1908 while climbing the highest mountain in the Shetland Isles.

Health was one of the most common personal reasons given for the decision to migrate. With the high incidence of tuberculosis in England, the healthy open-air life of the colonies was a ready prescription available to the family doctor. Those who came out for health were clearly from families who could afford the expenses of the voyage and the possibility of having to provide continuing maintenance, for the delicate were not likely to be strong enough to cope with the rough demands of a pioneering life.

There were those, too, whose disease today would be diagnosed as "alcoholism". Quaker families were not exempt from the temptation to protect respectability by sending the cause of embarrassment twelve thousand miles away for the sake of his "health". In the case of one wealthy and well-known Quaker family the younger son of twenty was despatched to the gold-fields of Victoria to sober down and perchance to find his fortune. After thirty years of wandering he ended his alcoholic safari by drowning in a Montreal lake. The newspaper heading in a Jersey paper — "A Wasted Life" — was a pertinent commentary on the folly of expecting that despatch to the colonies was a cure for the alcoholic "black sheep" of the family.

The only explicitly Quaker reason for migration discovered amongst the first settlers was that given by William May, who emigrated to South Australia with his parents, Joseph and Hannah May, eleven other members of the family, and an uncle, Henry, in 1839. In a letter to his sister Rachel thirty years later he described what had led the family to migrate. Initially, the reason was economic. His father's business worries had prompted William to suggest migration as a move to meet the crisis. The South Australian colonial experiment had caught William's imagination. His father, however, at first did not accept the suggestion, but a year later the economic reason was overlaid with a Quaker rationale, for he wrote to William to say that "on further pondering the subject of South Australia he believed it would be his duty to remove to that colony with his family". William then commented, "He had, it seemed, long hoped to be employed in higher service in the church and was led to believe he might be qualified for such service in a distant land."[21] The last line of this letter is particularly significant. William May concluded, "It was not in ordinary course of emigration the common motive". This observation sums up succinctly the great difference between the American and the Australian Quaker migrations. The common motive for the American migration was to seek a land where the Quaker faith could be practised in freedom. The common motive for the Quaker migrant to Australia was an economic one — to seek better opportunities for himself and his family. Joseph May was one of the few who formulated an explicit Quaker reason as well. His wife was remembered as adding, "and I hope we shan't get too rich".

A common reason, also economic, but not always explicit until arrival in Australia, was the lure of gold. The biggest single occupational group indicated in the survey of chapter two was the gold-diggers. Quakers were perhaps sensitive about reporting to their Meetings such a reason for migration. Quite a number of young Irish Quakers came out for a year or two to try their luck and then returned home, mostly with little more in their pockets than they came with. One was proud that he had at least found enough gold to make a wedding ring for his fiancée. In 1852 George Sayce wrote from Dublin to Edward Sayce to report to him that a dozen young Dublin Friends were about to leave for the "golden country". He had heard of the growing wealth of the new settlers and wanted to have first-hand reports. "A good report from thee", he wrote, "might tempt some of us to come and share."[22] Gold-rush fever was in the air and some of the Irish Quakers, in spite of warnings about the lure of gold, did not intend to stop their ears to the far-off sirens' call.

Finally there was a small group of ex-Quakers whose reason for leaving England was patently clear — being sentenced to transportation, they had no choice but to go. Identification of individuals in this group is beset with some difficulties. Frequently an alias was adopted to protect the family, or perhaps the Meeting, from embarrassment. In most cases those in membership had been disowned before the crime for which they were transported had been committed, or were disowned because of it. They were therefore unlikely to make any move to establish contact with Quakers on arrival in New South Wales or Van Diemen's Land, particularly as most of these would have arrived before there were any organized Meetings in these two settlements. Nevertheless twenty-seven convicts who had been members have been identified. Seventeen have been traced back to the Meetings by which they had been disowned. The crimes for which they were transported included rape, highway robbery, forgery, larceny, fraud, and petty thefts. One Irish Quaker, George Walpole, was transported for manslaughter but his was one of those rare cases where, after transportation, the sentence was reviewed and finally cancelled. He, with five other police constables, was clearing a hotel at closing time and in the struggle the man they were trying to arrest was killed. In 1827, two years after their arrival in New South

Wales to serve their sentences, the local magistrates in Ireland ruled that the accused had been wrongly sentenced for carrying out what was now judged to be an illegal order from their superiors and so Walpole and his fellow-accused were pardoned.[23]

Of the twenty-seven, six were claimed to be Friends through hearsay by people such as Backhouse, but proof of membership has not been established, and a further four are those who claimed membership in their own statements, three in the census of 1828 and one on arrival. This last one is of particular interest. Convicts on arrival in Van Diemen's Land were given the opportunity to make their statement of the nature of the crime for which they had been transported, as well as their personal details, date of birth, family, religion, etc. In some cases the information thus supplied was much more revealing than was available on the official card brought by the ship's captain. A Joseph Ritchie, who was listed as a "felon", protested that he was not a felon, but a political prisoner, convicted for his part in "The Orange Tree Conspiracy" against the British government in 1848. Following collapse of the Chartist movement after the rejection of a third petition by Parliament in 1848, a group of radicals planned an armed uprising in London. The conspirators were surprised by the police at their final conference in the Orange Tree public-house in Bloomsbury on 15 September 1848. The trial was held at the Old Baily on 18 September and the five leaders were transported for life.[24] Ritchie, one of these five, claimed that the crime was sedition and therefore not a felony. He also stated that he was a Quaker bricklayer from Newcastle-on-Tyne though attempts to trace his membership in Newcastle Quaker records have not so far corroborated his claim. Ritchie died in the Launceston hospital in August 1854.[25]

Two of the seventeen traced back to Meetings of origin were listed as transported in the records of Ackworth Old Scholars and given as members, but these two brothers have not so far been traced as having arrived in Australia. In cases of doubt change of name may be the obstacle to identification.

The reasons which led Quakers to migrate were varied.

They were far from being a homogeneous group, as the survey in chapter two has shown. Most of the migrants were single men coming out to try their fortunes, but at least fifty married men with wives and three or more children made the long voyage. The factors influencing the flow of migration were, in retrospect, the "expelling" effect of economic and social conditions prevailing in England and Ireland, and, in prospect, the enticing attractions of land distribution in the new colonies of South Australia and Victoria and of the gold rush which held out promise of adventure and quick returns. All these factors operated on the Quaker migrants, who, indeed, in motivation, were migrants first and Quakers second.

Corporate Concern

Given that the reasons for migration were economic and personal, it is important to determine what attitude was adopted to migration by London Yearly Meeting and by individual Monthly Meetings. The situation in the nineteenth century was far different from that in the seventeenth century, when Quakers, spurred on by bitter persecution, but also motivated by religious and political idealism, founded their Quaker settlements in America. When the Toleration Act was passed in 1689 the spate of emigration subsided but in 1714 London Yearly Meeting still considered it advisable to issue advice to members on emigration. "When any Friend removes into America, or other Parts, it is advised that their going be with consent of their Monthly Meeting; and that they take a Certificate of their Conversation and Unity with Friends; and if possible, clearness respecting marriage and that their Parents, if living, signify their minds there."[26]

Even before this it is evident that Meetings were beginning to exercise some discipline where members indicated intention to migrate. This was necessary particularly where Meetings were being asked to give financial support to migrant members. Thus in the records of Yorkshire Quarterly Meeting in 1683 there is a reference to a Robert Thompson of Guisborough who applied for permission to go to America.

The Quarterly Meeting ruled that it was "not free to yield him any assistance upon that accompt to further his transportation as aforesaid but rather desires him to rest contented in his own country".[27] Quite clearly Meetings were anxious to ensure that migration was undertaken for good reasons and not merely because of restless discontent. There was also an understandable desire to protect members from hasty, ill-considered decisions, particularly if members proposed migrating to areas where there were no settled Friends' communities into whose care they could be safely transferred.

Friends' interest in migration was stirred by reports of new settlements on the Swan River, Western Australia. *The Friends Monthly* in 1828[28] carried an account of this settlement under the direction of Captain Stirling. In the following issue[29] a correspondent referred to the "flattering expectations" held out by those who were trying to attract free settlers to Western Australia. He underlined the attraction this colony would have if Friends migrated in significant numbers.

There was talk of the possibility of a planned Quaker migration but this plan came to nought. Apparently a group of Quakers, calling themselves "Social Emigrants", consulted with Stirling in 1833 about establishing a settlement on Albany Sound, Western Australia. The support of people who could contribute £300 or more in capital and of artisans, farmers, and mechanics was solicited. There was a strong component of social idealism in this reported plan, for poverty was to be circumvented by setting up a co-operative society and Temperance was to be an important priority.[30]

Interest however switched quickly to South Australia when Backhouse and Walker, who visited the settlements at Albany and on the Swan River late in 1837, sent back discouraging reports. They found the land sterile and inhospitable. Apart from a climate suitable as a retreat for invalids, Walker saw few advantages for settlers.

> It is indeed a happy circumstance that Friends of the poorer class who we have understood it was a favourite project with one or two of our Society in London to induce to come out, did not make the voyage to King George's Sound. I think it is the last place a person

with independent means should come to while there are so many more favourable spots for the securing of the means of a comfortable subsistence, especially Adelaide and Port Phillip.[31]

It is probable that Backhouse influenced a number of Friends on his return to England by his personal endorsement of the settlements in Victoria and South Australia. His frank accounts also of what he called in his report to Governor Bourke "the prevailing immorality of the population of New South Wales" and his concern about the moral effect of a continuing convict presence on the rising generation in New South Wales and Van Diemen's Land meant that any Friends contemplating migration were not likely to look beyond Victoria and South Australia.

Friends' periodicals carried advance publicity about the South Australian experiment. *The Lindfield Reporter*[32] in its first issue, January 1835, carried a preview of the attractive immigration scheme proposed for the new colony of South Australia. It was announced that the settler would be charged one pound per acre, that ninety pounds would purchase ninety acres and that the proceeds would pay for the passages of six labourers to be brought out at the cost of fifteen pounds per head. The advantages of the new colony were summed up as follows, "To small capitalists having grown-up children willing to work and not able to pay for their own passage, the advantages of the arrangement will prove very considerable and will far exceed the advantages they could secure even were they to obtain land for nothing either in Canada or New South Wales."[33]

The number of August 1835 positively promoted South Australia over New South Wales and Canada. South Australia had, the paper argued, an advantage over the former, which "was exposed to the moral malaria of a convict population" and over the latter, because land in South Australia was four times more productive than in Canada.

In the next volume South Australia was projected as an opportunity for the establishment of a model colony, an ideal location for groups of Friends wishing to emigrate. Much publicity was also given in 1840 by *The Irish Friend* to reports of Lutheran refugees from persecution in Germany who were on their way to South Australia. *The Irish Friend* solicited help for them from Friends. There is no doubt that South Australia, with this active promotion in Friends' periodicals, was in the front running as the most attractive colony for Friends' migration. The first issue of *The Irish Friend* had been full of enthusiasm for the prospects of emigration to South Australia and had seen it as a promising area of Quaker growth at a time when English Quakerism was in decline.

> Whilst in the present day in this country the complaint continuing to exist among us that "there is not much growth in the Truth and but little appearance of convincement", it is truly cheering to learn that "the Truth spreads and increases in a region until recently the abode only of the sable sons of the forest".[34]

The Irish Friend sustained interest in the question of emigration. From 1837 it carried as a regular feature serialized extracts from Backhouse's journal and comments on matters likely to appeal to prospective migrants. Thus in 1838 Backhouse passed on the advice of R. Clint, assistant surveyor at King George's Sound: "He thinks Friends would be disappointed in migrating thither".[35]

By 1839 the number of Quakers emigrating to the Australian colonies was sufficiently significant for the subject of emigration to be raised at London Yearly Meeting. The following "minute of caution" was issued to all Meetings and was printed in full in *The Irish Friend* of 1 July 1839.

> This Meeting has been introduced into feeling, on behalf of our members who may be induced to contemplate emigration, either singly, or in families, to Australia, or other distant countries. We strongly recommend our Friends on all such occasions, to take counsel of their brethren, before entering on an undertaking of such great importance. We also desire, in much affection, to offer a word of caution to such, that they be not hastily induced by the prospect of outward advantage to engage in a movement so fraught with important consequences, but that in singleness of heart they seek for Divine direction, whereby they may be favoured to know the place of their right allotment, whether at home or abroad. We would especially entreat them to guard against the influence of an impatient and restless spirit, which would lead them under the pressure of present difficulties or discouragements, to seek in foreign lands those temporal advantages which may not seem to be readily available at home, and whereby they may expose themselves and their families

to much disadvantage, in reference to their religious interests. Many are the dangers attending a hasty and unadvised movement of this kind — our safety consists in being willing to commit all our ways to the most High.[36]

The accent here was all on the side of sober caution. *The Irish Friend*[37] commended London Y.M. for its "salutary" advice to migrant members and underlined the need for them to examine their motives. In 1841 an editorial linked what it called "this hitherto unprecedented era of abandonment" of the homes of their forefathers with the classic migrations of early Friends to the American colonies by reminding this new wave of migrants of the advice of Fox and Penn that, before a decision to migrate was made, they should obtain the goodwill of their kinsfolk and do all in their power to arrive at a "sober judgment". They were also reminded that their Christian faith would be subjected to severe testing in "climes where the Christian principle remains yet to be exhibited in its genuineness and true beauty".

Concern for the aboriginal inhabitants, wherever the white colonist settled, was a constant theme of Friends' advice to migrants. Friends were urged to maintain "considerate conduct" towards the aboriginal inhabitants of the lands in which they settled. This advice was reinforced by a special Meeting for Sufferings' epistle to members in the Australian colonies in 1841. Having reminded them of the importance of the Meeting for Worship on the first day of the week, even if this meant meeting on one's own, the epistle added:

> We feel much for the native inhabitants of the countries in which you are settled. In pity for that ignorance and darkness and for the oppression to which they have been subjected, be concerned yourselves to act towards them with kindness and to embrace every opportunity to plead with others to do likewise — that the Christian religion may be commended and adorned by the whole conduct of our countrymen toward them.[38]

The year 1840 might be regarded as a turning-point in Friends' official attitude to the Australian migrations. Up until then interest was random and attention cursory. Any statements made were such as to discourage migration. Warnings were issued about the difficulties that would face Quakers in isolation in the colonies.

The two factors which contributed to a change of attitude were, first, the authentic voice of Backhouse, particularly through the publishing of extracts from his journals. The second was the attractiveness of the prospectus of the South Australian commissioners, whose proposals were hailed by some over-zealous supporters as heralding a Pennsylvania of the South. This element of Quaker idealism was sufficient to cause London Yearly Meeting to take notice and *The Irish Friend*, reporting on this development, concluded: "The establishment of colonies of Friends in these remote regions, cannot but be viewed with interest by their Friends at home".[39] The editor clearly anticipated in the phrase "colonies of Friends" that the opportunity now presented itself for planned Friend group migrations with South Australia as the desired location.

Backhouse's influence on emigration to South Australia and Victoria has already been indicated. Quite early in his visit to the Australian colonies, Backhouse had begun to show his interest in giving guidance to emigrants. In a letter to John Cadbury, dated 1 October 1833 from Hobart, he had written, "With regard to emigration there can be no doubt but those who can make a living in England and have health there do well to stay: those who cannot but who are industrious do well to emigrate; and if a fine climate be required for health, here it is among Englishmen." When he returned to England on 2 February 1841 after nine and a half years in Australia and Africa, he published his *Narrative of a visit to the Australian colonies*. It is significant that he devoted the last two pages[40] to advice to Friends who were contemplating emigration. He warned them against extravagant expectations, which could only result in disappointment when they came to face the actuality of settlement in a new country. Few, he said, took into account the privations to be endured, the lack of companionship to which they had been accustomed, the necessity of having to do for themselves and by themselves what normally had been done for them by others. He warned them against emigrating from a "restlessness of spirit", for there was then a danger of projecting on to the new land "the plague of their own hearts". He urged them therefore to be sure that they had sufficient reasons for taking so important a step as to leave their native land. He also quoted the example of a young Irishman who, through intemperance, lost his money and his friends and had come to call on him for help. This led to a further warning to Friends at home. "Without persons have capital and conduct to take care of it, they should not emigrate to the Australian colonies."[41]

He had some practical advice for single men. Many, he said, on arrival in the colonies had discovered their mistake.

> Even if a man go into the interior, he is much more likely to succeed, if he have a wife to take care of what he may leave in his dwelling, be that ever so humble a one, while he is out attending to his flocks; if his residence be in a town, such a caretaker is still necessary, for respectable housekeepers are not so easily to be obtained, because persons of this class are generally soon sought out, by those wanting wives.[42]

By 1841 a more positive attitude to emigration seemed to be emerging in London Yearly Meeting. Monthly Meetings were advised to organize correspondents who would take responsibility to communicate with any of their members in the colonies. At the same time the Continental Committee,[43] a subcommittee of Meeting for Sufferings, was asked to give general oversight to the needs of overseas members. A list of migrant members was drawn up by the Committee in 1847. From this time onwards the Committee prompted Meetings to keep it informed of migrant members and encouraged Meetings "not to consider themselves released from that Christian care and interest for such members, which this Meeting has uniformly enjoined upon them".[44]

Meetings, however, were slow to respond to these promptings and some made no response at all. Lancaster Meeting did make some effort, though belatedly.

> Report is now received that the circumstances of the members of our several Monthly Meetings, resident in foreign parts, have received some attention from them. It is requested the particular nature of the care bestowed be reported to our next Meeting in writing — regard being had to the yearly Meeting Minute of 1841 under the head "Emigration". It is also requested that the names of such members be reported — and, as far as practicable their place of residence and when last heard from.[45]

The constituent Monthly Meetings[46] duly and dutifully reported. Lancaster indicated that it considered no further care was necessary "as in all cases the individuals have removed within the compass of some recognized Meeting". This may have been true of migrants to America, but not to Australia, where there were as yet no "recognized" Meetings. Hardshaw West Monthly Meeting was more thorough. A committee had been set up to meet with any intending migrants and to urge them to keep in touch by correspondence, though the clerk, Joseph Crosfield, added that it was "almost impossible to extend (to the emigrants) that care which is due to the individuals themselves and to the proper maintenance of the discipline of the Society".

The visit of Robert Lindsey and Frederick Mackie to the Australian colonies in 1852–54 may be seen as a direct result of this concern of the Continental Committee, for a determined effort was made by this Committee to get Monthly Meetings to supply up-to-date lists of any members known to be in Australia. These lists were used by Lindsey and Mackie in their attempt to contact as many as possible during their visit.[47]

The British Friend of February 1853 drew attention to another practical response to the contemporary interest in migration. It carried a report on the launching of the *Swarthmore*, an iron sailing-vessel of eleven hundred tons, from the building yard of Coutts and Parkinson at Willington, constructed specifically for use as an Australian emigrant ship. Ackworth Old Scholars recalled that Thomas Lidbetter came to the School with a model of the *Swarthmore* and as a result of this promotion several Ackworth teachers were amongst the Friends who took shares in the ship.[48] The owners, listed as members of the Society of Friends, "instead of giving money for a carouse, which is often the case after a launch, contributed fifty pounds towards a school for the education of the workmen's children". Further evidence of Quaker control of this shipping enterprise was reported by *The British Friend* quoting from a Melbourne newspaper item.

> The *Swarthmore* of 1384 tons register (Captain Thomas Lidbetter) arrived in our harbour on the 22nd instant from Calcutta. She is the

largest iron ship that has ever been built for sailing. We are informed ... that she performed admirably, doing fifteen knots with ease; but owing to calms, light and adverse winds, fifty-three days were occupied on the passage. The urbanity of her captain (who belongs to the Society of Friends) and his excellent lady, contributed much to the happiness of all. There were a number of discharged soldiers on board, amongst whom her captain endeavoured to instil those principles of total abstinence so strictly adhered to by himself, officers and crew. We much wish that these examples were more frequently imitated.[49]

The master of this Quaker vessel was Thomas Lidbetter, a member of Kendal Monthly Meeting and educated at Ackworth School. His first experience of Australia had been as an apprentice on the *Avon* which was in Sydney in 1840. By 1853, when Lindsey and Mackie spent a night on board his ship in Melbourne, he was a master mariner and plying mostly on the India–Australia route. His ship, the *Swarthmore*, bore an historical Friends' name, its crockery was stamped with a Friends' message, "nuncio pacis", and the master and crew were expected to run the ship as far as possible in accord with Friends' principles. Mackie, however, hinted that the *Swarthmore* was beset with difficulties. Most of her crew had deserted ship in 1854 to seek the goldfields[50] and the ship itself because of its unusual design was unclassified by Lloyds. This meant that it was severely limited in the freight load it was permitted to carry and also in the number of passengers, fifty instead of the five hundred it was designed to carry. The *Swarthmore*'s return voyage, with a valuable cargo of gold and wool, was beset with difficulties. It had a scrap crew, a mutiny when Lidbetter put in to Tahiti for repairs, a rough passage around the Horn, but a safe arrival home. The *Swarthmore* was wrecked in the Bahamas on its second voyage.

By 1860 Lidbetter had settled in Karachi, where he was employed in building the Indian River Steam Flotilla. When this was completed, he remained and entered the business of shipping insurance. Ruined by the financial crash of 1866 he transferred his family to Bombay and became an "average adjuster". Later the family moved to Melbourne and then Hobart. His wife died in Sydney in 1879 while Lidbetter was in Bombay on shipping business. In 1890 he returned to England and died there in 1908. He must have been one of the last of the Quaker seafarers in a tradition which stretched back over the eighteenth and nineteenth centuries.

At first sight this example of Quaker interest in emigrant shipping would appear to be an isolated one, at least on the Australian route, but shipping records of the period indicate that Quakers, well-known for their involvement in iron-manufacture, transport, and commerce, were also quite deeply engaged in ship-building and controlled a number of shipping lines. R. and J. Lecky of Ireland are reported to have built the first screw-propelled steamer, the *Rattler*;[51] Francis and Jeremiah Thompson established in 1817 the first regular packet ship between New York and Liverpool; and James Beale of Cork built the *Sirius*, the first steamship to cross from England to America under her own power. James Robertson Pim, known as "Captain Pim", was the founder of the St George Shipping Company, a leading Irish shipping company of the mid-nineteenth century.

Quaker interest in improving migrant shipping is evident in James Richardson's inauguration of a system of carrying steerage passengers at five pounds per head from Liverpool to Philadelphia, a sum considered to be so low that it would be attractive. However superior value was given, it was said, in terms of better accommodation and food. Quaker Richardson prospered by giving greater value at lower cost.[52]

The *Swarthmore* experiment, therefore, though an isolated experiment on the Australian route, was by no means the only indication of Quaker ship-owners' practical concern for improving the conditions under which migrants travelled.[53]

During the decade of the forties there had been a marked increase in the numbers of Quakers migrating. Attention was now being turned to ways in which emigrants might be helped. There was a committee formed to provide books for the use of emigrants on the long outward voyage. The Tract Societies produced tracts in quantity for distribution in the colonies. A correspondent to *The British Friend* wrote about assisting deserving Friends to emigrate. Having referred to the hundreds who had suffered religious persecution and gone to America in the time of William Penn, he continued:

In this our day the upright and conscientious tradesmen can scarcely live, through excessive competition and trickery in business; and there are hundreds who would, if they could, escape to a freer atmosphere.

Promote co-operation then; a splendid field is before us, of usefulness to those who stay behind and of advantage to those who go. Let us no longer see a family going from their native land and unclaimed. Let those who incline to emigrate have the company of Friends — yea, let's have a colony of Friends. A more interesting subject could scarcely be introduced, or one combining so much utility. A cargo of Friends for Australia would have the sympathy of the whole Society. Advantageous schemes are afloat, from some of which plans could easily be arranged . . . Dr. Lang's is a good model and his work a high authority. All that is wanted is to set the thing agoing; and as your Journal is the most direct medium, I trust you will devote some space to the remarks that may be made on the subject.[54]

The editor expressed "cordial Sympathy" and promised assistance. In subsequent issues various suggestions were made. The paper, it was felt, could be a contact point, providing a means of communication between Friends desiring to emigrate and Friends already in the colonies. An "intending" migrant hoped that in the colonies Friends could be found who would undertake registration of members as they arrived and thus both help the migrants and advance the work of the Society. An offer of such help eventually appeared twelve months later. Henry Tregelles Fox, a surgeon, member of Thaxted Monthly Meeting, who had arrived to take up a practice in Melbourne, replied that he would be glad to help new arrivals and put them in touch with Melbourne Friends. He attached his address, 31 Swanston Street, Melbourne, Port Phillip.

Such measures of communication and assistance were random and undirected and so, lacking any positive lead from London Yearly Meeting, migrants left their home Meetings with at first little notice being taken of their departure, or firm arrangements for assistance being offered. Hence many lacked the incentive to link up with Friends on their arrival. The results of this lack of strategy and planning for coping with the dispersal of its members will become clearer when the struggling efforts of a few Friends to establish Meetings in the colonies are discussed in later chapters.

PART TWO

Quakers in Australia: 1770–1861

Introductory Note

The first time that a Quaker set foot on Australian soil was in 1770. Sydney Parkinson, artist on Captain Cook's ship, *Endeavour*, was the son of Joel Parkinson, a Quaker brewer of Edinburgh. Originally a woollen draper, he was recommended to Sir Joseph Banks because of his skill in drawing and painting objects from natural history.[1]

From 1770 to 1832, the date of the arrival of the two Quakers, James Backhouse and George Washington Walker, in Van Diemen's Land, records of Quakers in Australia are limited to scanty information about a few convicts with Quaker connections, or early settlers, emancipist or free, who left traces of Quaker influence.

Backhouse and Walker must be regarded as the pioneers of Australian Quakerism. It is doubtful whether Quaker Meetings would have been established in Van Diemen's Land and New South Wales, had they not spent six years in these two convict colonies, or whether the Meetings that struggled to take root later in the free colonies of Victoria and South Australia would have survived without the continuing effects of their influence.

There is one point which becomes clear in a survey of this first period of Quakerism in Australia, and this is that there is little to record of Quakerism, the institution, beyond the establishment of Quaker Meetings, but more to relate concerning Quakers, as individuals. The Quaker Meetings in each colony arose at different periods and in response to different conditions. Van Diemen's Land and New South Wales were convict colonies. Victoria and South Australia were proudly hailed by their early founders as "free" settlements. The Meetings arose independently of each other and

Sydney Parkinson, artist on Captain Cook's ship, *The Endeavour,* was the first Quaker to set foot on Australian soil, in 1770. He died of fever at sea after the ship left Batavia. This portrait engraving is taken from Parkinson's *Journal,* published posthumously in 1773, and reproduced in the facsimile edition published by the State Library of South Australia in 1972.

were so concerned with taking root that there is little evidence of any Meeting response to the problems of early colonial life. The Minutes of Monthly Meetings until 1861 were lacking in any community concerns. Time was taken in answering London Yearly Meeting Queries, replying to Epistles, dealing with admission and disownment of members, and seeking London Yearly Meeting's help with raising the money to build Meeting Houses. The reports to London bore confessions of weakness and isolation rather than assertions of a pioneering Quaker spirit.

The interest therefore lies in observing how Quakers individually responded to the challenges of living in isolation in a distant colonial environment. The growth of Meetings and of an Australian Quakerism came later.

One reason for selecting 1861 as a convenient terminal point for an examination of the earliest period of Quaker settlement in the colonies has already been given. Eighteen sixty-one was the year when London Yearly Meeting gave formal recognition to the Quaker Meetings in Hobart, Melbourne, and Adelaide. An additional reason is that the dates of Walker's death in 1859 and Backhouse's in 1869 are close enough to 1861 to make this an appropriate year to mark the end of what might well be sub-titled the Backhouse and Walker period of Australian Quakerism.

Four
Backhouse and Walker

Backhouse and Walker earned a place in Australian history for reasons that went far beyond their reputation as founders of Quakerism in Australia. Though they came to Australia with the full support, moral and financial, of the London Yearly Meeting of the Society of Friends, they had no narrow vision of limiting their mission to those who might be connected with the Society of Friends. They made no secret of their Quaker beliefs, but they did not parade these beliefs to convert others. It is true that as a result of their visit Quaker Meetings were established firmly in Hobart and less firmly in Sydney, but these were fruits of their labours, not the sole purpose of their visit. Coming as it did in the eighteen-thirties, their visit is historically important because of the description they have left of the events of this decade, and because of their particular contribution to an understanding of penal reform and Aboriginal policy.

They were acute observers and gifted diarists. Both were meticulous in recording daily accounts of what they had seen and done. Though they collaborated in preparation of reports, they maintained in their journals and later in their published works a refreshingly independent eye-witness account of people, places, and events, so that the reader with access to both accounts gets, as it were, a stereoscopic, in-depth view of the eighteen-thirties, a significant decade in Australian history.

The partnership of Backhouse and Walker was an unusually strong one. Though Backhouse was the initiator and the dominant partner, Walker was by no means merely a subservient secretary-companion. They worked so closely together that it is often difficult to identify the individual contributions. They were "centred on the same stock and root", as Walker wrote when parting from Backhouse in Capetown, Backhouse returning to England and Walker to permanent residence in Hobart Town.

> I have parted from my friends in Cape Town and more particularly from my beloved companion and fellow-labourer in the gospel, James Backhouse, after an intimate association and fellowship on religious grounds of more than nine years' standing. It seems to myself like separating two branches that had long been united at the base and were centred on the same stock and root: for whatever may have been our differences of sentiment and dispositions (and with respect to the latter they were diverse) on religious grounds we were ever preserved in unity and harmony of religious labour — an unspeakable mercy which ought to inspire us with devout thankfulness.[2]

James Backhouse was born in 1794 in Darlington, County Durham, into a well-established Quaker family. After attending J. Tatham's boarding-school in Leeds he worked as an assistant in a grocery, drug, and chemical business in Darlington, but then for three winters was ill with inflammation of the lungs. In these winters of enforced idleness he took up the study of botany and thus began his lifelong interest in botany and his career as a nurseryman. He was only eighteen when in response to the ministry of Stephen Grellet[3] he first sensed a call to service in far-off countries. Three years later the focus of vision sharpened to identify the "far-off" country as Australia.

> I was first impressed with the belief that it was the will of the Lord that at a future time I should go on a gospel errand in to Australia. The impression was sudden but very clear. It occurred as I was standing in the nursery ground at Norwich, not thinking on such subjects. I felt as though I could have sunk under it, but I dared not to oppose it and I prayed in spirit that if it were indeed the will of God, He would be pleased to prepare me for it, and to open the way for it, both in my own mind and in the minds of my Friends.[4]

Another fifteen years were to pass before vision was translated into opportunity. Among his friends, however, there was one, Elizabeth Fry, who must have helped to keep his vision focussed on Australia during those years. Backhouse had visited Newgate Prison with Elizabeth Fry and heard

James Backhouse, 1794-1869 (from the Friends' Meeting, Hobart)

George Washington Walker, 1800-1859 (from the Friends' Meeting, Hobart)

from her about her concern for the convicts, particularly for the women, transported to New South Wales and Van Diemen's Land.

In 1830 Thomas Shillitoe, who had returned from travelling as a minister in America, had thoughts of going on to Australia, and James Backhouse offered himself as a companion, but Thomas Shillitoe withdrew and his cloak of concern fell upon Backhouse. This concern was then subjected to the usual sieving process[5] and was finally approved by the Yearly Meeting of Ministers and Elders in London. Approval also signified that London Yearly Meeting would accept responsibility for financing the visit to Australia and Africa.[6]

Backhouse chose as his companion George Washington Walker, who was born in 1800 into a Unitarian family. He first came into contact with Friends during apprenticeship to a draper, Hadwen Bragg, of Newcastle, who, with his wife, Margaret, was a member of the Society of Friends. Walker's contact with Backhouse began in 1820 when Backhouse came to value the stock of one of Margaret Bragg's tenants. He joined the Society of Friends in 1827.

Writing to Samuel Bewley, 3 June 1841, Backhouse recalled how, being unable to think of a suitable companion and no Friend having come forward to offer himself, the thought of Walker came to him in a dream. In the half-waking hours of early morning he seemed to hear a voice say, "Now look northward". Thereupon, not wanting to use a form of heavenly blackmail to persuade Walker of his duty to offer himself, Backhouse wrote, simply asking him to consider whether he felt any urge towards accompanying him. The offer came to him at a time when Walker needed such a challenge. He still felt keenly the loss of Mary Bragg, to whom he had become engaged in 1824. She became blind and died in November 1828. Backhouse's wife had died in 1827. The offer of his widowed sister, Elizabeth Janson, to look after his two children freed Backhouse to undertake the visit to the Australian colonies.

Backhouse, duly accredited as a travelling minister, and his companion-secretary, Walker, entered upon a remarkable partnership. Backhouse was the senior partner, responsible to London Yearly Meeting for carrying out the religious duty he had undertaken. Neither he nor Walker was vigorous in health. Backhouse was small in stature and his weight never apparently exceeded 111 pounds. He had a severe chest illness as a young man and there are references by Walker to Backhouse suffering from angina in Australia. If heart trouble was his problem, he unwittingly perhaps prescribed for himself the very treatment which modern medicine now insists on — walking. Most of their journeying in Australia was on foot. Backhouse kept as meticulous an account of daily mileage travelled as he did of any other details of his journeys. He reported in his diary[7] that the land distance travelled in Australia and Mauritius was 4260 miles, of which 3,000 miles were on foot, 1,000 on horseback, and the rest by coach or row-boat. Twenty-five to thirty miles in all sorts of weather was regarded as a normal day's walk. When the Quaker botanist, W. H. Harvey, met Backhouse in Capetown in 1838, he commented, "He takes four hours' exercise daily for health's sake, but is in the habit of walking in the heat of the day, which I am not able for, so I shall confine myself to his evening exercise."[8] Of the two it would appear that Walker was the less robust. He frequently complained of severe stomach disorders and, in the last days of their final visit to Hobart, he spoke of signs of heart trouble and difficulty in walking uphill. And yet neither bodily frailty nor outward dangers and difficulties daunted them. Such was the nature of their faith.

Backhouse and Walker embarked on the *Science* at St Katharine's dock on 3 September 1831. It was to be almost a decade before their visit to Australia and Africa was completed.

They came to the Australian colonies primarily, as Backhouse said, "to discharge a duty of Christian love". He set out four specific objectives within this primary purpose — to preach the Gospel to the scattered settlers, whether bond or free, to investigate the penal system, to see how the Aborigines were being treated by the white settlers, and to promote the cause of Temperance.

These four objectives are representative of the Quaker outlook of this period, described above in chapter one. There is the strong evangelical motivation, and the expressed intention of grappling with what they and their contemporaries identified as three of the major moral concerns of their day — penal reform, treatment of subject peoples, and Temperance.

Their analysis of these problems and their recommendations may fall short of what social reformers today would consider appropriate, but, limited as they may have been by a measure of paternalism and social naiveté, they had much to say which was well in advance of their times, and which is still relevant now, one hundred and fifty years later.

The Gospel of Christian Love

The underlying purpose of Backhouse and Walker's visit was to preach the gospel of Christian love. At this time in the history of Quakerism in England the Evangelical influence was strong. Many Quakers shared with the Evangelicals a common theological language. The themes of Atonement, Salvation, and Redemption were constantly recurring in the letters and spoken ministry of Friends. Backhouse and Walker's journals reflected this emphasis. Their strong feeling of religious duty gave them a sense of "mission", of being "sent" to proclaim the gospel of love to the outcast prisoner, the lonely settler, the rejected Aborigine.

Their mission had however already begun as soon as they left England on the *Science*. Backhouse had applied for a passage on a convict ship with a view to offering moral and religious instruction to the convicts on the voyage. Three well-known Friends, John Sanderson, Samuel Gurney, and Peter Bedford, formed a deputation to Lord Goderich in support of this request. Permission was refused, the reason given being that this was against established practice and would expose Backhouse and Walker to "much disrespect from prisoners".[9] Letters of introduction to Governors in New South Wales and Van Diemen's Land were however given to facilitate entry to the colonies and to convict settlements.

Instead of convicts, as they had hoped, they had as fellow-passengers forty-six steerage Chelsea pensioners who had commuted their military pensions for a four years' advance payment and a passage to Van Diemen's Land. There were also nine women on board, chiefly wives of pensioners, and six children. Backhouse summed up the situation in these words:

> From having been long accustomed to act in obedience to military discipline, instead of upon principle, these men were generally as incapable of taking care of themselves, when temptation was in the way, as children; and the state of confusion they were in was often appalling. From first going on board we read to them twice a day from the Bible or religious tracts. This was nearly the only time they were quiet. At first some of them tried to stop us by making a noise, but finding we proceeded without noticing them, they ceased: and at the conclusion of the voyage, some of them acknowledged that the time of our reading had been the only time in which they had any comfort.[10]

Backhouse and Walker however gave comfort in more ways than by reading and distributing tracts. Backhouse appears to have had considerable medical expertise and was constantly in demand for dealing with pensioners' ailments. He was also a marriage celebrant, being called on to conduct a wedding of two passengers whose lack of married status had been the cause of several fights. There were at least three occasions when drunk pensioners seized the captain and threatened to throw him overboard. The master of the *Science* considered he owed his life to Backhouse and Walker, who, he told Lieutenant-Governor Arthur, had saved him "from the frantic conduct of the turbulent characters he was bringing out . . . ten times more unruly and troublesome than these convicts".[11]

Quaker peace-making was severely tested, but was persisted in. Backhouse and Walker interviewed regularly the pensioners in steerage and did their best to counsel them on matters affecting their earthly as well as their heavenly welfare. They tried to tackle the drink problem by starting a Temperance Society on board, but the only response came from a poor widow. They may well have wished that their initial efforts to take passage on a convict ship had not been turned down by the Naval Board, for at least on a prison ship they would have had others to take responsibility for law and order.

Backhouse indeed carried unofficial responsibility for the duties usually performed by the surgeon on convict ships and when the *Science* at last reached Hobart Town, Backhouse presented to the Lieutenant-Governor a detailed report on each of the pensioners.[12] He also wrote a letter to Viscount Goderich urging that if there were to be further consignments of pensioners, they should appoint someone to be in authority over them and a doctor to look after them, for many had diseases for which they had been discharged from the army. He also questioned the morality of government policy whereby disabled people were shipped out and dumped, like convicts, to relieve England of an unwelcome burden, but to the prejudice of the Colony, for few of these army derelicts were likely to make good in a distant land with no-one to give them any moral guidance.

At no time did Backhouse and Walker shrink from their religious duty of preaching and caring, for this combination of evangelical fervour and practical concern was a special mark of their mission, and did not fail to convince even their anti-Quaker clerical critics that the main purpose of these two Quaker wayfarers when they set out on their journey was to minister to the needs of the derelict, the desolate, and the isolated.

They held meetings wherever they went. It is probable that no road-gang was missed out, no matter how lonely the spot where the convicts had been sent to cut through a road or build a bridge. Backhouse describes the procedure they followed.

> When we stop them during their working-hours, which we have liberty from the Governor to do, few plead excuses; and as we do not enjoin any forms of worship, but simply after a pause, say what is upon our minds, or pray for them, none seem to take it amiss. If it can be done, we always desire them to sit down, in order that they may rest at the same time; and if exposed to the sun, we request them to keep on their hats or caps. These little considerations for their personal comfort often prepare the way for the reception of our counsel.[13]

For these hardened men the sudden appearance of two strangely garbed Quakers was probably worth no more than a passing respite from an hour's unwilling slavery. For one or two perhaps it awakened a memory which harsh punishment had all but obliterated. And there was an occasional echo later from an ex-convict who thanked God the Quakers had passed his way.

Backhouse and Walker felt their responsibility as much to the lonely settler as to the lonely prisoner. Many a settler must have had the same surprised reaction that Backhouse recorded of one they visited on their way from Stroud to Dingadee in New South Wales, who said that "when he first saw a white man come from the hills behind him, his surprise was excessive, as he had no idea that his countrymen had penetrated the woods in that direction".[14]

They were tireless in carrying out what they felt to be their pastoral duty. No limits were set to their caring.

When they visited isolated settlers, they were often given a night's lodging. Wherever possible they asked to have "a religious opportunity" with the family. With the more affluent settlers this meant asking that the assigned servants also be permitted to attend. Sometimes discussions would follow on the "peculiar" views of Friends on silent worship, paid clergy, the sacraments, and oath-taking, but Backhouse and Walker rarely put forward views unless it was in answer to direct questions. During their journeys in Van Diemen's Land they visited about two hundred and fifty families, many of them more than once, because of the warm friendships formed. They were most impressed with the hospitality given them so freely. "The openness and hospitality with which we are received by those who are outwardly strangers to us is striking and such as we could hardly have expected."[15]

They were welcomed by affluent and needy alike and they were at home in Government House or in the rudest hut. Walker records their night in the hut of a J. Smith when a thunderstorm made it prudent for them to accept the offer of hospitality.

> We had no alternative but to accept or take to the bush which indeed would have been decidedly preferable, but there was a heavy thunderstorm passing over which rendered a shower more than probable. We accordingly took up our quarters for the night — the overseer giving up his birth (sic) to us, which by the bye was only accepted for one person, while he and another man slept on the floor and

two aborigines who were temporary inmates of the hut slept in their sooty blankets by the fire. The united influence of heat, bugs and filth added to extreme fatigue and irritation in my feet from walking banished sleep from my eyelids.... We breakfasted and subsequently had a religious opportunity with the inmates of the hut and three other men who called in passing. We then pursued our way.[16]

No day passed, as they "pursued" their way, without two or more meetings happening, mostly unarranged. In the towns they sought a public "opportunity" and this meant gaining permission for use of the court house or a church property. They sought and were freely given co-operation from government and ecclesiastical authority.

Dr John Service,[17] summing up what he felt to be the distinguishing character of Backhouse and Walker's religion, said, "The Quakers were philanthropists who, instead of preaching too much, kept accounts and kept them accurately. With a view to practical results they were careful to note facts with draper-like precision."[18]

As well as this combination of the spiritual and practical there was also a strong admixture of the spiritual and the adventurous in Backhouse's approach to life. Filled with a sure conviction that he was under God's providence, he accepted all the dangers and uncertainties of daily living with an exhilaration that overwhelmed any fears he might have had. Perhaps the best example of this is his own lively description of their entry into Macquarie Harbour. On 4 June 1832 they were within reach of Macquarie Harbour and the ominous-sounding Hell's Gates. The pilot was taken on board and immediately commanded everybody to go below decks. Backhouse, however, said that if they were lost, he "should like to see the last of it, for the sight was awfully grand". He was given a rope to hang on to, and Walker likewise, and thus they made their entry.[19]

Prisons and Penal Reform

Investigation of every aspect of the penal system was a major objective of the visit of Backhouse and Walker to the Australian colonies, but it was an investigation motivated by a sense of religious duty.

A week after their arrival in Hobart Town they launched into a programme of inspection with a visit to the newly-docked convict ship, the *Elizabeth*. They watched the interrogation process whereby the local authority through questioning produced its own documentary information on each convict. Backhouse and Walker then went over the ship with the Surgeon-Superintendent, Dr Martyn, and found it was

> perfectly free from unpleasant smell, notwithstanding the prisoners, 220 in number, had slept in it last night. The boys were separated from the men, and a system of discipline and instruction was pursued among them that was attended by very pleasing results. Some of the convicts were employed by the Doctor as assistants and monitors. Out of the 120 of the prisoners 76 could not read and many of them seemed never to have had any care bestowed on them before. Several of them learned to read and write and improved their conduct on the passage.[20]

From Martyn they learnt much about the backgrounds of the forty boy convicts, half of whom had already been confined in hulks with hardened criminals. From marks on the arms of some of his boys Martyn knew that they belonged to one of the child-gangs of London, known by the name of the "Forty Thieves". Walker devoted four pages of his journal entry for that day to a detailed Dickensian-like description of these gangs, their training in "bussing" (pick-pocketing), their defence funds, and their badges of brotherhood. One such badge was a verse tattoed on the arm:

> When this you see, remember me.
> And bear me in your mind.
> Let all the world say what they will,
> Don't prove to me unkind.[21]

Backhouse and Walker clearly thought that conditions on the prison ship under Martyn's enlightened leadership were preferable to those from which most of these boys, society's jetsam, had come. They praised particularly Martyn's educational programme and the use of rewards to encourage good behaviour of boys in the contingent. The Penitentiary was then visited, where the same boatload of convicts was addressed by Lieutenant-Governor Arthur, who outlined to them the prospects each had for going up the ladder of hope through ticket-of-leave, conditional pardon, and finally freedom. Backhouse begged leave to add some words of exhortation to enforce the moral thrust of Arthur's address.

On 23 February they paid the first of several visits to the House of Correction for Females, otherwise known simply as the Factory, where 230 female prisoners were housed and employed in teasing, carding and spinning wool, and laundering for the hospital and Orphan School. The wool was then sent to the penal establishment on Maria Island to be made into coarse cloth for convict wear. Following their visits each recorded much interesting detail of prison conditions such as the diet of prisoners, their occupations, treatment, access to moral and religious instruction — and their reception. "As they are in the habit of receiving all descriptions within their walls, some from the very lowest scale of degradation, the first thing that is put into practice is to immerse them in a cold bath where they are thoroughly cleansed and clothed in clean garments."[22]

During the years that followed Backhouse and Walker made visits to almost all the penal establishments scattered through Van Diemen's Land and New South Wales. For these they had not only the permission, but the active co-operation of the governors of the two colonies. Where necessary, transport and rations were provided for them on government vessels and after their visits Backhouse and Walker furnished detailed reports to the authorities. To Lieutenant-Governor Arthur they submitted reports on the penal settlement at Port Arthur, the state of chain-gangs and road-parties in Van Diemen's Land, the state of prisoners in Van Diemen's Land with remarks upon the Penal Discipline and Observations on the state of the colony, Spirituous Liquors, the penal settlement at Macquarie Harbour, the Aborigines on Flinders Island, the use of Quaker models for government records of births, marriages, and deaths, and the Van Diemen's Land Company. Reports were made to Governor Bourke on the penal settlements at Moreton Bay and at Norfolk Island and on various subjects connected with conditions in the colony of New South Wales, including some recommendations concerning treatment of the Aborigines.

It is clear that Arthur valued the reports submitted to him.

He regarded Backhouse and Walker as unprejudiced observers. "Individuals", he said, "unbiassed and unprejudiced as these gentlemen must be, are therefore very likely to afford not only wholesome admonition to the convicts but useful suggestions to the local government."[23]

The reports, based on personal observations, were carefully documented and, where necessary, relevant statistics were provided. Dr Service's description of Walker travelling with a draper's measuring-tape was very apt. In the report to Arthur on Macquarie Harbour details were given of names of absconders, of casualties, punishments, boats built, timbers cut, and work done in the first quarter of 1832 by blacksmiths, turners, coopers, bricklayers, masons, and shoemakers (323 pairs of boots). There were schedules of military duties, work schedules of all sections of the prison community, dimensions of buildings, costs of running the establishment, security measures, health records. Of particular note were Walker's descriptions of the prison on Rocky Island, of timber-cutting on Phillips Island and of the pilot station at the entry to Macquarie Harbour, where they had to wait eighteen days for a favourable wind to leave on the return journey.

These reports were meant primarily for presentation to the authorities on the spot in the colonies and only afterwards to Friends in England for information and for publication in Friends' journals. They were written in the hope that government policy could be influenced.

It is difficult to determine the extent to which their recommendations were heeded. There is evidence that their report on Port Arthur had some effect. On their first visit, not long after the opening of this new settlement, they made practical suggestions, such as the importance of green vegetables to prevent scurvy, the provision of solitary confinement as an alternative to flogging, the need for a catechist to give religious instruction, and a surgeon to supervise health. They urged that the construction of permanent accommodation should proceed without delay so that prisoners could be classified and housed separately. They praised the use of "indulgences" of tea and sugar as rewards for good behaviour and the opportunity given to classified prisoners to have garden plots of their own.

It was a great disappointment therefore to them when they heard six months later that the gardens had been abandoned as incompatible with the concept of punishment. On their second visit to Port Arthur, a year after their first, they found a regime of greater severity in evidence, with consequent increase in the number of attempts to escape. The withdrawal of the privilege of working garden plots was considered to be the cause of renewed onset of scurvy. The work, however, of J. A. Manton, the catechist, met with their approval. It was reassuring to receive a letter from the commandant, Major Charles O'Hara Booth, in June 1835, telling them that as a result of their recommendations on the need for fresh vegetables, scorbutic diseases had almost disappeared and only twenty-nine out of a total of 918 were unable to go to work.

Booth pointed out that a start had been made on increasing accommodation by building a penitentiary, that scurvy had been reduced by growing more field vegetables, and that public flagellation was reserved only for the most serious offences against prison order, such as attempted escape. He expressed gratification that in their report, his "humble efforts" had met "on the whole with the approbation of two such highly esteemed friends of the community as Messrs Backhouse and Walker".[24]

Lady Franklin's journal contained frequent references to Backhouse and Walker's reports on prison discipline, some of these being quoted at length, such as their recommendation that breaches of discipline by members of road gangs should be punished, not by flagellation, but by extension of sentence.[25] She also commented on Ronald Gunn's replies to Backhouse and Walker's criticism of his administration of the Launceston penitentiary.[26] She recorded their views on their visit to the Aboriginal settlement at Wellington in New South Wales[27] and their recommendations concerning Moreton Bay[28] and "ardent" spirits.[29] It is clear that Lady Franklin respected these reports as the product of honest and independent eye-witnesses.

Backhouse and Walker were commissioned by Elizabeth Fry to report personally to her on penal conditions on convict ships and in the colonies. Before coming to Australia

Backhouse had been in contact with her and it is likely that his lively interest in Australian penal institutions had its source in this association. Elizabeth Fry's work in Newgate, begun in 1813, was widely acclaimed, but her interest in female convicts sentenced to transportation is not so well-known. The Ladies' Committee at Newgate, all Quakers except for the vicar's wife, initiated a project with women inmates to make patchwork quilts for use by women convicts transported to Australia.[30] Elizabeth Fry saw to it that women convicts about to be transported, who were taken in open wagons from Newgate to Deptford, like condemned criminals on the way to the guillotine for the public to stare at, should be carried in closed hackney carriages. She herself went personally to comfort and reassure these women and supply clothing and lesson books and parcels of tea and sugar. In all, Elizabeth Fry saw off 106 prison-ships.

Shortly after his arrival in Australia Backhouse wrote to Elizabeth Fry at the request of Arthur to ask for her help in relation to a recent decision of the British government to send out boatloads of young marriageable women to redress the imbalance of the sexes in a preponderantly male colony.

Hobart Town
17 of 2nd mo. 1832

My dear friend,
Elizabeth Fry,

    At the request of Lieut.Governor Arthur I now address thee on behalf of those females that the British Government have determined on sending out to the Colony from the class of society, if I understand it correctly, that may be termed peasantry. The Governor is a man of sincere piety and indefatigable in labouring to promote the temporal and spiritual welfare of the Colony and he is deeply aware in a measure of the kind proposed, which meets his cordial approbation, how much depends upon the manner in which it is carried into effect and he considers it a matter of the first importance that the chastity of these females be most vigilantly protected on the passage out.[31]

With the problem thus stated Backhouse sought Elizabeth Fry's help in seeing that suitable captains and crews were chosen who would not threaten the chastity of their ship's passengers. He hoped also that some women Friends or missionary wives accompanying their husbands might be found to superintend these boatloads of unprotected females. Elizabeth Fry replied promptly, saying she regretted that one shipload had already left without her being able to provide any supervision, but she would exercise her influence with the government to see that any other ship would satisfy the requested conditions. Then there followed a request which indicated Elizabeth's expectation of Backhouse as one who would supply detailed information to her on the condition in which female convicts arrived in the colony. "And we think that very great good would result from an exact report of these things being taken upon the arrival of every ship and a copy of that report *always* forwarded to me because the women feel it a very strong stimulus to good conduct during the voyage."[32] The check-list given indicates the thoroughness of Elizabeth Fry's regulations for the welfare of the women during the voyage.[33] Elizabeth Fry then expressed the hope that the Ladies' Association in New South Wales would furnish regular reports on convict ships arriving in Sydney and that a similar association would be formed in Hobart. She concluded her letter:

> I cannot help hoping that thy companion and thyself may in many ways be of use where your lot is at present likely to be cast and, my dear friend, may you be 'wise as serpents and harmless as doves', I think you will find it difficult in a place where there is so much party spirit to keep clear of it. You must not listen at what one person says of another or only those who you find you can indeed trust. May a blessing rest upon you and your labours in every way and above all the choice blessing of preservation. My love to thy companion, though I believe unknown to me, and believe me
>
> Thy affectionately interested friend,
> Elizth. Fry.
>
> Excuse my letter being rather a scrawl, but I have so much writing and other engagements that I have not time to revise.[34]

Though some measures of reform had reduced the worst incidence of brutality in the treatment of prisoners, the reports given by Backhouse and Walker presented pictures of conditions that were horrifying enough. Hulks were used in Van Diemen's Land as well as in English ports. Here is Walker's picture of the Hobart hulks in 1833:

> In the afternoon of this day we had a religious meeting with the

Prisoners of the Hulks, about two hundred in number. This party is engaged chiefly in forming a new wharf on the South East side of the town which when completed will be a great acquisition to the shipping. The greater part of the gang are in chains. They sleep in the Hulks at night which are confined vessels with rows of berths one above the other in which three and four men sleep abreast. One hulk contains about 110 men, and the other about 90. In the summer season the places must be very close and offensive. It is no slight punishment to be obliged to sleep there amidst such a large number of men, and under the strictest confinement during the night season.[35]

But the Campbelltown gaol in New South Wales was admitted by Backhouse and Walker to be far worse. It was built below the Court House and consisted of one large ward for prisoners, 20½ feet long by 12½ feet wide and 8 feet high with two small inadequate ventilation tubes. Sixty convicts had at times been confined in it and on one occasion ninety. "The stench arising through the floor of the Court House is so bad that the windows have to be kept open during the time of business and sometimes the court is adjourned to another place. This is the worst prison we have seen in the colony."[36] Walker added: "I have seen nothing so like the Black Hole of Calcutta as is here verified".[37] Backhouse and Walker experienced also the horrors of travelling on the small prison ships that were used to ferry prisoners from Hobart Town to Macquarie Harbour or from Sydney to Port Macquarie. Here there was not only the stench of the small, confined, belowdecks prison, but the added misery of a pitching and rolling ship. To prevent the possibility of a convict takeover of a ship, prisoners were often chained not only singly but each fastened in turn to a long chain. Walker came away from reading to the men below decks with the conviction that subjecting men to such inhuman conditions and total lack of privacy outraged any finer feelings they might have ever had and left a permanent and debasing effect on their morals and habits. The same feeling lay behind Backhouse's observations, made after seeing in Perth, Van Diemen's Land, the corpse of a prisoner, who had been sentenced to hanging in Hobart, gibbeting in chains by the wayside.

Near Perth we passed a gibbet, lately erected; on which the body of a prisoner who committed a murder near the spot was suspended, with a view of deterring from crime. But so unsuccessful was this first experiment of the kind in Tasmania, that pocket-picking and drunkenness occurred among the crowd who resorted thither to view the hideous spectacle. Popular feeling was so strong, against the transfer of this political barbarism to the Australian regions, that it was officially resolved that this first experiment should be the last.[38]

Backhouse and Walker did not find Macquarie Harbour as bad as its dread reputation had led them to expect. The statistics they supplied, however, were a grim reminder of the horrors of this isolated outpost and its depraving effect on those condemned to exile there. In the eleven years of its existence since 1822, only thirty-five out of eighty-five deaths were from natural causes. The other fifty died violent deaths from drowning, accidental death while felling trees, shooting by the military guards, and murder by fellow-prisoners. Just as grim were the statistics of escape.

> Out of the 112 who eloped, 62 were supposed to have perished in the bush, and 9 were murdered by their comrades on the journey, for a supply of food. For this purpose the party proposing to attempt traversing the formidable forest, selected a weak minded man, and persuaded him to accompany them: and when the slender stock of provisions which they had contrived to save from their scanty rations was exhausted they laid violent hands on their victim. One party when lately apprehended near the settled districts, had in their possession, along with the flesh of a kangaroo, a portion of that of one of their comrades! An appalling evidence of how easily man, in a depraved state, may descend even to cannibalism.[39]

Backhouse and Walker however reported favourably on the regime of the current commandant, Major Bailee, who had considerably reduced the incidence of brutal flogging in favour of solitary confinement and appeared to have won from the inmates a reputation for fair and firm dealing. Some effort too was being made to separate from the toughened reprobates those who showed some glimmer of a wish to reform.

In their report on Norfolk Island to Governor Bourke Backhouse and Walker made a number of quite specific recommendations. They realized that Norfolk Island had more than its quota of what Walker called "depraved" prisoners, as judged by their profanity, their complete disregard for honesty, their proneness to crime, neglect of work, and insolence to overseers. Backhouse and Walker had a naive faith in the reforming effect of solitary confinement, and this is what they repeatedly urged as a substitution for flagellation. They believed that in solitude men would resolve to turn from a life of crime. What they did not perhaps see was that the solitary confinement cells designed by prison architects, shutting out light and all human contact, could have as brutalizing an effect as the lash. Though Norfolk Islanders complained of the food, Backhouse and Walker considered it coarse but wholesome. The serving of vegetables twice a week was approved as a preventative against scurvy. Moral education and religious instruction were in the hands of a lapsed Episcopalian trainee minister. Backhouse believed a free catechist was needed. He made the practical suggestion that the importation of bullocks would free convicts for productive labour and he also urged that competent boat-builders be engaged to repair the boats damaged in the surf, which pounded on the island shores and made every landing of men or stores hazardous.

Backhouse and Walker spent almost two months on Norfolk Island. They tramped all over it, meeting with working parties, talking with groups and with individuals and in general, acting as pastors to these outcasts of society "in the hope", said Backhouse, "that some of them may yet come under the power of the gospel".[40] Then just as they were about to leave the island, a number of prisoners asked to meet with them in the Court House during the dinner hour. About forty were present, but their spokesman said they represented a much larger number who were away with the work gangs. Backhouse and Walker, to their great surprise, were presented with an address by the prisoners. This must surely have been an unprecedented event in this "sea-girt prison".

Norfolk Island, 29th April 1835.

Gentlemen,

We, the prisoners of the Crown, embracing the tenets of the Protestant faith, cannot, from pure motives of unfeigned gratitude, allow you to quit this island without thus publicly expressing our sentiments for your unwearied zeal and attention to our best interests, since you came among us, viz. the salvation of our immortal souls.

Permit us to implore that you would convey to Major Anderson, the Commandant, the deep sense we entertain of his great anxiety, since he assumed the command, for our well-being, here and hereafter.

That a kind Providence may conduct you both, in safety, through the trackless deep, to the haven where you would wish to be is,

> Gentlemen,
> The ardent wish of
> This congregation.[41]

Backhouse, though he may have had unspoken reservations about the "pure motives" nevertheless acknowledged this unsolicited tribute as a "kind intention". Walker, however, recording the incident, was clearly very moved by this expression of gratitude from "our unhappy fellow-creatures, respecting whom our Christian interest has been so deeply excited".[42]

In June 1834 Backhouse and Walker presented to Arthur their "Report upon the State of Prisoners in Van Diemen's Land, with Remarks upon the penal Discipline and Observations on the General State of the Colony". This report, while based on conditions observed in their travels, is important for its general statement on the purpose of prison discipline, and as such it is relevant to modern penology. Backhouse and Walker's three objectives of imprisonment — restraint, restitution, reformation — are still considered to provide a valid frame of reference.

They acknowledged that restraint was necessary to prevent the wrongdoer from committing further mischief. They protested however that heavy punishments did not have the expected deterrent effect. Walker quoted in his journals several examples of punishments which seemed to him out of all proportion to the crimes committed. One woman employed at Government House in Hobart and an attender at Friends' Meetings had been sentenced to seven years for stealing one shilling and sixpence. The sentence of capital punishment meted out so freely by judges for any one of over a hundred offences had, in Walker's opinion, little deterrent effect upon the classes of people engaged in crime — the uneducated, the spirit-drinkers, the trained group of thieves, the "licentious" (those given to indulgence in theft and fraud). These, in most cases lacking moral perception or religious convictions, had no fear of death, because they had no belief in the ultimate Judgment Day. Hence dread of punishment was not likely to impress these classes.

Backhouse and Walker held that attempts should be made to counteract the causes of crime. Here they appear closer to modern social theorists who maintain that the causes of crime lie in the social conditions in which the poor and the deprived are reared. Backhouse and Walker however put poverty as the last of the causes of crime and illiteracy first. They listed education therefore as the first of the social measures needed, particularly moral education, based upon a knowledge of the Bible. The expectation of the Christian moral theorists of the nineteenth century was that once people had been taught to read and therefore had access to the Bible, crime would fall away. Education would make people morally responsible. This theory now appears naive, for it is clear that education does not make people "good". Backhouse and Walker consistently advocated the importance of religious instruction as an essential part of the prison discipline, and although as Quakers they did not hold with the idea of paid clergy, they urged the appointment of catechists in all penal institutions and the availability of a supply of Bibles in the prison ships, the road-gang camps, the scattered gaols, and the isolated penal settlements.

The second most obvious cause of crime to them, next to lack of moral education, was the drinking of "ardent" spirits. Certainly there was no lack of evidence appearing to support this theory. Again Walker's journals contained countless examples of drink cited as the cause of crimes. The attempt to establish Temperance Associations wherever they went in settled areas was as typical of their routine as the distribution of tracts and Bibles. From their own experience with the Chelsea pensioners on board the *Science*, they believed that alcohol should be prohibited on prison ships and indeed, ideally, throughout the colonies. They failed perhaps to give due weight to the causes which led men to take refuge in drink — the slums from which they came, the hulks, the appalling conditions below deck in the prison ships and, in a far land, the punishment which seemed to have no end, for it was but a very few who ever returned from forced exile to rejoin the families they left behind. The other measures proposed for the reduction of crime were the breaking up of the street gangs, the suppression of prostitution and of gambling, and the due observance of the Sabbath.

There was one aspect of the "restraint" component of punishment which became a hot political subject during Backhouse and Walker's period in Van Diemen's Land. There were those, both in the colony and in England, who were loud in their claims that transportation was no punishment, for had they not heard stories of hardened criminals released before their time was up, given grants of land, prospering and hence making a mockery of transportation as a deterrent?

Backhouse and Walker identified one way in which the idea had spread in England that transportation was no punishment. "Prisoners frequently represent their situation to their friends to be much better than it really is. . . . This is often done to induce their friends to emigrate, in the hope that they may be a benefit to themselves."[43] An example was given of a woman entreated by her husband to come out to join him and assured that he had a good position and good wages. On arrival the woman found that her husband was 250 miles away and without wages, whereupon the woman took to "immoral courses". Even if the detail of distance is questionable, for 250 miles' distance from Hobart, unless by a very circuitous route, would imply a watery place of work, examples of this sort were not infrequent. There was also the case of the well-known Henry Savery, author of *The Hermit of Van Diemen's Land,* whose wife joined him on the strength of the very rosy picture given of her husband's circumstances and prospects, but who soon returned disillusioned by the discovery of his continuing convict status.

Backhouse and Walker claimed that transportation, so far from being a soft option, was indeed a grievous punishment, for it meant the hard rigours of a long sea voyage, clamped like cattle below decks, assignment without choice of master or occupation, work without wages, liability to summary punishment in a chain-gang for offences provoked perhaps by a brutal overseer, himself a convict, "and in the midst of all these trials he is continually reminded of the sweets of liberty by numbers around who are free, and, by contrast, of the irksomeness of his miserable bondage with their freedom".[44] Arthur, under fire from critics at home who considered that transportation was no deterrent, sent reports from Backhouse and Walker to support his own view that the state of the convict was "wretched indeed, for nothing compensates for the loss of liberty".[45]

Transportation also met the second of their objectives of imprisonment — restitution, for the transportee, they said, whether assigned or employed on public works, had the opportunity to make restitution by his labour, not to the victim of his crime, but to the new society of which he was now an unwilling member.

Backhouse and Walker claimed that reformation should be the main aim of prison discipline. They would be strongly on the side of modern behavioural psychologists in penology, as well as in pedagogy.

> It is worthy of observation, as a fact well known to those acquainted with school discipline that the receipt or forfeiture of a single ticket, a certain number of which entitle the possessor to a specific reward of insignificant value, has a far greater influence in exciting to good conduct than the old, and now nearly exploded system of corporal punishment. And prisoners, generally, are but children in point of moral attainment, or true understanding of their own interests. If a plan, therefore, on a somewhat similar principle to the foregoing, were to be adopted with reference to them we are of the opinion that it would be attended with happy effects.[46]

They firmly believed that the judicious use of rewards, graduated and planned to be within reach, like stars in a child's school book, would do much to encourage the progress of the prisoner through the various degrees of servitude — the penitentiary, the ticket-of-leave, the conditional, and finally the free pardon. They were equally aware that, if inducements failed, movement could lead down as well as up the ladder of hope. Again, moral education and religious instruction were seen as essential to any possibility of lasting reformation.

Backhouse and Walker found themselves in agreement with much of what Captain Maconochie, Secretary to Sir John Franklin, was advocating in his paper on penal reform. They thought Maconochie's principles "Christian, humane, and rational".[47] They fully supported his criticism of the operation of the penal system in Van Diemen's Land and his central theme that moral principles should be brought to bear on prisoners to promote their own reform. They supported Maconochie's behavioural approach of using rewards to break bad habits. They also believed that Van Diemen's Land provided the appropriate setting for a fair trial of Maconochie's idea. Maconochie in turn acknowledged his debt to Backhouse and Walker, particularly for his Mark System whereby marks were to be used as a measuring-stick of a convict's progress towards rehabilitation.[48] In his reports to Franklin in 1838 Maconochie quoted freely from Backhouse and Walker and particularly the passage cited above.[49]

When Maconochie finally presented his case to the Houses of Parliament he acknowledged the valuable support and encouragement given him by Backhouse and Walker, attaching three of their letters to his as a proof of this,[50] and the following declaration:

> The well-known and highly respected Quakers, James Backhouse and George Washington Walker, who have been above five years in the penal settlements observing closely the operation of their existing constitution, not only cordially agree with the views which I have here attempted to explain regarding it, but also with those I entertained for amelioration. They have accordingly given me a testimony to this effect, which I subjoin, and also placed their journals and reports in my hands that I may select whatever passages I may find in them to my purpose. I feel extremely indebted for this kindness and avail myself of it gladly.[51]

Backhouse, just before leaving Sydney, had been engaged in correspondence with Maconochie about penal reform and in a letter to Maconochie dated 29 August 1837,[52] made some interesting comparisons between the penal systems in New South Wales and in Van Diemen's Land. Backhouse found that convicts in New South Wales were more insubordinate and reckless, one reason given being that the Irish were sent to New South Wales rather than to Van Diemen's Land. He said that discipline was more rigid, that flagellation was much more common,[53] it being not uncommon to find in some road-gangs that all of the members had been flogged on an average four times with twenty-five to a hundred lashes of the cat-o'-nine-tails. By contrast he applauded Lieutenant-Governor Arthur who believed in moral and religious influence and did what he could to introduce this in Van Diemen's Land through the appointment of catechists, the opening of schools, and encouragement of the attendance of prisoners at public worship.

In promulgating their ideas of penal reform, Backhouse and Walker had access to several influential people. In Van Diemen's Land they had, in effect, an open line of communication with the Lieutenant-Governors, Arthur and Franklin, and it has been shown that their reports were not only received but that attempts were made to act on some of the specific practical issues they raised. They also had direct access to the British Parliament through Sir Thomas Fowell Buxton, the ex-Quaker member of Parliament and brother-in-law of Elizabeth Fry, who had something of the stature of a Wilberforce in the social reform movement in Great Britain. Backhouse sent copies of his reports back to England and also personal letters to Buxton urging legislative action on penal reform and treatment of Aborigines.

Australian Aborigines

The importance of Backhouse and Walker's references to the Aborigines, particularly those in Van Diemen's Land, lies in their eyewitness accounts of the Tasmanians and of some of the mainland tribes. But to this valuable factual material were added some trenchant comments on black and white relationships — on indigenous landowner and white intruder. Social attitudes and official government policy alike came in for criticism and the issues raised then are still relevant.

At the time of Backhouse and Walker's arrival in Van Diemen's Land the last act of the Tasmanian tragedy had begun. After the disastrous and expensive fiasco of the attempt to round up the Tasmanian tribes, the government had turned to persuasion and given George Augustus Robinson authority to gather the remnants of the wandering tribes together on Flinders Island. From Robinson they gained information about this threatened race. Both Backhouse and Walker initially were impressed by him. "We endeavoured as much as we could to strengthen the hands of this worthy man, who has many discouragements and difficulties to contend with, but Divine Providence has hitherto eminently blessed his labours and we separated under feelings of much sympathy and interest for him and the object he was about to prosecute."[54]

It is interesting to note Walker's change of opinion of "the conciliator" when he met him some nine months later in Northern Tasmania where Robinson was bringing in some of the West Coast Aborigines to areas settled by the Van Diemen's Land Company. In his journal he foreshadowed Robinson's ultimate failure in leadership on Flinders Island.

> From the concurrent testimony of a great many individuals we cannot but fear, however disposed we might be to form a more favourable judgment could we do so with propriety, that George Augustus Robinson is a person who has either fallen from his steadfastness as a Christian, or that he is not the person that we once thought we had reason to believe him. In addition to flagrant instances of defective judgment, there is too much ground to believe that he has acted in several aspects in a manner unbecoming the character of a Christian, or even moral man. This is to us a matter of sincere regret. But we are quite confirmed in the opinion that to place him at the head of the Aboriginal Establishment as their instructor, and director in matters of religious or moral nature would be fraught with disadvantages. This is not the man who possesses the requisite qualifications, either as regards his judgment or his principles, if we be not greatly deceived in our conclusions respecting him.[55]

The reasons for this change of attitude are not made explicit, but it is probable that Backhouse and Walker had heard reports of Robinson's alleged intimacy with Trucanini,[56] and also of his apparently increasing tendency to think in terms of profit to himself from his Aboriginal mission.[57]

There is much in Backhouse and Walker's attitude to the Tasmanians which is reminiscent of the Quaker, John Woolman's, approach to the American Indians. When Woolman travelled amongst the feared tribes he declared that his first object was "if haply I might learn something from them". And this was the spirit in which Backhouse and Walker met the Aborigines. Walker set down, sometimes in great detail, his observations on the habits, customs, appearance, attitudes of these people who never ceased to fascinate him. He was particularly impressed by what he took to be their peaceable disposition.

> It is a pleasing sight in all their public amusements and as well in their more private intercourse, to observe the harmony and good humour that prevails. Was a like number of Europeans to meet for amusement, it would be a rare occurrence if they separated without exhibiting proofs of selfishness or discontent or other malevolent feelings, but the aborigines on these occasions are like so many brothers and sisters. Nothing but good humour, mirth and genuine and unsophisticated kindness prevails. Everything is done in uniting concert. Jarring, or quarrelling, is a thing unknown.[58]

Though Backhouse referred in his *Narrative* to the Aborigines as "savages", he took pains in his introduction to make it clear that this term was intended to "designate human beings, living on the wild produce of the earth, and destitute of any traces of civilization; and by no means, to convey the idea that these people are more cruel than the rest of the human race, or of inferior intellect".[59]

Through the co-operation of the Lieutenant-Governor arrangements were made for Backhouse and Walker to visit the new Aboriginal settlement on Flinders Island and to have the opportunity to study at first hand the characteristics of a people destined soon to become museum pieces. Each made copious notes. Their descriptions are complementary. Backhouse often adds summary comment to factual description, as in the following account of his first contact with the "original inhabitants" of Tasmania.

> The original inhabitants, whose forefathers had occupied it from time immemorial, were of the Negro race. They were of moderate stature, dark olive colour, and had black, curly, woolly hair. They were few in number, probably never more than from seven hundred to a thousand, their habits of life being unfriendly to increase. Excepting on the west coast, they had no houses, but in inclement weather took shelter in the thicker parts of the forest, in the valleys or near the sea. They wore no clothes, but sometimes ornamented

themselves by strips of skin with the fur on, which they wore around the body, arms, or legs. To enable them to resist the changes of weather, they smeared themselves from head to food with red ochre and grease. The men also clotted their hair with these articles, and had the ringlets drawn out like rat-tails. The women cropped their hair as close as they could with sharp stones or shells.

These people formed a few tribes, differing a little in dialects and habits; they were destitute of any traces of civilization; their food consisted of roots and some species of fungus, with shell-fish, grubs, birds, and other wild animals. The latter they took by means of the simplest missiles, or by climbing trees; they cooked them by roasting, and daily moved to a fresh place, to avoid the offal and filth that accumulated about the little fires which they kindled daily, and around which they slept.

In this state the first European visitors of their island found them, and mistaking some peculiarities in their manners for stupidity, set them down as lower in intellect than other human beings.[60]

Walker too mingles comment with descriptive details, but the comment is rather more of his own personal feelings towards the Aborigines he describes.

The expression of countenance and the general figure and appearance of these people is far from denoting that degree of ferocity, or of degradation that has been ascribed to them by their enemies. They are of middle stature on an average, tho' some individuals are six feet or more, and they are remarkably well proportioned, plump and athletic in person. The men are clothed in coarse woollen garments, consisting generally of a long jacket — the women wear a garb made from a blanket into a sort of loose cape which covers their persons pretty effectively, with the exception of the feet and neck, which with their heads generally go bare. Their countenances, both men and women, are far from unpleasing — not that they can claim to anything approaching beauty according to European ideas of beauty — but there is something agreeable in the expression and arrangement of their features, and which leads the observer to hope that there are good dispositions within.

They appear extremely good natured and when a remark is addressed to them, they smile and nod assent, and if addressed so as to exhibit a knowledge of any word in their language, or in terms that are familiar to them in English, they laugh and utter a sort of exclamation approaching to a shout, but strongly indicative of satisfaction. There are 44 men, 29 women and 5 children on the Establishment. Of the latter 2 are half-caste; or the offspring of European fathers by native women. It is remarkable that there should be so few children, considering that the females are generally young and healthy — which may also be said with regard to the men.[61]

Several stories are related to illustrate the kindly disposition of the Tasmanians. Backhouse describes how two white men of Cottrell's party, Cottrell being Robinson's assistant, were thrown into the water while crossing a river by raft.[62] Native women swam out and indicated that the men should get on their backs and they would ferry them to shore. The men refused — and were drowned. Though Backhouse might have commented that the white men preferred drowning to an admission that they needed the help of Aboriginal women, he chose rather to observe: "The kind-hearted women were greatly affected by the accident".[63] On another occasion Backhouse was staying with John Batman, who told him that one of the native women had lost a child and buried it near Batman's house. Next morning Batman, happening to be walking before sunrise, found the mother weeping over the grave. "Yet it is asserted by some", said Backhouse, "that these people are without natural affection."[64]

Backhouse did not meet Charles Darwin who was a visitor to Hobart in 1835 on *H.M.S. Beagle* and who was disposed to see a biological justice in the disappearance of the weaker Tasmanian human species. Bernard Smith, quoting Darwin in his 1980 Boyer Lecture, "How little can the hard worked wife of a degraded Australian savage, who uses very few abstract words and cannot count above four, exert her self-consciousness, or reflect on the nature of her existence", added the comment, "The conclusion is inescapable. Truganini possessed less intelligence that Darwin's dog". Backhouse would have strongly contested Darwin's view (or Smith's interpretation of it), which equated cultural difference with innate intellectual superiority.[65] Backhouse's summing up on the intelligence of the Aborigines, as he assessed it, is a masterly statement of the fallacy that underlies theories of racial superiority.

> After having seen something of the natives of Van Diemen's Land, the conviction was forced upon my mind that they exceeded the Europeans in skill, in those things to which their attention has been directed from childhood, just as much as Europeans exceeded them

in the points to which the attention of the former had been turned under the culture of civilization. There is similar variety of talent and of temper among the Tasmanian aborigines to what is to be found among other branches of the human family; and it would not be more erroneous in one of these people to look upon an English woman as defective in capacity, because she could neither dive into the deep and bring up cray-fish, nor ascend the lofty gum-trees to catch opossums for her family, than it would be for an English woman to look upon the Tasmanian as defective in capacity, because she could neither sew nor read, nor perform the duties of civil, domestic life. Were the two to change stations, it is not too much to assume that the untutored native of the woods would much sooner learn to obtain her food by acquiring the arts of civilization than the woman from the civilized society would by acquiring the arts belonging to the savage life.[66]

Backhouse and Walker no doubt shared the common view that the future of the Tasmanians depended on their willingness to be "civilized", which to them meant learning to eat like the white man, wear clothes, worship the white man's God — but not to drink the white man's poison. In New South Wales they were appalled by the evidence of white man's depravity and of its effect on the unprotected Aborigine. They noted the incidence of drunkenness, prostitution, and venereal disease. The Tasmanians, after being almost wiped out, were to be "protected" from these evils by being gathered into the sanctuary of Flinders Island. That this protection, so far from guaranteeing a future, might even hasten its eclipse did not become evident to Backhouse and Walker. Walker even tried to reassure the remnants on Flinders Island that they had a future — thanks to the good intentions of the government. He expressed this in a sort of "pidgin" English.

> Several have expressed their wish that we should stay with them. We have at different times endeavoured to make them understand that our object in visiting them was to promote their comfort and welfare. That we should tell the people of England who are interested about them whether they are treated kindly. That the white who were cruel and aggressive towards them were very bad men; that if they do so again people of England would be very angry. Governor be very angry. Encouraged them to look forward to their removal to Pea Jacket as the means of increasing their happiness —

there they are to have little 'Lehprennys' (that is, houses) to themselves — they then grow potatoes for themselves, corn to make bread — learn to read and write — to sew — be very comfortable and happy like the Lodowinnys (white men). That all this is very good — what we desire for them — and what is intended — because they are our brothers and sisters — same flesh and blood — men like ourselves; that the Commandant and Doctor love them — be good to them — give them plenty of gibla (eat) plenty tobacco. They must do as their friends and brothers desire them. Through the medium of Jambo and one or two others who know a little English, I think these leading ideas they are made acquainted with. In making them known to one another I frequently have heard the expression of 'narreh coopeh' (very good) introduced. I hope it will tend to increase their confidence in the benevolent good intentions of the government towards them, and animate them to act their part in bringing about a better state of things with reference to their own condition.[67]

It is unlikely that these reassurances were sufficient to assuage the land-hunger of the Tasmanians, evicted from the earth of their roamings, nor to guarantee that governmental good intentions would be translated into benevolent action. However good the intentions, the civilizing and Christianizing of this race served only to hasten the end.

Bernard Smith titled the third part of his 1980 Boyer Lecture "The Concerned Conscience". In it he described a sketch of an Aborigine of the Botany Bay tribe by the young Quaker artist, Sydney Parkinson, on Cook's *Endeavour*. Parkinson had drawn the tribal markings made on the front of the body as a crucifix in form. Was this, says Bernard Smith, evidence "that at the first moment of European contact on our eastern coast one conscience at least was troubled?"[68] Parkinson's own comments upon the attitudes of the ship's company to the natives of Otaheite would seem to corroborate the suggestions that his symbolic representation of tribal marks revealed his troubled conscience. In his journal he writes: "What a pity that such brutality should be exercised upon unarmed ignorant Indians."[69] Further support for the suggestion comes from his brother who published the journal. In his introduction he described what he understood to be Parkinson's feelings about the native islanders of the South Pacific. "While others for want of a more innocent curiosity or amusement were indulging themselves in those sensual gratifications which are so easily obtained among the female part of uncivilized nations we find him gratifying no other passion than that of laudable curiosity."[70] Revulsion against white brutality, and laudable curiosity, based on a respect for the Aborigines as fellow human beings, were also characteristic of Backhouse and Walker. This is why, if, as Bernard Smith suggests, the history of the "concerned Australian conscience" is ever written, Backhouse and Walker deserve a prominent place in that history, for their consciences were deeply troubled and they did their best to stir the conscience of their fellow-Christians in the colonies and at home in England. They wrote frank reports on Aborigine settlements not only on Flinders Island but also on the mainland. They also spoke the truth as they saw it to authority, to Governor Bourke in New South Wales, to Lieutenant-Governor Arthur in Van Diemen's Land, and to the British government, particularly through letters to Sir Thomas Fowell Buxton. In a personal letter to Governor Bourke, following a visit by Backhouse and Walker when Bourke commented that he was anxious to do something for "the Blacks" but didn't know what, Backhouse listed as major grievances the usurpation of Aboriginal hunting grounds as white squatters moved out in search of new land and the lack of any government land-rights policy. Lady Franklin apparently was impressed by the logic of Backhouse's advocacy of land rights for the Aborigines, for after copying out extracts from Backhouse's report to Governor Bourke in her journals, she added:

> Mr. Backhouse does not disguise that the expense of such a plea would be very considerable — he thinks it might be safely provided for out of the proceeds of Government sales of the very land which was the natural possession of the Blacks — this priority of claim must be admitted by anyone who wants equity and common justice.[71]

He also pointed to the appalling cruelties practised by the white man upon an almost defenceless race. If any retaliation was attempted the unmitigated vengeance which followed was pursued without any regard for law and without fear of legal consequence. Backhouse urged that the government should make every effort to give Aborigines protection under the law. They needed also material support, particularly by establishing settlements away from centres of population where white and black mixed to the detriment of both. He advocated the establishment of schools at mission stations and the payment of missionaries by the government. Aborigines, he said, should be encouraged to work by having inducements held out to them, but work should not be exacted from them. He concluded his letter with a prophetic peroration:

> Therefore I trust I shall not be accounted as improperly interfering in a political question in thus plainly, yet respectfully urging it: seeing it is in the cause of humanity and on behalf of the oppressed — of a people who require to have justice done to them speedily, or the opportunity will be gone for ever, and the unmitigated guilt before God of their extermination be fixed irremediably upon the British nation and its Australian descendants.[72]

It might be said that those Australian descendants are now facing the truth of that prophecy.

Though Backhouse and Walker did what they could to influence official British policy on land-rights and on legal recognition of the rights of Aboriginal peoples not only for protection but for citizenship status, they admitted that there was a gap between pious statements of government intention in Westminster and settlers' avid land-grabbing twelve thousand miles away in the colonies.

New colonies were springing up in Port Phillip and in South and Western Australia. Some attempt at formulating a land policy had already been made at Port Phillip on the initiative of John Batman and Arthur. Walker recorded a detailed account of the land "treaty" made by Batman with the Port Phillip Aboriginal tribes. He saw it as "a novel example in these modern times, but one which it is hoped will soon become general, of the rights of the Aboriginal possessors of the soil being respected". Walker was, perhaps, rather too easily disposed to see in Batman's treaty an echo of William Penn's famous treaty with the Indians, as he added: "I hope the arms mentioned merely allude to the tomahawks which, though they might be used as offensive weapons, are not generally converted to the purposes of warfare by the Aborigines of New Holland".[73]

Backhouse was inclined to see in the treaty evidence of benevolence rather than of self-interest or of an attempt to pre-empt government recognition of a "fait accompli" acquisition of new territory. He was concerned however and sceptical about government policy with respect to Aborigines in the new colonies.

> At the first settlement of Port Phillip a party of benevolent people attempted making a treaty with some of the chiefs and purchasing land from them, but this the British Government did not sanction and the whole scheme fell through when the country was taken possession of as a part of New South Wales. There is reason to think that the state of society among the Aborigines gave no power to the chiefs to sell on behalf of the respective tribes and they certainly had none on behalf of other tribes. If Europeans occupy the country of savages [74] the former must act justly from principle, if they would act as becomes Christians. The untutored natives, forming a thinly scattered and unorganized population can neither assert nor defend their own rights. It is in cases like this that principle is put to the test; and it is lamentable to see how little principle, in this respect, has been exhibited in these cases either by the British Government or by its European subjects. [75]

Officialdom found a legal technicality to justify breaking the treaty. No further obstacle was placed in the way of the free settlers' grab for land.

There was hope, however, that South Australia might provide a different example of fair treatment of the Aborigines. Soon after the breakdown of the "treaty" at Port Phillip Backhouse and Walker were on their way to Adelaide. They had been impressed by what they considered was the enlightened attitude of the South Australian Commissioners, whose first report to Lord Glenelg stated that a fifth of the land taken from the Aborigines would be set apart for their further use and benefit. The Commissioners had further pledged "to provide for these poor creatures the means of subsistence and of moral and religious instruction".[76] Whether Backhouse had had any part in influencing the Commissioners in the formulation of this policy is a matter of speculation. In 1834 he had written to Buxton along these lines and Edward Gibbon Wakefield had personal connections with the Buxtons and the Frys. In any case one of the first things

Backhouse and Walker set themselves to do on arrival in Adelaide was to remind the settlers of their obligation to carry out the commissioners' intentions. They were instrumental in setting up a South Australian Committee for the purpose of assisting the official Protector of the Aborigines in carrying out the Commissioners' land policy. At a meeting called for this purpose Backhouse and Walker seemed reasonably optimistic. Walker reported that the resolution to assist the Protector was carried unanimously,

> .. the greatest harmony and good feeling also prevailing during the discussion of the subject, so important for the Blacks, and also for the European Inhabitants whose comfort and prosperity will be in measure identified with those of the former. We pointed out the dire consequences of a less humane and equitable policy as illustrated in the history of New South Wales and Van Diemen's Land, particularly of the last-mentioned colony, which brought upon itself a frightful retribution for the oppression that had been practised under the tacit permission of its local government.[77]

Such optimism however was short-lived. When Backhouse wrote a letter to Buxton after visiting South and Western Australia, he had already begun to have doubts about the outcome of the land policy in South Australia. Genuine as the original intention may have been and laudable as the motives of the Commissioners may have appeared to those distant in Westminster, there was already lurking in Backhouse's mind a suspicion that a way would be found by the South Australian settlers to circumvent the one-fifth reservation clause. He feared that a legal technicality would be found as easily there as it had been in Victoria. Settlers indeed had already canvassed what Walker called the "legal sophism" of an interpretation of land rights, whereby proprietary rights are determined by cultivation or improvement of the soil, it being argued that as the Aborigines were nomadic and not tillers of the soil, they therefore had no legal rights to the land. Backhouse revealed in a succinct comment, "an apprehension . . . that the consideration of the rights of the original Inhabitants of the country would ultimately be merged in the supposed interests of the settlers. This arose from some sense of the general prevalence of self-interest among mankind at large, and especially among the emigrants to newly-settled countries, and of the annoyance that uncivilized human beings are apt to prove, to those from civilized countries."⁷⁸

There was one settler in South Australia, Robert Cock, who was to echo Backhouse's view on the justice of land-rights for the Aborigines. Cock was one of those whom Backhouse met with in his brief visit to South Australia. He had sought Cock's support in the forming of the committee to assist the Protector of the Aborigines.⁷⁹ On 15 September 1838 a letter appeared in *The South Australian* under the nom-de-plume of A. Tenant. Enclosed with the letter was £3.16.6,

> ... being the interest at the rate of 10% on one-fifth of the purchase money of the town land, purchased by me on the 27 March 1837. This sum is in accordance with the pledge given by the colonization commissioners for this province and in accordance with the principle therein signified in their first annual report, wherein it is stated that they were to receive one-fifth of the lands to constitute a permanent fund for the support and advancement of the natives. I beg leave to pay the above sum for that purpose, seeing that the commissioners have neither fulfilled their pledge in this respect to the public, or carried out the moral principle signified. Under these circumstances it is impossible to let the question rest and until that be done I feel it my duty to pay the proper authorities for the use of the natives this yearly rent — the above sum being 1½ years' rent, viz. from 27 March to 27 instant. I disclaim this to be either donation, grant, or gift, but a just claim the natives of this land have on me as occupier of their lands.

G. M. Stephen, acting-governor following Captain John Hindmarsh's recall, drew the attention of Lord Glenelg to this action in a despatch.⁸⁰ In this he identified A. Tenant as Robert Cock, "a member of the Society of Friends". Robert Cock certainly attended Meetings of the Society of Friends at Adelaide and Mount Barker, and was apparently regarded as a member by Stephen. Backhouse, however, did not name him as a member, referring to him simply as "a prudent Scotchman". Walker said that Cock was convinced of Friends' principles but was never in membership.⁸¹

Robert Cock was a lonely example of one settler who recognized the justice of recompensing Aborigines for land that had been taken from them. Stephen clearly sympathized with Cock's views, even if he found them a little embarrassing. He concluded his despatch with the observation, "Mr. Cock, being a member of the Society of Friends, his scrupulous regards for the rights as he conceived them to be of the Aborigines, and the mode of presenting the donation will not probably surprise your Lordship. His liberality has not produced a beneficial effect upon his brother colonists, for unfortunately it remains a solitary instance."

News of Cock's solitary protest travelled the world and featured in a leader of *The Irish Friend* of 1 July 1839.

> In connexion with the subject of emigration, a gratifying circumstance has been communicated to us, with respect to a Friend who has been sometime settled in Australia, and who has become dissatisfied with the title to his possessions there; although obtained in the usual manner from the Land Company, he has taken measures to remunerate the Aboriginal inhabitants for his location, but in what manner we are not informed. How desirable it would be, that all our Friends who emigrate to newly-settled countries, should imitate the Christian example of William Penn — a course consistent at once with justice and sound policy.

The second major theme of Backhouse's letter to Buxton concerned legal justice for the Aborigines. Again he pointed out the vast gap between policy and practice. Although Aborigines were supposed to be given protection under British law and Aborigine Protection Leagues were active in England, Backhouse could quote numerous cases where Aborigines were helpless in the courts, if indeed they could ever bring their grievances to court. Backhouse and Walker had just travelled to Mauritius with a certain Dr Guistiniani who had defended Aborigines in Western Australia without success.[82] In one case quoted by Walker the defendant had killed sheep in retaliation for kangaroos being killed by whites, but whereas the Aborigine suffered the extreme penalty, the whites were not even challenged in law. Further when a black was killed, no inquest was held and no investigations undertaken. In one such particularly blatant travesty of justice Guistiniani had happened to be present in the home when the white man returned boasting of despatching a black for whom a trap had previously been set. Though Guistiniani made the circumstances known through the *Government*

Gazette, nothing was done, except that he was made to feel his presence in the colony was not wanted. Backhouse therefore urged upon Buxton the need for giving Aborigines protection under British law, for had the government not promised the boon of civilization as compensation for land already lost to its original inhabitants? Finally Backhouse pleaded that "no more colonies be established, without taking the care that common justice and humanity, both towards the European and the native population, demand, respecting the rights and civilization of the latter, and the neglect of which in the older Australian colonies has caused much oppression, suffering and bloodshed".[83]

Perhaps it is not stretching the imagination too far to see in the following quotation a theological extension of land rights to support the claims of Aborigines to a place in Heaven! Backhouse had been addressing the remnants of the Tasmanians and their white caretakers during one of his visits to the Flinders Island settlement.

> Though able to understand little more than the general object for which we were assembled, and having scarcely any ideas of a Deity, or a future state, the Aborigines behaved with great reverence and attention. It was affecting and humiliating to be cut off from communication with them on these subjects, by the want of knowledge of their language: but there was a comfort in knowing that 'where there is no law, there is no transgression'; and that 'sin is not imputed where there is no law': and that they will be judged only according to the measure of the light they have received.[84]

The Temperance Cause

Of all the social evils of the day intemperance was rated as the greatest by Backhouse and Walker. To it, rather than to the social conditions of the day, they ascribed the major cause of crime. The outward voyage on the *Science* had confirmed them in this view. Subsequent experience of the part played by rum in the colonies made them fervent campaigners against what then were labelled "ardent spirits". The extension of the campaign from "Temperance" to "Total Abstinence" was the result of their observation of the havoc wrought by alcohol on the lives of convicts and free settlers alike. Both Backhouse and Walker quoted in their journals horror stories which were the equivalent of the "Don't drink and drive" campaigns of today. One sample will suffice from Backhouse's account of the problem in New South Wales.

> A short time after our visit to Molong, one of the men went off the road with a cart towards a house where spirits were sold illicitly. On the way he upset the cart, which fell across his breast: he had cut away part of the side of the cart with his pocket-knife but had died before he could extricate himself. When he was found a wild dog was eating his head and his own dog was eating the horse. Accidents from the use of intoxicating drinks are not infrequent in this land where the quantity of spirituous liquors consumed is very great in proportion to the population. We lately heard of a man falling, in a state of helpless drunkenness, on one of the large, flat, loose ant-hills that are common in the bush. When found, he was lifeless, the exasperated ants having eaten the interior of his nostrils and his throat.[85]

What concerned Backhouse and Walker most of all was to see the way the government had allowed rum to take control of the colony and the traffic in rum to be given government sanction, protection, and support. It appeared to them that the government was corrupting the morals of the people by holding out every temptation to them to become drunkards. Employers were permitted to pay up to a third of a man's wages in rum and, by becoming suppliers of rum themselves, they made a further profit on each man's wages. Backhouse and Walker ascribed to alcohol the parlous state of the Western Australian colony, the whole revenue of which (amounting to about seven thousand pounds) was derived, according to Backhouse, from excise on imported spirits.

In Van Diemen's Land Backhouse and Walker prepared for the Lieutenant-Governor a paper entitled *Observations on the Distillation, Importation and Sale of Ardent Spirits as sanctioned by the Government.* The paper was received by Arthur, who had to point out in defence that he would have some difficulty in carrying out the recommendations contained therein because the revenue of the government was largely dependent on excise. On this Backhouse reflected wryly, but with penetrating forcefulness, that "the state of a government which depends upon the continuance of the sins of the people for the support of its revenue is truly an awful state".[86]

Backhouse and Walker campaigned tirelessly for Temperance in every city, town, and in the homes they visited. They carried tracts, urged individuals to sign a Declaration of Support for the Temperance Movement, organized public meetings, and in most cases were successful in persuading prominent citizens of their duty to form local committees. In this movement they had the support of many public figures, including churchmen of all Protestant denominations, who, while not necessarily teetotallers, acknowledged the social ravages of drunkenness and were anxious at least to appear on the side of sobriety.

Backhouse and Walker have a claim for recognition as two of the most significant pioneers of the Temperance Cause in Australia.

A Place in History

Backhouse and Walker spent the greater part of the decade of the eighteen-thirties in the Australian colonies. The most detailed accounts were of life in Van Diemen's Land and New South Wales, but they paid brief visits to the new settlements which were being established in Moreton Bay, Port Phillip, Adelaide, Albany, and Perth. Their impressions of these fledgling colonies, though briefer, are of particular historical interest because of their timing.

The first of these, Moreton Bay, was still primarily a penal settlement. Backhouse and Walker sailed there in the *Isabella* in 1836 in the company of forty-four prisoners, fifteen soldiers, and sixteen crew. The early inhabitants of Eagle Farm were forty females, considered, they were told, the most depraved of their sex. It was easier perhaps to write enthusiastically about the natural wonders of this new land than about its inhabitants. Backhouse, the botanist and naturalist, described in detail the ecology of the mangrove swamps with their bird, shell, fish, and plant life, thus providing what must be one of the earliest authentic descriptions of this area by a trained observer.[87]

The historical significance of their accounts of Port Phillip is underlined by their description of meetings with John Batman, first in 1833 when he received them hospitably at Buffalo Plains on one of their foot-journeys through Van Diemen's Land, and then in 1837 when they called on him in his Port Phillip location and reported that he did not seem long for this world. The *Eudora*, on which Backhouse and Walker had berths to Western Australia, docked for little more than a week in Melbourne, but Backhouse's impressions of fifteen-months-old Melbourne are none the less interesting.[88]

Their stay in South Australia was also brief, but their accounts again have value for their closeness to the founding days of the colony. After tossing all night on the *Eudora* anchored in Holdfast Bay, they were rowed ashore in the morning, landing in a small creek at Glenelg. They were, however, lucky to obtain a ride to Adelaide in a light chaise past several settlers' "rude huts of rushes or of sods". They presented their credentials of introduction from Sir John Franklin to the Governor, Captain John Hindmarsh, and Commissioner James Fisher. There are detailed descriptions by Backhouse of flora, of walks by the Torrens, "one foot in depth and four in width", and observations on the cost of land and provisions and on discussions with the Governor on the rights of the Aborigines.[89]

Neither had encouraging words to say for the settlements at Albany, Freemantle, or Perth. Perhaps their judgment had been soured by ex-Western Australians who had migrated to Van Diemen's Land and brought reports of an inhospitable land and economic disaster. The variety of vegetation, however, merited some praise and the climate was rated "salubrious, adapted for persons who have lost their health in India; but to make this their retreat, they ought to have a tolerable income and be fond of solitude".[90]

Backhouse and Walker's comments on these new colonies even if they were made "en passant" and therefore liable through brief exposure to errors of judgment, provide nevertheless a lively primary source of information about the early years of their history.

The reports of Backhouse and Walker on Van Diemen's

Land and New South Wales are not open to this criticism. Their sojourn in Van Diemen's Land covered the years 1832-37, broken only by visits to New South Wales. They spent the equivalent of two years in this colony, including some weeks on Norfolk Island and a shorter period at Moreton Bay.

At the rear of the 1843 edition of Backhouse's *Narrative of a Visit to the Australian colonies* a map of Van Diemen's Land is included on which the journeys of Backhouse and Walker are traced in red ink, each book individually, presumably by Backhouse himself, for he had returned to England in time to supervise the publication of the book. From this map it can be seen that they tramped the length and breadth of the island and visited every settled district. They were frequent visitors to the East Coast, where there was a group of Friends centred at the "Kelvedon" home of Francis Cotton. On two occasions they sailed to Flinders Island to visit the Aboriginal settlement at The Lagoons and then later at the more permanent location at Wybalenna. They went as far west as Cape Grim around the north of the island to visit the properties of the Van Diemen's Land Company, and they also sailed around the stormy southern route past Maatsuyker Island and Port Davey to the penal settlement of Macquarie Harbour. In all their journeys they kept detailed and personal records. Backhouse made daily use of his botanical knowledge to identify flora and note botanical classifications, thus providing one of the earliest reference books of Tasmanian flora.[91] Collections of plant, rock, and animal life were carefully packed and sent back to England.

Both Backhouse and Walker appeared to be skilled in sketching. The *Narrative* included signed Backhouse sketches of views on the Clyde, of Ben Lomond, and of storm-tossed entry into Port Davey. It is probable that at least one of the unsigned sketches can be attributed to Walker.

Francis Cotton, writing in July 1851, in *The British Friend* confirmed that the drawing of his home at Kelvedon appearing in Backhouse's *Narrative* was by Walker. "The plate of our house in J. Backhouse's Journal is hardly correct: the person who transferred the plate to a lithographer, or wood plate, has taken a few licences. The original drawing, taken by G. W. Walker, was very like. I saw a copy of it at Sydney which I recognized at once."

Both had considerable gifts of expression and powers of conveying to the reader vivid impressions of what they saw, whom they met, and how they reacted to a land where all was new to them. They were also good story-tellers. Walker particularly delighted in setting down anecdotes about bushrangers, Aborigines, and conditions of living in the outback. These qualities of scientific training, keen observation, and literary ability, combined with a sympathetic understanding of people and a scrupulous regard for frankness and honesty in recording their impressions, make their writings especially valuable for a study of the period of the eighteen-thirties in Van Diemen's Land and New South Wales.

There were few free settlers' homes in Van Diemen's Land where Backhouse and Walker were not known and welcomed. Their journals therefore provide almost a "Who's Who" of colonial society in the eighteen-thirties. They visited all the penal establishments — the road-gang camps, the hulks, the town lock-ups, the penitentiaries, the female "factory", and isolated Macquarie Harbour. Few observers would have been so well placed to report on the closing stages of this notorious settlement and then the early years of the Port Arthur experiment. Similarly they were in Van Diemen's Land at a critical stage in the history of the Aborigines. They spent some time in the North West as the guest of Edward Curr, manager of the Van Diemen's Land Company. They visited the Company's stations at Circular Head, Woolnorth, the Hampshire Hills, and the Surrey Hills. They were very critical of the Company's employment policy, particularly of the agreement made when free labour was indentured in England. On arrival, the indentured labourer often found himself at a disadvantage when he learnt what wages were actually being paid in the colony. If he tried to escape he was punished as an absconder.

Backhouse and Walker were frequent guests at Government House.

> Our first interview with Colonel Arthur gave us a favourable impression of his character as a Governor and as a Christian, which further acquaintance with him strongly confirmed: he took great interest in

the temporal and spiritual prosperity of the colonists, and in the reformation of the prisoner population, as well as the welfare of the surviving remnants of the native Black inhabitants; and he assured us that every facility should be granted us in attempts to further any of these objects.[92]

They were open supporters of Arthur, who, they considered, had done much to raise the moral tone of the colony. They admired his courage and his willingness to risk unpopularity. Such support was not surprising, for they had in fact much in common with him, in spite of Arthur's military background and their Quaker anti-military principles. They shared an Evangelical approach to the Christian faith and a strong conviction that their lives were under the ruling of Providence. Backhouse and Walker were impressed by Arthur's humanitarian sympathies, though they may have regarded his handling of the Tasmanian Aborigines as unduly influenced by a desire to placate the white Tasmanian settlers rather than by a genuine effort to save a threatened race. They found much to applaud in his ideas on penal reform and in what they considered to be his genuine efforts to bring about the moral reformation of the prisoners.

Some of their reports were directly commissioned by Arthur, others supplied to him because Backhouse and Walker considered his attention should be drawn to certain observed evils in the colony. Some of the reports too were openly supportive of Arthur's policies, so that it was to be expected that they should lay themselves open to the charge of being partisan apologists for those policies.

Arthur's opponents, after the release of their report on Macquarie Harbour, labelled Backhouse and Walker "government spies" and the Hobart newspaper *The Tasmanian* called them "eleemosynary wanderers".[93] These labels did not worry Backhouse, who called Arthur's opponents "dissatisfied men, of party spirit, who, being in a wrong mind themselves, took great pains to prejudice others against this worthy man".[94] They were far from being mere rubber-stampers of Arthur's policies. Their basic honesty prevented them from uncritical acceptance of everything Arthur said or enacted. They were however well aware that Arthur was a controversial figure and that his enemies were seeking to destroy him. In this struggle they made no secret of their support for Arthur.

Backhouse and Walker were also in Van Diemen's Land at the time of Sir John Franklin's governorship. Initially Franklin merited Backhouse's approval because he appeared to have good intentions of continuing Arthur's policies. Walker thought him a man "of urbane manners, easy of access and very conversible".[95]

Lady Franklin was very friendly to Backhouse and Walker and appeared to have a high regard for them. She told them to call upon the family at any time, without waiting for a specific invitation.[96] She astonished Backhouse on one of their first meetings by producing a copy of Backhouse's *Extracts*, published in England and brought out by her.[97] Lady Franklin attended a Friends' Meeting for Worship on 29 October 1837 and Walker accompanied her back to Government House. "I had some serious conversation with Lady Franklin after Meeting, escorting her home, in the course of which she made several enquiries respecting our principles and practices as a community."[98] Some years later, when writing an invitation to Walker to attend the opening of the Lady Franklin Museum, she paid tribute to the scientific contribution made by Backhouse and Walker, and added: "I have always deeply regretted that we have known you less as a Resident than we did as a Visitor. Nevertheless we have never doubted your kindly feelings."[99]

The time spent in New South Wales was much less than in Van Diemen's Land and hence their account of life in the senior colony was not so detailed nor as colourful. It is not however without historical significance. On their first visit they arrived in Sydney Harbour in the *Henry Freeling*, a boat chartered by the Quaker missionaries, Daniel and Charles Wheeler, who had called in at Hobart on their way to the Pacific Islands and taken Backhouse and Walker with them to Sydney.[100] Backhouse and Walker found Governor Bourke friendly and helpful and had no trouble gaining his support and permission to visit Norfolk Island, Moreton Bay, and the penal settlements in New South Wales. Again they appeared to be welcome at Government House, both in Sydney and in Parramatta, even though on their first visit they made it clear they were not card-players or "socially" minded.

Their journals provide valuable comment on the development of towns in New South Wales, such as Maitland, with its soil rich and loamy from river-flooding and its packet-boats taking produce direct to Sydney; Bathurst, where lack of a bridge over the Macquarie River meant people had to wade through knee-deep water to attend church; Newcastle, already producing seventy tons of coal daily at a price of eight shillings a ton; Bourke, Castlereagh, Liverpool, the Hunter Valley. Here Walker recorded that they were asked to meet with Alexander McLeay, Colonial Secretary, Francis Forbes, Chief Justice, Sir John Jamison, and William Macarthur to examine three hundred varieties of vines imported from Europe and give advice on their suitability for Australian conditions. It is intriguing to speculate whether Backhouse, staunch advocate of Total Abstinence, was instrumental through his botanical expertise in laying the foundation of the wine industry in one of Australia's most renowned wine-producing areas.

There are interesting references in the journals to well-known personalities such as Samuel Marsden, Archdeacon Broughton, and Dr Lang, who is described in some detail because Backhouse and Walker were most upset by the court action brought by Dr Lang against L. E. Threlkeld, whose work among the Aborigines at Lake Macquarie had earned their highest praise. Threlkeld was awarded a farthing's damages — "a proof", said Walker, "that religious character and worth is held in cheap estimation in the Colony, if we are to form a general opinion from the verdict of a jury chosen from among the class that is regarded as the most respectable and intelligent in the community".[101] Backhouse and Walker had appeared in court in support of Threlkeld but had had to leave before judgment was given. They felt so strongly about the injustice of the court's verdict that they went personally to see Dr Lang to tell him plainly that he was quite mistaken about Threlkeld, that they had seen all the book-keeping accounts of the mission and would be writing a full account of their findings to the directors of the London Missionary Society.

Backhouse and Walker stayed with Captain Sturt at Mittagong in October 1836. They were most appreciative of his hospitality. The meeting led to a close relationship between Sturt and Backhouse. They were both keen botanists and Sturt gave Backhouse some specimens for his plant collection. Sturt's success in maintaining good relationships with the Aborigines without recourse to armed violence either in offence or defence particularly impressed the two Quakers.

Backhouse afterwards apparently kept up a correspondence with Sturt, for there is a letter to Backhouse, written by Sturt on 6 December 1848 in which he asked Backhouse's advice on what he could do to promote good relations between the white settlers and the Aborigines when he returned to South Australia.[102]

Recognition of Backhouse and Walker's place in the early history of the colonies has been slow in coming, perhaps because they may have been commonly regarded as Quaker missionaries working within the Society of Friends. Their contribution to penal reform, to the advocacy of enlightened treatment of the Aborigines, and to the promotion of Temperance belongs in a much wider context. It may be appropriate therefore to conclude this estimate of Backhouse and Walker with comments on them by nineteenth century writers who were in no way connected with Quakers.

One refreshingly lively account was given by the Irishman, Captain Foster Fyans, who was commandant at the Moreton Bay prison settlement when Backhouse and Walker suddenly appeared, unannounced, presented a letter of introduction from Governor Bourke and asked to see everything that Fyans could show them.[103] They had also brought with them four volumes of a botanical dictionary and nets for catching butterflies. Fyans was persuaded to let them go on an overnight scientific expedition, which tested their constitutional toughness. Fyans, having been cross-examined by them on the subject of "flagellation", which he proceeded to describe in lurid detail, finally offered to arrange a special demonstration of flogging for his visitors. This offer however they declined, but they agreed to find out by personal experience what it was like for a prisoner to be sentenced to the treadmill. Fyans gave a racy, unpunctuated account of the experiment.

> The Friends were anxious to see and to know everything, on the mill they would go, when round it went, it passed slowly for a few minutes, Quakers addressing me from above, Friend, severe work, very, very, Friend, the prisoners hate it — Friend that is sufficient for Friend Walker laughingly, and Friend, I want no more, I kept them for some time, telling them the idlers were always worked harder by the power of the windmill at full speed, after giving the Quakers a good heat of ten minutes, the mill was stopped and Friends came off with thanks, blowing and puffing and short smiles.[104]

Fyans was impressed by these two Quakers with their strange "Friend" language, their habit of beginning the day with prayers and readings from the Bible and their insatiable appetite for information on prisoners, Aboriginal tribes, and exotic flora and butterflies.

Lady Franklin concluded the letter which she wrote to her sister in praise of Daniel Wheeler with the following reference to

> two other delightful Quakers who had just quitted us for a long and circuitous route home, Messrs. Backhouse and Walker. They have been some years in these two penal colonies and have written much on prison discipline. Mr. Backhouse is an accomplished botanist and a very lively and clever creature. The other, Walker, very interesting and valuable. We expect him back to marry and settle here, but though I don't know that I don't altogether prefer old Daniel Wheeler to any of the others yet he seemed more to belong to us. Two days ago he sat by me for dinner for the last time on my right and the Roman Catholic priest (the Vicar-General) on my left.[105]

The historian of early Tasmania, John West, writing in 1852, called Backhouse "a gentleman of prudence and sagacity". "He lifted up his heart to God; took his pocket compass, and thus escaped some perils by sea and land: and carried to England a reputation, from which detraction has taken nothing and which friendship would scarcely desire to improve."[106]

And Dr John Service, commissioned in 1880 by the editor of *Master Missionaries: Chapters in Pioneer Effort throughout the World*, wrote warmly of the impression that Walker had made on colonists and convicts alike. "He and his companion were seen in places where no missionary had been heard of before, and left wholesome impressions of their sincerity, good sense and goodness upon the minds of men who had considered themselves abandoned, alike of God and men, to solitude, blasphemy and drink. There were many colonists and many convicts (some of them possibly still alive) who for years afterwards dated all events with reference to the visits of the Quakers".[107]

Five
Quakers in Van Diemen's Land

The six years spent in Van Diemen's Land and New South Wales by Backhouse and Walker led eventually to the establishment of Quaker Meetings in both colonies, first in Hobart and then less securely in Sydney. Backhouse and Walker shaped the development of Quakerism in Australia by being themselves the image of what was understood by the term "Quaker" in an Australian context. They played a supportive, encouraging and, where necessary, a disciplinary role in the guidance of individuals and Meetings and they laid down the basic organization of Quaker Meetings in Van Diemen's Land and New South Wales.

Australia's First Quaker Meeting

The little group that first formed a Meeting in Van Diemen's Land was a most unpromising collection of prospective members. Apart from Backhouse and Walker there were none who could be regarded as staunch and experienced Quakers. Walker said that some who claimed to be Friends did not seem to make their principles accord with their practices, "and would indeed disgrace any profession. We have found it necessary to be very guarded in our conduct towards such, whilst we should be truly sorry to withhold any encouragement we could extend towards those who are sincerely desirous to set about reformation."[1] Two years later he saw no reason to change his opinion about what was still "but a weakly company".[2] Backhouse said, as he pondered whether the moment had come to attempt to organize this weakly company into a recognized Meeting,

> I cannot say I feel any rejoicing in contemplating the establishment of this Meeting: though my judgment and I think my better feelings also approve the measure. The company is small and weak, more to be prayed for than rejoiced over. If they become anything in religious strength it will be through the blessing of the Most High upon that which is yet of its kind but like a grain of mustard seed.[3]

Seven months later Backhouse made a move to plant the seed. The preparation of the ground had begun on the first Sunday after their arrival in Hobart. Backhouse recorded in his *Narrative* on 12 February 1832:

> We sat down together to wait upon the Lord, in our sitting room, and were joined by the Captain of a vessel who had lately taken some of the aborigines to Flinders Island, where they are provided for by the Government — We continued the practice of holding our Meeting for Worship, on first days and once in the course of the week, for a considerable period by ourselves, unless, as on this occasion, anyone casually stepped in.[4]

It was nineteen months before the formal step was taken to establish a Meeting for Discipline. On 20 September 1833 such a Meeting was held in the home of the under-sheriff, Thomas Crouch. Thomas Crouch, though never a member of the Society of Friends, was most sympathetic to the Society. One reason for not seeking membership was that he felt that his office of under-sheriff, which involved swearing-in witnesses under oath, would conflict with the Quaker testimony against oaths. His wife, Sarah Crouch, however, was a former Wesleyan, whose convincement was regretted by the Wesleyans and a blessing to the Quakers. The Crouch home became a Friends' centre in Hobart, providing accommodation for Friends coming to Hobart for Monthly and Yearly Meetings and hospitality for Backhouse and Walker. Sarah Crouch came to be known by Friends as "a mother in Israel". James Backhouse wrote in a copy[5] of William Penn's *No cross, no crown*, which he and Walker presented to Thomas and Sarah Crouch:

> "From their sincere friends, J. B. and G. W. W., as a token of their affectionate remembrance and esteem, after a sojourn of between two and three years in V.D.L., the greatest part of which has been spent in T. J. and S. Crouch's family."
>
> 28 vii 1834.

That first Meeting held in the home of Thomas and Sarah Crouch was not a highly auspicious gathering, for only two members of the Society of Friends could be found to join with Backhouse and Walker in forming the Meeting. These were a girl of thirteen years of age, Ann Pollard, a member of Devonshire House Meeting, London, and Thomas Squire, who said he was a member of Albans Monthly Meeting. This statement was accepted, though on 1 November 1833 he was asked to write to his Monthly Meeting to send proof of membership. There is no record of a reply. Perhaps the reason was a Minute of Albans Monthly Meeting, dated 13 November 1829[6] recording that Thomas Squire had been disowned for insolvency and had already "emigrated to a foreign country without making satisfactory arrangements for the settlement of his just debts". He had gone initially to the Swan River settlement, but stayed only seven weeks and in April 1830 arrived in Hobart, where he tried various jobs, including opening a day-school for boys in Brisbane Street. Thomas Squire, therefore, so far from being a "pillar" of the Meeting, was a member by false pretences. There may be a charitable explanation of Thomas Squire's concealment of his disownment — that he left in such haste to escape his debtors that the decision of the Meeting had not caught up with him. Understandably he seems to have made little effort to find out or to notify Albans Meeting of his new address. He continued to be a burden on the Hobart Meeting, both spiritually and financially, until his second disownment on 3 December 1857, when the Meeting regarded him as beyond hope of reformation, because he had persistently refused to go to Meeting, living as a recluse in a mill some distance from Hobart.

Nor did the prospects seem more promising when this small Meeting sat down to draw up a list of all those who might be interested in joining the Meeting eventually. On this list were entered thirteen names of those who had attended Meetings for Worship at any time or who had been contacted by Backhouse and Walker in their journeys around Van Diemen's Land. Only one of these, David Stead,[7] was a member "in good standing", a farmer living some distance away at Falmouth on the East Coast and therefore not really able to be an active Friend in the Meeting in Hobart. Four others had been disowned before emigrating. One had been an attender in England; another, the keeper of the gaol at New Norfolk, was the brother of a disowned member.

There were no experienced, birthright Friends to act as a nucleus for the new Meeting. This provoked an interesting reaction from one birthright Friend, John Fisher, who believed that he had been disowned by his Meeting, but, having migrated to Van Diemen's Land before hearing of the decision of his Meeting, still cherished the hope that birthright membership might protect him. He was well enough

David Stead (1797-1886), one of the earliest Friends in Van Diemen's Land and in 1835 among the first of the settlers to go to Port Phillip, Victoria.

connected with Friends for him to be the subject of a letter of enquiry to Walker from Backhouse, writing on behalf of Fisher's father, Abraham, in Cork.[8] Yet Fisher made no attempt to link up with the little group of Friends in Hobart, but made the reason quite clear in a letter to his brother, Reuben. "There are four churches, two English, two Scotch, 1 Catholic chapel and four dissenting houses of worship and a Friends' Meeting House. I have not been much amongst them. They are quite different from the home ones. I believe there are only one or two that have been born in membership. The rest are all convinced."[9] John Fisher, the birthright Quaker, it seems, did not have much faith in convinced Quakers. After working as a fellmonger in Hobart, he went off to Canada to "see if the gold is to be picked up as reported",[10] and so disappeared from the Hobart scene.

The Hobart Meeting relied almost totally at first on the physical presence of Backhouse and Walker. This was demonstrated when they were absent in New South Wales. During their first absence there was a lock-out and a distressing disownment. The Meeting had been held at the homes of members. One Sunday when it was being held at the home of a member, William Holdship, members arrived to find the door locked against them. A verbal explanation had been given but not passed on. Holdship thought that the Meeting for Worship was too much dominated by Wesleyans and he had personal objections to some other members with prison backgrounds. For a member of six months' standing to have become so soon disillusioned and so un-Friendly was not a happy augury for the future of the Meeting. Another member, previously disowned in England and recently re-admitted in Hobart, had shocked the Meeting by marrying out in circumstances that were soon after discovered by Backhouse to have been bigamous, the first wife having been left behind in the Retreat at York. When on their next absence there were further troubles, Backhouse wrote to the Meeting: "We cannot help remarking the great inroads our unwearied adversary is making in our Society".[11]

Problems of membership and discipline occupied much of the time and energy of members during the first decade of the Meeting. At the second Meeting for Discipline held on

14 October 1833 the unusual status of the Hobart Meeting was acknowledged. Membership granted in Van Diemen's Land could not be transferred to any Meeting in Great Britain or the United States, because the Hobart Meeting was not officially recognized. Members however were encouraged to take statements of membership with them when returning overseas and London Yearly Meeting was requested to advise any members emigrating to the Colonies to bring notification of membership with them.

The Monthly Meeting operated under Backhouse and Walker's guidance in every way like an English Monthly Meeting, but it was nevertheless not recognized until 1861 by London Yearly Meeting. Yet for all practical purposes it functioned as an effective Meeting for Discipline, the parent body in London giving sympathetic rather than formal acknowledgment of its existence. In fact some members held a double membership, the first with their original English or Irish Meeting and the second with Hobart, Kelvedon, or Launceston Monthly Meeting.[12]

A Meeting was formed in Launceston on 4 January 1844. Until this date Monthly Meetings were held alternately in Hobart and Kelvedon, but from the date of Launceston Monthly Meeting's formation until 30 July 1851, the Launceston Meeting met in alternate months in Launceston and Kelvedon.[13]

The first Van Diemen's Land Yearly Meeting was held on 3 October 1834 and continued its sessions over several days. Apart from considering at length answers to the Queries sent out from London Yearly Meeting, some of which, such as those concerning payment of tithes, were quite irrelevant to Australian conditions, there was little business of consequence transacted. The Yearly Meeting's main function was to provide some communication between the three separate geographical locations and to give members the opportunity for mutual encouragement and sharing of spiritual experience. The Yearly Meeting also received and composed epistles. Members spent much time on this exercise, the language being exhortatory and evangelical and the message bearing little Australian content.

Monthly Meeting Minutes, similarly, tended to follow a

routine pattern, covering admission or disownment of members, notices of intention of marriage, records of births and deaths, and consideration of any property or financial affairs of the Meeting.

While Backhouse was in Van Diemen's Land, he was invaluable to the Meeting, not only spiritually but financially. Thus when Backhouse and Walker returned from their first absence to Hobart to find Friends in Hobart distressed by their lack of a settled and secure place for Meeting for Worship, Backhouse announced that he had arranged for the purchase of a house at 143 Murray Street, from William Nicoll and Bernard Carron at a cost of £350. The Meeting for Sufferings in London supplied a temporary loan and this was later repaid by subscriptions from English Friends. Furnishings were purchased and these also were charged to the Meet-

The first Friends' Meeting House, Hobart, at 143 Murray Street. The cottage was bought by Backhouse in September 1837 for £350 and was in use until September 1880 when it was replaced by a new Meeting House on the same site.

ing for Sufferings. The deeds of the Meeting House were transferred to the Hobart Monthly Meeting in 1859.[14]

Hobart Monthly Meeting fulfilled an important function by acting as "parent" Meeting to other Australian Meetings as they were established. First there was Sydney, which was attached to Hobart as part of the Van Diemen's Land Yearly Meeting until such time as it would be strong enough to be independent. Hobart members, Abraham Davy and R. A. Mather, who lived in Sydney from 1839 to 1844, attempted to form a Meeting. To help them J. B. Mather was "liberated" by Hobart Monthly Meeting to spend some months in Sydney. On his return he seemed pessimistic about the Sydney possibilities, reporting that the good seed sown by Backhouse and Walker had been overgrown by weeds. The chequered history of the Sydney Meeting is recounted below, but Hobart remained "in loco parentis" until Sydney was settled enough to take responsibility for managing its own affairs.

In 1856 George Story expressed a concern to visit the Meetings in South Australia, Victoria, and New South Wales. Thus by personal contact and by correspondence the Hobart Monthly Meeting endeavoured to discharge its parental duties with the limited resources available to it.

There was one particularly interesting example of the importance of correspondence as a means of meeting the problem of the isolation of individual Friends. Backhouse had written to Walker advising him that a Kingston (England) Friend, Elinor Clifton, had emigrated to Western Australia with her husband and a family of twelve children. Elinor was the daughter of Daniel Bell, Wandsworth, who was the uncle of Elizabeth Fry and of Edward, father of Edward Gibbon Wakefield. She was a grand-daughter of Robert Barclay.

Australind was a name devised by the founders to mark their aim to provide a port which would be the main Western Australian centre for the Australia–India trade, and the outlet for the agricultural produce of a large land-settlement scheme, based on Wakefield's principles. Wakefield himself was a member of the Company's Board of Directors. It is estimated that 460 people came out to settle at Australind in the years 1840–43.

Elinor Clifton (1793-1866), cousin of Elizabeth Fry and of Edward Gibbon Wakefield, was the first Quaker to settle in Western Australia at Australind in 1841 (Photograph by courtesy of Mr Bingham Clifton, Upton House, Australind).

The Friends' Meeting House brought out to Australind, Western Australia, in 1841 by Elinor Clifton (from the Friends' Meeting, Perth).

Marshall Walter Clifton, Elinor's husband, had been appointed Chief Commissioner of the Western Australian Company's settlement at Australind, situated on the eastern side of the Leschenault Inlet near Bunbury, Western Australia.

The Cliftons came out on the *Parkfield*. Elinor Clifton seems to have had high hopes of promoting Quakerism in the new settlement, for she brought with her a small prefabricated Meeting House donated by some of her Kingston Friends. The Company Prospectus described the plans made for a thousand-acre township and the community facilities which were to be provided. Sites were allotted for a library, museum, recreation centre, seven places of worship, and a Quaker Meeting House. Quaker interest in the settlement is also indicated by the purchase of Lot 25, one of 52 town lots, by Samuel Gurney, for his sister Elizabeth Fry. But on her death in 1845, the Cliftons bought the house erected in 1844 on the site, and this has remained the Clifton family home, with the name of Upton after the address of Elizabeth Fry's London home in Upton Lane. In 1843 the Company closed down its activities in Australind and transferred its interests to Port Grey. The Cliftons decided to remain. The little Meeting House, erected near the Clifton homestead became the centre for family worship.[15] In her isolation Elinor Clifton wrote, probably at Backhouse's suggestion, to Hobart asking to be admitted as a member of the Van Diemen's Land Yearly Meeting, which recorded its sympathy in the following Minute:

> This Meeting having been introduced into near sympathy with Elinor Clifton in her peculiarly lonely situation as regards religious association with members of her own Society, believes it right to accede to her request of admitting her as a member of this Yearly Meeting and appoints George Washington Walker and Joseph Benson Mather to inform her thereof and to hand her such religious counsel as may appear suitable to one in her very secluded allotment.[16]

Hobart maintained a regular correspondence with Elinor Clifton until her death.[17]

Elinor Clifton finished a letter to Friends in England in 1858 with a description of her situation as a solitary Friend in an isolated corner of the Australian continent. Quoting Scripture, "Although I have cast thee far off amongst the heathen and although I have scattered them amongst the countries, yet will I be to them as a little sanctuary in the countries where they shall come," she added, "Although a very unworthy member I still hope I am bound up in the bundle of life with Friends".[18]

Mackie was quite sure that, though a Friend in isolation, she had nevertheless by her faithful persistence in her "little sanctuary" and her Quaker witness in her family and in the community exercised a Quaker influence on the colony at large. She is therefore deserving of an honoured place in any history of Quakers in Australia.

Backhouse and Walker thus established and nurtured in Van Diemen's Land a Meeting which played the parental role with respect to other Meetings in Australia.

Their influence however is seen most clearly in the impact they made upon the lives of an extraordinary assortment of people, who might be classified as the convicted, the disowned, and the convinced.

The largest component was the convict group. No Quaker Meeting had yet faced the challenge of such a group. In Van Diemen's Land there were men and women who had met with Backhouse and Walker during their visits to penal institutions and settlements, and had been won over by the power of their ministry. Now they were anxious to be united with Quakers because of the image of a Quaker which Backhouse and Walker represented to them.

There were some who had had previous contact with Quakerism in England but who had been disowned and would therefore have been unlikely to seek re-admission to the Society of Friends in Australia, if it had not been for the influence of Backhouse and Walker.

The third component, added a little later, was made up mainly of Wesleyans, who, having come out as free settlers, had met with Backhouse and Walker and been convinced by their witness. Yet from this assortment of the convicted, the disowned and the convinced, came the leadership which was to ensure the continuity of a Quaker witness in Van Diemen's Land, when Backhouse and Walker were no longer present to give guidance and support.

The Convicted

The most significant of these three components — the convicted, the disowned and the convinced — was the convicted. It is of particular interest therefore to examine in some detail the history of this group's experience of Quakerism and of Backhouse and Walker's influence upon them.

There were six with a convict background in the original list drawn up at the first meeting and during the early years of the Hobart Meeting there was a total of twenty-two convicts and ex-convicts who came in contact with the Meeting. Of these all except two owed their interest in Quakers to Backhouse and Walker. Ten had had a previous link with Quakers, twelve no such link until then. Of these twelve, seven applied for membership, five being accepted and two rejected. Of the five accepted, three were subsequently disowned and two retained their membership. Of the ten with previous links two had had connections with Quakers by schooling or attendance at Quaker Meetings, eight had been members in England or Ireland and been disowned. Three of these disowned were readmitted to membership in Hobart, one applied but was refused, and one of the three was again disowned and again readmitted. The remaining one lost contact with the Society. Of the twenty-two therefore only five retained membership.

Backhouse and Walker had to handle two specific problems with the convict component. First, they undertook the demanding task of educating those who had had no previous understanding of the implications of membership or who had lapsed and then had to be re-educated. Second, they had to help members of the Meeting to an understanding and acceptance of a group whom the general community regarded as outcasts. A reflection of the latter problem is provided in a letter which the English Quaker, Edwin R. Ransome, wrote in 1893 to the American Friend, Samuel Morris.

> These little isolated churches seem somewhat like outposts of the main body and thus they claim our sympathy as the foundation for a nucleus in any of the respective localities. In not a few cases some of the units have scarcely been of a kind that one would select as very likely material with which to build up a congregation, but we

may well be thankful for all and any signs of spiritual life, come where it may. Even the Meeting in Hobart when first started with seven members had a convict or two amongst them, so we may well say, "What hath the Lord done".[19]

That the convict component had been the subject of some raising of the eyebrows is hinted at in Ransome's final words of caution. "Please do not refer to this anywhere, for our Friends are, perhaps naturally, a little sensitive on this point."[20] In 1833 Walker, commenting on the ministry of a convict in the Meeting for Worship, said, "It will appear a little singular in the eyes of many that this kind of person should be called upon to labour".[21] Backhouse and Walker had to combat a certain amount of prejudice among some Friends who resented the acceptance of convicts into the Meeting. One, who was applying for membership, refused to be interviewed when she heard that an ex-convict was one of the two members of the Meeting appointed to visit her. A measure of the success of Backhouse and Walker's powers of persuasion is perhaps reflected in a decision of Hobart Monthly Meeting in 1836 to take a firm stand against any anti-convict feeling in the Meeting. William Holdship[22] was disowned, ostensibly for non-attendance at Meetings, but in the minute of disownment the reason for his non-attendance was disclosed. "He has given way to an un-Christian objection to meet with persons who have been prisoners, on which ground he publicly declines meeting any more with Friends in Van Diemen's Land. We endeavoured without success to convince him of his error."[23]

The most dramatic example of Backhouse and Walker's influence on a convict is that provided by the change in Abraham Flower, alias Richard Edwards, who had been transported for larceny, first to Bermuda and then to Van Diemen's Land. His convict record[24] disclosed that when he was a prisoner in the hulks he was "repeatedly ironed for long periods and well known to have had a knife in his hand on the evening of the affair of stabbing Mr. Pickthorn and others and a leader in all tumult and riotous conduct, and a clerk to the gang of refractory prisoners". His general conduct was summarized as "contemptuous and mutinous". He would therefore appear to have been the reverse of a peaceable Quaker.

Backhouse and Walker first met him at Macquarie Harbour where he had been sent because of his truculence in Bermuda. He still retained the reputation of a trouble-maker, but under the influence of the Reverend W. Schofield there had been signs of a change. On board the brig which brought prisoners and Backhouse and Walker to Hobart from Macquarie Harbour, Flower had several talks with the two Quakers. The contact, begun in the gaol below decks, was continued when Flower on arrival in Hobart was assigned as a servant to Government House. He began attending Meetings for Worship. Permission had been sought for this attendance and been granted by the Lieutenant-Governor. Soon there was a little group of four assigned servants from Government House attending Meeting. When one of these was prevented from attending, the Meeting protested and the restriction was withdrawn.[25]

Flower was one of the first to be admitted to membership in the newly formed Hobart Monthly Meeting, October 1833. In June 1834 he was recorded as a minister in recognition of what was felt to be his gift for speaking acceptably in Meeting for Worship. Some years later, in one of his reports published serially in *The Irish Friend*, Backhouse expressed the exhilaration which Flower's transformation had aroused in the hearts of Friends, and particularly by his recognition by the Meeting as a minister.[26] "That one of the despised, hated and persecuted little band at Macquarie Harbour should become an accredited minister of a body of Christians . . . cannot but be considered as one of those glorious triumphs of Grace which cause the saints to rejoice, to adore and to love the Saviour with increasing ardour."[27] Flower gained his freedom at the same time as he was admitted to membership, but this should not be construed as implying that admission was conditioned by release from convict status. It was to be expected that Flower's progress as a Quaker would be the subject of more than usual interest to onlookers. The Society of Friends, too, would have been regarded as on trial by association. There is one amusing but revealing story recounted in Boyes' Diary.

> At 11 a.m. I left my office for Roseway where I had made an appointment with Mr. Harbottle who was to look over the house and

see what repairs were required, by way of making an estimate. I waited until 1, but the painter and glazier did not appear. It appears that he came while I was at the Parsonage eating a mutton chop with Ewing and his wife (the Incumbrant and the encumbrance). I found Mr. Quaker Flower putting up a fence upon what I considered very suspicious ground and upon a slight examination I found my view was correct as the holes where the old fence ran along were visible enough as soon as I had removed the stones which the honest Quaker had covered them with. It is a pleasant prospect to have a neighbour of such approved honesty as one of the Society of Friends.

I called upon Mrs. Scott and acquainted her with the pleasure I anticipated in having such an ally as her friend Mr. Abraham Flower, who was not only detected in removing his neighbour's marks but avowed his intention of carrying his fencing property away through my garden, thereby cutting me off from the stream that ran at the bottom and appropriating to his own use the only portion of the ground that could be made ornamental as well as useful. This mathematical love of the straight line was so strong that he was induced to abandon the appropriation of the garden, as before mentioned, solely out of regard to his landlady's interest, as he did not wish to deprive her of a good tenant by refusing to sacrifice on this occasion his disinterested love of geometry.[28]

There are no means of judging whether Boyes' insinuations were based on malice, cynicism, or fact. It is however probably fair to comment that membership in the Society of Friends did not guarantee a subsequent blameless record and that the Society's reputation for honesty was a plant of fragile growth in this new climate.

In 1843 Flower departed from the path of strict adherence to the truth when he recorded himself in the Census as having "arrived free". Desire to distance himself from a distasteful memory was perhaps understandably strong enough to silence any momentary promptings of a Quaker conscience. Walker quoted in his journal on 23 October 1834 what he called "a pleasing proof of the sincerity of his (Flower's) repentance". He had received news of a legacy of three hundred pounds left to him by his father. In spite of his own very slender means to support his wife and family in Van Diemen's Land, he asked Walker to arrange through the English Friend, Peter Bedford, to restore sums of money amounting to half the legacy to two individuals "as a restitution for monies wrongfully obtained of them during the period of his folly and wicked career".

Flower's subsequent history illustrates the problems that beset any ex-convict struggling to rehabilitate himself. First he tried butchering in partnership with Henry Propsting, who was similarly placed. Backhouse observed, "They are very industrious, but have many discouragements to contend with".[29] Three months after this observation the *Hobart Town Courier* carried an advertisement stating that the partnership of Flower and Propsting was being dissolved by mutual agreement.[30] Flower then carried on for a time as a milkman and a small dairy farmer and when this did not succeed he became insolvent. The Hobart Meeting was sympathetic to his difficulties, for it cautioned but did not disown him. In February 1844 he moved to Launceston. When members move from one Meeting to another, the procedure followed is for the Meeting of origin to furnish a certificate of identity and clearance to the Meeting of destination. This Hobart at first refused to furnish, because Flower still had some debts unpaid, but within a year Launceston Monthly Meeting notified Hobart that he was paying off his debts to the best of his ability and that he was therefore clear to be admitted to membership in Launceston.

In 1847 however Launceston Monthly Meeting called on Flower to account for his membership of a "secret society", the Rechabites. The minute noted[31] that the "adoption of badges, insignia, passwords and signs" were "inconsistent with Christian simplicity and gravity", that many meetings were held at coffee-houses, that "unnecessary frequenting of public houses" was inconsistent with his position as a minister of the Society of Friends, and that the money thus spent on secret societies and public houses should have been used to pay his creditors. When Flower refused to discuss the matter with his fellow-members, he was disowned "in order that the Society may be clear before the world of any participation in dishonesty".[32]

This disownment highlights the great difficulties that confronted the small Meetings in these early days of Quakerism in Van Diemen's Land. The smaller the Meeting the greater was the likelihood of clashes of personality. The Launceston

Meeting was at no time a strong Meeting. Members tended to drift in and out, mostly for short periods of residence while making a decision about ultimate location. There was also the difficulty of establishing credentials of such members. At least one of the members who participated in the decision to disown Flower for dishonesty was himself far from guiltless, for Backhouse wrote to Walker on 23 August 1845 warning him about George Yates. Backhouse had discovered that Yates had migrated from Sheffield, leaving a wife and unpaid debts. Backhouse summed him up as "having artfully played the hypocrite".

In a letter to Backhouse, dated 21 August 1849, Walker recounted the whole sad story of Flower's alienation from the Society of Friends. "Poor Abraham Flower is much to be felt for", said Walker. He had apparently again been unsuccessful in the business of exporting fruit to Port Phillip and had been tempted to leave Launceston to avoid facing his creditors. Walker had advised him against this and Flower had accepted this advice. Walker perceived that one of the reasons that Flower sought membership of a "secret society" was that he found little real fellowship within the Launceston Friends' Meeting and the other reason was that his family, to use Walker's description, was an "incubus" to him.

Disowned by Launceston Monthly Meeting, Flower had appealed to the Van Diemen's Land Yearly Meeting, which upheld his appeal and cancelled his disownment. Thereupon two members of the Launceston Meeting declared that they would appeal to London Meeting for Sufferings against this reinstatement. "Abraham Flower", wrote Walker, "on being witness to this state of feeling generously and in a true Christian spirit and after having made a full acknowledgment of his faults, as regards the offence for which he had been dealt with by the Monthly Meeting (viz. connecting himself with the Rechabites) and refusing to yield to the counsel of his friends on the subject . . . to relieve Friends here and at home from the trial and responsibility of an appeal to the Meeting for Sufferings tendered his resignation." To Walker's great dismay the Van Diemen's Land Yearly Meeting accepted the resignation. Walker felt that Flower had acted entirely properly by admission of fault and out of concern for others' difficulties. In any case Walker regarded the alleged offence as somewhat trivial. Flower received the acceptance of his resignation "like a death blow to every good thing in him". Walker's verdict was, "I still believe that much lies at the door of those who shut up the bowels of compassion against an erring brother".

Not long afterwards Flower left Launceston on the *Swan* on 1 March 1849 for Victoria and was lost to Friends until two Quaker travelling ministers, Joseph Neave and Walter Robson, discovered him in 1868 living alone about seven miles from Castlemaine. Neave reported, "There was nothing of unkind feeling towards those who had been instrumental in his separation from Friends. Those who advised him to resign his membership may have been right in so doing, though we could not quite understand it."[33] And Walter Robson gave the following picture of the old man:

> His wife being deceased and his family married and settled elsewhere, he lived alone, his occupation, gold-digging, which brings him in an income of about five shillings per week. He is in a most happy and thoughtful state, telling us his wants were well supplied, his little two roomed hut, of his own building, enabling him to live rent-free. He keeps some goats which supply him with milk. We had a very precious time with him, a brook by the way.... A few months ago he was put to jail for a little debt which he had offered payment of, but his creditor, an unprincipled man, who has since been sold off, and ruined himself, refused to accept the money when offered and from spite, we suppose, put the poor old man to jail. Even here he was happy and it was very instructive to us both to see how humble and tender and sensible of his many shortcomings he was, yet so full of the love of Jesus and gratitude to him.[34]

There are several observations to be made about the story of Flower's association with Quakers. He became a Quaker because of the influence of Backhouse and Walker and he would probably have remained one if members of the Hobart and Launceston Meetings had shared Walker's understanding of his problems. Though he was regarded by Backhouse and Walker as a "prop" to the struggling Hobart Meeting during their periods of absence, the Meeting was not mature enough to hold him, fragile as he was, within its fellowship. The smallness of the Quaker Meetings in Van Diemen's Land made personal clashes more likely to erupt and more damaging when they did. While the Meetings were within the pastoral care of Backhouse and Walker, such clashes were less volatile: without their presence the future of these Meetings was always in doubt.

A second example is that of Henry Propsting, who was transported to Van Diemen's Land in 1831, having been convicted of stealing two tame geese on the evidence of a ten-year old boy.[35] He was assigned first as a labourer to H.H. Ridler, who later became a member of the Society of Friends.[36] He was then assigned to Isaac Sherwin in Launceston. Possibly it was here that he first met Backhouse and Walker, who were frequent guests of the Sherwins. He gained his ticket of leave in 1835 and his full pardon in 1837. It is clear that by December 1835 he had already absorbed some of Backhouse and Walker's Quaker ideas, for Walker recorded in his *Journal* on 2 December 1835 that Propsting had "applied for permission to have his son's birth registered in the Meeting, as he feels a conscientious objection to having him sprinkled by a priest". Ten months later he was admitted to membership, though he became restive at the five months' interval between his application and his admission.

Propsting's membership led ultimately to an unprecedented increase in membership figures, for he eventually had twenty-eight children, fourteen by his first wife, Ann, who died in 1857 and the remainder by his second wife, Hannah, whom he married in 1858. Isaac Sharp, who visited the Propsting family wrote in *The Friend*, "Few can tell of having had so large a family as Henry Propsting. The youngest of them sat on my knee. A fine boy, under two years old. I do not know his name, but it might have been Zed (Z or last) for he is the twenty-sixth."[37]

Propsting's membership was not without its problems. By temperament he was impulsive and hotheaded. On 7 June 1838 he was tried in the Hobart Police Court for engaging in a fracas with a previous employee. He refused to enter into a bond of good behaviour as this, he said, would have implied an admission of guilt. The magistrate called him a "great goose" and sentenced him to three months' gaol. Quakers intervened on his behalf and managed to secure his release after nine days in gaol.[38] Another instance of his fiery temperament is disclosed in the minutes of Hobart Monthly Meeting. A dispute between Propsting and his one-time employer, Ridler, finally was submitted to arbitration by the Meeting. Propsting accepted the decision and was generous in expressing a spirit of reconciliation. In a letter to the Meeting he expressed contrition for having been "in a moment of unwatchfulness betrayed into a very unchristian warmth of temper and serious quarreling with a neighbour under circumstances which I believed at the time to have been towards me unwarrantable and oppressive".[39]

His marriage to Hannah Cater in 1858 in a registry office raised embarrassing problems for the Meeting. Propsting was an Elder of the Meeting and as such had been responsible for upholding the discipline of the Society against those "delinquents" who married non-members. Up to this time there had been no relaxation of this discipline.[40] The Meeting wrestled with the problem, which in the same year was being debated in London Yearly Meeting. Members of the Meeting appreciated Propsting's forthright admission that the discipline should take its course and his consideration in being married in a registry office and not by a priest in a church. So the Meeting reached the only sensible solution of not disowning him, even though this created, for Hobart, a precedent. "He had", the Minute recorded, "aimed as far as he could under the circumstances to meet the views of the Society."[41] This decision was followed soon after by London Yearly Meeting's relaxation in 1859 of the rule of disownment for "marrying out". Hannah Propsting did not apply for membership until 1874. In her application she stated, "In so doing I do not see eye to eye with you in all things, but with the desire to create a still greater unity in our family I make the present application."[42] She was accepted without the usual preliminary visitation by two members of the Meeting, thus creating a second precedent in the history of that Meeting. Henry Propsting had many handicaps to overcome. He had little formal education. He had served a seven year sentence for what was a trivial offence. When he applied for membership of the Hobart Monthly Meeting, he had little money and a family to support. The Meeting perhaps was fully justified in making no hasty decision — but they accepted him, and Propsting's subsequent life fully justified their confidence. Sensitive though he must have been to the shadow of his past, he was able to free himself from any negative effect and live a life of remarkable worth.

He had a frank honesty that sometimes led him into trouble, for he did not hesitate to speak his mind about the truth as he saw it and he could not abide anything that smacked of insincerity or hypocrisy. When one Friend asked him for a loan of fifty pounds to build a glasshouse, he questioned the Friend's sense of values, thinking he should have waited for the glasshouse until he could afford to pay for it. However generosity prevailed, but when some time later the Friend wrote, suggesting that, since they were both members of the Meeting, Propsting might forego repayment, Propsting is said to have replied in forthright language: "Payment I will have. What are religious convictions to do with the debt you owe?" For Propsting religion meant helping those in need and not seeking to escape one's obligations.

Francis Cotton recognized Propsting's solid character. Having tried unsuccessfully to borrow a small sum of money from a fellow-member of the Society, Cotton commented in a letter to J. B. Mather, on the "avariciousness" of this fellow-member and contrasted it with Propsting's generosity of spirit. "Avariciousness, meanness, selfishness are the dark spots of his character. The sordid, avaricious character could not lend me a few shillings for a few days, when he has £280 of mine for near twelve months. How different the conduct of one with the slur of conviction about him. Verily, Henry Propsting is a prince compared to him."[43] Just how much Propsting felt "the slur of conviction" is difficult to estimate. It may have sometimes inhibited him from seeking public office, though he became an alderman of the Hobart Town Corporation from June 1857 to December 1859.[44] When he was defeated in the elections at the end of 1859, the Corporation recorded a minute of appreciation of his services as an alderman and praised him "for the attention, the perseverance and ability which he exhibited while acting as one of the municipal council and for the moderation which he invariably displayed as a member of the Corporation".[45]

This same moderation was one of the qualities for which he was remembered in the *Dictionary of Quaker Biography*[46] in which were listed "his truthfulness, punctuality, moderation and generosity to those in need". There was much in the life of Henry Propsting which would have made Backhouse and Walker rejoice.

A third example of the influence of Backhouse and Walker on the "convicted" is that of Abraham Davy, who had met them during their visit to Macquarie Harbour. His father, a Quaker woolcomber, had married out and been disowned. Orphaned at eight, Abraham was brought up by his half-sister. At the age of twenty-two he was tried at the York Assizes on two indictments, for feloniously stealing from the warehouse of his employer, George Rodger, silver and cutlery manufacturer, and for embezzlement from customers. He was sentenced to transportation for seven years on each of the two charges. Backhouse was impressed by hearing of Davy's honesty in pleading "guilty" when a plea of "not guilty", according to Backhouse, might have reduced his sentence from fourteen to seven years.[47] This honest confession was seen by Backhouse as evidence of a tender spirit, awakened, it is said, by reading the Bible while awaiting trial in his York prison. There is also evidence of some residue of Quaker upbringing, because, before meeting with Backhouse and Walker on his arrival in the *Larkins* in Van Diemen's Land on 19 October 1831, Davy gave his religion as "Quaker".[48] His association with Backhouse and Walker began in Macquarie Harbour, continued when he was assigned as clerk to the Police Office in Launceston, and became closest when Backhouse applied for and was granted Davy's services as an assigned servant during his visit to Sydney. Here Davy acted as a secretary to Backhouse and Walker. He was pardoned in 1837, returned for a brief period to Launceston, but finally settled near Sydney later that year.

Through Backhouse and Walker's influence Davy joined the Society of Friends in Hobart in 1834. Even before this Walker had recorded in his diary an example of what he saw as Davy's religious principles in action. Davy had been given permission to board privately and to act as scribe for a shopkeeper who gave him his board in return for his services.

Davy expressed concern about selling sausages for the shopkeeper on the Sabbath. He spoke with his master, who agreed. Sausages were therefore delivered on Saturday evenings.[49] After his admission to membership he became even more determined to be a fully practising Quaker. Walker reported[50] that Davy had been gaoled for a night in Launceston for refusing to take off his hat to the authorities. To support this member's correctness in refusing to pay "hat-honour", the Hobart Meeting sent a petition to Lieutenant-Governor Arthur.

> To Colonel George Arthur, Lieut-Governor of Van Diemen's Land and its Dependencies,
>
> We, the undersigned, professing with the Society of Friends, commonly called Quakers, being assembled at our Annual Meeting . . . respectfully solicit the attention of the Lieut.-Governor to the suffering in which the Prisoners of the Crown professing with us may be involved, from their conscientious objection to touch or take off the hat to their superiors, which they are required to do by an existing Government order . . . We gratefully acknowledge the attention that has been paid by the Lieut.-Governor to the claims of Prisoners of our Religious persuasion (whether members originally or having become such by convincement in the Colony) in regard to the privilege of attending our Meetings for Worship. We desire that the Divine Blessing may rest on the Colony and that its Rulers, acting in the fear of God and in conformity with his Will, may prove a terror to evil-doers, and a praise to them that do well, that thus the present and future well-being of all classes may be effectually promoted.
>
> Signed by James Backhouse, G.W. Walker, Wm. Rayner, Thomas Squire, A.C. Flower, R.A. Mather, H.H. Ridler, J.B. Mather and Francis Cotton, Clerk.[51]

The Lieutenant-Governor in reply agreed to draw the attention of the Secretary of State to the need to recognize the conscientious scruples of prisoners. Walker said that he understood that the Lieutenant-Governor had previously "expressed his opinion that, as he tolerated Quakers' hats in his office, on account of their being kept on from conscientious motives, and not out of disrespect, they might be tolerated in other offices also".[52]

Davy, in contrast to Propsting, suffered from the Monthly Meeting's rigid application of discipline to his application to marry Jane Dawson, who, in anticipation of marriage, had applied for membership in Hobart. At the time of Davy's settling in Sydney there was no organized Meeting, apart from the one in Hobart. Davy, upset by Hobart Meeting's slowness in attending to the application, decided to proceed with wedding plans and was married to Jane Dawson in a Presbyterian church, there being no recognized Meeting in Sydney. A Hobart Friend, R. A. Mather, then resident in Sydney, reported that the marriage had taken place against the advice of Friends both in Hobart and Sydney. Davy was thereupon disowned for "marrying out". The rigidity of attitude is seen from the unwillingness of the Meeting to recognize that, though Jane Dawson was not a member, her application for membership had been before them for some time. The Minutes of disownment underlined this rigidity.

> Abraham Davy having forwarded to this Meeting a notification of intended marriage to a female not a member of our Society, but merely applying for membership, this Meeting feels called upon (however unwilling to hurt the feelings of either party) to testify its decided disapproval of such a departure from the Rules of our Discipline, at the same time earnestly desires that Abraham Davy may be brought to see the impropriety of his procedure and to be willing to retrace his steps.[53]

It is doubtful whether such rigid application of the rules would have been agreed to if Backhouse and Walker had been present at the deliberations of Hobart Monthly Meeting, but by this time they were thousands of miles away on the African continent. It would have been understandable if Abraham and Jane Davy had severed their links with the Society. That they did not is perhaps due to a counselling of patience by Backhouse, who kept up a regular correspondence with Davy. At any rate, when the Sydney Meeting was linked with the Van Diemen's Land Yearly Meeting in 1842, Abraham and Jane Davy both appeared to have been accepted as members in Sydney.[54]

Davy, ex-convict, prospered and, in spite of some carping criticism by fellow-workers, remained a staunch Friend. Meetings were held regularly in his home and he was host to numbers of visiting Friends from overseas and from other Australian Meetings. Some Friends, particularly J. B. Mather, had some Quaker qualms about Davy's speculative ventures in land and business deals. Davy managed to elude most of Mather's attempts to counsel him and Mather returned to Hobart with the impression that Davy's business gave evidence of "the most perfect confusion and disorder being displayed in every corner".[55] There is evidence however to indicate that he became a Quaker of some substance. By 1853 he was ready to move from a store in George Street, Sydney, to a thousand-acre estate, thirty miles from the city and not far from Campbelltown.[56] In 1870 his daughter, Helen, recorded in her diary[57] on 19 September that there were forty cows in milk and "plenty more to carve" (*sic*), that 200 pounds of butter were being marketed each week, that there were twelve acres in wheat and plentiful supplies of potatoes. Evidence of growing wealth is also given in a letter he wrote to Sir William Macarthur in 1862, forwarding specimens of iron ore and coal from the Fitzroy mine at Mittagong in which he held a substantial interest.[58]

But with the growing wealth there was coupled a philanthropic interest, which was revealed in a further letter to Macarthur on 12 June 1870. Davy was soliciting donations for the establishment of a Public School in the isolated bush district of Kincumber, "settled only by savages noted for ignorance and intemperance who have numerous families of fine children growing up in the most lamentable and gross ignorance and thus untrained and uncared for may become a curse to society and the country". He had already persuaded sixty or seventy families to agree to send their children to the school and had collected twenty-five pounds from their meagre resources. He aimed to augment this to a hundred pounds by canvassing the more affluent of his neighbours.[59] This concern for what he called "the moral and intellectual advancement of society" was typical of the Quaker espousal of the cause of education in the first half of the nineteenth century. Davy would have been present in Sydney when Backhouse and Walker at public meetings spoke strongly in favour of the British and Foreign School System as the most suited for adoption in the colonies.[60] In their report to Governor Bourke on the state of the colony of New South Wales education was advocated as the first essential in combating the "low state of morality" in the colony.[61] Davy's support for public education was an echo of his previous close contact with Backhouse.

Davy's resources, carefully husbanded over the years, were instrumental in enabling his son-in-law, Joseph James Neave, to "travel in the ministry" for several years in Australia, England, and Russia without financial anxiety. Indirectly therefore Davy's contribution to the support and strengthening of Quakerism in Australia was considerable.

Three other convicts, besides Propsting and Davy, who remained in membership, were the ex-highwayman, William Rayner,[62] Edward Rowntree, and Thomas Willington. None of these took any very active share of responsibility as members by comparison with the former, but all in a measure responded to the faith that Backhouse and Walker had in them.

Judgment on the success or failure of Backhouse and Walker in their attempts to help the convict members of the Meeting must be tempered with an understanding of the dimensions of the problem, and it was a problem for the solution of which neither they nor the members of the Meeting had any precedent. The handling of a convict component was an entirely Australian problem, presenting itself at a particular period in colonial history. The establishing of a Meeting in the colonies, so far away from the home base, would have been difficult enough, even if the Quaker migrants had all been members in good standing and intent on seeing Quaker Meetings flourish in a new environment. Backhouse and Walker had to face an almost complete lack of such support initially and then to mould unpromising material into an approved Quaker cast. In the process there were successes and failures. The failures were not always due to the insensitive handling of delicate issues by inexperienced members of the Meeting, for some who applied and were admitted, perhaps too hastily, into membership, made little effort to change their ways and relapsed into delinquency.

Backhouse and Walker had not only to help the inexperienced to exercise, where necessary, the discipline which would give some structure to a new Meeting, but they also had to help members to temper judgment with compassion. The most difficult task was to get the self-righteous to accept the branded sinner. With one member, who showed little evidence of Christian charity, Walker reasoned as follows: "But, my dear friend, why shouldst thou be surprised or unduly discouraged because offences have arisen? Was there ever a community of Christians who has been favoured with a measure of the Divine blessing that were exempted from this trial of their faith. Nay truly, 'Offences must come'."[63] Backhouse and Walker had no illusions about the dimensions of the problem; the offences came not necessarily from those who had previously offended. The one to whom Walker addressed the above plea had no convict record.

The Disowned

Of the two other components of the Hobart Meeting, the disowned Quakers and the convinced ex-Wesleyans, space permits only one example of each. Again each of these illustrates the depth of Backhouse and Walker's influence on individuals and on the shaping of this first Quaker Meeting in the Australian colonies. Each also in turn influenced the development of the Hobart Meeting and reflected the Backhouse and Walker image.

Francis Cotton was disowned by Southwark Meeting for marrying Anna Maria Tilney, of Kelvedon, Essex, member of the Devonshire House Monthly Meeting, in a church.[64]

Francis Cotton had been apprenticed with the help of his Meeting to a builder in London and he himself set up in business as a contractor. Ill-health led to his decision to emigrate in 1828 to Australia. The voyage took six months and came close to disaster. Their ship was dismasted in a storm after leaving the Cape of Good Hope and limped, jury-rigged, into Hobart. The Cottons, by now thoroughly weary of the sea, and attracted by the beauty of Hobart, decided not to go on to New South Wales, but to settle there. After six months in Hobart, Cotton selected a grant of fifteen hundred acres on the East Coast near the Government Station at Waterloo Point, where a friend of the Cottons, George Story, was assistant-surgeon and stores officer. Their short trip from Hobart to the East Coast was as eventful and

Francis Cotton (1801–83) settled at "Kelvedon" on the East Coast of Van Diemen's Land in 1830.

"Kelvedon", the Cottons' residence. This illustration (from Backhouse's *Narrative*, p. 142) was taken from an original drawing by G. W. Walker.

as near-disastrous as their voyage from England. Shipwrecked near Maria Island on their way to Swanport, they finally took to an open, overloaded boat and landed on the beach at Waterloo Point. Story had prepared a rough sod hut, thatched with grass, as a temporary shelter for them. All their belongings were lost in a fire which destroyed the hut, the family escaping in night attire. Story had been searching with a candle for a side of bacon hung amid the thatch, but being short sighted, had held the candle too close to the thatch. William J. Sayce, writing a history of Australian Friends for *The Australian Friend* of 6 April 1894, said that Story was so upset by his carelessness being the cause of the disaster, "that he counted no personal sacrifice other than due to the family; to whom he became the instructor of their youth and life-long friend and inmate of the Kelvedon household to the day of his death". Cotton, though his hand had been injured by a falling tree, went back to Hobart in an open boat to procure clothing and supplies.

From this disastrous beginning grew a Friends' settlement at Kelvedon which became a pivotal centre for Friends in Van Diemen's Land.

Backhouse and Walker's first visit to Kelvedon was by sea on their way back from Flinders Island. Their landing, like that of the Cottons, was a near-disaster. "We gladly took leave of the *Shamrock* and were conveyed through the surf by the intrepid mate. . . . In the haste of our departure the plug-hole of the boat was left open and the state of the sea admitted no delay; to remedy this inconvenience, I therefore stopped the hole with my thumb, and we were favoured to reach the land in safety, the men jumping out of the boat and running it quickly through the surf."[65] Backhouse and Walker spent several weeks at Kelvedon. Much of this time was taken up with discussions about the future of Quakerism in Van Diemen's Land. Backhouse said that he thought it was his place "to encourage them to truthfulness in bearing the testimony of Friends in all things".[66] He also pointed out to them their great responsibility to raise their family in the Quaker faith so that they would be an influence for good in their neighbourhood, "where I believe", he said, "it is the design of the Lord to have a people to bear testimony to the simplicity and purity of the Gospel of Christ and have no doubt but if this family be faithful to their convictions, they will have a part in this matter". Backhouse's vision of the role of a Quaker family in a pioneer neighbourhood was fulfilled in the lives of Francis and Anna Maria Cotton and their friend George Story, but sadly the vision was to fade in the next generation.

Francis Cotton and Anna Maria, urged on by Backhouse and Walker, applied to Hobart Monthly Meeting for readmission to membership. Francis Cotton was admitted on 14 October 1833, Anna Maria on 4 April 1834. Both agreed to write to their respective Meetings, Southwark and Devonshire House, to have their readmission confirmed.

The contrast between the reactions of these two Meetings illustrates the difficulty of handling questions of membership at long distance. Southwark responded positively to the letter of support in which Backhouse had stressed "the growing exercise of Francis Cotton's mind in the things that pertain to salvation", his faithful support of Friends' testimonies on simplicity and spirituality, his recognition as a minister by the Van Diemen's Land Yearly Meeting and his sorrow for his previous "deviation". Cotton was readmitted in Southwark as well as in Hobart.[67]

Much to Backhouse's dismay, no such response was given by Devonshire House Monthly Meeting to his equally warm letter of support for Anna Maria Cotton. The judgment of the Meeting was against readmission "while it rejoices in the state of her mind as conveyed in a letter on the subject from James Backhouse and George Washington Walker". Her request, after a year's delay, as was explained nine years later, when she was finally readmitted by Devonshire House Monthly Meeting, had been refused "on the grounds of her residing at so great a distance from us and where no recognized Meeting of our Society exists, which can exercise a right care and oversight over its members".[68] Backhouse's comment was, "There is more care of Friends over one another in Van Diemen's Land than is generally the case in London".[69] It was the perceptive understanding of Backhouse and Walker that brought these disowned Friends back into the Society. Meetings were held regularly in the

Kelvedon home of the Cottons; until 1843 Monthly Meetings were held in alternate months at Kelvedon and in Hobart.

Not only did the Cotton home become a Quaker centre on the East Coast, but Francis and Anna Maria Cotton, in their personal and family life, in their support of the Meeting, and in their public image, expressed what they felt to be a Quaker witness. In the isolation of the early settlement at Kelvedon the Cottons had to face considerable trouble with the Aborigines. Two of Francis Cotton's men were speared, but he himself applied his Quaker peace testimony and refused to carry arms. He insisted on going out himself to look for stray cattle instead of exposing his men to further risk.

He was a pioneer of the wool industry on the East Coast. An unsuccessful venture in the export of whale oil made him a primary producer rather than a merchant. He had a reputation for shrewdness. George Meredith is said to have had Francis Cotton,[70] his neighbour, in mind when he remarked: "A Jew sleeps with one eye open, but a Quaker with two".[71] By 1851, when Cotton wrote a series of articles for *The British Friend* in February, April, and July, he stated that he had 170 acres of cleared land at Kelvedon and in cultivation, a hundred acres at the "Grange", where his eldest son, Henry, was installed and a further eighty acres at "The Bend" for his son, Francis. In addition he said that he rented 2200 acres for his sheep and that about five thousand sheep were on the Cotton runs.

The Cotton establishment at this period consisted of the large Cotton family of fourteen sons and daughters, Dr George Story, and twenty assigned servants. Many of the plants growing in the Cotton garden were a reminder of Backhouse, who had sent the seeds, making every Spring, said Cotton, "an earthly paradise: the richness, the beauty, the variety and abundance of the flowers are quite beyond my description".[72] As he surveyed his domain, Cotton must have felt like a Hebrew patriarch. Indeed, this is perhaps how he did see himself, for in his last article in *The British Friend* he wrote, "These countries remind us of patriarchal times, except that some of our graziers have flocks and herds far exceeding Job's when his prosperity was at the highest. Would that, if it were possible, they as far exceeded him in holiness."[73]

Cotton was a most responsible citizen, but his Quaker testimonies placed limits on his seeking public office. The Quaker testimony on oath-swearing precluded him from accepting appointment to the office of a justice of the peace, for this would require him to administer the oath to others. On one occasion he was asked to stand for Glamorgan in the Tasmanian House of Assembly, but he was unsuccessful because, it was said, he refused to solicit votes or to woo voters by alcoholic enticements. He did not shirk civic responsibility in his district. He was a leader in the struggle to get roads built to ease their isolation and he was a member of the Road Trust from its inception. He was also a pioneer in district council government, topping the poll in the first district council election in Van Diemen's Land, and he was the council's first treasurer.[74]

He did not always agree with his fellow-Quakers. His dependence on assigned servants led him to oppose vigorously moves for the cessation of transportation. Walker tried just as vigorously to convince him that the continuance of a convict population was a recipe for moral disaster. Cotton also disagreed with Walker's support of Captain Maconochie's view on penal reform and wrote to Maconochie protesting that Maconochie had quoted from Backhouse and Walker's journals and correspondence in his report without the permission of Backhouse and Walker or of Friends in Hobart. Maconochie in reply assured him that he had in fact received permission from Backhouse and Walker[75] to quote any passages he felt were suited to his purpose. He added that Backhouse and Walker never entertained the scruples expressed by Cotton about Friends engaging in politics for they did not see penal reform, he said, as a political question, but as a moral, religious and scientific one.[76]

Cotton took issue with the Hobart Monthly Meeting on the question of disownment for marrying out. This was an intensely personal issue for Francis and Anna Maria Cotton, for they had to face the Meeting's unyielding attitude and see four sons disowned for marrying non-Friends. It says much for their strong attachment to the Society of Friends that their own loyalty to the Society survived both their own initial disownment and the alienation of so many of their family. Francis Cotton's letter to Walker is a very convincing statement of the case against Friends' rule of disownment for "marrying out".

> My wife is much distressed by the decision of the Monthly Meeting in regard to Henry. I was taken by surprise at your Monthly Meeting when I heard his disownment read. He addressed the Meeting, if I mistake not, apprizing them of the step he was about to take and could not do more. Not only is he much hurt by the treatment of Friends — but they have suffered much in the estimation of several who are aware of the circumstances. Henry had a value for Friends and did a good deal to preserve his consistency, though under much discouragement, and it seems hard to be turned out for moral delinquency when he has at the mature age of 34–5 taken a pious young woman to wife — his own Society being unable to furnish him with one.
>
> I think we could not have taken more effectual means in our small sphere to reduce the numbers of our Society, and I now question the propriety of our Disownment in regard to Marriage contrary to our rules *except in marriage by a priest.*
>
> In disowning I do not think we follow the example of our Holy Head, nor act in unison with his holy will.
>
> Thou wilt excuse my plain speaking but I do not think that our rules of discipline in this matter are in accordance to the love of the Gospel, and that we are influenced in our decision by these *Rules* more than by our love for Christ.
>
> This may lead to resignation of membership — such being talked of — because of a belief of a want of charity on your part and this makes the matter to me still more serious, nor can I think it well to incur the displeasure of pious persons of other denominations by an act which may be misinterpreted, nor to break the heart or discourage a weak brother in his passage through a world quite full enough of trouble without our adding this too.
>
> Hoping that thee and other Friends in Hobart Town may never have a trial of this kind,
>
> Francis Cotton.[77]

This letter summarizes very aptly the sad results of trying to apply an English Quaker disciplinary code unalterably in an Australian context. In the thirty years 1832 to 1862 of the history of Friends in Van Diemen's Land there were fifteen disownments for "marrying out". The threat of disownment placed intolerable restrictions on the range of choice of marriage partners, even allowing for the prolific

Propstings being available for matching up with the half as prolific Cottons. However, no Cotton married a Propsting! Cotton saw that the inevitable result of this dogged and blind adherence to Quaker discipline would be the extinction of the Society in one or two generations. "I think", he said, "we could not have taken more effective means in our small sphere to reduce the number of our Society."[78] He also questioned the manner of disownment. His son, Henry, about to marry, had placed his position — and his dilemma — frankly before the Meeting and had been treated as though he were a moral delinquent. The father's letter to Walker carried something of a personal remonstrance by expressing the hope that Walker would never have to face a similar conflict of loyalties between the family and the Society. Walker, however, was not unsympathetic or unaware of the difficulty. In a letter on 28 June 1847, when he heard of a young Friend marrying out, he commented, "Young men in his circumstances are much to be felt for, as suitable companions for life are not easily made in these parts".[79] By the time that the "marrying out" rule had been relaxed in 1859, much damage had already been done and as a result the Society of Friends lost many of its second Australian generation to other churches. Backhouse's vision of the Lord's design on the East Coast did not survive the movement of the original Quaker stalwarts from the Kelvedon scene.

The Convinced

The third component of the Van Diemen's Land Meeting was the group of the "convinced", that is, of those who through the evangelical message and the Quaker witness of Backhouse and Walker became convinced that the Inward Light of Christ in the heart was the true guide and that therefore they wished to join the Society of Friends. This meant a break with their own previous religious denomination. Backhouse and Walker had been careful in their public meetings to speak as evangelists proclaiming the gospel of Love and not to appear as Quaker proselytizers. When questioned, however, they did not shrink from making their Quaker testimonies known. Written statements were made when they felt these timely. Thus they wrote *A Concise apology for the peculiarities of the Society of Friends commonly called Quakers, in their language, costume and manners*. The last sentence of this pamphlet stressed that they did not wish to appear censorious of those who differed from them. "On the contrary", Backhouse wrote, "we desire to regard with Christian love all who fear the Lord and work righteousness: and constantly to bear in remembrance the saying of the apostle: 'Who art thou that judgest another man's servant? to his own master he standeth or falleth'."[80]

The "convinced" were drawn mainly from the Wesleyans in Hobart. There were some Wesleyans, like William Shoobridge and his wife, who were greatly influenced by Backhouse and Walker, and were said by Walker to be entirely convinced of the soundness of Friends' principles, but who did not break with the Wesleyans, even though they were regular attenders at Meetings for Worship with Friends. William Shoobridge was a frequent contributor to ministry in these Meetings. He came within the orbit of Backhouse and Walker's pastoral care. Walker records in his *Journal* on 16 September 1833 how he and Backhouse devoted the morning to a twofold pastoral mission, first to try to help the parents understand the problems of their two daughters, and second to explain that William Shoobridge's lengthy readings from Scripture and his prepared sermons were not appropriate to a Quaker Meeting. They linked these two matters by pointing out that ministry should not be offered in Meeting if any "reproachful conduct" of the one ministering was known to his hearers. There is no record of the successful outcome of their visit, or whether family reconciliation led to the resumption of William Shoobridge's lengthy ministry. He has left, however, one permanent reminder of his Quaker leanings. He sold to Backhouse for the nominal sum of five shillings half an acre of land in Providence Valley, West Hobart, for the use of Friends as a burial ground and "with liberty to build a meeting-house thereon".[81] Uncertainty of allegiance pursued William Shoobridge to the grave, for he was buried in the Friends' burial-ground, but Wesleyans directed the burial service and Friends present were left somewhat disconsolate.

The influence of Backhouse and Walker on individual Wesleyans is perhaps best illustrated by the effect which their ministry had upon a well-established Wesleyan family, the Mathers of Lauderdale. Robert Mather arrived in Hobart with his wife, Ann, and family in the *Heroine* in 1821 with a number of other Wesleyan families who had responded to the Reverend William Horton s plea to Wesleyans to emigrate as free settlers.[82] Ann was the daughter of Joseph Benson who was widely regarded as an outstanding preacher, second only to John Wesley himself. Before his meeting with Backhouse and Walker, ten years after his arrival, Robert Mather's only contact with Friends had been a chance purchase from a street barrow in London of a copy of Barclay's *Apology*,[83] which had been seized from a Quaker, Edmund Fry, as a distraint for his refusal to pay tithes. Mather took up a grant of land at Lauderdale, Muddy Plains, near the narrow neck between Ralph's Bay and Frederick Henry Bay. Much of his capital was drained away by fruitless attempts to bring the marshy land into profitable cultivation. Because of the high cost of labour he applied to Joshua Spode, the Principal Superintendent of Prisons, for assistance. The assigned servants sent by Spode had apparently been "the sweepings of the ship" and so Mather had had to see more of his capital drained away to pay his five free labourers £130 per annum each.[84] He also lost his best drainer, in spite of protests, to the Lieutenant-Governor. It was during this period of financial anxiety that Robert Mather had his first contact with Backhouse and Walker. Backhouse recorded in his *Narrative* this first meeting held in Robert Mather's house.

> 18.8.32 Having received an invitation from a settler named Robert Mather, to pay him a visit at Lauderdale, on Muddy Plains, we made our way to his house, crossing a salt marsh on the side of which were large bushes of shrubby samphire. R. Mather sent notice to his neighbours of our wish to have a meeting with them....
>
> 19.8.32 We had a meeting on R. Mather's premises, with about twenty-five persons, some of whom were prisoners, in which the people were warned against habitual sins.[85]

Three members of Robert Mather's family, his sons, Joseph Benson and Robert Andrew, and his daughter, Sarah Benson, joined the Society of Friends. Mather's wife, Ann, had died in 1831, her frailty having been one of the reasons which had prompted the family's migration ten years earlier. Robert Mather himself did not apply for membership until 1837, when the threat of court action against him for insolvency no longer hung over him. His image of a Quaker quite clearly led him to determine to clear himself financially before seeking membership. He knew that Quakers were disowned for insolvency and he deduced that he would be an embarrassment to them if he did not first clear himself of this stigma by paying back his creditors in full.

Backhouse and Walker fully appreciated this demonstration of honesty. They did what they could to help him. They supported Mather's requests to the Colonial Secretary for some financial recognition of the services he had rendered voluntarily to travellers by ferrying their boats overland between the two stretches of water. This duty had been carried out at any hour of day or night for ten years with neither recognition nor recompense from the authorities. Often during stormy weather he had furnished crews with rations.[86] When finally after three years he appealed direct to Lieutenant-Governor Arthur for a grant of land in recognition of services rendered, a request he said he would not have made had not the adversity of his family forced him, the Secretary had replied that the Lieutenant-Governor had no power to make the grant because the Port Officer had never given written authority and that the answer was "no".

Backhouse then sought a loan for Mather from John Tawell in Sydney, but was unsuccessful because Tawell was then setting up one of his sons in business and did not have capital available.

Walker, as Mather's prospective son-in-law, felt deeply about this financial anxiety and in a letter to Margaret Bragg, 10 November 1834, he reported that the Lauderdale land was to be subject to forced sale at prices that would not cover the debts. Mather's creditors gave him eight months to wind up his affairs. By his determination to pay off his creditors in full, he gained their respect — and then felt free to apply for membership of the Society of Friends.

Robert Mather had been one of the foundation trustees of

the Wesleyan Church in Hobart. The loss of four of the Mather family to the Quakers understandably cooled the original warm feelings which the Wesleyans had shown towards the Quaker evangelists. The Wesleyans' minus was certainly a plus to the small Quaker Meeting, for much of the leadership in the Meeting and also much of the witness of Quakerism in business and community life in Hobart was given by members of the Mather family. Walker saw their addition to the Meeting as wonderful evidence of the working of the Lord.

George Washington Walker

It was fortunate for the struggling Hobart Meeting that Walker regarded his return from Africa to Van Diemen's Land in 1840 as providential. In this view he was supported by a letter written to him from the Meeting for Sufferings, London, in which the writer saw his proposed return to Tasmania to marry Sarah Mather as "a providential opening for promoting the stability and encouragement of the little band there, who profess the simple and spiritual views of Christian doctrine as held by Friends".[87]

Walker's presence in Hobart for the next twenty years was not only a source of great encouragement and strength to the Quaker Meeting but his life set a pattern of Quaker citizenship which influenced his fellow-members and also won wide recognition in the community.

First, he endeavoured to conduct his drapery business on Quaker principles of honesty and simplicity. Having made the decision to try linen drapery, he sought the help of his friends in England to furnish the required capital. He asked Charles Bragg to be his partner and London buyer. Bragg agreed to be his buyer but was not willing to risk what he said was his meagre capital in a partnership. Sufficient capital however was raised by donations or loans from friends such as Backhouse himself and George Bennington, and his capital enabled him to lease premises at 65 Liverpool Street, Hobart, at £125 per annum. The considerable renovations necessary to make a somewhat dilapidated two-storey house suitable for a drapery store cost £247.6.0d. When he wrote to his English friends for assistance he set out very clearly the principles on which he intended to conduct his business. There were to be no "fancy", only "useful" goods in stock. He aimed, he said, at moderate profit on first-class quality. Christian morality was to be applied to trade.

He soon found out that cottons and woollens, not linen goods, were in greater demand. He also discovered that the dividing line between the "fancy" and the "useful" was not always clear. In this he ran into some criticism from Friends, from one for not faithfully applying his Quaker testimony of simplicity to his advertised goods, from another for not indulging a little harmless interest in attractive adornment. To George Bell's attack on him for advertising the sale of "Military drills" and "operatics", Walker patiently reasoned that those were but trade names for useful articles like "Wellington" boots or "Lucifer" matches, which were neither warlike nor devilish. He said that if he had suspected that these might be a stumbling-block to Friends he would not have used these terms. Nevertheless Walker was upset because George Bell had written to *The British Friend* exposing what he regarded as inconsistency in Walker as a Friend. Walker said he deplored Bell's "petulant and censorious spirit".[88] The opposite reason for rebuke came when he received an order from Anna Maria Cotton for white gloves. Thinking that this was not in keeping with the testimony of simplicity as applied to dress, Walker substituted light kid for white, saying that light kid was sufficiently a la mode, but "white would be yet more incongruous".[89]

When he received Anna Maria Cotton's rebuke in reply, he again reaffirmed the Quaker testimony to plainness in dress and ended with a Pauline appeal. "And now, my beloved friends, let us all renewedly seek for ability to obey the injunction of an inspired apostle — 'to live as brethren' — be pitiful, be courteous! If I have in any way infringed upon this precept, I ask your forgiveness. And in whatsoever degree you have infringed upon it (which I do not undertake to decide) I desire sincerely to add, I forgive you, as I hope to be forgiven."[90] The issue of the "fancy" goods continued to be irksome and became a cause of friction between him and his main assistant, Robert Andrew Mather. In 1846 he crossed off several of Mather's orders in baby linen, which apparently Mather defended as "plain goods adapted for Wesleyans". "But", added Walker, "there is a great deal of unnecessary work and expense bestowed on children's clothing, even among Friends."[91] Walker had scruples, too, about selling lace. Mather called these "idle scruples". When Walker at last decided in 1848 to simplify his business, he parted company with Mather, who thereupon set up his own drapery business. Walker sold his stock of "idle scruples" to him at below cost and with conscience eased withdrew from linen drapery and concentrated on the plainer fabrics of wool and cotton.

Apart from his image as a Quaker shopkeeper, Walker was also building up an image as a Quaker citizen and philanthropist. His most lasting contribution perhaps was a direct outcome of his concern for the victims of alcohol. Not only was he a leader in the Temperance movement[92] but he saw the necessity for some practical application of his concern, some positive move to counteract the rum trade. In January 1845 he wrote:

> I have for some time past been of the mind that few things would tend more to the moral welfare of our working-classes here, who have been notorious for their recklessness and prodigality than the establishment of a savings bank, especially now that hundreds, nay thousands are discontinuing their visits to the public house, so that they begin to find that money *remains* in their pockets, it may be after providing for all essential wants.[93]

Two months later he opened up a savings bank in a corner of his Liverpool Street store. He enlisted the support of a group of well-known and respected citizens as trustees. These included the Lieutenant-Governor, Sir John Eardley Wilmot, and the Colonial Secretary, J. E. Bicheno. At a meeting on 15 January 1845 thirty citizens agreed to the founding of "The Hobart Town Savings Bank", Walker being appointed honorary manager for a six months' trial period, to give the bank time to establish itself. Operations commenced on 1 March 1845.

The bank prospered and after the trial period of six months Walker was appointed manager on a salaried basis of

G. W. Walker's drapery shop at 65 Liverpool Street, Hobart, where in 1845 he opened a Savings Bank. This bank, now known as the Savings Bank of Tasmania, has operated continuously up to the present.

£100 per annum. Within two years there were fifteen hundred depositors and a capital of £20,000. Walker said that he had no scruples about admitting that the bank was also good for business, as depositors tended to buy from the stocks displayed nearby. "I am of the opinion the Savings Bank has done good in drawing custom to the shop, many of the depositors expressing thankfulness for the privilege afforded them for their securing their earnings at a moderate rate of interest and giving the shop a measure of their custom. It is an indirect benefit in this way that we may fairly enjoy without scruple."[94] In the one location the depositor could operate on his pass-book, spend his savings on a new outfit, buy a Bible from the Bible Depot in another corner, and sign the pledge. In Walker's drapery store philanthropy, commerce, and thrift were mutually supportive.

Walker was one of the nine original members of the

Council of the Hobart Town High School, which was founded in 1850 to provide unsectarian secondary education.[95] Walker wrote to his English friends seeking contributions to the public appeal for five thousand pounds, which was to be raised in twenty-five pound shares.[96] Walker was also invited by the Colonial Secretary to be a member of the new Board of Education, set up in 1856 to supervise education in the southern area of Tasmania. The image that Walker called up by his involvement in education is illustrated by a phrase used in his obituary appearing in *The Hobart Town Advertiser* of 5 February 1859, which wrote of him as having "a characteristic sympathy for the cause of education".

Not so well-known was his willingness to be drawn in to public endorsement of good causes. He was a member of the Irish Famine Relief Committee which raised £1,350 and a consignment of wheat for Ireland. He wrote a very spirited protest to the editor of one paper who had to some extent sabotaged the appeal by alleging that benevolence to the Irish was misplaced because it would simply "furnish the lawless Irish with the means of bloodshed and plunder".[97]

When an employee of the Gas Works, James Cunningham, was blinded in an explosion in the works, Walker, with a fellow-director, C. M. Maxwell, organized a public appeal to help Cunningham and his wife gain an income by setting up a working-man's hostel. He was vice-president of the Auxiliary Bible Society, a member of the Committee of the Mechanics' Institute, and a member of the Council of the Royal Society of Tasmania. The breadth of his philanthropy is underlined in a tribute by Lady Denison. When she was planning to set up a house of refuge for homeless, "unfortunate" women in Tasmania, but in doubt concerning the success of such a venture, she was advised, she said:

> . . . to call to my assistance the person, who, I was told, was, of all others, the most competent to assist in a work of this kind. This is a linen-draper in the town, the very personification of a mild, benevolent and excellent Quaker. Even here where sectarian and religious party feeling run higher than anywhere I have ever known, men of all denominations unite in speaking well of George Washington Walker. He is never mentioned but with respect by those who, I fear, are too indifferent on the subject of religion to belong to any party at all; and whatever good is to be done, he is sure to have a hand in it.[98]

Walker became, as the Quaker Committee in London foresaw, a providential source of strength to the Hobart Meeting. He also became the image and the example of a Quaker philanthropist in action.

Six
Quakers in New South Wales

When London Yearly Meeting established in 1861 a "disciplinary connection" with the Meetings existing in Tasmania, Victoria, and South Australia, there was no reference to the Sydney Meeting which had to wait until 1887 for recognition.

The history of the Sydney Meeting before 1861, and for some years afterwards, is one of repeated failures to establish a settled Meeting for Discipline. William J. Sayce, writing a brief survey of the development of Australian Meetings for *The Friend* in 1894,[1] attempted to analyze the reasons for the apparent failure of the Quaker plant to take root in the Sydney climate. "The cause at Sydney did not prosper", he said, "even in the days of James Backhouse: discord entered in amongst the flock and was the object of much concern and labour. The contrast between the history of this meeting and that of Hobart Town is very marked, owing, of course, to the character of those constituting the meeting." Sayce attributed this lack of success to the character of those Quakers who happened to settle in the colony. Or did the difficulty lie also in the conditions operative in the colony itself?

In March 1837 Backhouse and Walker left Sydney to return to Hobart on their way to Africa. Daniel and Charles Wheeler had returned a few weeks before from their mission to the Pacific Islands and remained in Sydney a while longer. Daniel Wheeler would seem to have doubted whether Quakerism could ever flourish under the conditions he observed in the "wicked" city of Sydney. He recorded in his journal the desolation felt when Backhouse and Walker departed, a desolation all the more desperate because of the sense of being unable to cope with what they saw as the terrible wickedness of the convict city Sydney. Sydney, in Daniel

Wheeler's denunciation, was almost worse than Sodom and Gomorrha combined.

> Our dear friends, James Backhouse and George W. Walker, took their departure from these shores last First-day, the 12th inst. (12th 3 mo., 1837), so that we are sitting desolate, and somewhat resembling those that are forsaken; but, alas! not amongst an afflicted people; Would that I could say so. But instead of this, I think this is as wicked a place as any I have seen, which have been not a few in my day. Pride and haughtiness abound and lamentable ignorance of spiritual religion is manifest on every side; indeed, few seem to make even an outward profession of it. Drunkenness appears to be the prevailing sin, which leads to the most deadly callousness amongst the working part of the community, although it is not confined to their grade. The major part of the lower order are bound in the fetters of Popery; and for the most part are prisoners who have obtained tickets-of-leave, or they are what are called assigned servants, many of whom have been accustomed to crime from their very youth. . . . Cursing and bitterness resound continually through the streets; and extortion and deceit prevail almost universally among the shopkeepers, on whose promises hardly any dependence can be placed. Many have amassed considerable wealth by extortion and the sale of spirits; and having arisen only as from a dunghill, are living as if there was no God, no judgment, and no world to come — as if length of days was at their command.[2]

Only a Backhouse or a Walker, one can almost hear Wheeler saying, could cope with such iniquity. Whether convict Sydney was so much worse than convict Hobart is a matter of opinion, but at least Hobart Quakers had the presence of a Walker to steady and guide them. Sydney Meeting had no such assets. Indeed it had serious liabilities — as the case study of one of its earliest supporters will presently reveal.

There were Quakers in New South Wales before the arrival of Backhouse and Walker, but identification and verification of membership have been difficult because of the loss of early Quaker records. Over thirty names of people known to be Quakers or connected with Quakers and to have settled in New South Wales by 1834 have been traced. About half of these were free settlers and half had been transported.

There is a story that after the Castle Hill rebellion of 1804 the subsequent hanging of the rebels greatly upset some

Quakers who lived in Church Street Parramatta, known as Quakers Row. It was said that they offered to bury the bodies of the rebels. Records, however, have yet to be found to verify the identity of these "Quakers". It was also said that William Joyce, who escaped on horseback from his farm at Toongabbee Hill[3] and was sent by the commanding officer at Castle Hill to raise the alarm at Parramatta, was a Quaker. Joyce's part in summoning help for Castle Hill was confirmed by a letter from the wife of Samuel Marsden.[4] Details of Joyce's trial at Croydon on 3 August 1789, his subsequent transportation to Sydney on the *Albermarle*, and his grant of freedom and land in 1804 are all attested, but his Quaker connections remain unconfirmed.

Also unproven are the Quaker origins of a Thomas Harvey whom Rita Ashton in her *History of Quakers Hill* identified as a Lincolnshire farmer and Quaker, and therefore as the one after whom the area now known as Quakers Hill has been named.

Two claimed to be Quakers in the census of 1828, a William Reilly and Catherine Walker, a Quaker seamstress from Dublin. Neither made contact with Backhouse and Walker. Quaker links of others were recorded by Backhouse and Walker in their journals, but few of these seemed likely to retain any interest in the Society of Friends. Thus Walker recorded of one, formerly a member, that he had "since put off the appearance and profession of a Friend".[5] Of another, however, whose downfall Walker attributed to drink, he said: "The young man seemed feeling, humble and tender and received my council very gratefully and I have considerable hopes respecting him."[6] One elderly convict, David Richards, sought the help of Backhouse and Walker in obtaining a pardon. Though a disowned Friend, he clearly wished to remain within the care of Friends; he was one of those present in 1842 when a Meeting for Discipline was first formed in Sydney and for some years until his death at the age of eighty in 1853, he occupied a cottage on the Friends' burial-ground. He was greatly respected as one who "truly adorned his religious profession".[7]

Although Abraham Davy spent several years in Van Diemen's Land[8] he finally settled in New South Wales and, like David Richards, not only maintained contact with Friends, but through the encouragement and help given to him by Backhouse and Walker, became one of the most consistent supporters of the Sydney Meeting. Meetings for Worship for a time were held in his George Street house.

John Tawell

There was one, John Tawell, who of all those in Sydney connected in any way with the Society of Friends proved to be the most helpful to Backhouse and Walker and the most concerned to support a Meeting in Sydney. Yet John Tawell's name has been almost expunged from any account of the early days of the history of Friends in Sydney, understandably perhaps in view of the nature of his death — he was executed at Aylesbury, England, on 25 March 1845 for murdering his mistress by administering prussic acid in a glass of porter. As a result of this notoriety little attempt has been made to consider with any sympathy this man's complex personality, the extent of his contribution to the development of a Quaker Meeting in Sydney, or the nature of the tragedy which overtook him. Further, horror at what one Sydney journalist called a crime of "singular atrocity" has not only meant that some would gladly consign him to oblivion, but others, judging all his actions in the light of his subsequent crime, have denigrated the help that he tried to render or labelled any good thing he did as further evidence of his hypocrisy.

There are several reasons for a more detailed treatment of this complex, enigmatic man. First, he is an example of one, who, by personal effort and ability — and some strokes of luck — managed to rise from the lowest status of a convict to that of a wealthy and respected citizen of Sydney in spite of being an emancipist. Second, he had a very strong attachment to Quakerism, even though he had been disowned and had been refused re-admission at least twice by his English Monthly Meeting, Devonshire House. The period of his attachment to Backhouse and Walker, however, and its significance because of his "de facto" membership in Sydney, was most productive and was probably the happiest period of his life. Third, there are the questions posed by the curious sequence of events between 1838, the year of his return with his wife, Mary, to England, and 1845, the year of his death. Was the double Jekyll-Hyde type of life he seemed to lead simply the emergence at last of the real Tawell, or was it the result of a life-long conflict between his longing to be regarded as a respectable Quaker and his self-indulgent desire to be a man of affairs? Was his clumsy removal of one, who, he may have finally realized, destroyed his claim to Quaker respectability, the tragic result of his attempt to resolve this conflict?

Tawell's life-story, from his conviction in 1814 for forgery and his transportation to Sydney, to his return to England in 1838, a wealthy respected land-owner,[9] who had "made good" in the tough early days of Sydney, was a remarkable success story. The main facts of Tawell's life — and particularly his death — are well documented. He was born in 1784. His first contact with Friends was in 1798 when he was employed by a Quaker widow in a shop in Suffolk. When he went to London, Friends helped him to obtain a position in a draper's shop with William Janson in Whitechapel. On 8 December he was admitted to membership of the Devonshire House Meeting. A year later he was disowned. A hasty marriage with his employer's housemaid had been insisted on by Janson as a matter of necessity, not of choice, and as the marriage had been conducted by a priest, he was disowned, Tawell admitting "his disorderly and unchaste conduct". Soon after this he left Janson and became a traveller with a drug firm. He still appeared to value his connection with Friends, for he let himself be known as the "Quaker traveller".

It is said that the cause of his subsequent downfall was an unwise friendship with a Joseph Hunter, a Quaker linen-draper, who was eventually executed for forgery. Tawell was fortunate not to have suffered the same penalty for committing forgery on the Uxbridge Bank. When apprehended, he had a forged Bank of England note in his possession and the managers of the Uxbridge Bank, Quakers, refused to prosecute on the major charge, leaving Tawell to face the lesser charge of possession of a forged note. He pleaded guilty and was transported for fourteen years to Sydney in 1814. Because of his knowledge of drugs he was assigned on arrival to the convict hospital. On 7 December 1818 he petitioned and was granted ticket-of-leave.[10] In 1820 he was given a certificate of qualification by the Medical Board to act as a chemist,[11] and thereafter practised as an apothecary, first in Hunter Street, then in Pitt Street, with groceries as additional stock. He purchased a whaling vessel and made money by cornering the whalebone market, exporting the product to London for manufacture into combs and brush-handles. He also speculated in whale-oil and, it is suspected, in the common currency of rum, though he disclaimed to Backhouse and Walker responsibility for ordering the consignment of rum which he later poured dramatically into Sydney harbour. Backhouse described this unusual scene in his *Narrative*:

> We had the satisfaction of witnessing the destruction of five puncheons of Rum, containing four hundred and ninety-two gallons, and two hogsheads of Geneva, containing one hundred and sixteen gallons. They were the property of one of our friends, who had received them as part of an investment, from his agent in England, who had not been apprized of a change of views of his correspondent, respecting the use and sale of spirits, in which he cannot now, conscientiously, be concerned. He therefore represented the case to the Governor, who allowed them to be taken out of bond, free of duty, under the same circumstances as if for export, and under the charge of an Officer of Customs, placed on board a staged boat, which took them out into the Cove, where the heads of the casks were removed, and the contents poured into the sea. A few friends of the owner accompanied him, to witness this "new thing under the sun," in this Colony. We were much pleased with the hearty manner in which the custom-house officer superintended this sacrifice of property to principle. Some persons, from neighbouring vessels, looked on with approval, others with surprise, and others, not yet awake to the evils of spirit-drinking, expressed regret. A man, from a little vessel, cried out, "That's real murder." One of the puncheons, being too near the edge of the boat, went overboard, and brought its top above the surface of the water, with much rum in it. It floated close by the same little vessel, and a man dipped a horn into it, to try to get a drink of the devoted fluid. It was now rum and water; but happily for the man, it was rum and salt-water! even his vitiated

palate rejected it, and he poured it back to the rest, which was soon mingled with the briny flood.[12]

In the directory of 1837 Tawell's name appears as "John Tawell, merchant and agent for London and the Colonies, 1, Macquarie Street". He had prospered quickly, for in 1820 he had sold out his original business for £14,000 to Ambrose Foss, who also seemed to have some link with Quakers, and invested the money in land and mortgages.

It is difficult to judge the validity of the claims that though Tawell grew rich in the colony he sent no aid to his wife, and that it was only because Friends subscribed to her passage that she was able to join Tawell in 1823, but was not welcomed by him because he "had formed one of those female connections which are more consistent with convenience than sanctioned by morality".[13] In 1822 he applied to have his wife and two sons sent out from England to join him.[14] They arrived on 13 March 1823 on the *Lord Sidmouth*. It would seem therefore that the initiative came from him. From the time of his wife's arrival to her death in 1838 he appeared to carry out his responsibilities as a faithful husband and father. Both sons were educated at Sydney Grammar School.[15] By 1829, when he took his family back to England for a visit, he had accumulated, it was said, a fortune of £35,000. Tawell returned alone to Sydney on 20 July 1830 on business and went back again to England in 1831. On this occasion he was given a farewell dinner by prominent citizens, "one of the most convivial parties we witnessed in the colony", according to the report in *The Sydney Gazette* of 1 November 1831, though another newspaper *Truth*,[16] reporting the occasion years later, attempted to downgrade its importance by alleging that it was only the emancipists who attended. The last period he spent in Australia was with his wife and family from their return in July 1834 until the final departure in 1838. His younger son had died in England in 1833 and the older son in Australia in 1838. This and his wife's poor health led to his decision to return. She died on 12 December 1838.

However much Quakers may have tried to forget Tawell's part in the early history of the Sydney Meeting, he was not forgotten by others. In one of his articles on early history

"Old Sydney" called him "one of the most extraordinary characters in early Australian history".[17] Roger (later Sir) Therry, commissioner of the local court of requests, occupied a house opposite to Tawell's in Hunter Street. His assessment of Tawell, is quoted by Arthur Jose.[18]

> He struck me as being a remarkably well-conducted person. He had once been a member of the Society of Friends; he wore the broad-brimmed hat, appeared always in a neat and carefully adjusted costume and his whole appearance and manner impressed one with the notion of his being a saintly personage. He always sought the society in public of persons of reputed piety. Tawell was himself a liberal contributor to charities,[19] and the opinion of his character was so favourable that the act for which he suffered created a general astonishment in Sydney.

Jose, in a sympathetic appraisal of Tawell, added:

> He was rich, surrounded with affection, honoured by men whose judgment was worth respecting and — this for him was the greatest honour of all — readmitted, as fully as was possible, in that distant settlement, to real membership in the Society of Friends.[20]

By 1838 therefore he seemed to be at the peak of his acceptance as a respectable citizen of Sydney.

Jose noted Tawell's strong attachment to Quakerism. This is borne out by evidence from Backhouse and Walker and from the extraordinary lengths to which Tawell was prepared to go to regain membership. John Tawell was the first contact made by Backhouse and Walker with Friends in Sydney. The initiative came from Tawell who visited them shortly after their arrival on the *Henry Freeling* in Sydney Harbour on 22 December 1834. Walker recorded the meeting. "John Tawell, a person whose wife we believe to be a Friend and who is himself attached to the Society visited us this morning, kindly offering his services in any way we might be disposed to avail ourselves of them."[21] The first Meeting for Worship was held on board ship on 28 December 1834, and attended by Backhouse and Walker, Daniel and Charles Wheeler, and seven whom Backhouse described as "somewhat connected with Friends".[22] Besides Tawell and his wife, Mary, there were Thomas and Amelia Brown, Mary Keane, Gabriel Bennet, and Samuel Cross. Thomas and Amelia Brown had been attenders in England. Amelia apparently felt sufficient attachment to Friends to wear the plain Friends' costume. Gabriel Bennet had been a member in Cork, for Walker said that he had given up a position as an officer of the Orange Lodge to join Friends,[23] but Mackie[24] described him as a former member of the Society of Friends and he must therefore be regarded as having resigned or been disowned. Samuel Cross was an attender from Nottingham, but nothing is known of Mary Keane.

It was at the house of John and Mary Tawell on 4 January 1835 that the first Meeting for Worship on land in New South Wales was held at six o'clock in the evening. Twenty-two persons were present. Both Backhouse and Walker made frequent reference in their journals to the Tawell's thoughtfulness and hospitality. A typical entry is Walker's on 30 December 1834 saying that Tawell was "extremely attentive and useful in rendering every aid in his power". The Tawells' house became a Friends' centre during the visits of Backhouse and Walker. They regarded it as their home and often took meals with the Tawells. Backhouse commented[25] that "their kindness has far exceeded that of administering a cup of cold water in the name of the disciples and surely will not fail of its reward". Backhouse, writing to his sister, Elizabeth, spoke most warmly of Mary Tawell's kindness. "Mary Tawell is the greatest comfort. She is really a valuable woman."[26]

Tawell was an unofficial co-ordinator of Friends' activities, distributing Friends' tracts, notices of public meetings, and acting as Friends' representative in any negotiations with the authorities. He showed much concern for any young Friends arriving as strangers in the city. When three arrived on Tawell's doorstep, Walker was confident that Tawell with his contacts would be able to find employment for them. Tawell's house seemed to be a clearing-house for Friends' letters and parcels. When one young ex-convict, working some distance from Sydney, wanted someone to be willing to collect a valuable parcel of belongings from home and forward them to him, Walker assured him that Tawell was one whom he could safely consult "on any matter of the kind on which help or advice may be needed, as we have had many opportunities of observing the interest he is disposed to

The earliest Friends' Meeting House in Australia was erected by John Tawell for Friends at 195 Macquarie Street, Sydney, in 1835. Copper engraving attributed to John Carmichael. In the *Picture of Sydney and strangers' guide in New South Wales for 1838* by James Maclehose, Sydney, 1938. NK 1477. In the Rex Nan Kivell Collection, National Library of Australia.

Friends' second Meeting House, Sydney, on the site of the Friends' burial-ground. From a drawing by Frederic Mackie. By kind permission of Mary Nichols, editor of *Traveller under concern* Hobart: University of Tasmania, 1973 and Nancie Hewitt.

take in promoting the welfare of young men circumstanced as thou art".[27]

In 1835 Tawell gave convincing proof of his desire to promote the cause of Quakerism in the colony and to support the labours of Backhouse and Walker. In 1827 he had purchased land at 195 Macquarie Street, directly opposite the "Rum Hospital" where he had worked as a druggist. The price was said to be £1,380.[28] On this land he built and furnished a Meeting House with the inscription "*John Tawell — to the Society of Friends*". The first Meeting in the new Meeting House was held on 1 November 1835, the Colonial Secretary, Alexander McLeay, being present with his son and daughter. Walker said that one Friend, Jeremiah Bigg, had expressed the opinion that there was some prejudice against meeting at Tawell's house, where meetings had been held previously. Whether the prejudice was against the size or location of the house or against Tawell as an emancipist is not clear. Whatever the motive for his generosity, Tawell quite clearly aimed to provide a suitable Meeting House. Backhouse spoke of it in his letters as "a neat little Meeting House . . . a pattern of simplicity combined with becoming proportions, is well finished, seated with cedar and is capable of accommodating 150 persons comfortably".[29] Walker described it as "a neat structure of brick, containing one large room and calculated to seat 196 persons ... The seats are all of cedar, which from its resemblance to mahogany gives them a neat and finished appearance. In short, the building is all that a Friends' Meeting House needs to be, simple, commodious and convenient."[30]

Some mystery surrounds the reason why this Meeting House did not finally become the property of Friends, for this was Tawell's intention. When he returned to England in 1838, he wrote to the Meeting for Sufferings, informing Friends that he had explained the proposal to Backhouse and Walker and had appointed six trustees, James Backhouse of York, Joseph Story Jun. of Southwark, and William Manley of York, together with three in Australia, G. W. Walker, Francis Cotton, and Joseph Benson Mather. The closing paragraphs of his letter are particularly significant:

> I do not possess the privilege of church-fellowship with Friends — and it is love to the Society — and, I would also trust, with regard to its principles — by which I have been induced to make this offer, as a free gift — I may also remark that my circumstances enable me to do this; from a successful persevering industry in a respectable profession and business — a Licensed Apothecary — and a Chemist Druggist — and as there was no other party in Sydney — who met as Friends, that could have well afforded contributing — to even the hire of a room.
>   The Meeting for Sufferings concluded on its acceptance, I give directions for its conveyance to my private agent in Sydney — James Norton — a solicitor of high respectability and integrity.
>   4th of 12th mo. 1839
>   John Tawell,
>   24 Bridge Street, Southwark Bridge.[31]

Tawell was anxious to stress his attachment to the Society of Friends and his success in a "respectable profession and business". The Meeting for Sufferings, after referring Tawell's offer to the Continental Committee, accepted the Meeting House.[32] Yet the transfer, which was to have been made by James Norton, was never finalized. One writer[33] alleged that "the Quakers would not accept the gift". This judgment may have been due to the writer not being aware of Meeting for Sufferings' acceptance of the offer, or it may have been a reflection of the wish in some Friends' minds to disassociate Friends from any reminder of Tawell's link with Friends.

A summary of the nineteenth century history of Sydney Friends[34] gives 1840 as the date of sale of the Meeting House by auction. Yet Hobart Monthly Meeting Minutes recorded on 4 August 1842 that the first Monthly Meeting of Sydney was held on 2 and 3 May 1842 in the Macquarie Street Meeting House. A letter from Sydney to the Van Diemen's Land Yearly Meeting of 5 December 1845 said that the Meeting House was not the property of Friends, though this does not necessarily mean that it was not being used by Friends. By the end of 1845 it had probably been disposed of by those who had been authorized by Tawell before his execution. In any case its use was lost to Friends after 1845 and this was a serious setback, for Friends were now without a centre for their activities.[35]

It was in the years 1840 to 1845 that Tawell's desire to be readmitted into membership of the Devonshire House Meeting became an obsession and yet at the same time his personal life was such that, if the details of his liaison were to become known, readmission would be more remote than ever. His wife, Mary, died on 12 December 1838. He had meanwhile formed a liaison with Sarah Hart who had been nursing her. Not only did he maintain her in a house at Salt Hill near Slough, but he set his sights on marrying a wealthy Quaker widow, Eliza Cutforth, who kept a girls' school in Clerkenwell. One wonders whether Tawell perhaps thought that such a respectable marriage would improve his chances for readmission. It resulted however only in Eliza Cutforth's disownment for marrying Tawell, a disowned Friend.

Tawell persisted in reapplying for readmission, even though his application had been refused in 1840. He tried at least once again in January 1844. The minutes of Devonshire House Meeting recorded the judgment of the interviewing committee. "He manifests an attachment to the Society of Friends and, on enquiry, we do not find that his conduct since his last application has been consistent therewith . . . but we have not been able to discover in him that abiding tenderness, and self-abasedness of mind, which true repentance for past deeds leads into."[36]

The events which led to his crime and immediate apprehension and the attitude he assumed during his trial had a certain bizarre quality which makes one question his mental condition. It was as though he laid the trail to his own apprehension. On an afternoon of September 1844 he purchased some prussic acid from a druggist, then, dressed in Quaker garb, visited his mistress in Slough. A neighbour, hearing screams, came out to see Tawell leaving in a hurry, ran in, found Sarah Hart dying and summoned help. Tawell meanwhile had gone to the Slough railway station at 7.00 p.m., discovered that no train left until 7:42, caught a bus to Windsor, got out before the bus had gone far, walked back to the Slough Station and was seen entering the train by the doctor who had been called to attend Sarah Hart, and who had then run to the station to see if he could trace the man in Quaker garb. The station-master was persuaded to send a message by telegraph to Paddington, the first time that the telegraph had been used to apprehend a suspect. The telegraphed message became historic. "A murder has just been committed at Salt Hill and the suspected murderer was seen to take a first class ticket for London by the train which left Slough at 7.42 p.m. He is in the garb of a Kwaker (no letter Q yet being devised for telegraphic transmission) with a brown great-coat on, which reaches to his feet. He is in the last compartment of the second class carriage."[37] Tawell, on arrival at Paddington, was shadowed by the police to a lodging-house kept by a Quaker and arrested next morning.

Right through the trial Tawell persisted in claims that he was innocent, making such declarations as, "Thou must be mistaken in the identity. My station in society places me above suspicion".[38] He was so certain that he would be acquitted that he had a new set of Quaker clothes ready and had arranged for a celebration banquet at the White Hart Inn. He was found guilty and hanged before a crowd of thousands at Aylesbury on 25 March 1845. At the last moment apparently Tawell confessed to his crime. John Tawell wrote to Hannah Backhouse, one of the Friends who visited him in prison.

> My deeply interested friend, H. Backhouse, I feel the more desirous for the deep interest thou hast evinced on my account for my eternal

welfare thus to address thee if only briefly and in unison with thy desire, for giving thee at this late hour an assurance that a full confession has been made by me. Awful is my condition in the sight of that pure and holy Being unto whom my account is soon to be given.[39]

Several factors perhaps contributed to the moral deterioration and mental instability of the last five years of his life. He had lost his wife and both his sons. He had left Australia a wealthy man and this material success had given him a certain glow of self-respect. The depression years 1842-43 saw a big drop in the value of his property assets in New South Wales and therefore of his income. His acceptance in the Quaker community of Sydney and encouragement from Backhouse and Walker had revived his hopes that he would regain the Quaker respectability which he had once but briefly enjoyed. He must have been confident that the Quaker credit he had built up in Australia, and particularly the proposed gift of the Meeting House, would assure a favourable credit balance in the Devonshire House Meeting, and indeed Sarah Bacon testified at his trial that he had said in June 1840 that he was about to be reinstated in membership.[40]

His rejection by Devonshire House Meeting in August 1840 may have intensified the inner conflict between "the good that he would" and "the evil that he would not" by pushing him further into a moral morass. On the outside he did his best to preserve his unofficial Quaker respectability, in garb, in family life, in attendance at Meeting. And behind this facade he carried on a furtive Jekyll existence visiting Sarah Hart, by whom he had two children. Did the rejection then of his further appeal in 1844 make him realize that this hidden life was perhaps suspected and that, if revealed, would destroy for ever his Quaker image? and so had led him in desperation to seek a prussic acid solution of the conflict? Or should the question be posed another way? If Devonshire House had accepted him into membership in 1840, would this have helped Tawell to resolve his conflict in a way acceptable to society and to fulfil the promise he gave in Sydney, under the pastoral care of Backhouse and Walker, of becoming a worthy Quaker? Arthur Jose phrases the enigma of Tawell's character in two other questions. Was he, as almost everybody seemed to judge, "an accomplished hypocrite, concealing his sensual and murderous designs under a cloak of Quakerism?" Or does Tawell rather represent "an intensely human problem, the strife between godliness and sensuality in a single brain?"[41]

This leads to a further question — how did Backhouse and Walker view Tawell's downfall? In their journal entries they gave no hints of any uneasiness about him and indeed they were generous in praise of their "kind friend". Backhouse, on his return to England, had evidently kept in touch with Tawell by correspondence and had seen him at least once, as the following letter, written to Tawell on 16 November 1844, indicates. "Often since I last saw thee I have had thee in remembrance, as well as thy dear wife, with desires for your welfare. I hope by this time you may both have been enabled to feel benefit to have arisen from the bitter cup you had then but recently drunk and the taste of which was still painful to the palate."[42]

The date of Backhouse and Tawell's last meeting here referred to is not clear, nor is the reference to the "bitter cup" recently drunk. Since this sentence is addressed to both Tawell and his wife, it may have referred to the disownment of Eliza and to Tawell's failure to gain readmission to Devonshire House Meeting. Then in a letter a fortnight later to Walker he reported that he had received a prompt reply from Tawell and that "he has got an agreeable wife and a fine little son".[43] Two months later Backhouse broke to Walker the painful news of Tawell's arrest. It is clear that Backhouse, and presumably Walker, after the event claimed to have seen a flaw of evil in his character.

> I must turn from the pleasant to the painful. Probably before this reach thee thou wilt have been informed of the awful situation in which John Tawell is placed. Thou art so well aware of the evil that has often shown itself in his character that I conclude no fresh development of moral turpitude on his part would greatly surprise thee! but he now stands fully committed to take his trial for wilful murder! ... If he be guilty, as I fear he is, the greatest comfort would be to see him truly penitent, confessing his faults and seeking the pardon of his sin, but I am not aware that there is any present prospect of this.[44]

Backhouse seemed, therefore, to have no doubt about Tawell's guilt. Of two later letters referring to Tawell, the first on 11 April 1845 reported on the execution "under circumstances which just leave some room to hope the poor culprit might be penitent".[45] In a second letter on 8 July 1845 Backhouse reported that he had seen Tawell's daughter-in-law, Isabella. "She has felt much the dreadful conduct of her father-in-law and its consequences to him, but she was too well aware of his character to be surprised."[46] Though some Friends visited Tawell in prison Backhouse does not appear to have gone to see him.[47]

Tawell's crime and the publicity given to it in England clearly came as a great shock to Friends and it was thought necessary to set the record straight by publishing a tract on *The history of John Tawell, with his life, trial, confession and execution,*[48] and to issue a formal denial in *The British Friend*[49] that he was a member. It was pointed out that the Society had disowned him many years before and had "even refused to reinstate him". One Friend, William Tallach, in the midst of denunciation, at least acknowledged that Tawell's record was not all black. "It would appear that, notwithstanding Tawell's gross hypocrisy, so long and successfully assumed, there were better moments in his life, at various periods, when he was awakened to earnest desires and resolutions of amendment. But each time he again yielded to the influences of passion and temptation, and finally beyond recall."[50]

In Sydney the impact on the small Quaker Meeting was quite devastating, for Tawell had achieved some standing in the community as a respected citizen and he was identified as a Quaker. The story must have been current in other States, as well as in New South Wales, for a Melbourne Friend felt it necessary to disown any connection between Quakers and Tawell by writing a letter to *The Argus* stating that Tawell was never a Quaker. This was an error of fact, if not of intention. When Frederick Mackie, visiting Sydney in 1835, saw the Meeting House Tawell had built for the Society of Friends, he said, not naming the original owner, "the site was calculated to awaken serious reflection to remind one of the depths of Satan and of the deceitfulness of the heart of man".[51]

And so, as far as it was possible, Sydney Friends tried to forget Tawell — and the very useful contribution he had made to the early development of the Sydney Meeting.

Two by-products of Tawell's unhappy end seemed to ensure that the ghost of Tawell would not depart. One has been mentioned — the fortuitous link of his arrest with the historic use of the telegraph. The second concerned what was known as The Great Seal Case. The disposal of Tawell's Australian assets became a bone of constitutional contention between Her Majesty's government in England and the Legislative Assembly in Sydney which was beginning to flex its muscles of independence. Normally the assets of the condemned reverted to the Crown. On 31 January 1845 Tawell had conveyed his real estate and personal assets to his brother, William Tawell, and William Bevan, as trustees for his wife and his son by her. He appointed two attorneys, James Norton and George Turner, in Sydney. Clearly Tawell hoped that conveyance before possible conviction would be legally valid. It was over three years later, on 30 December 1848, that Earl Grey informed the authorities in Sydney that Her Majesty the Queen had been pleased to grant Tawell's property to his widow and child. The trustees, however, in the meantime had instructed the attorneys to sell the property and the blocks were sold on 12 February 1849. One of the attorneys, Turner, absconded to America, taking with him part proceeds of the sale. The conflict of legal opinion concerned the forfeiture of the lands and the custody of the Seal where Australian property was involved. Did the Secretary of State for the Colonies have the right to make grants of land without reference to the Crown Law officers in the colony where the land was sited? In whose custody was the Great Seal? In England or in Sydney? The Governor, Sir William Denison, meanwhile, exercising his authority, affixed the seal in accordance with instructions from England and successfully evaded colonial displeasure by going to Mauritius.[52]

The publicity given to the trial, magnified by public interest in the telegraph and the Great Seal Case, had echoes in newspaper articles well into the twentieth century and must have had an effect on the already insecure Sydney

Meeting. It was even possible that some who would otherwise have joined the Society of Friends were deterred by what they considered the disrepute brought upon the Society by Tawell.

The Sydney Meeting

The Tawell affair indeed cast its shadow over the struggling Meeting in Sydney, and this shadow remained for many years. Even in 1867 when Walter Robson and J. Neave "laboured" in Sydney, they were conscious of this shadow. Robson recorded in his diary: "Ever since the late John Tawell resided here it seems as if an evil spirit has hung over Friends in this city".[53] At no time however had this Meeting shown any signs of strength. Backhouse on 21 November 1836 reported to the Van Diemen's Land Yearly Meeting that the number of those in New South Wales who claimed any connection with Friends was very small and that there were none "sufficiently consistent in their practice to make the organization of a Meeting for Discipline expedient".[54] Though the environment of Sydney, as Daniel Wheeler saw it, was hostile to Quakerism, or indeed to any religious body, it was the lack of a strong nucleus of concerned Friends which delayed the establishment of a recognized Meeting for Discipline for so many years.

Weakness tended to promote rigidity and defensiveness. As a result some who came from England with strong recommendations from their Meetings drifted into indifference and then into membership of other churches. The arrival of the Huntly family in Sydney in 1836 gave promise of a valuable accession to the Meeting. Robert and Isette Huntly and five of their family came with a certificate signed by members of their Longford Meeting, London, which had appeared to be willing to do its best to keep its distant members in touch by sending Yearly Meeting epistles as "expressive of the interest this meeting entertains on account of their best welfare".[55] Huntly's decision to migrate had been due to an accident which he had had in his phaeton. He became a doctor in Balmain. The appearance of the family at their first Meeting for Worship in Sydney was the occasion of critical comment rather than of warm acceptance. J. B. Mather, a visiting Friend from Hobart, commented in his diary on the Huntly family. "They make an external appearance of being Friends neither in dress nor address: the daughters wear ringlets and their back hair is plaited and hanging from under the back of their bonnets. . . . The gay appearance of members of our Society who generally set a pattern of plainness, is so painful to me that I could submit to clothe myself in sackcloth, if such were needful as a testimony against such inconsistency."[56] J. B. Mather, though a Friend of only a few years' standing, was apparently determined that all who bore the name of Friends should conform to the testimony of plainness of dress. It is not surprising therefore that the two daughters who were the object of Mather's stern disapproval did not long remain in membership. They were both disowned for marrying out. The son, Robert, however, received much more understanding treatment from his Witney Monthly Meeting. Rather than let any Sydney member inform his Witney Monthly Meeting about his intention of marriage, Huntly himself took the initiative to explain to the Witney Meeting that he had no choice but to "marry out".

> As there are none of our persuasion here with whom such a connexion could be formed, and if so, no properly constituted meeting where the ceremony of marriage could be solemnized, I shall be compelled to adopt other means of accomplishing this object. In doing so, I assure you, I shall do it with regret, being still attached to the principles of Friends, in which I have been educated and it would give me pain to forfeit my membership.[57]

By the time a reply could reach him, he had married. Witney wrote with some understanding "that although the Meeting regrets him having accomplished the marriage in the way he mentions yet under the peculiar circumstances of the case concludes to retain him in membership".[58]

The lack of a core of experienced Friends in Sydney and therefore of a continuing and organized Monthly Meeting meant that decisions of any Meeting, when in existence, were arbitrary and often ill-judged. There are two examples of this, the first resulting in the loss of a prospective member, the second in a near loss.

Dr George Cox came out to New South Wales before 1836 and settled near the Nepean River at Winbourn in what Backhouse described as "a substantial mansion, having the features of an English gentleman's seat . . . situated in a country resembling an English park".[59] Walker too was impressed, for he estimated that George, with his brothers Edward, Henry, William, and James, constituted one of the most opulent families in New South Wales. George Cox had contact with Friends in Thaxted and on arrival in the colony he seemed to conduct himself in the manner of Friends so that others assumed he was indeed a member. He was on J. J. Neave's list of members in 1874 and Rachel Henning rated him a Quaker because of what he said about peace at the time of the Crimean War.

> Dr. Cox who sometimes comes here to see Biddulph puts me out of patience with the nonsense he talks about peace. He is a Quaker and considers such texts as 'If thine enemy . . . ' as applicable to our relations with Russia. It is of no use to argue with him as Tregenna said, for he only goes off into a long string of heterogeneous and misapplied quotations. I told him I was thankful the English Government did not think like him and went off to feed the fowls.[59]

Cox's son-in-law, Walter Robson, told in his diary the reason for Cox not being in membership of the Society of Friends. Having been a "thorough" Friend for thirty years, he applied to Sydney Friends for membership. It was a year before two Friends, Abraham Davy and John Palser, came to interview him about his application. Robson then explained what happened. "He had then in his house a poor relative whom he had rescued from destruction thru drink and when the Friends paid the visit this man was drunk and insulted them. The result was they declined to receive Dr. Cox into membership because he had a drunkard in his home!"[60] This handling of Cox's application is a sad commentary on the state of the Sydney Meeting, which could be so dilatory in taking action and so lacking in sensitivity when it did act.

Sydney Meeting's handling of the marriage of John Palser and Ellen Eliza Metford is a further example of the mistakes that can be made by an inexperienced Meeting, whose members, perhaps in an excess of zeal to gain recognition from English Meetings, applied rules rigidly without sensitivity or understanding of the implications. Palser had been accepted as a member by Sydney Meeting in 1854. In 1856 he married a widow, Ellen Eliza Metford, who was a member of Newcastle (England) Meeting, but Sydney Meeting disowned Palser because the marriage was solemnized in a Presbyterian church. Ellen Metford meanwhile had explained to her Newcastle Meeting that the reason for not marrying in the Sydney Meeting House was because she thought such a marriage would not be recognized as legally valid, the Sydney Meeting not having been recognized by London Yearly Meeting. The Palsers were most upset at the decision of Sydney Meeting, particularly because Palser, soon after admission to the Meeting, had been clerk of that Meeting. Newcastle, however, accepted Ellen Palser's explanation and recommended that Sydney admit both.

The drift of faithful members into other churches is illustrated by John Cash Nield's experience. Nield came with his family from Bristol in 1853, first to Sydney, then to New Zealand, but he returned to Port Macquarie at the onset of the Maori wars and there tried unsuccessfully to establish a sugar-cane factory, for sugar, not for rum, he was careful to explain. In an article which he wrote for *The Friend*,[61] explaining that though he had by then linked up with the Congregational Church, he and his wife prized their membership of the Society of Friends, he exposed, perhaps unwittingly, a picture of the Sydney Meeting and of its limitations. He confessed that by education (at Ackworth Friends' School) he had been led to believe that Friends alone were right. Mixing however with men and women of other denominations had taught him to value their friendship, to respect their different views, and to reject what he felt was the uncompromising rigidity into which some Friends had fallen.

Until Joseph James Neave came to Australia in 1867 and then returned in 1876 to settle in New South Wales, the Sydney Meeting alternated between glowing and guttering like a candle-flame. Hobart Monthly Meeting had tried to provide some support and guidance,[62] by correspondence and by personal links through such members as R. Andrew Mather, who left Hobart to work in Sydney from 1838 to

1842.[63] On 7 December 1838 the Van Diemen's Land Yearly Meeting authorized Sydney Friends to hold Meetings for Marriage and this made possible a Quaker marriage between R. A. Mather and Ann Pollard in Sydney on 22 August 1839. J. B. Mather travelled to Sydney to attend his brother's wedding and stayed until November 1840, "labouring among Friends". By 1842 the Sydney Meeting seemed so much in danger of guttering that Francis Cotton offered to go to Sydney to see what he could do to establish a Meeting for Discipline there. He was given a Minute by Hobart Monthly Meeting on 24 February 1842, and with the support of R. A. and Ann Mather a Two Months' Meeting was organized on 3 May 1842 with Mather as the first clerk. It was agreed that those members who held membership with English and Irish Meetings should retain this link and that the Sydney Two Months' Meeting should seek recognition as part of the Van Diemen's Land Yearly Meeting.

For four years Sydney Meeting corresponded with the Yearly Meeting in Hobart, by supplying answers to the Queries, but from 1848 no word from Sydney reached Hobart. One reason was undoubtedly the loss of the use of the Meeting House in 1845 and the unfavourable publicity following the execution of Tawell. A further reason was the lack of committed members. Abraham Davy who might have given leadership had been disowned by the Hobart Monthly Meeting in 1839 for "marrying out".[64] Deprived of a Meeting House the remnant members turned their thoughts to the Friends' Burial Ground over which they had some security of tenure. Backhouse had taken the initiative in 1836 to approach the Colonial Secretary for a grant of land and on 25 May 1836 Walker recorded in his journal that the Governor had ordered a quarter acre of ground in the vicinity of the town to be appropriated for use by Friends. The three signatories to the application were Backhouse, Walker, and Tawell. The burial ground was situated in Devonshire Street and bounded by the Roman Catholic and Congregational sections. David Richards had been given permission to build a cottage on this ground and he lived there as a caretaker until his death in 1853.

Mackie and Lindsey arrived in Sydney on 11 August 1853.

Their first impressions of Quaker prospects in Sydney were not propitious, for on arrival they were greeted by a stranger who said he was glad to see any of the Society of Friends in Sydney, "but he was afraid", said Mackie, "we should find that we stood alone".[65] They were surprised therefore to trace afterwards about forty who were either members or connected in some way with the Society of Friends. At a Meeting for Worship held at Samuel Darton's home they counted over fifty present. They found that no Monthly Meeting had been held since November 1845, that Meeting for Worship had been held intermittently in such places as a Presbyterian school-room in Jamieson Street and in homes such as that of Abraham Davy in George Street. Before they left Sydney for Van Diemen's Land they arranged for a Monthly Meeting to be re-formed. This Meeting was held on 14 December 1853 and was recognized formally by the following Van Diemen's Land Yearly Meeting on 8 December 1854. On 15 July 1854 Lindsey and Mackie made a brief return visit to Sydney to follow up their strenuous attempt to revive the Sydney Meeting. They came to the conclusion that priority should be given to finding a permanent Meeting House and that the only possible site available was the tenement on the burial ground.[66] Some idea of the depressed state of the Sydney Meeting is reflected in its acceptance of the adaptation of this two-roomed tenement as a Meeting House.

Yet Lindsey and Mackie were not dismayed. Between 19 July, when they first inspected the small cottage and arranged for it to be vacated by a temporary tenant, and 20 August, when seventeen gathered there for the first Meeting for Worship, Lindsey and Mackie personally undertook the supervision of the alterations. A sum of fifty pounds was spent on the transformation.[67]

The revival of the Sydney Meeting illustrated the need such a Meeting had for a small core of committed Friends who were free to devote their whole time and energies to the service of the Meeting. It was not a matter simply of attracting more members of the Society from England to settle in the colonies. J. B. Mather, during his visit to Sydney in 1840 saw this. In a diary entry of 2 February 1840[68] he commented on an offer which he heard had been made in England by John Tawell, who promised to pay a premium to Friends willing to emigrate to New South Wales — an indication that Tawell still nourished thoughts of promoting the cause of Quakerism in the colonies. Mather, however, noting what he estimated to be the low level of enthusiasm of birthright and disowned Quakers in Sydney for the Quaker cause, was of the opinion that such an influx would be but a stumbling-block to the attainment of the purpose that Tawell had in mind. "The golden bait", he said "is taken by mercenary persons who so soon as they arrive here are so overwhelmed by the acquirement of wealth that nothing else is thought of by them."[69] Mather identified materialism, "the acquirement of wealth", as a major obstacle to the growth of Quakerism in Sydney. Materialism, however, was equally an obstacle to the growth of any religious cause. Backhouse would seem to have held the view that religion would not take root easily in the colonial environment with its accent on making fortunes, on material display, and the pursuit of pleasure.

> The state of society seems to be widely different, in the thickly populated parts of Europe, from what it is in the thinly-inhabited regions of Australia. In the latter few persons are to be found, willing to devote their time and energies to endeavouring to raise the moral and religious tone of the population. Most of the settlers, who rank above the lowest class, have come hither to try to better their fortunes; this object they seem chiefly to pursue; and when they are successful, pleasure, and a measure of display are, with most of them, the chief additional objects, combined with the original pursuit.[70]

What Quakerism lacked in particular was a core of members, free of material cares or aspirations, who could nurture the growth of Quakerism in a new and challenging environment.

No other Meeting perhaps demonstrates more clearly than the Sydney Meeting the need of these early scattered groups of Friends for a Friend of the calibre of a Backhouse or a Walker, a Mackie or a Lindsey, to stay and provide guidance and leadership. Van Diemen's Land had been fortunate in attracting Walker, as South Australia was to be in holding Mackie.

Seven
Quakers in South Australia

By contrast with New South Wales and Van Diemen's Land, where the first motive for settlement was the establishment of convict outposts, South Australia could claim that it was a planned, deliberate, well-organized colony of free settlers. The idealistic land settlement programme proposed by Edward Gibbon Wakefield, who had been brought up by a Quaker grandmother and who also had connections by marriage with Quakers, appealed to members of the Society of Friends and led some of them to hail it as a Pennsylvania of the South.

A further attraction was the announcement that the church was to be disestablished in South Australia. Mackie during his visit was impressed with this feature of the colony. "None of the colonies are at present so free from ecclesiastical domination as South Australia. The voluntary system has free scope and all state aid to religion has been refused. The colonists have not secured this amount of freedom without a struggle, and it is probable that they will yet have many contests to maintain this position."[1]

Backhouse and Walker had little direct influence on the development of Quaker Meetings in either South Australia or Victoria. Their contacts with both were limited to shore leave from the ship which was carrying them westwards on the next stage of their journey to Africa. They did however meet with John and Bridget Hack, the first Quaker settlers in South Australia. After being landed in the rough surf in Holdfast Bay on 28 November 1837 they rode in a light chaise cart to the embryo city of Adelaide and were welcomed to the Hacks' home. Hack had brought out two prefabricated cottages, one being erected at Holdfast Bay and the other in Adelaide on a block situated where the Adelaide Railway station now stands. Backhouse had known the Hacks in England through family connections. Backhouse and Walker spent almost three weeks in South Australia and were able to accomplish much in spite of the severe heat and the "moschettos". They held a Meeting for Worship in the Hacks' home on the morning of 3 December 1837, nine persons including Backhouse and Walker being present. Two days later, with the co-operation of the Governor and the Episcopalian clergyman, a public meeting was held, at which over two hundred people were present. Not only did Backhouse "labour with them" on the central Quaker theme of the importance of yielding to the promptings of the Holy Spirit, but he took the opportunity to remind his audience of their responsibility to "the Black population and the danger of bringing a curse upon themselves if they neglected these things".[2] Six days later Backhouse arranged a meeting for the promotion of Temperance, at which Governor Hindmarsh was in the chair and Hack was appointed treasurer. At the close of this meeting the Governor vacated the chair and Backhouse initiated a discussion on the need to appoint a committee to assist the Protector of the Aborigines. While Backhouse and Walker's stay was limited, their work on behalf of two of their objectives, Temperance and Aboriginal welfare, was unwearied.

John Barton Hack

In a letter which Hack wrote to his brother-in-law, Henry Watson, he forecast that Backhouse's reports of the colony would have a great effect at home.

> Have been enjoying more than we can well express the company of James Backhouse and George Washington Walker. I think their report on the state of the colony and its prospects will have a great effect at home. They said they had seen nothing like this country in the other colonies — which, as J.B. is a bit of a judge, is an opinion worth having.[3]

Jane Sanders, the daughter of an early Quaker migrant, recalled years later that her father had been influenced, first by Backhouse and then by Hack. She said that the three reasons her father migrated were his meeting with his friend Backhouse and hearing from him glowing accounts of the delightful climate and fertility of the soil, his own business failure, and the "alluring" letters of Barton and Bridget Hack.

This reported meeting between Sanders and Backhouse could not have taken place after Backhouse's return to England, which was in 1840 and by this time Sanders and his family were in South Australia. Jane must have remembered her father recording his being impressed by Backhouse's accounts of the colony, but these would have been the ones sent ahead of his return and serialized in English Friend periodicals.

The story of Hack's rise — and downfall — is important to an understanding of the special problems that arose in the development of a Quaker Meeting in South Australia. Hack described in his diary[4] how his thoughts were first turned to migration by reading Colonel Torrens' "The New Idea of a self-supporting colony to be founded in South Australia". Some anxiety about health and a desire to try his fortune sharpened his interest and led him to seek an interview with E. G Wakefield and with Robert Gouger, the first Colonial Secretary for South Australia. Gouger recorded it in his journal for 29 May 1835. "Two gentlemen called today at my office, having rather important errands. Mr. Barton Hack, a Quaker, called to say he has some friends, persons of capital, desirous to emigrate. He appears to be a highly respectable man and is very well connected. The other is a Captain Hindmarsh, who wishes to be appointed Governor."[5] Hack was clearly regarded as a man of some substance. Walker had noted that Hack and his family were living in greater comfort than other migrants and that he had promising material prospects. "Few seem to have better prospects of success than Hack, who has already materially improved his circumstances by several favorable coincidences in the purchase of allotments, letting out bullocks for hire, sale of the produce of the dairy and other means."[6] He had the backing of family capital and this meant that he was well placed to take advantage of the opportunities which the new colony offered. He arrived with his family in February 1837,

John Barton Hack (1805-84), the first Quaker to settle in South Australia, ruary 1837.

Jacob Hagen (1809-70), Quaker merchant, financier and politician in early days of South Australia.

only a few weeks after the initial landing by Hindmarsh. Delay had been due to Hack's shrewd calculation that success would come to the colonist who brought not only capital but the means to operate quickly on that capital. So the *Isabella* put in to Launceston, where he bought 350 ewes, 45 wethers, 6 heifers, 1 Devon bull, 10 red Devon bullocks, 3 mares, a Timor pony, goats, pigs and poultry, seed wheat, a large wagon and dray, and a plough. A stormy crossing of Bass Strait and the hazards of landing in the surf at Holdfast Bay robbed him of most of his sheep, but he had also taken the precaution of bringing with him what he reckoned as "a few hundred sovereigns". The shelter problems that early pioneers faced Hack forestalled by bringing with him two "Manning" prefabricated houses that could be erected in a day or so. Each house had three rooms, each ten feet square, and one of these was a kitchen with a Belgian stove. He had foreseen too the need for labour by engaging in Launceston an experienced stockman and three ticket-of-leave men.

It was possible therefore, equipped as he was with capital, agricultural implements, livestock, and labour, for Hack to exploit immediately the opportunities presented to him. His letters home to his mother and to Henry Watson, whom he encouraged to migrate, were full of ebullient optimism. His bullock team was the first to be seen in the colony and was soon fully engaged at £15 per week in transporting the goods of newly-arrived settlers from Glenelg to Adelaide. By quick importing of cows and heifers from the Cape he was able to be a major supplier of milk, clearing £35 per week. At first he seemed to have a Midas-touch with everything he undertook. Bullocks bought at £8 to £10 were selling for three times that price. A canal was needed at Port Adelaide to facilitate the landing of goods — Hack was the only one with the equipment and the resources who could dig the canal, at a contract price of £700. Town acres were up for sale. Hack bought sixty-four of these at £180 per block. The rising value of town land meant that Hack could ask up to £2,000 for each block. On 5 July 1838,[7] a year after his arrival, he wrote to his mother that he had "prospered beyond all expectations", that his dairy alone was bringing in sufficient to provide subsistence and that he had just made £1,000 on a cattle transaction; his whaling interests brought in eighty tons of oil when forty-five were sufficient to cover costs; he had bought a forty-ton cutter for trading. Five months later[8] he was still on a crest of optimism. He had just finished stock-taking and estimated his personal property was worth at least £18,000. He had nine hundred head of cattle, the only herd in the colony, his investment in fisheries was £2,500, and he had built a new trading store for £1,000.

By 1839 Hack was at the zenith of his material success and influence. He was the mainspring of a family investment in the South Australian enterprise. His brother, Stephen, who came out with him, specialized in the cattle section of the business and acquired considerable experience as a bushman, experience which he was to put to good use in exploration.[9] Two of his sisters, Ellen Maria Knott and Priscilla Philcox, and their husbands, had joined him. He tried unsuccessfully to persuade another brother-in-law, Thomas Gates Darton, who had already invested in land in Hindmarsh Square, to come too. In 1838 his wife's brother, Henry Watson, and wife Charlotte emigrated, to be followed by the parents, William and Martha Watson. The loss of one of his infant children in 1840 led Hack to transfer his home from Hindley Street, which he now regarded as an unhealthy location, to Mount Barker, where he had taken up a large selection of land.

Hack had control of so much property in the city, at Para and Mount Barker that he was able to offer help to other Quaker migrants besides his family. When Jacob Hagen arrived from Southwark Monthly Meeting in 1840, he stayed first with the Hacks at Mount Barker while he looked around and decided where to invest his capital. Alfred Capper from Hertford Monthly Meeting, who came from a wealthy Quaker merchant family,[10] but who had arrived according to Hack with a meagre hundred pounds in his pocket, lived with the Hacks and helped them on the farm. George Deane from Witham Meeting was set up as a wine-dealer and accountant and was given a loan of £1,000 by Hack for speculation in Van Diemen's Land. When the large May family arrived in September 1839, Hack made a section of his Mt Barker land available on lease to them until they decided where they wanted to settle finally. Another member of Witham Monthly Meeting, Joseph Barritt, arrived early in 1840 with a letter of introduction to Hack, who seems to have been regarded as the key Quaker contact in the colony. Hack set Barritt up with a loan of thirty cows on one of his properties on the River Para, agreed to pay him a percentage on butter produced, and lent him two horses to pull the cart that Barritt had bought for £25. Two months later, after Hack had come to visit him at Strangways Valley, Barritt reported Hack saying as he left, "Joseph, if at any time thee want anything, send me a note and thee shall have it".[11] He summed up his feeling of gratitude to Hack with the words, "He has behaved more like a brother to me than a stranger". Henry Watson painted an impressive picture of his brother-in-law's success.

> We find them in most affluent circumstances. Barton is indeed a prosperous gentleman. No one in the colony is more universally respected or more influential. We find him occupying the best house in town, a large store in course of erection, he is doing a large business as commissioner or merchant, he is also engaged in whaling in Encounter Bay, he has a splendid estate at Mount Barker that a Duke might envy, he is engaged in getting cattle overland from Sydney which is much lucrative.[12]

Henry Watson shared Hack's speculative enthusiasm, was even dazzled at first by it, and had no misgivings about possible disaster. In fact he wrote home urging that the marriage settlement money of his wife, Charlotte, should be invested in South Australian property, for he said he could conceive of nothing which would affect the security of property. After relaying Hack's latest prospects for making a fortune on property deals in Adelaide's choice town area, he added, "The only marvel is that so much could have been done with the small capital which Barton brought out. Nothing but the most unparalleled exertions of mind and body could have succeeded in establishing such a fortune as he is on the point of realizing."[13] Hack's very success, while it was the means whereby he was able to help fellow-Quakers settle in South Australia, was also the source of grave difficulties which were to disturb relationships, not only between members of the Quaker community, but also between members of the Hack family constellation.

The crisis was precipitated in 1841. A fortnight before he left the colony Governor Gawler was instructed by the South Australian Commissioners not to draw any bills on the Commissioners in payment of government debts amounting to about £30,000. As a result there was no cash and an almost complete cessation of capital inflow. Property values slumped. Hack was badly trapped. He had tied up too much capital in buildings and improvements. Hack's letters home, which initially had been so full of optimism, were now less frequent and bore witness to the severity of the blow which had struck him. In one letter written in 1842 he revealed that he must have been the target of some criticism from his family in England, which was also involved because of family investments in the colony. He wrote tartly to his mother, saying that he didn't want "cautions or expressions of disapprobation" from family or friends, but simply a letter of kindness and affection to "thaw the frost".[14]

There was to be a much more frigid season of financial ruin before any thaw could set in. All Hack's properties were sold up to pay his debts. His Echunga properties were taken over by a fellow-Quaker, Jacob Hagen, who appeared to drive a hard bargain, for Hack was cast in the role of a mendicant to Hagen and was humiliated to the point of having to ask for a loan of a hundred pounds from Hagen to pay off wages due to his farm-workers. He was given notice to quit his farm and further allowance of provisions was refused. By renting a property of 160 acres for £27 per year he was able to attempt to make a living by farming and carting wheat, £65 being contributed by his friends to enable him to purchase a team and dray to do his carting. At one time he seemed, Job-like, to be plagued by one disaster after the other. He wrote to his sister, Margaret, telling her of being flooded out, one room only in the house being roofed, and of his children having to go without shoes. "I could not bear", he said, "to see them go into the milking yard on cold mornings nearly to their knees in mud."[15]

Hack never recovered from his insolvency. He tried a variety of jobs, including carting ore at the copper mines of Kapunda and the Burra and digging for gold with four of his sons in Victoria. He finally entered the government service, retiring in his seventieth year as comptroller of accounts in the government railways.

Hack's collapse soured relationships between him and members of his family and also between himself and members of the Friends' Meeting. His brother, Stephen, was declared insolvent and had to spend two weeks in gaol. Margaret May, writing of his condition, said that "they had not seen a house that bore such marks of poverty since they had left England".[16] George Deane never really recovered from Hack's financial collapse and his wife and daughters kept him by needlework. John Godlee was reported as "disadvantaged" by being linked with Hack.[17] The Hack-Watson partnership was dissolved and the financial settlement was submitted to arbitration. Though Hack came off the worse, Watson also faced considerable privation. His house in North Adelaide was sold and he and his family moved in with the Philcox family at Mount Barker, and he feared his wife's furniture which was being sent out from England would be sold on arrival to meet debts due to Jacob Hagen. Watson remarked that all this had brought "an end of Friendly feeling", for money "had hardened their hearts".[18]

Hack's relationship with the Society of Friends was also broken by his misfortune. It was not his insolvency which in itself caused the break. In accordance with the practice of the Society his insolvency was reported by members of the Adelaide group of Friends to Hack's home Meeting of Lewes and Chichester and after a year's deliberations this Meeting approved its committee's recommendation. The committee, while "sensible of the great suffering to individuals and to the cause of Truth", and of Hack's speculation and overextension, yet, "on the other hand, considering that such failures may have been accentuated by the extraordinary monetary panic and sudden depreciation of property which appears to have extensively prevailed in South Australia and considering the real difficulty which this Meeting has in arriving at the real state and circumstances of the case in a religious and moral point of view, it has come to the conclusion not to proceed further in the subject".[19] This judgment was an indication that Adelaide Friends had assessed the situation with some sympathy for Hack in his misfortunes and that English Friends had been sensitive to his difficulties.

It was probably a combination of several factors which led Hack finally to resign from the Society of Friends and join the Wesleyans. The strain which his financial collapse placed upon his relations with some of his fellow-members must have been one contributing cause of his withdrawal. Yet he never ceased to feel that he really belonged with Friends and he continued to express this sentiment when he was visited from time to time by Friends from England.

Hack's life-story raises some important questions concerning the practical application of Quaker principles in what might be called a primitive colonial context. The strength of the first Quakers in the seventeenth century lay in their thoroughgoing attempt to make practice cohere with principle. In the face of persecution and suffering they gave each other strong mutual support. A "Meeting for Sufferings" was established to ensure that no member "suffering for the Truth" was allowed to feel separated from the "Friends of Truth".

While it is true that there was no planned Quaker migration to South Australia, there were sufficient Quaker families to make possible a Quaker approach to the solution of the problems confronting them in the colony. Hack was a key figure in the Quaker community. He was acknowledged leader of the early Quaker colonists and assisted them to find land and employment. Like Tawell in Sydney, he was one who had the contacts to make it possible for him to find employment for young Quakers who came to him for help on arrival. His early letters home were full of promise and hope for the colony and he appeared to hold every expectation of being able to organize a regular Meeting of Friends. He superintended the erection of the first Meeting House on land made available by him on his property at Pennington Terrace, North Adelaide, and when several of the families moved to Mount Barker, his barn was the gathering-place for the Meeting. The division of members between Adelaide and Mount Barker and the difficulties of transport delayed the formation of a Quaker Meeting for Discipline until mid-1843, and by this time the financial crisis had already gravely threatened the cohesion of the group. At a time when members might have helped each other to weather the crisis, they found themselves involved, some in mutual ruin, others in foreclosing on mortgages held on other members' properties. Watson spoke of the prevailing climate of "mutual distrust"[20] and when Hack received the verdict of the arbitrators in the dissolution of the Hack-Watson partnership, he muttered that this was "the end of all friendly feeling".[21] To "live in love as Christian brethren", as Quakers have often reminded their members, was only a pious platitude if not practised in daily living. Hack himself was partly to blame for the fading of the early promise, for his letters home in the period 1838 to 1843 reveal one who has been caught up, not only in the difficulties of a pioneer facing the uncertainty of colonial life, but in the lure of wealth. Each letter tended to be a catalogue of his assets, indicative indeed of a growing acquisitiveness, so that his mother saw fit apparently to reprove him for his "mercantile speculation" and to advise his brother Stephen, who had gone home for a brief visit, to dissociate himself from this area of Barton Hack's activities.

There were occasional references to keeping up Quaker Meetings for Worship, but the excitement of making money had begun to take possession of him and provide proof of the dangers of which the Society of Friends had warned its migrating members. There is probably therefore some substance in Captain John Hindmarsh's bitter estimate of him in a letter to Sir Pulteney Malcolm, dated 22 June 1838, concerning his recall, which he blamed on a conspiracy engineered by the agents of the South Australian Company, Mr Morphett, and by "Mr. Hack, a rich Quaker, a man of education and more like a gentleman than any one of the party, but unfortunately notwithstanding his riches, he is the most avaricious person I ever knew, he appears to care but little what he does for money. This led him to be a party to most of the jobbing transactions that individuals had entered into."[22]

There was no Monthly Meeting to exercise discipline or urge forbearance and mutual assistance in time of crisis. Each member therefore tended to act independently and without giving thought to what might have been a Quaker solution to their common difficulties. Henry Watson's observation — "I have little expectation of seeing a second Pennsylvania here" — was close to the reality. The early promise had faded. But the same Henry Watson, commenting on the way the May family seemed to have weathered the crisis, attributed their success to the way "they have all pulled together".[23] If this had been descriptive of the community of Friends, there might have been a significant second Pennsylvania in the South.

Adelaide's Quaker Meeting House

A further reason for examining in some detail Hack's Quaker role in the South Australian colony is his personal involvement in the unfortunate misunderstanding which arose between Friends in England and Friends in South Australia over the Meeting House at North Adelaide. This may also have been a further factor leading to Hack's resignation from the Society of Friends.

The Friends' Meeting House, Pennington Terrace, Adelaide, a prefabricated building sent out by English Friends to Adelaide in 1840 and still in use (from a woodcut for a Christmas card by Mary P. Harris).

The misunderstanding stemmed from the difficulty which English Friends sometimes had in comprehending some of the problems which faced Friends in a pioneer situation and also from Friends in the colony assuming such comprehension. English Friends had already generously responded to Backhouse's initiative in securing a Meeting House for Hobart Friends. In this second demonstration of practical help, the initiative seems to have come spontaneously from the Yearly Meeting of 1839, when it was decided that a framed building should be shipped out to provide a Meeting House for Adelaide Friends, and that a subscription list should be opened to cover the anticipated cost of four hundred pounds. A circular was issued to the Quarterly Meetings.

> Several families of Friends having emigrated to the Colony of Adelaide, in South Australia, and being settled within a moderate distance to each other, it has been thought desirable to provide a Meeting House for their accommodation, and a framed building, capable of seating 160 persons, has been purchased, the cost of which, with seats and freightage, will be nearly £400.[24]

There is no record of Friends in South Australia being consulted about details of the project. A committee of Meeting for Sufferings was appointed to arrange for the purchase and the shipping and Samuel Darton, whose son, Thomas Gates Darton, married Mary, a sister of John Barton Hack, undertook the responsibility for arrangements. His letter of 16 October 1839 to Barton and Stephen Hack is important for it was on the interpretation of this letter that misunderstanding subsequently arose.

> Dear Friends,
>   On behalf of a committee of the Meeting for Sufferings I have to advise you of our having shipped on board the 'Ragasthon', Captain Richie, a wooden framework Meeting House with verandah and iron pillars completed, packed and numbered with contents of each package as per annexed list of particulars. A plan and elevation of the building will also accompany this for your guidance in erecting it.
>   Unless a piece of ground can be readily procured gratuitously for it, you will please do the needful in purchasing a piece and transmit to me the particulars of purchase money and conveyance into the names of Samuel Gurney, Josiah Forster, George Stacey and Robert Forster, as Trustees for the same on behalf of the Meeting for Suffer-

ings, London, at the same time please furnish me with particulars of the expense of landing and cartage to your town and of the erection and I will take needful care to repay it to your order.

I need scarcely add that this Meeting House for the use of Friends and those professing with us at Adelaide has been erected by the voluntary contributions of many Friends, chiefly at the time of the late Yearly Meeting. Trusting that the Divine Blessing may attend the use of the building,

I am, your affectionate Friend, Samuel Darton.

P.S. I have to request on behalf of the committee your acknowledgment of the receipt of the Meeting House when any particulars of its use will be acceptable.[25]

To Hack the letter seemed to indicate that in addition to the cost of the prefabricated building, which had been met from Friends' contributions in England, the further expenses of the cost of the land, if this had to be purchased, cartage and erection would also be met in London. Hack made two errors of judgment, the first being that it was land owned by him in Pennington Terrace which he proposed to sell to the Trustees. The second was his precipitate action in erecting the building on that land without obtaining approval for the site from all Friends available to meet for that purpose. One family in particular, the May family, was not consulted, for some twenty years later, Edward May, writing to Josiah Forster about the need for repairs to the Meeting House which had proved unsuitable for the colony's climate, said that it was "lamentable to see how much trouble the Meeting House has been to Friends in England. It appears to have been left entirely in the hands of one or two Friends here to act on behalf of English Friends without any reference to others of the Society who were in the colony at the time of its erection".[26] It may be said in Hack's defence that distance made it difficult for the Mays and any other Friends not in the immediate vicinity of Adelaide to come together. Henry Watson at least was one who was consulted, for on 13 March 1840 he wrote, "we have not done anything yet about putting up the Meeting House. The Friends have all gone up to Mount Barker".[27] This puts the date of erection at no earlier than March 1840. The consignment, in sixty-nine separate packages, arrived in Adelaide on 6 February 1840.

The land which Hack sold for the Meeting House was part

of Town acres 704 and 705, part of an original land grant made to him on 23 December 1837. A sketch of the land is given.

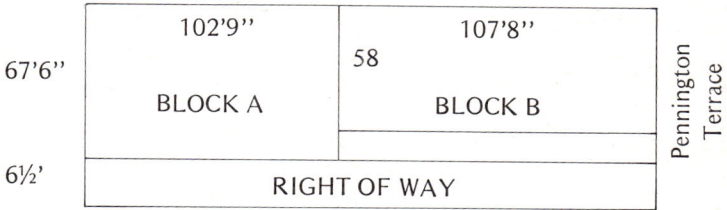

The expenses of cartage, erection, land, and legal fees amounted to £431.14.0, of which £200 was due to Hack for the purchase of the land, blocks A and B. When the bill for the total expenses was presented in England to Thomas Gates Darton, his father, Samuel, having died, the bill was not accepted and Hack received a curt note to this effect through a lawyer in July 1841, just at the time his own difficulties with the bank were becoming acute and his relationship with his brother-in-law, to whom he owed money, was becoming strained. Josiah Forster wrote to Hack to explain why his brother-in-law, Thomas Darton, did not accept the bill. English Friends, he said, had bought the prefabricated Meeting House as an encouragement to Adelaide Friends, but that it was expected that this would be the limit of English Friends' commitment and that "our Friends abroad would themselves find the land to set up the building thereon. I am sorry that any misapprehension should have arisen in this case".[28]

By the end of the year the dishonoured draft had risen from £431.14.0 to £607.19.3. At this stage two Friends, Jacob Hagen and Henry Phillips, both of whom had been associated with Hack in business as well as in Meeting affairs, wrote a long letter to the trustees, saying that at Hack's request they had examined all the correspondence and that they had concluded that the land at Pennington Terrace was the most suitable available, that the expenses of cartage and erection were reasonable, that section B with a cottage thereon should be sold, that the bill for the total expense should be re-presented. English Friends replied that the maximum amount they would meet was £307.19.3, for they considered that one-eighth of an acre, not one-third, was ample for a Meeting House, and that, allowing £50 for the value of the eighth, the said amount was more than ample to cover the original expenses of cartage, erection, and legal costs. It is to the credit of Hagen and Phillips that they came solidly to Hack's support by not only writing a strong letter of protest to the English trustees at their intransigence and refusal to accept that Hack had acted fairly and with the best interests of the Society in mind, but by each contributing £150 as a loan to the Society to clear Hack of debt and to honour the good name of the Society. They pointed out that English Friends, by persisting in their demands, would contribute to Hack's immediate bankruptcy. They hoped that the initiative they had each taken in lending £150 would close "this unpleasant correspondence".[29]

Samuel Gurney seems to have played a decisive role in bringing this unhappy affair to its conclusion. Perhaps he began to have doubts about the validity of the trustees' contention that Hack had exceeded his commission in conveying more land than was necessary for a Meeting House, particularly land belonging to himself and at an inflated value. Thomas Darton, indeed, admitted that he could not find a copy of his father's original letter, but he felt that Hack would have acted honestly in accord with what he understood to be his father's instructions. He regretted the misunderstanding, he wrote to Josiah Forster, but "whether it rests with poor Barton — my father, or Friends in London, I am quite unable to form an opinion".[30] Samuel Gurney came apparently to the conclusion that it may have been Samuel Darton after all who exceeded instructions by promising Hack more than the Meeting for Sufferings had ever contemplated. Samuel Gurney indeed came to the conclusion as early as February 1843 that misunderstanding had led English Friends to make too hard a judgment on Hack's part in the Meeting House affair. "I am quite willing", he said, "to bear the amount beyond the authority of the Meeting for Sufferings. I am quite certain that so doing has been judicious and due to John Barton Hack from us, notwithstanding the want of caution evident in his proceedings."[31] Samuel himself paid the remaining £300 to reimburse Hagen and Phillips for the loans they had offered, for there is a receipt issued on 28 June 1845.

> Received of Samuel Gurney, Josiah Forster, Robert Forster and George Stacey (trustees of Adelaide Meeting House) £300, being amount advanced by Jacob Hagen and H. W. Phillips on account of J. B. Hack's dishonoured bill which we acknowledge in discharge of all claim on the said trustees or the Meeting for Sufferings on account of the Adelaide Meeting House.
>
> Sgd. H. W. Phillips
> Jacob Hagen[32]

Minutes of the Continental Committee of the Meeting for Sufferings reveal no reference to the Meeting House or authority given to Samuel Darton to meet the cost. It would seem therefore that Samuel Darton acted from a spontaneous desire to help far-distant Friends, particularly as a significant proportion of them had family links with him. It was only when Samuel Gurney became directly involved that the Continental Committee took note that "the case is involved in some difficulty".[33]

To make sure however that colonial Friends did not again commit English Friends to unforeseen expenses the Continental Committee recommended that Meeting for Sufferings, following Samuel Gurney's action, should direct Adelaide Friends to sell the whole property, including the Meeting House if possible, to reimburse English Friends for the original outlay. It was however added that if Adelaide Friends were really desirous of retaining the Meeting House as a place of worship, they might have first refusal of a fair price. It was further suggested that in the present reduced state of the Meeting a smaller and less conspicuous place might be suitable. One of the trustees, George Stacey, objected, for he thought that if the building was retained as a place of worship, Adelaide Friends should not be expected to pay for it.

By this time Adelaide and Mount Barker Friends had formed a Two Months Meeting and could therefore act in unison. They reported that an agreement had been made with an Edmund Trimmer to purchase the cottage and land on Section B at a price of £80. They queried whether the Meeting House having been purchased with money contributed by a number of Friends could be sold without the consent of these contributors. They also pointed out the difficulty of selling land wherein several Friends were buried, one Friend already having indicated intention of applying for an injunction to prevent any such sale, and they reminded English Friends that those Friends who met for worship would be deprived of a place to meet in, as they were not "in circumstances to afford to erect another". As Adelaide Friends had for some time been upset by the long delays in obtaining action from English Friends, they concluded with a subtle reminder. "Your early attention is particularly desirable since should any death in the meantime occur it would be a matter of extreme difficulty to decide whether the interment should take place on Friends' ground or in the public burial ground."[34] Adelaide Friends had conducted a masterly campaign of delaying tactics, but it was more than a year before Adelaide Friends could rest in peace in the burial ground or cease anxiety about the future of their Meeting House. This was one of the very few instances of any serious difference of opinion between English Friends and Friends in these distant Meetings. A Minute of Meeting for Sufferings, 6 August 1847, finally recognized the validity of Adelaide Friends' request for suspension of the sale, but added a very firm reminder that Friends in England must not be held responsible for further expense of any kind. This injunction was either forgotten, or English Friends renewed their sympathy for their distant members, for seventeen years later English Friends contributed the major portion of the cost of alterations to make the prefabricated Meeting House more suited to Australian climatic conditions. A donation of £50 was acknowledged in a Minute of the Two Months Meeting of Adelaide, dated 4 December 1864. Adelaide Friends met the balance of £32.7.9.

Situated in what is now a prime residential area and in the shadow of the Cathedral, the Meeting House still remains as the meeting-place for Adelaide Friends. As one of Adelaide's oldest buildings, it has perhaps an historic rather than a functional value. William May, writing to *The Australian Friend* reflected the misgivings which some Friends had about the Meeting House's cramped site. He clearly sided with English Friends, "the generous donors", and considered that they were aggrieved for good reasons.

> Whatever those circumstances were, the knowledge of them in the Colony was entirely confined to two or three; to the rest of Friends they were absolutely unknown, but they led to the action of Friends in selling away a block of the land on which the Meeting House now stands, comprising nearly the whole frontage of the street. On this block a cottage residence was built by the purchaser and land enclosed, leaving only a narrow roadway to the back of the ground. Thus the North Adelaide Meeting House was, as it were, put in disgrace, and has had to be content with a back seat ever since.[35]

The misunderstanding concerning the Meeting House was undoubtedly one of the additional reasons for Hack's resignation from the Society of Friends. Though in hindsight it was an error of judgment on his part to sell his own land to the Society, thus arousing amongst English Friends some queries about his motives, there is no doubt that he was genuine in his belief that he had authority to buy land to erect the building. His own financial collapse occurring at the same time aggravated an embarrassing situation.

It was also unfortunate that the Meeting House arrived at a time when the centre of Friends' population was shifting from Adelaide to Mount Barker. A physical division occurring so early in the history of Adelaide Friends made consultation particularly difficult and hampered the growth of the Meeting.

A Quaker Community of Families

The time taken, seven years, to clear up this misunderstanding between the English trustees, representing the Meeting for Sufferings, and the handful of Adelaide Friends supporting Hack illustrates the difficulties of communication. An act which in origin was spontaneous and generous became the source of misunderstanding, suspicion, and even harsh and arbitrary action, which was completely out of keeping with the usual response of English Friends to the needs of their members in the colonies.

In spite of the serious effect which Hack's financial collapse and subsequent withdrawal had upon the Quaker group in South Australia there was a coherence about this group of families which distinguished the Quaker Meeting in South Australia from Meetings in New South Wales and Victoria. Reasons lay in similarity of background, in linkages by family, intermarriage, and business. Similarity of background is indicated by the relatively high proportion of these families engaged in farming, both before and after migration. They seemed to share also a greater degree of involvement in the Quaker Meetings from which they came. This may have been due to the feeling that, as South Australia was held to be a noble experiment, they came with the blessing of their Meetings and hence with a clear conscience and a sense of support at the home base.

They appeared also to come from a more affluent upper middle-class background, for most families came out with reserves of capital, some with a prefabricated house to provide shelter on disembarkation, and with a well-planned stock of food and equipment. Some of them were able on arrival to settle on land which, though it demanded initially much hard work, nevertheless assured them of a comfortable living, typical perhaps in their minds of an English "gentleman". Class consciousness did not take long to show itself. Henry Watson commenting on a fellow-Quaker, who was going home to England disillusioned, said of him, "He is not a gentleman, but a Manchester man".[36]

Linkage of family has already been illustrated by reference to the Hack constellation of families. The May family is perhaps the only complete family that came out for explicitly Quaker reasons.[37] The father, Joseph, was over fifty at the time of migration. With him came his wife, Hannah, and eleven sons and daughters, as well as his brother, Henry.

The May family was a ready-made Quaker community, ideally constituted for colonial success. There were five able-bodied sons immediately available on arrival as a strong labour force. Such a supply of labour was invaluable in a colony where labour was in great demand. Six daughters supplied the domestic back-up. Writing to Josiah Forster in May 1841 Joseph May said that one of the main reasons for thankfulness, besides good health, was the favourable circumstances of having "five sons very able and willing to work, which in a country where labour is so excessively dear makes us so independent that we have very little experience of that kind. Our daughters too with their mother do all the household work."[38]

By contrast with the Quaker community in Tasmania, there was considerable intermarriage among the South Australian Quaker families and no convict stigma to complicate the situation. Five May daughters married within the Society and the remaining one married an ex-Friend who had resigned because of the marrying-out restriction but later rejoined the Society. Of the five sons two died before marriage, two married into Friends' families, and one moved out of the close Mount Barker family circle, went to the goldfields, married out, and was disowned.

The May family might be called a typical Quaker family "of the olden time". This was the description which W. L. May recalled from one of his aunt Maria's letters. "They were a Quaker family of the olden time, and had brought with them from the old country the language, manners and principles and to some extent the dress of the early Friends. And here they began their colonial life, farming, gardening and dairying, all putting their shoulders to the wheel, even the little girls helping. And what a life it was. The work was new to them, for they were town, not country people."[39] The strong sense of their migration being what Friends describe as "in right ordering" comes clearly through the quite voluminous family correspondence that survives. William May, writing many years later of their settling at Mount Barker, said that Providence had determined the selection of this site. "Arrived in the colony our location was fixed for us, we were placed at Mount Barker.... How little we had to do with it. In a quiet valley over the hills, cooler and moister, wooded and diversified, our new home was given to us. We were helped and led there, protected and preserved."[40] The Mays settled first on land leased from Hack, but then took up a property nearby, named Fairfield. The homestead was completed by mid-1846 and became well-known as a gathering-place for Friends from overseas as well as for Friends visiting from other Australian Meetings.[41]

Though the Meeting House sent out from England was erected in Adelaide, the Mount Barker settlement in the early years of Quakerism in South Australia was the centre of Quaker activities. English migrants, finding the dust, flies, and fleas[42] intolerable, welcomed the countryside around Mount Barker. To Maria May it was "exactly like a gentleman's park in England and I think none that I ever saw excelled it in beauty". Most of the Quaker families on arrival went to Hack for advice, and as Hack had taken up some thousands of acres in the Mount Barker district, it was through him that these families settled there. The Mount Barker community was a farming community, with the May family forming the core of the Meeting. They were the prime movers behind the building of a simple Meeting House on a corner of a paddock belonging to Frederick May, adjoining the family home of "Fairfield". English Friends encouraged the building of the Meeting House by contributing £60 towards the total cost of £215.15.5.

Early Difficulties

The first attempt to set up a Meeting for Discipline took place in a school room of James McGowan, who had been engaged by Barton Hack to teach his children. The date was 5 February 1843. The motive for the Meeting was to enable a marriage to be conducted according to Friends' usage. On 7 March 1843 the first marriage was held in the North Adelaide Meeting House between Joseph Barritt and Mary Ann Harrison. The Meeting House however continued to fulfil little of its original purpose for some time because of the paucity of Friends in Adelaide. Meetings were infrequent and because of the distance of Mount Barker and the difficulty in negotiating the steep climb through the hills, Adelaide Friends took little part in the Monthly Meetings at Mount Barker, even when the frequency was reduced to a Two Months' Meeting in May 1843. In the following year a Two Months' Meeting was held in Adelaide and it was decided to hold Meetings alternately thereafter in Mount Barker and Adelaide.

Joseph May (1787–1878), pioneer Quaker settler at Mount Barker, South Australia.

"Fairfield", the home of Joseph and Hannah May and their eleven children at Mount Barker and a gathering-place for Friends from 1846 until 1905 when it was destroyed by fire.

It is evident however that with Friends scattered between these two centres and also with families such as the Barritts at Lyndoch and the Colemans in the Barossa Hills, the Meeting faced considerable difficulties in functioning effectively. A depressing lack of confidence is revealed in the answers to queries sent out annually by London Yearly Meeting. In 1843 the query concerning the spiritual state of the Meetings was answered "We fear there is but little growth in the truth amongst us". The unsettled state of the colony as well as the effect of financial depression upon the Meeting is reflected in the statement that members were facing severe problems because of the "extreme financial difficulty of the colony".[43] Yet, because of the strong inter-familial links and the largely rural membership, Friends made real efforts to gather together at least every two months, sometimes, as in the case of the Colemans, travelling eighty miles to attend the Meeting.

In 1849 there was the first sign of concern on the part of the "parent" Meeting in Hobart to help South Australian Friends by offering to send George Story and Thomas Mason to visit them. Story and Mason's recommendations at the conclusion of their pastoral visit were quite specific. They noted a lack of spiritual power in the Meetings and, not perhaps realizing the almost insuperable difficulties which distance placed upon Meetings with small membership, they attributed this to lack of a Quaker discipline. So they recommended that Meetings for Discipline should be held in each of three areas, Mount Barker, Adelaide, and the Barossa so that members could "admonish" and help one another. A reading of the listed recommendations gives, perhaps unfairly, the impression that admonition was given undue weight and mutual help undervalued. An attempt, it was urged, should be made to draw up a list of members and to contact all those who had had any connection with the Society before migrating.

In cases where breaches of discipline were discovered, as, for example, by marrying out, Friends were advised to disown and report action to the appropriate home Meetings in England, rather than to report first and after long delays act as agents for those distant Meetings. This advice reflects the inherent difficulty of discipline by remote control. Though, as will be shown later, South Australian Friends were reluctant to take responsibility for discipline, Story and Mason recognized the weakening effect of a Meeting which seemed to have little purpose other than a formal coming together every two months. The Minutes of these Meetings were devoid of any matters of consequence. There was no record, for example, of discussion of the effects of the 1843 financial collapse upon members of the Meeting. This is not to say that there was no caring of members, one for another. It simply underlines the impression that a properly constituted Meeting could have taken the initiative in creating a much more Quakerly approach to the crises and divisions which such a financial depression produced.

The exhortation with which the visiting Friends concluded their report was a challenge to be "separate". "Finally, dear Friends, we would encourage you to come out of the world and be separate."[44] The fear which these Friends had — and one which was shared by those South Australian Friends who took their membership seriously — was that the distinctive message Friends felt they had for the world was being threatened by the tendency of Friends to join other religious communities. "To come out of the world", therefore, meant "come out of the churches you worship in" and "resume your rightful role as members of the Society of Friends". This interpretation of the call to be "separate" is supported by an article which William May wrote in *The Australian Friend* in 1891. May frankly admitted the lack of spiritual power in Meetings for Worship "where no one broke the ice and no one spoke". Members would have felt keenly the contrast between their home Meetings, where recorded ministers generally assured some spoken ministry in Meetings, and the Meetings in the colony, where there were no recognized ministers and few felt the call to speak. Meetings therefore tended to be "habitually silent". It was no wonder then that the temptation was constantly before members, "this handful of professing Christians", to unite with fellow-Christians in the community and cease to be "separate". May, echoing the theme of Story and Mason, urged Friends to be true to their testimony that worship "consists not in a service or performance . . . but in a reverent approach to God as a living Presence". He concluded: "And so believing they were bound to be separate and to hand on their separation to those who might succeed them".[45]

The call to be "separate" could expect no response, for "separateness" can flourish only from a position of strength. The paucity of numbers allied to the isolation of members by distance from one another constituted weakness, not strength. Isolation, therefore, was often the forerunner to withdrawal and the members charged in 1850 with the duty of following up those who had not linked up with the local Meeting, though they had retained membership with their Meeting of origin, found that isolation had already led some to link up with other denominations.

The lure of the goldfields led to further loss of members. The Meeting, 5 September 1852, considered the situation of those going to the goldfields and urged them to be careful to maintain their religious principles and in particular to refuse to carry arms for personal defence. It was not easy for Quakerism to thrive on the goldfields.

Though Hobart Monthly Meeting endeavoured to provide reassurance by maintaining contact through annual epistles, in which South Australian Friends were exhorted to remain faithful though isolated, a sense of discouragement prevailed, and when the Meeting for Sufferings reminded them that no reply had been received to epistles from London they confessed that the reason for lack of communication was a feeling of weakness.[46] They expressed profound disappointment not only at the loss of members going to the goldfields, but at the apathy of birthright members who, whatever their attachment to the Meeting of their birth, showed no interest whatever in the Meeting of their adoption. They were but names on a list.

It was into such an atmosphere of defeatism that Robert Lindsey and Frederick Mackie came in May 1854. Robert Lindsey was from Yorkshire and had been a fellow-pupil of Francis Cotton of Kelvedon, Tasmania, at Ackworth Friends' School. He was to meet up with numbers of Ackworth old scholars in his travels around Australia and on the goldfields. He chose as his companion Frederick Mackie, a teacher at

Ayton Friends' School. There is a parallel here with Backhouse and Walker, for Lindsey went back to England (though he paid a return visit with his wife, Sarah, in 1860) and Mackie, like Walker, remained in the colonies and married Rachel May. He became a source of strength to Meetings, first in Hobart, where he and Rachel conducted a successful Friends' School[47] and then in Mount Barker, where the Mackies made their home with Rachel Mackie's father,

Frederick Mackie (1812-1893) visited Australian Friends with Robert Lindsey 1852-54, opened a Friends' School in Hobart in 1856 and settled at Mount Barker, South Australia, in 1861. This photograph is reproduced by kind permission of Nancie Hewitt and Mary Nichols.

Joseph May. Mackie provided the sort of leadership which the South Australian Friends needed, if they were to retain sufficient numbers to support a Meeting and make some impact on the community.

Both Lindsey and Mackie kept very careful records of their journeys. In their journals they gave the details of the day's travels, their impressions of each colony, and in particular the results of their visits to individual Friends, whether active or nominal, past or present. They found Adelaide a welcome relief after "that filthy place", as Mackie called Melbourne. "I cannot but feel astonished", Mackie said, "at what man will forego for the acquisition of wealth", but in Adelaide he felt immediately the contrast. "Here I observe neat gardens and agreeable residences, indicative of comfort and contentment."[48] What makes Mackie's journal so valuable in a study of Quakers in Australia is the care with which he identified those he visited, giving their occupation, their Meeting of origin, and any connection they might have with well-known English Friends.

There is a wealth of incidental detail in Mackie's journal. Two examples will suffice; Mackie said that William Watson told him that the horse which threw the well-known English evangelical Quaker, J. J. Gurney, and caused his death, formerly belonged to him but was sold to J. J. Gurney when the Watsons left England to join their daughter, Bridget, and her husband, Barton Hack. The second concerned the discovery of gold in the Echunga district. Mackie recorded: "Our friend George Sanders' wife was one of the first discoverers of gold in the district and in a singular way. She was dressing a pair of ducks for dinner, when she perceived a particle of gold which one of them had doubtless swallowed while feeding in a creek by the house."[49] Lindsey and Mackie came to appreciate how difficult it was for Quakers in isolation, scattered throughout sparsely settled South Australia, to receive the encouragement and fellowship of a Friends' Meeting and to retain a lively interest in Quakerism. "These very solitary allotments", Mackie observed, after journeying by jolting mail coach over unmade roads to Gawler and the new copper-mining towns of Kapunda and the Burra, "are not favourable to the development of Christian character and principles and though it be needful for all daily to strive to live near to the source whence all grace and power flow these solitary individuals especially need it."⁵⁰

They saw also the impossible situation in which young members of the Society were so often placed when the time came for them to seek a marriage partner. Some members of the South Australian Meeting, particularly following the visit of Story and Mason, had been attempting to apply the marrying-out rule as an essential part of Quaker discipline in a rigid and inflexible manner. As a result already a number of young people had been lost to the Society. At the Two Months' Meeting on 2 July 1854 the question of mixed marriages was discussed. Mackie held the view that much needless "mischief" had been done by Monthly Meetings in England disowning at a distance their members in the colonies who would have sought to remain within the Society if they had been given the opportunity.

This advice bore fruit, for two Meetings later members considered the case of Thomas Willington, who had joined the society in Van Diemen's Land, transferred to South Australia and then married a non-Friend. The members appointed to visit Willington recommended relaxation of the rules of the Society because his wife had "shown partiality for the doctrines of our Society".⁵¹

A similar position was taken with respect to David Joslyn, a member living at Gawler, who was reported to have married out. There was one difference however. Joslyn was still a member of Witham Monthly Meeting, England, whereas Willington had joined in Hobart. Joslyn's case therefore had to be decided in England and the responsibility of South Australian Friends was limited to reporting on the details of the case, though they were at liberty to make recommendations. Joslyn was said to have expressed a wish to retain his membership and his wife was reputed to have some connection with the Society and to be in some agreement with its principles. Witham Monthly Meeting took four years to reach a decision, Joslyn having first written in 1855 to plead his reasons for marrying out in a church, first that there were few female Friends in the colony, and second that the registry office was a hundred miles distant. The first reason was closer to fact than the second, for Witham Friends could not have been expected to know that Gawler was twenty-five, not a hundred miles distant from the registry office in Adelaide. Witham Meeting deferred a decision, but on 29 June 1859 the Meeting finally took no action to disown him. Joslyn therefore was not lost to the Society for marrying out, but his membership continued to be little more than nominal, for when J. J. Neave visited him about ten years later his verdict about Joslyn's effectiveness as a Friend was summed up in two words, "lifeless professor".[52] Mackie also expressed concern about the practice of people in England sending out "unsteady" (by which Mackie meant those who were probably alcoholic) friends or relations to the colonies in the hope that a change of air might effect a change of character — or at least keep them out of sight. "It is almost ensuring their ruin to send them here, it is opening the way for them to pursue unchecked their downward course and too often friends neglect to keep up their correspondence with them, which adds tenfold to the evil."[53]

In spite of the encouragement, which the visit of Lindsey and Mackie and the visit of Francis Cotton in 1856 gave the scattered Friends in South Australia, epistles of South Australian Friends to Friends in Melbourne, Sydney, and Hobart continued to sound a note of defeatism. They clearly felt a sense of being cut off from their Meetings of origin. Instead of facing the realities of conditions in the colonies they tended to be rendered inert by nostalgia. To fellow-Friends in the colonies they wrote: "Similarly situated as we are in these colonies, cut off from close and refreshing intercourse with the body at large, which many of us have enjoyed from the land of our birth, we are at times brought to feel very sensibly our poverty and weakness."[54]

In replying to this epistle other Meetings tended to reinforce the note of self-pity rather than engender some positive rallying of the spirit. Melbourne placed the blame on circumstances — on "the unsettled state" of the colonies and on the migratory habits of members. Samuel Darton, clerk of the Sydney Meeting, was very critical of the lack of participation by birthright members.

It has been to us from time to time cause for sorrow to see how many of those who come to these shores, who once bore our name, and whose earlier years would testify (and who might be said to owe their all) to the guarded and excellent education provided by the Society for all its members, cease to regard the principles thus carefully instilled and after perhaps a casual or occasional visit to our Meetings, wander away, in too many cases at last throwing away all that is honest, lovely or of good report.[55]

This impression reinforces the observation that many members did not really recognize any responsibility to the Meetings struggling to find a footing in the colonies. They retained membership with their English Meetings; they resisted the plea to throw in their support behind the Australian Meetings.

And so, while from London Yearly Meeting there were signals that it was time for Meetings in Australia, at least those in Hobart, Adelaide, and Melbourne, to take full responsibility as Monthly Meetings of London Yearly Meeting, Friends in the colonies showed reluctance to accept this challenge. For them such a move was seen as the breaking of a link and not as the forging of a new chain of stronger and more self-reliant Meetings. Friends in South Australia at this point complained that English Friends did not understand the conditions operative in the colonies and that they had an inflated idea of the number of Friends in the colonies. There was also a financial component in the proposed recognition of Australian Meetings. Though distance made the operation of the policy difficult, English Meetings still retained, at least in theory, responsibility for assistance to their poorer members. This responsibility they were now asking the colonial Meetings to accept. South Australian Friends protested that few of their members would be able to contribute to such assistance and they feared too that some Friends, not in good standing, might migrate and expect to be supported on arrival.[56] The letter to Meeting for Sufferings concluded on a note of discouragement and despair.

> Having thus a lively sense of our low condition and our discouraging circumstances as a collective religious body, we shrink from dismemberment and are generally disposed to prefer remaining as outlying members of our different Monthly Meetings rather than to assume a position of responsibility which we feel unequal to and unprepared for.[57]

One cannot help noting the contrast between the mood of optimism which prevailed in the early days of the colony when Friends appeared to be exercising no small influence on the development of what they then called the "Pennsylvania of the South" and this apparent acceptance of defeat. While however the institution of Quakerism in the form of the Two Months' Meeting seemed to have accomplished little and to have made negligible impact on the community, Quakers individually did endeavour to practise in daily living their Quaker principles. There were others who might be termed "vestigial" Quakers, that is, they showed traces in their actions of Quaker influences that they had once been exposed to, either by education in a Quaker school or by some form of association with Quakers or Quaker Meetings.

Attention has been drawn[58] to the lead which Backhouse and Walker gave during their brief visit to the South Australian colony in 1837 with respect to treatment of the Aborigines. Friends who migrated were given specific reminders of the need to respect the rights of their Aboriginal neighbours. They were urged to treat them with "Christian kindness" and to "befriend these poor destitute fellow-creatures".[59] Backhouse was impressed with the way Hack received his neighbouring Aborigines and let them sleep on his verandah. The letters of the Sanders and the Mays also indicate that relationships between these Quaker families and the Aborigines were friendly, though there was a hint of paternalistic attitude in the assumption that they were a dying race and therefore deserved some compassion. Jane Sanders wrote in her diary that the white man had much to answer for in the way he had treated the Aborigines, but she believed that they were anyway a dying race before South Australia was settled because of the diseases such as smallpox which they had caught from crews of whaling ships. She assumed that it was only a matter of time before they died out. The Mays, in their relations with the Aborigines, endeavoured to apply the Quaker Peace Testimony, which bade them "live in the virtue of that power that took away the occasion of all wars".[60] So they felt no fear, kept no watch. William May said that the Aborigines never pilfered from them. He had a great respect for the character of what he called "the uncontaminated

Australian native". In an article which he wrote for *The Australian Friend* he lauded the qualities of what he called "the free child of the wilderness".[61] William May, like Backhouse, affirmed the view that the Aborigine had a native intelligence in no way inferior to that of the European. "Let the traveller find himself in perplexing circumstances, his saddle at his feet and his horses strayed away in unfamiliar country and he will quickly console himself, whether he confess it or no, with the superior intelligence of the Native, who will infallibly run down the tracks and bring the horses to the camp."[62] The squalid blackfellow who haunted the fringes of towns and camps was not in May's eyes the true representative of his race, but the dreadful result of contamination by contact with "civilized heathenism".

One young Friend, Rolles Biddle, a farmer, who had taken up land in the Port Lincoln district in 1840, was speared by Aborigines. At the trial of two of the Aborigines[63] evidence was given that Biddle had endeavoured to treat the Aborigines in a kindly fashion and, attacked unexpectedly by thirty-six members of a warlike tribe, had held his fire until his stockman, Fastings, was speared. Fastings, Stubbs' wife, and Biddle all died from spear wounds and only the shepherd, Charles Stubbs, escaped. On his evidence two of the Aborigines were convicted and hanged. Whether Biddle had had any contact with South Australian Friends is not clear. His name appears on none of the early lists. The notice of his death appeared in *The Annual Monitor* of 1844. The date of death was given as 28 March 1842 but there was no description of the circumstances surrounding his death. He was a member of Poole Monthly Meeting. The only clue to possible links with Friends in South Australia is that the surviving shepherd, Stubbs, was then employed by the Friend, Jacob Hagen. The trial would have attracted considerable attention and perhaps it was not until then that Friends even knew of Biddle's existence.

Even if communications were difficult, there was still a network of Friends' families linked by marriage and business, and some of these families made significant contributions to the communities where they settled. They were known and respected as Quakers. Sometimes actions were interpreted as

Quaker-motivated when a settler, acting in accord with acknowledged Quaker practice, was labelled Quaker by others. Thus, for example, Robert Cock was assumed by the acting-Governor, G. M. Stephen, to be a member of the Society of Friends, because the stand which he took in insisting on paying rent to the Aborigines for their land which he occupied was considered to be typical of a Quaker.

Isolated Quaker families became valued pioneers in a number of farming areas. Joseph Barritt, founder of Riverside and Highlands estates near Lyndoch, established a reputation in his district for "high character, infinite resource and indomitable pluck and perseverance". This was the estimate made of him by the writer of an article on his life in *The Adelaide Stock and Station Journal*, 29 August 1923. The writer acknowledged that Barritt came "of old Quaker stock", as if this stamp ensured quality of character. Barritt took an active part in district council affairs, but, unlike most Quakers, who still retained an inhibition against involvement in politics, he also agreed to serve in the Legislative Assembly of South Australia for the district of Barossa until failing eyesight led him to resign on 1 March 1864.

Another well-known Quaker, Jacob Hagen, also entered politics, being a member of the Legislative Council from 1843 to 1861. Hagen was at first very active, with Hack, in establishing a Friends' Meeting in Adelaide, and indeed was the first clerk of that Meeting. For marrying the sister of his business partner, John Hart, a non-Friend, he was disowned by his Southwark Monthly Meeting, much to the chagrin of one of his admirers, Margaret May, who had written, "I hope Friends in England will not disown Jacob Hagen for we really cannot spare him. He is one of the pillars of our little church and by far the best disciplinarian and appears to have the interests of our little body at heart."[64] Though he occasionally attended Meeting after his disownment he became more and more involved in business, finance, mining and politics. Some of his political actions may have stemmed from vestigial Quakerism. Thus he was the spokesman for the opponents of State Aid to religion which Quakers traditionally regarded as opening the way for ecclesiastical domination.

The year 1843 seemed to mark a turning-point in Hagen's

application of Quaker principles to the world of business. His foreclosure on his fellow-Quaker, Hack, and his subsequent prospering on Hack's former estates[65] must have not only strained friendly relationships but also provoked unfriendly comment. Hack was most grateful to Joseph May at this difficult time. He called on Joseph May for help "or Hagen would have tried what he could do".[66] His biographer in the *Australian Dictionary of Biography*[67] noted a change in the nature of the legislation supported by Hagen. "By 1850", he said, "his work as a reformer ceased." Thereafter he appeared to be supporting what Quakers would have been expected to oppose — class legislation, such as the introduction of a colonial peerage. Even more un-Quakerly was his unsympathetic instruction from England to his agent, George Sanders, who was managing his Echunga properties for him. Hagen once threatened Sanders with foreclosure, because he had failed to evict a widow and six children, who had unfailingly made payments on time over a period of twelve years but were temporarily in arrears.

The history of Friends in South Australia up to 1861 illustrated very clearly the forces which operated against the growth of Quakerism in the colony. South Australia had presented the best prospect for healthy growth of Quaker Meetings. This was Walker's hope for the new colony, for he wrote from South Africa to his friend, George Richardson of Newcastle in July 1839, saying that he had heard via Robert Mather that Hack had reported the arrival of the two Quaker families of George Deane and Edward Coleman in South Australia. Walker added: "I am expecting many more ere long. It seems as if it was the merciful design of the most High that the pure doctrines and principles of Christianity as maintained by Friends should have a place in these lands, rising as they daily are in importance and under the influence of the principles which recommend themselves alike to the conscience and reason of unsophisticated and sincere enquirers after the truth."[68] There was a nucleus of committed Quakers, who came with the blessing of their English Meetings and who quickly formed links by business and intermarriage. Quakers, like Hack and Hagen, were leaders in the community and exercised considerable influence and even power. Hack's opposition to Governor Hindmarsh was alleged to have contributed to Hindmarsh's recall, and Hagen who was chief creditor to the government in Governor Grey's time was similarly held responsible for Grey's transfer to New Zealand. Others like Stephen Hack and William Darton Kekwick were leaders of early exploration, Hack leading a successful expedition to open up the north-west of Eyre's Peninsula, Kekwick being John McDouall Stuart's valued assistant.

Pike, makes the point that the settlement of a number of the more prosperous Friends in country districts removed them from the opportunity of exerting political influence in the early days of the colony. "Most of the more prosperous Friends however moved to the country districts, where they maintained their high principles and with the exception of Jacob Hagen, were cut off from the main movements of the struggle for religious liberty."[69]

Friends corporately made little impact by 1861 on the community, even in the Peace Movement, where traditionally they had particular interest and been most active. In the late fifties there were signs of the stirring of a martial spirit with the government proclaiming a Militia Act and volunteers being sought for the army, but there was no sign in Minutes of the Two Months' Meeting of any initiative being taken to resist the growth of a war spirit in the community. The only reference is one in a letter of Edward May to a friend, dated 13 March 1860, in which he reported that he and his brother, William, had attended a meeting in Adelaide to form a Peace Society, but he added that the initiative had come from young men outside the Society. "The young men who have been most active in commencing the peace movement are not members of our Society. This circumstance I thought more interesting and encouraging than though it commenced among ourselves. It is nothing now for a Quaker to be a peace man but it is something encouraging to have others agree with us here."[70]

There were two main factors contributing to the ineffectiveness of the Meeting. The first was the early division of the Meeting between Mount Barker and Adelaide and the second was the impact of the depression years of 1842 and

1843 upon the fortunes of most of the Quaker families. Another factor was that of distance separating members. Distance brought a sense of isolation and isolation dampened interest and led eventually, if Quaker bonds were not strong enough, to alienation from the Society.

Quaker impact upon the community came largely from the lives of individual Quakers striving to apply their Quakerism to their daily living. Hence while the Society of Friends was not widely known, individuals bearing names such as Coleman, Sanders, Barritt, May, were recognized and respected as Quakers and won for themselves a firm place in the early history of their localities.

Eight
Quakers in Victoria

The Lure of Gold

The discovery of gold in 1851 was the biggest single factor influencing the nature and the development of Quakerism in Victoria. Victoria had the largest concentration of Quaker migrants[1] with a total of 410, compared with New South Wales, 225. The great majority of these (seventy-one per cent) came out in the gold rush years of 1851 to 1856. Victoria's pre-1851 intake of 49 however was smaller than South Australia's total of 136, the former being unplanned and random.

Though not all who came in the years 1851 to 1856 were directly engaged in gold-digging, the economic prosperity which the discovery of gold heralded was a powerful lure. However atypical the Quaker gold-digger might appear against the stereotype of the sober, industrious, honest Quaker artisan, farmer, and merchant, the survey of occupations of Quaker migrants[2] revealed gold-diggers as a significant numerical group. It must be conceded however that for most Quakers in this group, as indeed for most who came to the goldfields, gold-digging was a temporary occupation and when once they had found out for themselves how fickle was Dame Fortune, they returned either home across the seas or to the more stable occupations which they had hurriedly abandoned in the grip of the fever that affected all the settled colonies. Numbers of Quaker young men already in Australia left their farms in Van Diemen's Land and in South Australia to try their luck. Those coming to Victoria from overseas were more concerned with reaping a quick material reward than with the propagation of Quakerism. A significant proportion therefore was transitory, seeing the journey to Australia as a way to temporary adventure and not to permanent settlement. Gold-rush fever and impermanence inhibited the growth of the Quaker movement in Victoria.

Amongst a preponderantly non-committed and even indifferent body of Quaker migrants there were some who believed that Quakers had a message and who were prepared to devote time and energy to proclaiming it. These eventually formed the core of the Quaker Meeting in Victoria, gave the Meeting leadership, and laid the path for the development of an Australian Quakerism.

Backhouse and Walker exerted little or no influence on Quakerism in Victoria. They spent only nine days in Port Phillip while they were on their way westwards to Africa and the colony was in the very early stage of settlement. Most of their contacts were with those whom they had known before in Van Diemen's Land or in New South Wales, such as John Batman, John and Mary Gardiner from Van Diemen's Land, and George Langhorne, formerly catechist at Goat Island and lately appointed to take charge of a mission station at Port Phillip. The "old acquaintance" reunion in Port Phillip included also Captain Foster Fyans, now Police Magistrate at Geelong, James Simpson, former magistrate in Van Diemen's Land, and Thomas Watson, whom Backhouse and Walker had met in Temperance work in Launceston. It is unlikely that these would have come within Backhouse's classification of Port Phillip settlers, many of whom, Backhouse wrote, came "from an unsettled disposition, others from dissipated habits and others from greediness of gain".[3] The judgment of one of the early chroniclers of Melbourne's history was that Backhouse and Walker "during their short stay exerted themselves laudably to render the few residents God-fearing and temperate, but they did not succeed quite so much as they deserved".[4]

The only Quaker who might have provided a link with Backhouse and Walker was David Stead,[5] but he was not within walking distance from Melbourne, having settled forty miles from Geelong on the banks of the Devon. Although he was a member of the Society of Friends by birth, his contacts with Friends in Van Diemen's Land where he migrated in

1833 from Glasgow were limited because he was overseer on a property at Falmouth on the East Coast and rarely was able to attend Meeting at Kelvedon or Hobart. On the 11 November 1835 he was one of the original settlers of Port Phillip who left Van Diemen's Land with John Batman's group on the *Norval*. Like Hack, early success seemed to dazzle him somewhat, for his letters told of the increase of his flocks of sheep from five hundred to five times that number and of an anticipated wool clip worth £500. And in a letter to a friend, Isaac Robson, he urged him to come out, bringing as much capital as possible, for, he said, fifteen per cent interest was common and twenty-two to twenty-five possible. Though he was already drifting away from the Society in spirit as well as in distance, there was nevertheless a wistful nostalgia in his statement to Robson that he was the only Friend in the colony. "I feel a good deal", he wrote, "the want of the Society of Friends. It is a great loss to be without it. Therefore I would have thee take that into consideration."[6] Backhouse kept in touch with him by letter from Cape Town and met him when Stead attended a Quarterly Meeting in England in 1845. On his return to Victoria he married a daughter of a Dr Belcher and when he acknowledged this in a letter to an overseer of Barnsley Meeting some four years later, he was disowned for marrying out.[7]

David Stead's story was a typical illustration of the effect of continued isolation on membership of the Society of Friends.

The first record of an attempt to counter that isolation was a brief comment on a page of a pocket-book belonging to Edward Sayce which read, "The first Meeting for Worship at my house, Little Bourke Street, Melbourne". The date was 23 July 1843.[8] There is some justification for the claim made that he was one of the founding fathers of Australian Quakerism.[9] Certainly that claim could be acknowledged as applying to his role in the establishment and development of a Quaker Meeting in Melbourne. The Sayce family had a deep attachment to the Society of Friends. Edward and Deborah Sayce brought with them a strong commendation from their Cheshire Monthly Meeting. "We cannot but apprehend that they and their offspring will suffer great privations in being entirely separated from the social intercourse and the Christian care and example of their fellow members in religious communion."[10] Though there is no record of a specifically Quaker reason for migration as there was in Joseph May's decision to go with his family to South Australia, there is evidence of a similar commitment to the service of the Society. The Sayce home became the early Friends' centre in Melbourne, providing not only a place of worship but hospitality for visiting Friends. Edward Sayce was an old scholar of Ackworth School and to give his older children a Friends' School education he returned to England for a period of nine years. During this time he travelled widely "in the ministry", visiting at least five Quarterly Meetings. When he returned to Victoria in 1863 he provided valuable leadership for the Meeting and became the first clerk of Melbourne Annual Meeting.[11] Edward Sayce was one of the few Australian Friends who could have been classified perhaps as "gentleman".[12] He was successful in business, was able to travel back to England to educate his children, and had the leisure to spend some time in the service of the Society and of the community, for he was mayor of Hawthorn in 1875.

The second entry in the early records of Melbourne Friends is for 30 November 1847 when there is a note of the grant of a burial ground to the Society of Friends by the Governor of New South Wales. In addition to Edward Sayce there were three more names of members who might have been expected to continue to help with the establishment of the Meeting in Melbourne, but it was to be otherwise. The first, Robert Dunsford, a wine cooper in Devonshire, died in Melbourne a week after recording his signature to the burial ground document. John Bakewell arrived in 1840 with his brother Robert and their brother-in-law, Godfrey Howitt and his family. John became a stock and station agent, his business being taken over later by Goldsborough. His brother, Robert, took up land for farming at Plenty, but returned to England by 1857, having resigned from the Society. Nottingham Monthly Meeting accepted his resignation because "he had entirely discontinued his membership during his long residence in Australia".[13] Apart from lending his signature to the trust deed for the burial ground John Bakewell seemed to play no further active part in the early Meeting in Melbourne, for he disappears from notice in Melbourne Quaker records. The clue to his apparent disinterest may have been provided by a comment which William Howitt made on his brothers-in-law's farm at Plenty. "The English stamp and the English character", he observed, "are on all their settlements."[14] Was it perhaps that the Bakewell brothers never really accepted settlement in Australia as anything more than a temporary diversion and that membership of the Society of Friends was seen as having little to do with active support of an as yet unestablished outpost of Quakerism in the colony of Victoria?

The third name was that of Godfrey Howitt, one of the earliest doctors in the colony, who, unlike his brothers-in-law Bakewell and brother William, did indeed remain and make a significant contribution to his adopted country. He came from a yeoman family and was a member of Nottingham Monthly Meeting at the time of his migration in 1840. He graduated in medicine from Edinburgh and on arrival in Melbourne was a leader of the medical profession, being a member of the first Medical Board and of the first honorary staff of Melbourne Hospital.[15] Yet Godfrey Howitt's links with Friends tended to become limited to professional attendance on Friends in sickness. By 1854 Frederick Mackie's conversation with him concerned the current "colonial fever" epidemic and the "increasingly unhealthy" state of Melbourne, rather than Howitt's dwindling relationship with Friends. Howitt's gradual alienation from Friends followed his increasing identification with "upper" classes of Melbourne and with the established church. When his Nottingham Meeting requested Melbourne members to visit Howitt concerning his membership, it was already too late. He told the visiting members that he "had long ceased to consider himself a member of the Society" and that his sons had never considered themselves members, but he added that nevertheless he was "not disposed to resign".[16] As he had already joined the Church of England Nottingham Monthly Meeting disowned the whole Howitt family.

A similar pattern is seen in the movement of the fourth

signatory, Jonathan Binns Were, a brother-in-law of Robert Dunsford, from the Society of Friends to the Church of England as he gained prominence as a Melbourne citizen. Like Howitt he came of yeoman stock, from the Bristol area. That he was comfortably placed is indicated in a letter which he wrote to his brother on arrival in Melbourne in the *William Metcalfe* on 15 November 1839. "J. B. Were's party consisted of Sophia, his wife, Sophia Louisa, their daughter, Jonathan Henry, their son, Frederick Dunsford, Mrs. Were's brother and Rhoda, their maidservant and John Joachim a clerk...."[17] To this was added a message "to those who are active and wish to better their condition I have only to say 'come hither'. Your affectionate brother, Jonathan". He brought with him a prefabricated house and merchandise worth £1,500.[18] With these assets he was well placed to make good use of his opportunities for business success. Though he was twice bankrupt (a condition far from unusual in the disordered commercial world of the early colony) he was the first chairman of the Melbourne Stock Exchange, the first president of the Chamber of Commerce, the first Justice of the Peace for Port Phillip, and in 1856 was elected a member of the Legislative Assembly for Brighton, but resigned on account of his second bankruptcy. He held several consular posts and was knighted by Sweden and Denmark. In 1881 he was a member of the Commission for the International Exhibition and for his service he was awarded the C.M.G. On his death on 6 December 1885 he was praised on all sides for his success. "Few citizens of Melbourne have been more highly esteemed or more sincerely regretted", recalled the writer of an article in *Melbourne 1903*.[19] His biographer in the *Australian Dictionary of Biography*, was less fulsome when he commented on "the strange admixture of worldly ambition and idealism".[20] His idealism he owed largely to his Quaker background. His worldly ambition, to which he gave free reign in the early heady days of the colony, took him further and further away from that background. Though he joined the Church of England, his wife, Sophia, retained her membership in the Society of Friends and when her Meeting, Devonshire West, questioned her attending another church with her children, she said that she did not want to dissociate herself from the Society. Devonshire West therefore accepted her assurance and did not disown her. It is clear from comments of the deputation which London Yearly Meeting sent out to Australia in 1875 that Jonathan and Sophia Were retained some interest in the Society of Friends, for members of the deputation reported that on their visit to the Weres they were received with much cordiality. The Weres attended Meeting during the period of the deputation's visit to Melbourne, but the deputation recognized that their continuance in doing so afterwards could not be expected. Interest in the Society and sympathy with its principles did not necessarily cease with withdrawal from membership.

All four who signed the burial ground trust deed were men of some substance and standing in the community, but only one of these, Edward Sayce, did not allow material success to break the bonds of membership or dilute the quality of his service to the Melbourne Meeting.

The third significant entry in Melbourne records was on the 20 February 1853 when the gold rush was in full swing and Friends were aware that numbers of their persuasion had come to the colony and either did not know of the existence of a small Meeting or had not troubled to find out. To remedy this a group of fourteen members gathered together to attempt to draw up a list of those who might be interested in seeing a Meeting established in Melbourne. Brief explanatory comments on the backgrounds of these fourteen members will serve to illustrate how personal problems and difficulties limited the effectiveness of these fourteen as "foundation" members of Melbourne Meeting.

Edward and Deborah Sayce. Described above.

Sarah and Rachel Raleigh. Sisters of Joseph Raleigh, who had been disowned in England for bankruptcy and had come with his wife and three sons to Australia in 1843. Both parents died in Melbourne and the two aged aunts, 64 and 60, had to bring up the three sons.

James Hope, single. His marriage on 10 February 1855 was the first Friends' marriage in Melbourne. He took over Edward Sayce's china and glass business, became insolvent, but was not disowned.

Joseph Sayce. Brother of Edward Sayce. He was disowned twice for insolvency. He was readmitted after the first disownment, "he appearing to be in a humble state of mind and we believe that his future conduct may be in accordance with our Christian profession, we recommend his re-instatement".[21] He was disowned a second time, because he left debts unpaid when he left for Australia in 1852. The minute of disownment was on 5 April 1854.

John Veevers. He had been disowned by Preston Monthly Meeting for marrying out, but he was readmitted in 1854 on the recommendation of Lindsey and Mackie, who had visited him in Melbourne. In 1872 he resigned from Friends because of his interest in spiritualism.

Charles Levitt. Nothing is known of him, except for his presence at this Meeting.

Samuel Strong. On a visit from New Zealand.

Lucy Birchall. Wife of William Harding Birchall who had been disowned for insolvency in 1851 and had then migrated to Victoria. Lucy Birchall kept a boarding-house at St. Kilda. When Mackie visited her there in 1854 he spoke of her as "a bright example of patient cheerful perseverance under accumulated difficulties in providing a maintenance for herself and her children".[22] William Birchall went to the Bendigo goldfields with his family in 1855. Later, Lucy Birchall conducted a school to provide for the family.

William Smith. Migrated to Victoria in 1853, became insolvent in 1854, but was not disowned. He died in 1858.

William Harvey Jackson. From Ireland, an example of those who, Melbourne Meeting held in a letter to the Meeting for Sufferings, disadvantaged the Society because they "had no fixed purpose to settle amongst us".[23] Jackson had come from Ireland to Victoria, then went to Tahiti, returned to Victoria and finally went back to Ireland, where he resigned his membership.

William James Creeth. Was one of five brothers who came to Victoria in 1853. He became a mining agent on the goldfields in Bendigo. He became insolvent in 1871 but was not disowned. The Creeth family came from Lisburn, Ireland.

William Robinson. One of three brothers from Dublin who came to Melbourne in 1852. He kept a boarding-house. Later he joined the firm of Brooke, Robinson and Company and then became auditor of the Savings Bank of Victoria. From 1893 to 1902 he was its general manager. He was a keen member of the Society of Friends and was the first clerk of Melbourne Monthly Meeting.

The first observation to make on the above group is that insolvency figured either directly or by association in the history of several of its members. Insolvency was both a reason for migration and also a result of the fluctuating and unpredictable economic conditions in the colonies. That Melbourne Friends realized this and appreciated the probability that insolvency was a common hazard and not a Quaker "crime" is indicated by the decision not to disown or to recommend disownment to the Meetings of origin. Insolvency however would have had an unsettling effect and only a few of this group remained to give service to the Melbourne Meeting.

The Irish Connection

The second significant characteristic of this group is the Irish component. William Robinson was regarded by Dublin Monthly Meeting as the unofficial Quaker representative in Melbourne of Ireland Yearly Meeting. His boarding-house became the first place of lodging for many of the young single Irish Quaker migrants. When Dublin Monthly Meeting recognized the considerable number of Irish Friends who had been drawn to Victoria, it decided to collect the names, Meetings of origin, and the probable colonial addresses of its overseas members. It was to Robinson that this list was sent by Henry Russell on behalf of Dublin Monthly Meeting on 3 December 1853. The purpose, Henry Russell said, was "in order to thy being in possession of such information as may enable thee to extend any care or oversight of them that may be in thy power. The number from our Meeting (i.e. Dublin) is large: it will be interesting to us to learn any particulars respecting them, from time to time, that thou mayst send us. . . . How many attend your Meeting on first day? have you any meeting for discipline?"[24] Dublin Meeting, rather more than the majority of English Meetings, seemed anxious to maintain contact with its members in the colonies and to give what practical help it could. As early as 1842, when Dublin was concerned to follow up Annabella Locke, who had emigrated to Victoria with her disowned husband, William, a committee was appointed "to consider whether any further care is required to be bestowed by this Meeting on those of its members who are resident abroad in places remote from Friends".[25] That Dublin Friends felt a special sense of responsibility to their members in Victoria is further indicated by their contribution of £354 to the Melbourne Meeting House in December 1858. Of the forty-eight names on the 1853 list half came from Dublin, with the rest spread over eleven other Irish Meetings. Of the supposed destination of these Irish Friends thirty-one were thought to be in Melbourne or its environs, including the goldfields, nine in Sydney, two in Adelaide, and one in Queensland.[26] The main concentration of Irish Friends was therefore in Melbourne. It was a concentration of time, as well as of place, for the main thrust of Irish migration came in the years 1852 to 1854, whereas, by contrast, the migration of English Friends was much more dispersed both in time and place.

A majority of these Irish Quaker migrants consisted of young single men from well-known upper middle-class families, such as Fennell, Jacob, Grubb, Pim, and Fisher. They were well-educated, perhaps too much so to adjust to the rigours of life on the goldfields. At least this was the opinion of one Irish Friend, Joseph Beale, writing to his wife, Margaret, on 17 August 1853.

> I was very much pleased indeed last evening with a visit from Joseph Phelps, thou may recollect he served his apprenticeship to Jas Pim & Sons — thou often remarked to me what a well inform'd young man he was then. He still is the same, quiet, easy manner'd gentleman, he and his brother have stations and are *very* well off.... In the course of conversation I said to Joseph Phelps, people at home imagine that here there is nothing like society, *'like MtMellick Society'* — he laughed very heartily, and said, 'thou and I know what *that* is' — there is *no* comparison to be made, for unfortunately too many people who come out here, are unfitted for the Colony, too highly educated for the work to be done.[27]

One such, whom Beale had in mind, was Edward Ebenezer Barrington, a graduate of Trinity College, Dublin.[28] Beale said that Barrington had no job and added, "A great number of young men come here of the learned professions and they can do no good. A good accountant is worth three scholars of Trinity College, Dublin."[29] Barrington, called "Doctor" by other young Irish Quaker migrants, tried a variety of jobs, including setting up a reading-room for young men. He was also clerk of Melbourne Monthly Meeting for a short time, from November 1854 to April 1855, but by 1860 he had had enough of Melbourne and returned to Ireland.

At the age of fifty-one Beale had set off with his two oldest sons, Joseph and Francis, to try his fortune in Victoria. His letters home give a very lively picture of life in the colony, where he found that he had to turn his hands to any job, no matter how menial. "In this colony one must work, labour is the most expensive item of expenditure. A number of first class passengers are glad to mingle amongst us who have become working-men. We acknowledge them, do them an act of kindness, but here every man is for himself."[30]

Beale and his sons set up a carting business on the goldfields route and also contracted with the government for road-making. What impressed him about this country was that men were valued because they worked with their hands. He felt a new sense of independence. He liked being hailed by name and "shaking hands with pleasurable countenances". He faced the future with optimism. This was something he could not do in Ireland. One of his letters to his wife, urging her to persuade her father to sell their interest in the mill so that the family could be re-united in Melbourne, ended with the words, "Oh my love come here if at all in thy power and I believe we shall end our days without the anxiety we have endured at home".[31] The anxiety and hopelessness of the famine years in Ireland led many like the Beale family to seek a new future in the colonies.

The small Quaker community in Melbourne, fostered by Edward and Deborah Sayce, and centred for the Irish migrants around William Robinson's boarding-house, provided support for Beale. "Quakers here", he wrote, "are very kind to each other, there is great cordiality in a short converse with each other after meeting on first day. They are raising a subscription to buy land and build a meeting-house. I gave £2 for Joseph and £2 for Francis as they could not take it from me."[32] Beale found that to be connected with Quakers brought some direct advantages. He was given employment with William Locke, whom he had known in Ireland.[33] Locke had prospered in what was really an ex-Quaker firm of Locke, Raleigh, Thorp and Company, merchants, shopowners and wharfingers.[34]

Young Irish migrants often came out in groups of two or three to try their luck. Gabriel Fisher Unthank and Reuben Fisher Alexander, schoolfellows at New Town Friends' School, Waterford, for example, came out together, even packing their belongings in one big case, which proved, they admitted, a regular "white elephant" when they had to transport it to the gold-diggings.[35] Unthank returned with only enough gold to make a wedding-ring eventually for his wife. Alexander also returned to Ireland by 1860, even though miner's rights had been issued to him in that year at the Ararat gold-diggings. Another boarder at Robinson's was Alfred Webb[36] who linked up then with his friend, Thomas Walpole. Later he found lodgings with a Wesleyan family, the Johnstons.

Alfred Webb, like many young migrants who arrived full of hope, found reality did not conform to his expectations. When he left home, high prices were reported as being paid for imported goods and so he arranged for his uncle to send out a consignment. But when this arrived, prices had fallen and he lost his money and his optimism. He also lost faith in Friends. Having failed in business he had tried working as a wharf clerk at four pounds per week, his job being to tally stocks arriving by lighter from ships anchored in Hobson's Bay. His Quaker background led him to question handling cargoes of spirits. Exercised about this he decided to consult "a Friend minister". "A Friend minister visited Melbourne about this time and had a sitting with me as with all other members. I asked his advice but could get no light. Difficulty on this head was, if I remember rightly, one of the causes of my eventually giving up the situation."[37] Equally unhelpful was his reception by his aunt and uncle, Deborah and John Thompson. Thompson was a Quaker from Manchester, but had been disowned by Hardshaw East Monthly Meeting during the Crewdson controversy. His wife, Deborah, an Irish Friend, had not attended the Friend's Meeting in Melbourne and, in sympathy no doubt with her husband, did not encourage Alfred to associate with Friends. He found the Johnston family most congenial and attended the Wesleyan church with them. Here he felt more satisfaction than in the Friends' Meeting, which had as yet no Meeting House of its own.

Like numbers of Irish Friends he never really felt drawn to settle in Australia. Perhaps he came out in 1853 with no such intention, or, if he did, the harsh reality of having to earn a living by tough manual work was more than he could accept. Having given up his work of tally clerk because of conscience, he contracted to build wooden bridges, an unpromising enterprise for a young Irishman inexperienced in handling work parties of tough, possibly escaped convicts from Van Diemen's Land. While in a despondent mood from failure to cope with such a job, he met with the Quaker botanist, William H. Harvey, who was on a scientific voyage around the world collecting algae. His bearing and conversation, said Webb, were far different from that of the sort of society that he had met with in the colony. This struck him so forcibly that he was possessed with a desire to return home at the earliest opportunity. Webb however wanted to see more before he sailed. He therefore set out on foot for Sydney, stopping to dig for gold, which seemed to be a required part of any Irishman's Australian experience. He found enough to make rings for his sisters, who generously returned the rings later so that he could make them into a wedding-ring for his wife, "Lizzie".

Most of the Irish Quakers who came out to seek their fortunes on the goldfields were in no mood to settle down, still less to accept any responsibility for assisting in the establishment of a Quaker Meeting. Those Quaker migrants, Irish or English, who came out for other reasons than gold were however also exposed to the general malaise of spirit which resulted from the craze for quick material gains. It was even more evident in Victoria than it had been in South Australia that a particularly strong Quaker allegiance was needed if Quakers were to resist the blandishments of wealth.

Lindsey and Mackie

Lindsey and Mackie were very much aware of the effects of what they called "goldmania" on the Melbourne Meeting and to a lesser extent on Sydney, Hobart, and Adelaide, because of the sudden urge to quit the farm or the shop and hurry off to claim the promise of fortune on the goldfield. Entries in Mackie's diary give voice to his concern. "We have to mourn over many of our friends who, overcome by the unfavourable influences with which they were surrounded, conceal their principles, ashamed to own them; thus gradually losing their strength they renounce Quakerism, assimilate with the world and sustain, too often, I fear, irreparable loss."[38] He met with Gabriel Unthank and Reuben Alexander and placed Unthank in charge of a library of forty Quaker volumes in Geelong. That same evening, 19 November 1855, he walked to Emerald Hill and visited three young Friends lodging together. Again he came away with the same depressing feeling. "Many and grievous are the entanglements for our friends in these parts, and one is ready to tremble for any of them lest any should make a shipwreck of faith."[39] Mackie formed the firm view that many had migrated who would have done much better to have stayed at home.

> They must endure severe privations and such are the temptations with which they are beset that they can hardly be expected to escape. It is plain that many here make gold their god and regardless of the means are in haste to be rich that they may leave this land of misery and return home. The state of morals is far worse than any place we have visited.[40]

Such was Mackie's damning verdict on the effects of "goldmania".

Using somewhat different evidence ex-Quaker William Howitt also had much to say about the effect of "goldmania" on the colony. From the moment the eager migrant stepped on shore, he said, he found that "all seem bent on fleecing their neighbours to the utmost in their power".[41] "My effects will cost me more", he continued, "in getting them up to town from the ship than they did in bringing them hither from London."[42] The reason for this deplorable state of affairs he considered was that everyone was out for himself and no-one looked upon this new country as his home. What he observed on the goldfields — the firing of guns and the felling of trees — was an ecologist's nightmare, with diggers leaving a trail of desolation as they left one worked-out concession to exploit the next.

He saw also the rise of a class society in a country which prided itself on its egalitarian, anti-establishment ideas. "The new hairystocracy (sic) seem to indemnify themselves for the subjection in which they are kept in England." Howitt foreshadowed the "Ocker" of the future in his description of the "diggers in their shirt sleeves and most of them their pipe or cigar in their mouths; an actor being occasionally saluted with 'Bravo'. Bray away, old woman!"[43] Yet, critical as he was of this brash new colony and having no intention of regarding his stay there as anything more than an adventurous interlude, he saw Australia as a country with a great future, not as an outpost of European culture, but, from its position in the new world of Asia and the Pacific, as one of the greatest and most fortunate regions in the world.

Howitt's reports on the colony received wide circulation through *The Friend* in England. Though this paper thought that Howitt, by meeting the violence of bushrangers on the goldfields with guns of his own, had departed considerably from the Quaker Peace Testimony in which he had been educated, it used Howitt's description of sludge, filth, and confusion of the diggings to issue a warning. "Well could it have been for thousands could they have seen Mr. Howitt's volumes, before committing themselves to the search for gold in the far-off colonies of the South."[44] The reports of Lindsey and Mackie on the unsettled state of the colony, like those of Howitt, had wide circulation amongst Friends and acted as a brake on the enthusiasm of some Friends for migration.

The visit of Lindsey and Mackie, travelling "under concern" had several important results. They provided the sort of pastoral care that was desperately needed in the colonies at this time. When ministers were "liberated" to travel amongst Meetings in England, they were expected not only to give spiritual encouragement by ministry in Meetings for

Worship but to visit with Friends in their homes and have a "religious opportunity" with them. This duty Lindsey and Mackie took very seriously in their travels around the colonies. By their tireless visiting they awakened interest amongst many who had shown little attachment to the Society of Friends in the colonies. During their two visits to Victoria they met personally with sixty-five individual Friends and with twenty-one families. They tried to track down many who were still members of Meetings in England but who had never made any attempt to contact Friends in Melbourne. They found it particularly difficult to trace Friends on the goldfields where, said Mackie, "mate" was the usual term of address and few used more than Tom, Joe, or Jack to identify neighbours.

They thus provided, though only temporarily, that pastoral care which the scattered and discouraged Friends in Victoria so much needed. Their visit to the goldfields illustrated the thoroughness with which they pursued this task. Though they found only one member of the Society, they traced a number who had once held membership. The formation some years later of a Meeting at Ballarat can be traced to the groundwork laid by Lindsey and Mackie. When they arrived at Ballarat, they found it crowded with a thousand troops in addition to armed police and under martial law. The timing of their visit to the goldfields came just a few days after the Eureka riots and so they were not permitted to hold public meetings, but were restricted to visiting and to distributing tracts. The tracts, Mackie reported, were eagerly received by the diggers.

> There was a good deal of excitement in this, many supposing they had reference to the present crisis and they began running towards us from all quarters which excited some little alarm in us and we found it needful to pocket our tracts and walk off in another direction. However by many they were very gratefully received knowing the subject of them. One said, 'We should have had them a fortnight ago.' Another observing the title of one, 'Unlawfulness of wars and fighting', seemed much interested. At length when our tracts were finished the disappointed man said, 'You should have brought a thousand'.[45]

Mackie made no secret of his sympathy for the diggers and

for the justice of their opposition to the system of collecting licensing fees. He felt that the police had exercised their powers in a way which would not have been tolerated in England.

The Melbourne Meeting

The most obvious result of their Victorian visit was the formation of a Meeting for Discipline in Melbourne. Early in 1853 moves had been made to secure land for a Meeting House and a school. The mention of a school marked the first indication of what developed later as a very strong concern in Melbourne Meeting for the establishment of a Friends' school. In the request, drawn up by Edward Sayce and William Robinson, it was stated that financial assistance from the government was not sought, but that the presence of ninety Friends in the colony and the prospect of rapid growth by the accession of Friends from England and Ireland made this request necessary. Promises of several hundred pounds were received and a decision was made on 14 December 1853 to purchase the western half of No. 10 allotment of Section C 21 in North Melbourne for £365. In the meantime Meetings for Worship were held in a succession of places — the Mechanics' Institute, a room in a building owned by William Overton, at that time an attender, St Paul's parish school-room, Great Bourke Street, and the school-room attached to the Independent Church, Collins Street. On 8 February 1854 the "Melbourne Monthly Meeting of Friends" was established at a meeting held in Sarah Raleigh's home, twenty-two Friends being present. William Robinson was appointed clerk and Alfred Clemes assistant-clerk.

Though not yet officially accepted as a recognized Monthly Meeting by London Yearly Meeting, it received a letter of support from the Meeting for Sufferings, which had been notified by Lindsey of the decision to form a Meeting. Meeting for Sufferings expressed the hope that Melbourne would recognize those who held membership in English and Irish Meetings and requested that a list of those considered to be members should be forwarded by Melbourne Monthly Meeting. Melbourne replied that "those persons are members, who, being members of some Meeting in Great Britain, Ireland or America, express a wish to become members of this".[46] A request for recognition was forwarded.

Melbourne proceeded to operate as a "de facto" Monthly Meeting, admitting and disowning members, issuing epistles, and planning for a permanent Meeting House. A petition signed by forty-one members and attenders requested that the meeting-place hired from the Mechanics' Institute should be registered as a place of worship so that marriages according to the usage of Friends could be legally performed and recognized. The request for registration was turned down, but the Meeting was given the assurance that marriages could be solemnized there. James Hope and Mary Skinner Green were the first Friends to be married in the colony. William Overton and Charles Mould were the first to be admitted to membership by convincement. Overton was one of the earliest settlers at Port Phillip, having come over from Van Diemen's Land in 1837 and set up the first confectioner's shop in a wattle and daub hut in Collins Street. Later, when he moved to Swanston Street, his premises were the first to be lit by gas. Even before joining Friends he had given practical support, first by making a room available for Meeting at no charge, then by donating a hundred pounds to the Meeting House Fund, and also by lending a further sixty-five pounds. Charles Mould, too, had liberally responded to the appeal with a donation of twenty-five pounds.

The guidance of Lindsey and Mackie was particularly helpful in the first few meetings when procedures were being established. Thus when the Meeting was faced with its first case for disownment for "marrying out", its assistant-clerk, Alfred Clemes, being the one in question, Lindsey reported in his Journal on 26 November 1854 the action taken by the Meeting.

> A report from the committee appointed to visit a young Friend (Alfred Clemes) on his marriage to a person not in connection with our Society, obtained the solid and deliberate consideration of the Meeting which came to the conclusion to dismiss the case, in which my dear companion and myself both united, believing that in this instance the requirements of the discipline would be fully answered

without proceeding to disownments. At the same time our young friends were affectionately cautioned not to allow this decision of the meeting to be any encouragement to them to transgress the wholesome rules of our Discipline in this respect and I am thankful in the hope that from the views which were elicited whilst the subject has been under the consideration of the meeting that it will not have this tendency but rather the contrary.[47]

The Meeting pursued with some vigour the question of a Meeting House, for it was clear that the lack of a suitable Meeting House was restricting growth in the Meeting. A Sydney Friend, Theodore West, writing to George Story in 1857, said he had heard that Melbourne Friends were building a Meeting House. This he felt was encouraging news, "showing that there were at least some who desire to see the Society live and have a place of abode".[48] At the end of 1856 land became available in Russell Street, but when those appointed by the Meeting went to conclude the purchase, they decided instead to buy the adjoining block on which there was a disused iron store. To finance the purchase price of £900 the North Melbourne land was sold at a figure of £250 and donations were then sought from English and Irish Friends. The iron store was converted for use as a Meeting House at a cost of £50 and the first Meeting for Worship was held there in the first week of January 1857. A Friend writing in 1893 recalled the "memorable" day, "a bright summer morning, as the members gathered with expressions of delight, in that simple room, so neat, so daintily clean and cool".[49] One wonders whether this initial delight at the acquisition of a Meeting House was tempered by experience of the Melbourne summer sun on an iron shed, for the Meeting, probably thankfully, accepted the offer by the owner of the original block inspected to exchange blocks for a credit of £300. A tender of £939.18.0 for the building was accepted and the new Meeting House was occupied for the first time on the first Sunday of March 1860. The total costs of the land, building, and furnishing came to approximately £2,000.

English Friends responded to Melbourne's appeal for help by contributing £500 in 1858, but Melbourne rather ungraciously considered the amount "was smaller than anticipated".[50] Hence a request for a further £500 was made to London Yearly Meeting, which was reminded of the peculiar and difficult circumstances in which the Melbourne Meeting was labouring. A supplementary amount of £354.8.11 was forwarded from London in 1859 and Irish Friends, in recognition of the number of Irish Friends who had emigrated to Victoria, sent £323.

Melbourne Meeting, which had a significant proportion of members who retained membership with English Meetings, appeared to expect English Friends to maintain a high level of financial support for their members in the colonies and so a third appeal was addressed to them. English Friends, however, while generously responsive to a request for help, showed signs of wanting Australian members to begin to assume some responsibility for themselves.

This expectation is clear from an examination of the correspondence leading to the recognition of the Monthly Meetings of Adelaide, Hobart and Melbourne by London Yearly Meeting in 1861. Melbourne Monthly Meeting[51] had made a direct request to London for an answer to a previous query, which concerned reimbursement of Australian Friends for relief moneys spent on Friends who were still members of

The Friends' Meeting House, Russell Street, Melbourne, opened March 1860, and was used until the move to Orrong Road, Toorak in 1953.

English Meetings. It saw no reason why English Meetings should not look after their own members, for Friends struggling to make a living in the colonies could not be expected to shoulder responsibility for maintenance of England's indigent.

The Yearly Meetings of 1858 and 1859 put forward proposals for the transfer of membership to Australian Meetings by giving full recognition to these as Meetings for Discipline responsible to London Yearly Meeting. The main point at issue seemed on both sides to be not the encouragement of the Australian Meetings to take responsibility for decision-making, but the financial question of whether all claims on English Meetings for maintenance of overseas members would cease when these members became members of Australian Meetings. London believed that this would indeed be the situation. Two Australian Meetings replied that "the pecuniary means of the members constituting these Meetings are such as would prove wholly inadequate to meet the demands which such an arrangement would entail on them".[52]

The Continental Committee however pointed out that any Friends migrating should, when making their decision, have taken into account the likelihood that Friends in the colonies would not have the resources to render much assistance and therefore any assistance given would be of a voluntary and not an obligatory nature. The Yearly Meeting of 1860 accepted this, but all three Australian Meetings continued to avow unreadiness to accept this financial responsibility. Adelaide members said bluntly that they were not able to extend financial aid and further that they preferred to remain "as outlying members of Monthly Meetings in England rather than assume a responsibility to which they feel themselves unequal"[53]

Melbourne Meeting, seeming still to be sensitive to the presence of those who were Friends in nothing more than name, wanted some plan whereby members who committed "flagrant breaches" of the Society's rules might be reported to their English Monthly Meetings "in order that the conduct of such may not go entirely unnoticed".[54]

This sensitivity to the problem of nominal membership seemed to have been particularly strong amongst Melbourne Friends. It was perhaps a logical outcome of migration to a colony where the main motive for such migration and the main preoccupation on arrival were the search for gold. In no other colony was there such a gap between nominal and active members, and in no other Meeting was such time and energy spent by active members in drawing up lists and in attempting to induce the nominal to become active. Something of the feeling of disappointment and even of despair is exposed in a letter written by a Prahran Friend to *The Friend*.[55] A statistical return of the number of Friends in the colony had been reprinted from the Melbourne *Argus* of 19 July 1856 at the time of public controversy over State Aid to religious denominations. This report showed that there were 211 Friends out of a total population in Victoria of 235,768. The Prahran Friend felt that this gave English Friends a false impression of the actual situation. Many of those 211 were, he implied, "census Quakers"; that is, their Quakerism was confined to a census entry, and even when within reach of a Meeting, they made no effort to attend. He continued:

> It is melancholy to reflect that in numerous instances those who have left their native land have left behind them their principles and their consistency and on arriving amongst circumstances unfavourable thereto, enter upon an ever-widening divergence and, so far as their fellow-members are concerned, 'walk no more with them' . . . What shall be said of those who on their arrival here have cast off to all appearances their allegiance to all good and run greedily astray. In a large number of instances of which the writer has heard their career has been very brief and their end wretched indeed; they have perished almost unknown and their friends have looked vainly for their return, or for any tidings of them.[56]

By 1860 there were signs of greater confidence in the Melbourne Meeting. William Tallach, visiting Victorian Friends in 1860, evidently felt it necessary, following some briefing from Melbourne Friends, to discount some of the unfavourable impressions that the two earlier Friends had given about the state of the colony. "It is very important for Friends at home to bear in mind that the state of exceeding unsettlement which characterized this colony at the time of the visit of the two latter Friends (viz. Lindsey and Mackie) has now become entirely a thing of the past."[57] Tallach said that it was a great mistake to think that the description of Victoria in 1854 at the time of the visit of Lindsey and Mackie was applicable six years later. He urged that English Friends should give greater weight to the claims of their countrymen in these distant colonies.⁵⁸ It would appear that William Tallach's more optimistic report on Melbourne had been successful in modifying English Friends' hesitation about granting Monthly Meeting status to Melbourne Meeting. When discussions were initiated by London Yearly Meeting on this subject it had then been felt that Melbourne Meeting was still too unsettled to be granted Monthly Meeting status. In August 1858 Melbourne Friends reported to Hobart that members in Melbourne Monthly Meeting were too scattered and that the Meeting itself was "in an infant state".⁵⁹

In 1861, Melbourne, as well as Hobart and Adelaide, was recognized as a Monthly Meeting by London Yearly Meeting.

PART THREE

Quakers in Australia: 1862–1901

Introductory Note

It was almost thirty years after the arrival of Backhouse and Walker in Hobart Town in 1832 that three Australian Meetings were finally recognized by London Yearly Meeting. In 1861 London Yearly Meeting issued specific regulations to cover the granting of Monthly Meeting status to the Meetings in the colonies. Following the establishment of "a disciplinary connexion between this Yearly Meeting and the Meetings existing in the colonies of Tasmania, Victoria and South Australia" arrangements were to be made for certificates of membership of all those holding membership of Meetings in England[1] to be sent to Australian Meetings. Those whose certificates were accepted in Australia would then cease to be members of their English or Irish Meetings and be recognized as members of Australian Meetings. If members failed to communicate with Australian Meetings within a reasonable time after their arrival, Australian Meetings were to be at liberty to return the certificates and hence to disown responsibility for them in Australia. If however any members were to find themselves so far distant from the nearest Australian Meeting that there was no possibility of personal contact with that Meeting, they were to remain members of their original Meetings, provided that contact was maintained by correspondence.

From 1862 there should have no longer been any reason, apart from isolation and distance from Australian Meetings, for Friends to cling to membership with Meetings of origin, though some did, nor to withhold support from Meetings of adoption. The "de facto" status of Meetings up to 1861 had led to uncertainty of identity. Friends were in a limbo, not knowing where they belonged. Some seemed more concerned to preserve links with the past than to work out the implications of Quaker commitment in the contemporary Australian context.

The question now to be considered is whether the conferring of "de jure" status did anything to change the climate of defeat and depression and the mood of reluctant compliance which seemed to prevail amongst the Australian Meetings in 1861. Would the action taken by London Yearly Meeting against the wishes of these Meetings result in a further retreat into dependence or in an advance towards an Australian Quakerism?

The second period of the history of Quakers in Australia from 1861 to 1901 reveals the difficulties which the Australian Meetings faced as Meetings dependent on each other, but linked rather to a parent body, London Yearly Meeting, twelve thousand miles away. The tendency was to attempt to apply the English rules to the Australian situation, rather than to seek an answer appropriate to Australian conditions. This had already been demonstrated with respect to marriage regulations, where the rigid application of the marrying out rule had led to the loss of almost a whole generation.

Further, many Friends were unwilling to transfer their membership to Australian Meetings after 1861. This was perhaps only symptomatic of the early colonist's reluctance to cut ties with the mother country and of his expectation of returning as soon as practicable from what many regarded as a period of exile. Birthright membership tended to fortify such an attitude and to inhibit commitment to full participation in Australian Meetings. In many cases birthright members were merely nominal members and this is why there was considerable weight of opinion amongst Australian Friends in favour of asking London Yearly Meeting to abandon automatic qualification for membership by registration of birth.

There were some valiant attempts made by individual Quakers in Australia to keep Meetings and scattered Friends in touch with each other and to encourage them to be faithful to their traditional testimonies. London Yearly Meeting endeavoured to do what it conceived to be its duty to its distant constituent Meetings in the colonies by correspondence, visitation, and financial support. It also consistently urged the separate Meetings to come together in a Yearly Meeting or, if that was felt to be too precipitate a step, at least to meet annually in a General Meeting, which was seen as exercising the general functions of an English Quarterly Meeting by providing an opportunity for mutual encouragement, for review, exhortation and, in cases of dispute, a court of appeal. This step was delayed by Australian Meetings until 1901 and even then taken with some misgivings.

Eighteen seventy-five is chosen as a suitable turning-point between a period of stagnation, frustration, and faintheartedness and the following years which saw the foundations laid for an Australian Quakerism. A change of attitude and of direction was the result of a growing realization in Australian Meetings of the threat of extinction and in London Yearly Meeting of the need for a rescue operation. Eighteen seventy-five was the year of the Australian Deputation. Three experienced members of London Yearly Meeting were sent out in that year to investigate and to recommend measures to aid the struggling Australian Meetings.

Nine
The Years 1862-1875

Dear Friends, if we have inherited a rich legacy of Christian Truth, surely the Lord will not be honoured by our keeping it buried in a napkin.[2]

This statement, though written some years later than the period under review in this chapter, is particularly descriptive of a time when discussions of Friends assembled in their Monthly, Two Monthly, or Annual Meetings appeared to centre on the preservation of Truth rather than on its propagation. The direction of sight was backward-looking, rather than to the present and the future. The Truth was buried in a napkin when it should have been broadcast as seed.

This attitude is reflected in records of Annual Meetings. The first of these was set up in Hobart on 3 October 1834 as the Van Diemen's Land Yearly Meeting and this term continued in use until 1865 when the Melbourne Monthly Meeting, now duly recognized by London Yearly Meeting, asked that "Yearly" should be changed to "Annual". The reason, Melbourne explained, was that the term "Yearly Meeting" connoted a disciplinary function with respect to Monthly Meetings, and Melbourne, though it had appreciated Hobart Monthly Meeting's guidance as the older Meeting, no longer felt that Hobart should assume any such role. Hobart Monthly Meeting, now numerically inferior to Melbourne Monthly Meeting, conceded the point. Melbourne and Hobart therefore proceeded to hold Annual Meetings independently.

The main purpose of these Annual Meetings was to give distant members an opportunity to meet together, to gain and give mutual encouragement, and to provide time for review of the spiritual state of the Monthly Meeting. The agenda invariably followed the routine of reading the Queries framed by London Yearly Meeting and of composing replies in language which was stereotyped and barren. Epistles were read and replies drafted by sub-committees and brought back for adoption by the Meeting. Exhortation, with liberal quotation from the Scriptures, rather than information seemed to be the main purpose of the Epistles, though some review of the Meeting's activities was sometimes attempted. When Meetings were relieved in 1875[3] of the necessity to answer in strict sequence all the numbered Queries, much more factual reporting was possible and more time could be given to the discussion of matters pertaining to contemporary life. This can be seen by comparison of reports of Melbourne Annual Meetings in the sixties and the eighties.

In the sixties members laboured over each individual query and framed replies in carefully non-committal phrasing, such as the following:

> It is hoped that . . .
> They are believed to be . . .
> Meetings for Business are tolerably well attended . . .
> With some exceptions to punctuality Friends are believed to be just in their dealings, punctual in fulfilling their engagements and clear of defrauding the public revenue.
> The necessities of the poor where there are such among us are properly inspected and relieved.
> The advice to Friends in their outward affairs has only partially been given . . .

These answers, though qualified and repetitive from year to year, do however indicate the disciplinary purpose of the Queries. They had both a spiritual and practical purpose. Members, by facing the Queries, were expected to be alerted to any unfaithfulness in word or deed. On the practical side they were reminded, for example, of their responsibility to the poor and of their duty to keep their outward affairs, such as the making of wills, in proper order.

In the eighties, since written answers were now required to only two queries, time was available for consideration of matters such as the Peace Testimony, the education of Friends' children, and religious instruction in State Schools.

Quakers in Ballarat

The only extension of Friends' activities in Victoria in the period 1862–75 was in Ballarat. Here the initiative came, not from any members of the Society of Friends, but from a small group of men who knew little about the Society of Friends, except from casual acquaintance in England, but who felt dissatisfied with the ways of worship practised by the churches and with what they considered to be the "money-grubbing" ways of ministers. A James Lambert, Ballarat storekeeper, who had known something of Friends as a lad when working as a journeyman, John Phillips, a cooper, who had had contacts with Friends in Cornwall, and William Tunks[4] inserted at their own expense an advertisement in the Ballarat papers of intention to hold a Friends' Meeting for Worship. A report of this group was made to *The Friend* in England through a Quaker, Algernon Wallis, who wrote to his brother, Marriage Wallis, describing how he had found this group meeting in a store, only one being a member of the Society.[5] They were so keen to have their own meeting-place that they were proposing to build one with their own hands, a log hut, expected to cost about a hundred pounds. English Friends responded to this report with their usual generosity and by 7 March 1869 Wallis had reported to Melbourne Monthly Meeting that the money had been received.[6]

In 1867 a deputation of three Friends had gone from Melbourne to investigate. One of the members of this deputation recalled thirty years later their arrival in the bustling city of Ballarat and attending the next morning the meeting in a public hall, next to a church with a noisy organ. The story of a spontaneously generated Friends' Meeting in Ballarat was a source of encouragement to Friends in other centres. Tasmanian Friends featured the news in their epistle to London Yearly Meeting. "It appears that these dear people (i.e. in Ballarat), having been drawn away from the religious ceremonies of several different sects to worship the Almighty more in accordance with the views of the doctrines contained in the New Testament, have been led without human intervention to adopt our manner of holding meetings for divine worship."[7]   But when Joseph Neave and Walter Robson, English Friends "travelling in the ministry", visited Ballarat in 1868, Robson saw this Meeting also as a reproof to members of the Society who had been living in Ballarat but had done nothing to establish a Meeting, while others who knew little about the Society had taken the initiative.

There was however further cause for reproof in that several members of the Society of Friends, resident in Ballarat, not only did nothing to promote a Meeting, but held aloof from that Meeting when it was established. The reasons may be inferred from the correspondence of Henry Slater, a member of Melbourne Monthly Meeting, originally a member of Pontefract Monthly Meeting. He was regarded as a man of considerable talent; he had been a student in the Flounders Institute, but his career of teaching was abandoned when he decided to try his luck at gold digging in 1857. His intentions with respect to the Society of Friends had evidently been commendable, for he wrote to Samuel Darton offering to look up Friends in Ballarat, because, he said, he valued "the beneficial association" with his co-religionists and "the salutary effects" of Quaker Discipline.[8]   Later, however, when taxed with the query why he did not appear to be supporting the little group in Ballarat, he is said to have replied that he would have attended "if social influences favoured it".[9]

Slater was not alone in his aloofness. Another Friend, Solomon Clemesha, with a strong Friends' background, and married to a Friend, Rachel Green, in the Melbourne Meeting House in 1864, was manager of a business in Ballarat. It was reported by Neave in 1874 that Clemesha and his wife kept "rather aloof from the rest".[10]

These two reactions raise the question whether a certain class consciousness caused Slater and Clemesha to look with some amount of disdain upon the efforts of these new "working-class" adherents who had actually established a Friends' Meeting without having had any Friends' education or background. This disdain may have been aroused, or at least reinforced, by the state of the log-hut Meeting house, which had been erected by the willing, but unsophisticated Friends' adherents. When the deputation of English Friends from London Yearly Meeting visited Ballarat at the beginning of 1875, they were taken aback by this structure and were of the opinion that its dilapidated condition had much to do with the unwillingness of some Friends to go to Meeting. Among these apparently were Sarah Williamson, a Friend from Warwickshire, who said that she would have attended if Meetings had been held "in a place of proper respectability",[11] and Joseph Jones,[12] a Friend of some standing in the community, who did not attend Meeting because "the place of Meeting is so dirty and dilapidated as hardly to be fit for persons in better walks of society to sit in'.[13] Jonathan Dymond sent a colourful report of the building to *The British Friend*.

> It is in plain terms a dilapidated cottage, apparently on the eve of complete ruin, standing in an obscure position near the edge of a vast hollow, covered with the melancholy debris of gold-mining operations. In one part of the tattered interior the spider reigned supreme: and still more objectionable insects (we were told) had chosen the place for their abode.[14]

It was no wonder therefore that the deputation recommended that high priority should be given by Melbourne Friends to helping Ballarat Friends build a more suitable Meeting House. The deputation also betrayed a slightly patronizing air in its view that the members of the Ballarat Meeting, while they were undoubtedly of good solid character, lacked education and belonged to "but humble walks of life". The predominantly middle-class composition of the Quaker migrant groups was perhaps one reason why Quakerism in Australia did not present any real appeal to the working-classes. Ballarat represented an opportunity that was not exploited.

Quakers in South Australia — and India

The Adelaide Meeting was in a dormant state, showing little evidence of growth in the decades of the sixties and seventies. The membership record in table 11 confirms this view.[15]

The unusually high birth-rate of the sixties, and not any addition of members by convincement, was responsible for

Table 11. Membership Records of Adelaide Monthly Meeting

		1860-69	1870-79	1880-89
Transfers in:	Adults	4	2	19
	Children	5	—	9
Reinstatements		1	—	—
Convincements		4	1	9
Application of parents		1	—	6
Births		33	17	18
Total inward membership:		48	20	61
Transfers out:	Adults	5	6	8
	Children	2	15	6
Resignations		3	2	5
Lapse		—	7	—
Deaths:	Adults	7	4	11
	Children	2	6	—
Total movement outward:		19	40	30

the increase of the sixties but this was offset by a marked downturn in the seventies. The pattern altered again in the eighties because of the influx, by transfer, of a number of Friends from other Meetings — a second Quaker migration which brought new life to the Adelaide Meeting. However inactive the South Australian Meetings at Mount Barker and Adelaide may have appeared, if the Minutes are taken as a guide, individual Friends continued to seek what they held to be the Truth and not to bury it in a napkin.

The most interesting example of this was the concern of two South Australian Friends, Frederick Mackie and Edward May, to "travel in the ministry". Mackie, the travelling companion of Lindsey, like Backhouse's Walker, settled in Australia and gave to South Australian Friends the spiritual leadership which Walker gave in Tasmania. He, like Walker, also married in Australia. His brother-in-law was Edward May. The concern to "travel in the ministry" was not new amongst Australian Friends. Tasmanian Friends, such as Francis Cotton, George Story, and Joseph Mather, had already done considerable visiting amongst Australian Meetings in the tradition of English Friends. This was a much needed service. Just how important it was is indicated by the influence which the travelling ministers, Backhouse and Walker and Lindsey and Mackie, had exercised on Quakerism in Australia. The acceptance of a similar responsibility by

Australian Friends was an encouraging sign of a growing independence and maturity. The expenses of these visits had been borne by the Friends themselves with some support coming from the Hobart Meeting.

What was new in the concern of Mackie and May was that their objective was to travel to Calcutta to give support to a most unusual group of Quakers, who, like those in Ballarat, had spontaneously generated a desire to adopt the principles and practices of Friends. Mackie and May had apparently been greatly moved by reports in *The Friend* of a visit paid to London Yearly Meeting in 1861 by two Indo-Portuguese, Mariano d'Ortez and his wife, Cecilia, from Calcutta, representing a group who had read Quaker books and who had for fifteen years been trying to practise what they had found in their reading. Their reception by London Yearly Meeting is described by Marjorie Sykes, an English Friend, who has spent many years working with Friends in India. She called it "one of the most moving and dramatic incidents in the history of the Society of Friends".

> Mariano and Cecilia carried with them a letter of introduction from their fellow Quakers in Calcutta, and it must have seemed to them a simple, natural thing to ask the London body for admission and a hearing. To the Yearly Meeting the request was so novel and unexpected that the old Quaker habit of defensive withdrawal asserted itself, and instead of giving a warm welcome to those who had come so far with such a wonderful story they kept their visitors waiting all morning outside closed doors, while technical objections to their admissions were raised and overcome. Finally Thomas Hodgkin was allowed to bring them in, and their letter was read. It contained an appeal to British Friends for 'a Quaker missionary' to help the Calcutta group to grow in the faith. The appeal, like the visit, found London Yearly Meeting unprepared, and after about three weeks in England Mariano and his wife returned home, taking with them more Quaker books, but no assurance of the kind of help they most needed.[16]

Whether Mackie and May were moved to offer their services after sensing the slow and less than wholehearted response by English Friends to the plea from Calcutta for help is not clear, but when a further letter, written in September 1861, from Calcutta was read to Yearly Meeting in 1862, Josiah Forster had already received from Mackie and

May the offer to go to Calcutta and this was accepted. They left for Calcutta on 6 September 1862 and after surviving a stormy passage arrived in Calcutta on 3 November unannounced. They appeared, said Edward May, as "strangers in a strange land: for we knew no-one and landed without any of our friends hearing of our arrival. But we have met with an open-hearted welcome and that feeling which unites and destroys strangeness".[17] By looking up the name of d'Ortez in the Post Office directory they were able to make contact with the group, which Mackie called "this little body of professors". They then settled down to help the group by worshipping with them, instructing them in Quaker testimonies, and showing them how to keep their records according to established procedures laid down by the Society of Friends. Their help was gratefully accepted. Mackie and May felt that India was ripe for the sort of spiritual, uncluttered, and unpriestly Christianity represented by Quakerism. One of the Hindus they met was reported by Mackie as saying that "had Friends been the first missionaries, India might now have been Christianized".[18] Education, they felt, was the field of service where Friends could be most effective in India.

Just as they were about to leave India a group of three English Friends arrived "in the love of the gospel". Marjorie Sykes leaves no doubt as to which of the "missions" was the more effective. Not only was the Australian response to Calcutta's plea for help more direct and spontaneous and indeed appeared to pre-date, if not to inspire, a belated move by English Friends, but in her view the simple approach of Mackie and May did much more to meet the real needs of the Calcutta group for Quaker fellowship. The English Quakers, she said, were never at ease amongst the Indian members, perhaps because they seemed to share the current British belief in Britain's special mission to Christianize and civilize India. Mackie and May, though they were strongly evangelical in their approach, were non-judgmental and did not have any affectations of cultural or religious superiority. Their influence did not cease when they left Calcutta. For years afterwards Calcutta Friends continued to correspond with Mackie and to keep him informed of their activities.[19]

Though the concern of Mackie and May to travel in the ministry overseas is an isolated instance and was not followed up by further visits, it illustrates the potential of Australian Friends to accept responsibility as members of London Yearly Meeting.

The visit to Calcutta also revealed a problem of procedure. In England any member who felt he had a concern to "travel in the ministry" had to test this concern before a series of Meetings — Monthly, Quarterly and Yearly. What then was the procedure to be when members of an Australian Monthly Meeting, like Mackie or May, wished to undertake a journey, not simply to other Meetings in Australia, but over a considerable distance to India? Which Meeting was to bear the expense, their Australian Monthly Meeting or London Yearly Meeting? In this case London accepted the bill. "In consideration of the circumstances of our friends in South Australia, few in number and of limited means, several members of the committee of this Meeting, appointed to correspond with Friends in foreign parts, met and agreed that a letter should be written authorizing our friends in that colony to draw on this country for pecuniary aid in prosecuting the visit."[20]

In sending his statement of accounts to Josiah Forster on 20 January 1863[21] Edward May raised the question of procedures and pointed out the difficulty of a member of one Monthly Meeting gaining support from both the other recognized Meetings in Australia, when these were so far distant from each other. In the absence of any superior Quarterly or General Meeting he suggested that recognition by one Meeting, if recognition was not accorded by other Meetings, should be followed by two "weighty" Friends of the supporting Meeting corresponding direct with the Meeting for Sufferings.[22] In reply the Meeting for Sufferings made it clear that the recognition of Mackie and May for service in India was not to be taken as a precedent. It was only because Mackie was known personally as an English Friend to members of Meeting for Sufferings that the recommendation of only one Australian Monthly Meeting was considered sufficient. The death of Edward May[23] at the age of forty-three on 24 December 1862 on the eve of his marriage to Sarah Coleman was a sad blow to the South Australian Meeting.

Quakers in Hobart

Hobart Monthly Meeting minutes for the period 1862 to 1875 are indicative of an aging membership and of growing concern about the younger generation. There is evidence of little more than the maintenance of routines. It must be remembered however that these minutes do not record the public and philanthropic work of individual members and in this the example of Walker was well followed by the Mathers, the Cottons, and the Propstings. The Hobart Monthly Meeting continued to play the role of a senior Meeting, particularly by providing a travelling ministry. In 1867 Francis Cotton was in Adelaide, Melbourne and Sydney, "under concern".

In 1868 J. B. Mather visited Melbourne Meeting and in 1870 George Story went to Victoria and New South Wales. He returned his certificate with the comment about the Sydney Meeting that he had "never felt more emptiness and helplessness".

Quakers in Sydney

Sydney was the problem Meeting of this period. It had never reached anything approaching a settled state. The difficulties it encountered were rendered the more serious because there was not only a lack of really committed and experienced members in the Meeting, but its isolation from other Meetings, and therefore the lack of corporate guidance which would have been available from a Quarterly Meeting, aggravated personal clashes into Meeting schisms. The history of a dispute in the late sixties illustrates the dangers of a Friends' Meeting operating, as it were, in a spiritual vacuum.

The central figure in the dispute was Alfred Allen, whose parents William Bell and Ruth Allen, came out to Sydney in 1842 from Belfast and set up a soap and candle works in Sussex Street, Sydney. William Bell Allen and both his sons, William Johnston and Alfred, became members of the Legislative Assembly of New South Wales, the father 1860-69, the sons William 1888-89 and Alfred 1887-94.[24] Alfred Allen had a somewhat volatile character and his career was a stormy one. Trained as an engineer, he was dismissed for associating himself with the Eight-hour movement. His father having been disowned by Lisburn Meeting, Alfred Allen joined the Congregational Church, but on reading the Quaker Barclay's *Apology* he was convinced that the early Friends held the truth and that Sydney Friends were far from it. From his reading of the *Apology* he regarded, he said, "the Friends as a waning people and passing away. Their tenets I considered as manifestly unscriptural".[25] His mother had remained a Friend.

Allen had poems published in Sydney in 1883 under the title *Australian Verse Drift*. One of these, entitled "A tribute to my mother", revealed his great respect for her as a Friend:

> An aged 'Friend', a quaker dame,
> Whose bond was ever 'yea' or 'nay'.

He now rejoined Friends and became a very active and vocal member. He bewailed the paucity of Friends in Sydney and the prevailing air of inactivity and claimed that the Discipline of the Meeting was too much in the hands of one Friend, Abraham Davy. Backhouse may have unwittingly encouraged Davy to assume a special air of authority with respect to Friends' affairs in Sydney. When Sydney Friends wrote to Backhouse to suggest four names of trustees for the transfer of Friends' burial-ground (the original trustees being Backhouse, Walker, and Tawell), Backhouse replied that it was a matter of decision between himself and Davy, his personal friend, and that their decision would therefore stand.

Allen claimed that the Society could have been expected to flourish in a city which prided itself on being a city of religious liberty. He called for action from what he considered a dormant Society and set about arousing it with an excess of zeal. He wrote letters to English Friend publications, representing himself as a spokesman for the Society of Friends in Sydney. He became a pamphleteer in the tradition of early Friends, calling down wrath upon the priesthood in "this apostate age of pharisaic profession: who take unto themselves titles which belong only to God and desire of men to be called 'Reverend'. . . . Now this is the mystery of Godliness — Christ *within*, not *without*."[26] He and four of his followers issued in 1867 a printed letter as a Declaration of their claim to have been "visited by the Lord". "This, beloved, hath given us to see, that modern Friends have, generally, much degenerated from the purity, power, life and spirit, of the very precious ancient ones. The tone and spirit of the present state of the Society is that of continued complainings of shortcomings and unworthiness. This was not the testimony of our fathers."[27]

Then he proclaimed his main theme of Perfection, of freedom from sin, in which state they declared themselves to be. His criticism of the Sydney Meeting was probably well-founded, but its effect on the Sydney Meeting can well be imagined. William Benson, who came out to Australia in 1867 as a young man of twenty, wrote a very perceptive analysis in his diary of the effect Allen had upon these members.

> There being no leading spirit among them they have sunk into a sort of sleep of a very unrousable nature ... Allen himself being very energetic and earnest, he beset himself to the task of endeavouring to rouse to some degree of life the community into which he had gained admittance. Being a very fluent speaker he began to attract the attention of outsiders and quite a little congregation assembled at the Meeting. That they should be worked at by a young man, a comparative stranger, and that the drowsy quiet of the meetings should be invaded by soldiers, sailors and others who came to hear the young preacher considerably disgusted the ancient Friends who did not at all like the new state of affairs and accordingly they in a most unchristian spirit trumped up charges against Allen and turned him out of the Society.[28]

Benson later met Allen in Melbourne and was impressed by his forceful personality, though he confessed he could not agree with some of Allen's extreme views, such as his doctrine of perfection. "Allen", he said, "considers himself free from all sin whatever." This extravagant assertion irritated those who might otherwise have supported him. His trumpeting of Barclay's theory of Perfection and assumption of its embodiment in himself were anathema to them. Allen maintained that, through direct access to that of God within, man attains perfection and therefore cannot sin. His opponents seized on this and retorted: "Allen's conduct and untruthfulness by no means corresponds with this".[29] His wife, according to a member of the 1875 deputation, was said to have drily remarked "how well it would be if there was less talk of perfection in theory and more show of it in the daily walks of life".[30]

Reports of the difficulties in Sydney Meeting reached London Yearly Meeting and were the subject of much concern to British Friends, who were faced with the prospect of having to deal with a dispute which threatened to disrupt an already crippled Meeting. The visit of the English Friends, Joseph Neave and Walter Robson, was the direct result of London Yearly Meeting's anxiety about the future of Sydney Meeting.

Neave was born at Leiston, Suffolk, on 27 May 1836. He entered business with his half-brother, Edward. His wife, Eliza, died in childbirth in 1863. His first journey "in the ministry" was with William Norton to North Carolina during the American Civil War. To a soldier who queried his reasons for such a journey he replied that "we were all one people from the world over and I did not think it strange that someone from a distance should feel it a duty to come and see them and try to help and comfort them".[31] In 1867 he had the concern to visit Australia and New Zealand with his cousin, Walter Robson, who was appointed to be his secretary-companion. Robson returned to England and on 5 September 1869 married Christina, one of the daughters of Dr Cox.[32]

One of the major purposes of their visit was to attempt to reconcile the contending parties in Sydney Meeting. By the time they arrived in Australia on 17 October 1867 the split was open and the parties bitterly divided. Neave found that there were now two separate Meetings in Sydney, the original one in Devonshire Street and the breakaway group in Pitt Street. The Devonshire Street Friends had disowned Allen on three charges — immorality, unsound doctrine, and disorderly conduct. Allen had therefore set up a separate Meeting with his handful of supporters in Pitt Street. He issued an epistle which he circulated amongst Meetings in other States. This led other Australian Meetings to decide that something should be done. Now both English and Australian Friends were involved in an attempt to conciliate.

Joseph James Neave (1835-1913), a tireless traveller amongst Friends in Australia and New Zealand. In 1892-93, he went on a mission to Russia to the Czar to plead for the cessation of persecution of the religious dissidents, the Stundists.

Francis Cotton was in Melbourne when the Pitt Street epistle arrived and he was urged to go to Sydney to meet with the contending parties. He confessed that, like Jonah going in the opposite direction to that which the Lord required of him, he went to Adelaide, but with Frederick Mackie he composed a long letter in an attempt to answer Allen's doctrinal arguments. In the meantime Melbourne Friends appoined Edward Sayce and Samuel Levitt to go to Sydney: they were said to have come away sorrowing because they felt they had made no progress, but they did recommend that Sydney Meeting should rescind the minute of disownment. Francis Cotton was by now also in Sydney and with Joseph Neave visited Allen. Allen was cleared of the charge of immorality, the disownment was rescinded and on 28 June 1868 the separated groups of Friends met together for the first time since the division. Neave recorded in his diary[33] for that day, "I think it tended to soften down some hard feeling and shake the kinks out of us".

The kinks however remained and when Neave returned from a visit to Queensland in December 1868 he recorded pessimistically that he had come to a scene of renewed strife and conflict. "Our actions", he said, "are misunderstood and every hope and expectation of a brighter future for the Society of Friends here seem removed."[34]

Allen had been disowned a second time by the Meeting, now on charges of disrupting meetings. Friends had built a new Meeting House in Sydney, again with considerable financial support from London Yearly Meeting, but when Allen demanded entry and created disorder, the new Meeting House was closed and Friends held their meetings in a room elsewhere, bolted against Allen's expected disruption.[35]

Though berated by both sides for his peace-making efforts, Neave remained remarkably undeterred and his summing-up of the main elements of the dispute reflects his sound judgment and scrupulous fairness.

> The differences in the beginning were very much of a personal nature which a kind and christian interference on the part of one or two sound friends might have set right: then two earnest-hearted zealous young men read and embraced the doctrines contained in the writings of our early friends; but alas they have gone in some matters beyond them and withal have drunk deeply of the controversial spirit of those times so that while intending in word for some precious truths, they do not dwell in and under the power that they plead for and often say things very hurtful to the tender-hearted believer in Jesus to whom *all truth* is alike precious. . . . Now it is too much the case that each party contends for the mastery, rather than the truth: with the spirit manifested by the leading men in both companies I have no unity.[36]

Yet Neave did not lose hope that time would heal the wounds. Most of the Pitt Street group withdrew to set up in Queensland what would now be described as a "commune". Neave had high hopes that the quiet of the bush would have a healing effect. From his landing on 17 October 1867 in Adelaide to his departure from Sydney in September 1871 he covered many miles, much of it on foot, in all the Australian states except Western Australia, and he spent eighteen months visiting Friends in New Zealand, as well as some weeks in the South Sea Islands investigating the exploitation of native labour by Queensland sugar planters.

Two things about Neave impressed a non-Friend, Cornelius Appleton, and led him to write to both *The Friend* and *The British Friend* about Neave's visit to Copperfield, Peake Downs, Queensland. The first was Neave's capacity to undertake the most arduous of journeys through the Australian bush. "Our friend started in good trim, though by far too heavily laden. His weighty knapsack and rug thrown over the top, hanging over his shoulders, together with a 3 quart bottle of cold tea in his hand, was enough for any man to carry a mile on a cold day; but to plod on twenty and thirty miles a day in the boiling sun, and most painfully footsore, was no light work for the good man."[37]

A summary of this solitary journey can be compiled from Neave's record in his diary, commencing 17 September 1868:

> Train from Rockhampton to Westwood, coach to Gainsford, then walking, "bushed", 28 miles in moonlight to a house "honoured by the name of Springton", 18 miles carrying water to camp number 1, six miles to water and breakfast at a house, 17 miles to camp No. 2, 6 miles to public house for breakfast and dinner (total walked thus far 101m.) 6 miles to Corura station, 5 miles to water and billy tea, 15 miles to public house, 2 miles to the Downs, Capella and camp No. 3, 5 miles to Retro Creek, 22 miles to Clermont, stayed with Dr. Mackintosh, rested for a week to let feet heal, then walked 3½ miles to Copperfield.

The second impression he made upon those who met him was his willingness to co-operate with ministers of other churches. For him preaching the gospel was his prime concern; whether in church or meeting house was a secondary consideration. Appleton found him a very "liberal minded man". "I am under the opinion that many Friends travelling in the ministry would object to taking part in service other than their own form. By our friend having done as he did, he was thereby enabled to meet larger bodies of people together than would otherwise have been the case."[38] Neave, indeed, was regarded as too liberal-minded by some of his fellow-Quakers. Melbourne Monthly Meeting[39] expressed concern at reports that Neave and Robson had been holding meetings not in the manner of Friends, "but in a manner hardly to be distinguished from those of other denominations".[40] Apparently the objection was to the congregational singing and the "pre-arrangements" which characterized their public meetings. Melbourne Friends felt that important principles had been compromised. Any move to meet with fellow-Christians, except in strict accordance with Friends' testimonies against priests and ritual and prepared services, was unacceptable. An English Friend, J. B. Braithwaite, issued a strong reproof to Robson, based on a report apparently forwarded to him by a Friend in Sydney to the effect that Robson, during Neave's absence had held a meeting in a Baptist Meeting House (sic) "in which thou hadst given out a hymn and engaged in preaching and in prayer, *timing* thyself by thy watch — also asking the minister to engage in prayer". Braithwaite did at least grant the possibility of Robson's action having been misrepresented. "We accept these statements", he continued, "with great reserve, not doubting but that they may have been a good deal coloured",[41] but he warned Robson to exercise great caution. In his reply to Braithwaite's warning he stated that he regretted that he had been a source of concern to Melbourne Friends for entering a Baptist church. He felt that he should also let it be known that he had been baptized, in case this should reach the ears of Melbourne Friends. His reason for seeking secret baptism by water, he said, was because he felt he should fulfil the scriptural demand that "ministers should baptize".

Robson acknowledged that this was an error of judgment and therefore decided that he should accept the verdict of Friends in Melbourne and Sydney, that he should take the blame and return home, so as not to embarrass Neave in future contacts with Meetings. It was unfortunate that Neave and Robson's visit to Sydney coincided with such a difficult time in Sydney Meeting. They were called on to attempt to reconcile two parties who were bitterly opposed to each other, each party berating them because they refused to take sides. Robson's diary reveals how deeply he was hurt, not only by the Sydney divisions, but by Melbourne Friends, who, after a visit by Allen in Melbourne, came to Sydney to tell them that they did more harm than good by staying on further in Australia Robson's restrained comment in his diary after this announcement was: "Blessed be God: the truth will ultimately prevail".[42] Whatever judgment is passed on Robson, it is evident that he was not embittered by his rejection by some Friends in Australia.

Robson later travelled in America among Friends and became involved in the controversial issues which were dividing Friends at that time. Edwin Bronner, in his introduction to Robson's account of his American visit, says that Robson maintained a degree of objectivity during these extensive visits which enhanced the value of his observations.[43] A reading of Robson's diary of his Australian visit would tend to confirm Bronner's judgment. Unhappily some Sydney and Melbourne Friends at this time seemed unable to accept objectivity and labelled it as interference.

Neave himself was well aware of a critical attitude among Australian Friends towards his ecumenical spirit. After taking a regular service in a Toowoomba church he wrote in his diary: "I think at times it is our duty to become all things to all men that we may be the means of doing them good, if the truth as it is in Jesus be not injured".[44] Later he again commented on his participation in a church service as being something which Friends at home might not approve of, "but I hope", he said, "I did rightly in not allowing my feelings as a Friend to prevent my labouring among them in the Gospel".[45]

There was in Neave a largeness of spirit and a breadth of understanding which enabled him to minister most acceptably to the Australians he met. He avoided the doctrinaire attitude which seemed to mark some of the Australian Friends of this period and which left them unable to adjust to the conditions of life in Australia and to speak helpfully to others. Though Neave was a staunch teetotaller he understood enough of Australian water supplies to know why alcohol was a much preferred alternative for many Australians. "Teetotallers hereaway (and there are few) can sing 'Give me a drink from the crystal spring', but there are no crystal springs for many miles."[46] He had that characteristic generosity of spirit which many associate with St Francis. He was himself an example of the truth of his own words. "A loving heart and a Christian spirit can enliven and cheer the roughest spot on earth and make it to a weary pilgrim a little paradise."[47]

Quakers in Queensland

In the sixties a number of Quakers, both individuals and families, had settled in Queensland, first in the area around Brisbane and then, as a result of the financial depression in the years 1866 and 1867 in the districts of Buderim and Rockhampton. Neave spent five months of 1868 visiting these scattered Friends.

The history of Friends in Queensland is a history of individuals rather than of Meetings. Two of the first families to arrive were the Smith and Hopkins families. The Smith family, consisting of two brothers, Granville and Howard, and the sister, Rosamond, arrived in 1861 and the Hopkins family — Rachel, the mother, and her family of two sons, William and Francis, and daughter, Anne — in 1862. Two other sisters of the Smith family followed, Felicia in 1862 and Lyra in 1877. Felicia gave a lively account of her voyage in *The British Friend* of 1 July 1863. The Hopkins family arrived in the *Sultana* on the evening of 5 November 1862, a date verified by their report that they noted bonfires celebrating Guy Fawkes on the banks of the Brisbane River. Most of the Friends emigrating to Queensland had been educated at Croydon, Saffron Walden, and Ackworth Schools. Initially there was an evident eagerness to promote migration of other Friends to Queensland. A correspondent of *The Friend* who signed himself "a Queensland Friend", urged not only that migration would be a remedy for a country suffering the "disease" of a surplus population, but that Quaker emigration would be the means of propagating the truths of Quakerism.

Surely if the truths of Quakerism are worth cultivating they are worth propagating; and why not by transplantation? There is plenty of room in Queensland for all the surplus Quakers in England and much need of them too; for honest men are at a premium the world over . . . Friends in Brisbane would only be too glad to give employment as far as they could to Friends from home, especially domestic servants, of whom I am sure half a dozen could be disposed of to advantage, if not amongst members of the Society, yet in respectable families here.[48]

The young Friend, Rosamond Smith, soon after her arrival in 1861, proceeded to do something along the lines suggested. She established a Home for female servants, run on liberal and unsectarian lines. She had first floated the idea in a letter to *The Friend* of 1 October 1863. "It seems to me almost like taking trouble for nothing, for emigration societies at home to be doing so much to send out young women here in a comfortable manner, under a well-regulated system, if they are to be neglected and unprovided for when they arrive."[49] She indicated that she had already written to the local press and received support from the editor and a favourable response from the public. Five months later she wrote again reporting that the Home had been established, that government support had been given, and that a representative committee of members of the Legislative Assembly, clergymen, lawyers, and tradespeople had been set up. She was also hopeful that local Brisbane women would be stirred by her initiative to contribute to the care of young women arriving in the colony. The government showed its approval by contributing a sum of £500 to provide a "lying-in" hospital at the Home. The early decease of Rosamond Smith on 20 February 1870 at the age of thirty-three years brought to a close a life which set an example of community service to Queensland Friends.

Meetings of Friends in Brisbane were first held in the homes of members. Rosamond Smith in her letter to *The Friend* of 1 October 1863 indicated that Friends met regularly at E. Barrymore's house. Later meetings were held at the Milton home of Rachel Hopkins. There was sufficient initial interest and support for Barrymore to seek help from English Friends for the building of a Meeting House in Brisbane. He pointed out in his letter to *The Friend* of 1

August 1864 that Friends in Brisbane were mostly young men of limited means and that the anticipated growth in numbers would shortly make it impossible to continue meetings in private houses.

Again English Friends responded, as in the other states, quickly and generously. One Friend, Theodore West, who had spent nine years in Australia, arranged for the appeal to be placed before London Yearly Meeting and he himself laid the concern before English Friends in an article in *The British Friend*. He also raised contributions from members of his own Meeting.

Theodore West spoke feelingly of his own experience as an isolated Friend in Australia. "When living in the bush for years together, myself and family were prevented attending Meetings and sometimes, when opportunity occurred, were fain, through social feeling alone, to try other modes of worship and communities, but neither the paid ministry, the swelling music, nor the lengthy word-services of those fashionable throngs, can ever satisfy those who love to worship in spirit".[50]

By May 1865 English Friends had contributed £160.14.0. A block of land in Mackerston Street, Brisbane was bought for £160 and a brick Meeting House, measuring twenty-four feet by fifteen feet was opened on 7 October 1866. The

The first Friends' Meeting House in Mackerston Street, Brisbane, opened on 7 December 1866.

The Friends' Meeting House, Rockhampton, on land purchased by Friends in 1868. It was opened on 28 November 1880.

opening however coincided with a serious financial depression and the Friends' community was depleted by the departure of some families northwards to Rockhampton. The two pioneer families of the Hopkins and the Smiths were among those who left Brisbane. Francis Hopkins had married Felicia Smith in Brisbane on 18 December 1865, the first Friends' marriage recorded in Brisbane.

It was not long before the Friends who moved to Rockhampton acted to find a meeting place. A block of land was purchased in 1868 by six Friends on the Fitzroy River, but further dispersal of families led to the block remaining unused for some years. A second area of activity was opened up on the north side of the Fitzroy River, where "a school room was subsequently erected by general subscription on the commonage near the ferry and was used by Friends in the morning and Congregationalists in the afternoons for many years".[51] This building was removed in 1881 when the Baptists and Methodists erected chapels in the area.

The other activity of Friends in Queensland before 1875 was the establishment by the breakaway Pitt Street group of Sydney Friends of a Friends' community experiment on the Mooloolah River in 1869. To neighbours it was known as

Francis and Felicia Hopkins, pioneer Quakers in Rockhampton, North Queensland.

William Hopkins, brother of Francis, mayor of North Rockhampton in 1883.

"The Friends' Farm". Alfred Allen, Arthur Hood, Joseph Dixon, Marshall Mitchell, and a Hungarian, Gustaphus Reibe, were the members of this community. They were credited with having designed and built one of Queensland's first sugar mills, but a disastrous flood in 1871 ruined the experiment and the members scattered, Allen being the last to leave.[52] He was taken ill and nursed by Aborigines before finally making his way back to Sydney.

Dixon and Reibe cleared land at Buderim Mountain for sugar plantations. The rich volcanic soil proved most productive and with crops of sugar, coffee, and bananas these Friends prospered. They relied on Kanakas for their labour force. When Alfred Wright, who had been a member of the 1875 Deputation returned to Australia in 1891 and visited Queensland with another English Friend, William Jesper Sayce, he reported favourably on Dixon's treatment of his Kanaka labourers. Clearly the difficulty of finding labour to service his sugar and banana plantations outweighed Dixon's espousal of traditional Quaker attitudes to "slave" labour. Dixon, indeed, would have contested the application of such an epithet to his Kanaka labour force. This is reflected in Wright's report of his visit.

> Joseph Dixon's house (where a warm welcome was received) is situated on the summit of a mountain with an extensive view over the broad Pacific. . . . J. Dixon's plantation has been cleared by him at great labour; he employs about twenty Kanakas and grows bananas and sugar-cane; he has also erected a crushing mill and other machinery. These Kanakas come from different islands in the South Seas. They do not often bring their wives with them, and sometimes marry Australian Aborigines or low Irish women; They are mostly heathen, and spend the Sundays in shooting or fishing, of which they are very fond. They are a shy people, but J. Dixon enjoys their confidence, and hopes to commence a school amongst them, though at present he has a class in a children's school. These poor people seem to prefer living here to being in their own islands, and when their three years' engagement is expired they often come back and settle. They are not paid much wage, but are well fed and clothed, and not overworked. J. Dixon kills a bullock weekly for his family and the Kanakas and his wife with her Kanaka woman bakes all the bread. . . . The Queensland Government has put a stop to the introduction of these people, fearing that it may degenerate into slavery,

but probably more from the fact that it tends to shut out white labour by lowering the wages; and working men have great power with the Government here.[53]

Joseph Dixon opened his school some months later, for there was an enthusiastic report by him in June 1891[54] of the school which was open three nights a week and had up to thirty Kanakas learning to read and write.

The importation of Kanaka labour for the Queensland sugar plantations was a subject which should have aroused Australian Friends to action, but which so far seemed to have excited little comment. When Neave and Robson were in Queensland on their pastoral visit, they met with William Brooks, who was the leader of a section of those opposed to the importation of Kanaka labour. The Polynesian Labourers Act had had the assent of the acting-Governor of Queensland in April 1868. What they heard from Brooks convinced them there was the germ of slavery in this legislation and they determined to investigate the practice and to bring it to the notice of the Anti-Slavery Society in England in the hope that the Imperial Government would disallow the Act. Neave gave background information on the subject to *The British Friend*,[55] outlining the commercial reasons for the legislation, which ensured a supply of cheap coloured labour in conditions unacceptable to white workers. While the Act purported to control the conditions of employment and safeguard the interests of South Sea Islanders, Neave feared that the professed good intentions of the employers did not guarantee the protection of the interests of the employees. He summed up his opinion "The grand question, 'Is it right or is it wrong to bring them thus?' seems kept behind, and the uppermost one I fear is 'Does it pay?' Now it seems clear to my mind, if it does not pay — and I do not think it will if the provisions of the Act are enforced — it will either be abandoned, or the Act evaded."[56]

Neave and Robson visited the Hon. Charles Cowper, "for many years Premier of the colony" and spoke with him about the South Sea Islanders. He acknowledged that though the two hundred Kanakas on his Queensland estate were "comfortable, the whole principle was bad".[57] A further approach to the government came from a meeting of ministers of religion, at which Neave and Robson were present, when it was decided to "memorialize" the government on the issue of the South Sea Islanders.[58]

Not all Friends were united with Neave and Robson in their opposition to the Act. Neave was cautioned against accepting Brooks' opinions. Nevertheless Neave and Robson were determined to see for themselves and arranged a visit to the South Sea Islands on a London Missionary Society vessel, the *Samoa*, whose tour of the Islands occupied several months, because, Neave said, "the sad doings of unprincipled men in kidnapping and deceiving the poor islanders in some of these islands needs bringing to light".[59]

Neave did his best during the visit to warn natives wherever he went about the dangers of trusting any white men who tried to enrol them for work in Queensland. He urged them "not to be led to join the vessels who would kidnap them for slaves under false pretences".[60]

In 1871, at the end of his first period in Australia, Neave summed up his views on the state of the Society of Friends in the colonies. Though he saw some promising signs, the overall picture, he said, was indeed dark. "The body at large is in a sickly state, the dead are not awakened, the sleepers sleep on, the feeble mourn over their weakness and the burden-bearers are ready to faint." But he was not without hope, for he concluded: "In all those Meetings, though the enemy has sown the tares, there is a seed that the Lord hath planted and blessed".[61]

The Australian Deputation — 1875

London Yearly Meeting now began to realize that some positive action was needed to nurture that seed if the Society was to have any future in the Australian colonies. The reports of Neave and Robson and their views given in person to the Yearly Meeting of 1874 did much to reinforce this feeling. Neave stressed the result of isolation — the growth of a suspicion, even if unwarranted, among Australian Friends that London Yearly Meeting knew little about them and cared little. He pointed out that Australian Meetings had no superior Meeting to which they could appeal for help, except London Yearly Meeting, half the world away. He said that there was division on matters of doctrine and discipline and strife which required judicious counselling. The Yearly Meeting was clearly greatly moved by the assessments which Neave and Robson gave of the situation in Australia and agreed to send a deputation of three members, chosen for their experience, tact and wisdom. The members were J. J. Dymond, William Beck, and Alfred Wright. Alfred Wright let his name go forward because he confessed to having been greatly influenced by James Backhouse. The strength of this influence is indicated, not only by his wish to join the deputation from London Yearly Meeting in 1874-75 but also by his return journey in 1890-93 in the tradition of the travelling ministers. The "Australian Deputation", after a farewell meeting with Friends on 19 September 1874, left England on 21 September.

The deputation's impressions conveyed in their letters were in much more direct and forthright language than in their official reports which were more restrained, because, as J. J. Dymond said in a letter to Edwin Ransome, Australian Friends were "terribly sensitive".[62] They noted in each Meeting the disheartening effect of small numbers and the evidence of drift away from the Society. At one Meeting they overheard two old Quaker "patriarchs", the heads of long lines of children to the third generation, remark, as they sat on the "long unaccustomed forms, what a change it would have been if 'we and all ours had kept in the Society'".[63] They saw how the old marriage regulations, so inapplicable to colonial conditions, had alienated many of the young members of Friends' families and deprived Australian Friends of a whole generation of leadership. A phrase that was frequently to be found in their reports was that there was "a harvest waiting to be gathered, but the labourers are very few".

Although the deputation, wherever possible, visited individual Friends, they concentrated on the settled Meetings, believing that Neave and Robson had carried out pastoral visiting of outlying Friends much more effectively than they could do in the limited time available to them. Newspapers in Melbourne carried news of their arrival with the announcement that the purpose of the deputation was "the healing of certain differences and the correction of doctrinal errors".[64] The deputation, however, was engaged in no inquisitional task. They soon realized that their main objective must be to arrest the disintegration of the Society of Friends in the Australian colonies.

For the first time perhaps London Yearly Meeting was given what it recognized as an authoritative assessment of the state of the Society in the Australian Meetings and of the almost insuperable difficulties of isolation, distance, and paucity of numbers. Dymond pointed out graphically the crippling effect of lack of contacts with fellow Quakers — contacts that English Friends took for granted.

> Look at our Yearly Meetings, we cannot imagine how it would be if we had not this annual opportunity of meeting together, for as iron sharpened iron, so doth the countenance of a man his friend. Fancy London Yearly Meeting swept away, then fancy the Meeting for Sufferings and all such institutions gone with it. Then sweep away all the Quarterly Meetings, but one, and that one perhaps only meeting annually. Then most of the Monthly Meetings. Then fancy Ackworth School gone, and then every private school to which we are accustomed to send our children. Next abolish all our Christian work organizations; and not only so but all such organizations as the British and Foreign Bible Society, Peace Society, Anti-Slavery Society, &c., and where would be the 'rising generation'? Should we be surprised if here and there we found deadness, some drooping spirits, hands that hang down, and feeble knees. But that is not all. Take away forty-nine out of every fifty of our members, and leave only one, and then take these, one out of every fifty, and scatter them abroad over a tract of country two thousand miles across, with only four or five meetings, about five hundred miles apart.[65]

He believed that the effect of this would be like taking the coals comprising a burning fire and scattering them all over the world. The surprising thing to Dymond was that after the scattering there were any coals left at all.

The deputation saw that the main difficulty was the distance separating Friends from each other, in the cities as well as in the outback, and therefore the lack of social contact so necessary for mutual encouragement and inspiration. From this also stemmed the lack of corporate concerns and the prosecution of any social or religious work. The deputation believed that young Friends, missing these things, had sought association with more active Christian bodies.

Some specific recommendations were made to Meetings, particularly to Melbourne Meeting, which was urged to assist the Ballarat Meeting by recognizing it as a Preparative Meeting and helping it with the building of a new Meeting House. It was also recommended that the Melbourne Meeting House should have an additional building for use in social and practical work. Young Friends needed special attention if their loyalty was to be retained.

Strong support was expressed for the moves to set up an Australian Yearly Meeting, to promote inter-Meeting contacts. The need for personal visitation from Friends in England and America was stressed as a means of developing a more confident ministry in Australian Meetings.

> The more we see of things in Australia the more we are convinced that, if our Society is to keep its footing, there must be a mission from other lands of qualified and faithful men and women to preach the unsearchable riches of Christ and to guide the energies of the various members into channels of usefulness and profit. We see repeated evidence that a church without a Gospel ministry, and with no ground of union in religious labour, cannot be maintained.[66]

The highest priority however, was to be given in establishing a Friends' School. Members of the deputation would have known the history of Melbourne Meeting's abortive attempt to establish a Friends' School in Melbourne. Their strong recommendations may therefore be taken as implying criticism of Melbourne Friends for their failure to back initiative with action or as expressing the hope that the deputation's support might inspire in them more faith and courage. It is important therefore when considering the significance of this recommendation to trace briefly the story of Melbourne's proposed school. There had already been five attempts in Hobart to set up a small Friends' school and for some time there had been considerable discussion about a school among members of Melbourne Meeting. In 1865 the idea surfaced in *The British Friend* in a letter written by a Melbourne Friend, Rachel Horsfall. She made a plea that some concerned Friend or Friends would come out to set up a school for children of Friends in Melbourne. The Minutes of Melbourne Monthly Meeting of 20 January 1867 show that members had opened up a discussion on the possibility of doing something to make a school possible. By the end of the year Neave was in Melbourne and in his diary[67] he recorded that the subject of an inter-colonial school was seen as of great importance to the scattered members of the Society. He also saw that the cost of such a school would be more than Melbourne Friends could manage and that therefore the liberal help of English Friends would be essential.

Early in 1868[68] Melbourne Friends formulated a definite proposal to English Friends. The capital costs of establishing a co-educational day and boarding school to serve the needs of children of Friends from all the Australian Meetings were estimated at £6,000. Income, based on a prediction of forty boarders and eighty day scholars, was given as £3,520.[69]

English Friends reacted cautiously to this proposal, believing that a more modest project would be more within the reach of Friends. There was also an expectation that Australian Friends should now be able to shoulder a greater share of financial responsibility. There was a hint of annoyance at the attitude apparent in a letter such as the following from a Melbourne Friend with its suggestion of a lack of sympathy on the part of English Friends.

> Friends here feel greatly their distance from the main body, which is accompanied (we think) by a lack of sympathy for us. Could you only make them believe that we were jet black, were inclined towards cannibalism, or had embraced the tenets of Hindooism, we think the sympathy would flow in a broad stream from your hearts and pockets; but, as we are not all that, you do not care about us; and yet we feel as much attached to the Society as when we lived in England or Ireland.[70]

The committee of Meeting for Sufferings, which was considering Melbourne's request, asked Melbourne Friends why they would not accept any state aid for the acquisition of land, for example. They replied that there was no unanimity on the question of acceptance of state aid. In any case, they said, they felt that such acceptance would imply joining the state system of education and therefore running the risk of interference.

Meeting for Sufferings turned down the request for aid,

but pointed out that Ackworth School had agreed to accept children of non-resident Friends and sending children to board at Ackworth might be cheaper than setting up a separate school in the colonies. At the same time it was admitted that this was perhaps unrealistic, since it was unlikely that Australian Friends would want to send their children so far away to school in England.[71]

By the time the deputation arrived in Melbourne, the scheme for a school had been shelved. A Minute of Melbourne Monthly Meeting of 14 May 1871 resolved that no further action on a school should be taken for the present, in view of the growth of the state school system and the likelihood that there would not be sufficient children of Friends to make the enterprise viable. William Beck, a member of the deputation, was critical of this faintness of spirit. "Their strength", he said, "is to sit still."[72]

Their experience in Australia convinced members of the deputation of the vital importance of a school. They considered that a generation had been lost to Friends because there was no Friends' school. When the report of the deputation was presented to Yearly Meeting there was general support for the idea of a school and for financial support to be given, though some speakers stressed the need for Australian Meetings to stand on their own and not to be propped up from England.

The Minute of London Yearly Meeting expressed support for the establishment of a school in Melbourne, and if a suitable Friend should offer for service in such a school, London Yearly Meeting agreed to assist him in that service.

J. J. Dymond saw in the weakness of the Society in Australia a judgment on Friends for burying truth in a napkin, or as Dymond put it, for allowing, through unfaithfulness and apathy, the light to be hidden under a bushel. "Does it not appear", he asked, "as though God were righteously taking away the kingdom from us and giving it to others, who shall bring forth the fruits thereof?"[73]

Members of the Australian deputation saw it as a question of survival. They also saw education as a means to survival.

Ten
Towards an Australian Quakerism
1875-1901

Progress towards an Australian Quakerism was determined by the interaction of two factors — by the influence, advice and help of London Yearly Meeting, and by the willingness, sometimes reluctant, of Australian Quakers to listen and move towards a more mature independence. The Australian deputation was clear that the time had come for Australian Meetings to consider forming an Australian Yearly Meeting. The Australian Meetings however, were not yet of this mind. Indeed their very weakness and diffidence might well have made too early an acceptance of this advice a mistake. It was clear that in 1875 the Meetings did not feel ready to take responsibility. They had still to grow into it.

The Role of English Friends

In the earlier part of the nineteenth century, when the colonies were being settled by an increasing number of Quakers from English and Irish Meetings, London Yearly Meeting seemed almost unaware of what was happening. It was the visits of Backhouse and Walker and later of Lindsey and Mackie which brought home to English Friends that they had a responsibility to help their distant members.

Care of distant Friends was given over to the Continental Committee which held an umbrella-like responsibility for all Friends living outside England. It was not until 1904 that Australia ceased to be classified with the Continent of Europe and merited its own "Committee for Australian Affairs".

The key figure in helping Australian Friends to develop a measure of self-confidence and to move towards an Australian Quakerism was Edwin R. Ransome, the convenor of the Continental Committee. He was regarded by Australian Friends as a confidant — and as a court of appeal. Whenever an Australian Friend had a problem, Ransome seemed to be the one whose judgment was sought and advice heeded. Here again Australian Meetings had not yet built up sufficient strength for such advice to be sought in Australia. Yet in giving advice Ransome tried to make it clear that the decision must be seen to be made in Australia and not thought to be dictated in England. But, having been asked, he did not sidestep giving whatever advice he felt might be helpful.

Thus to one malcontent in Queensland who had written a confused and rambling hate-letter against a Queensland Friends' family and asked for a doctrinal pronouncement from Ransome, the reply was given, but not before Ransome had taken good care to receive a briefing from any English Friends known to have visited Queensland.

> The only way to make all men act exactly alike is to deprive them of freedom of conscience and compel them to act on the convictions of one spiritual director. This is the papal system and the reverse of the Society of Friends. ... Whilst not doubting thy sincerity of purpose we must remind thee that no human judgment is infallible and that by showing a criticizing spirit thou may be doing quite as much to hinder the work of Christ in the hearts of men as those whom thou condemns.[1]

The lack of any Quarterly Meeting in Australia meant that there was no superior body to which a Monthly Meeting or a member could appeal for guidance, except to London Yearly Meeting — or to Ransome. Melbourne Monthly Meeting, for example, was divided on the question of the use of the Meeting House for purposes other than for those of Friends. The point at issue was whether permission should be granted to a member of the Meeting, a keen worker for women's suffrage, to hold a women's suffragette meeting in the Meeting House. A majority of members favoured granting permission, but a small minority maintained objection, claiming that by the local Government Act of 1890, Section 246, the Meeting House was exempt from rates on the condition that it was used exclusively for public worship. The real reason for members to withhold permission was rather more likely to have been a prejudice against giving votes to women. Ransome discussed the problem with the Continental Committee and the advice given was that, since women's suffrage was regarded as a political matter, permission should not be given unless there was unanimity in the Meeting. Ransome gave also a more liberal interpretation of the phrase "exclusively for public worship", by indicating that social gatherings might be regarded as an extension of worship.

It was to Ransome that reports were made on the condition of Sydney Meeting and in 1886 it became clear to him that the time had come when recognition of Sydney Meeting should be recommended to London Yearly Meeting by the Continental Committee. Two Friends who had recently visited Sydney, Isaac Sharp and Rufus King, spoke warmly in support of recognition. In London Yearly Meeting 1887 recognition was finally given.

Ransome's standing in the eyes of Sydney members is indicated by the variety of requests made to him — for library books for the Adult School, for hospitality to Sydney Friends visiting England, for help to indigent Friends in Sydney Meeting and for adjudication in a dispute which had reappeared between Alfred Allen and some members of the Meeting. When answering a member's claim that one of the contending parties should be disowned, Ransome wisely answered of parties A and B that it was "six of one and half a dozen of the other", and of A he commented: "As far as I am able to gather from his own many pages of notes, he seemed to imply that he is the only one who is right. Can this really be the case?"[2]

Sydney Meeting had need of such advice. Ransome's influence contributed to the resolution of differences and the growth of a much healthier spiritual condition in this Meeting.

Ransome's major contribution, however, was to the building of a partnership with Australian Friends in the establishment and development of a Friends' School in Hobart.[3] Though he never visited Australia, Ransome maintained an unbroken correspondence with J. Francis Mather in Hobart concerning the affairs of the School until his death in 1910. An explanation which Ransome gave to an English Friend applying for a position on the staff of the school in Hobart aptly sums up what he conceived his role to be. In a letter to J.B. Mather, chairman of the School Committee in Hobart, he reported what he had told this Friend. "I told him all I could and advised him to write either to Samuel Clemes or to the secretary of your committee, informing him that the School was entirely under your care and management. . . . If there is anything we can do in this matter, let us know and we will do our best."[4]

Ransome demonstrated great wisdom in his ability to respond to the fluctuating needs of Australian Friends, sometimes for an experienced Friend to lean upon for guidance, sometimes for a reminder that the goal was independence. He would give advice, but avoid direction. He accepted the need for patient care, but sought to wean Australian Friends of dependence and reliance upon English Friends.

Edwin Ransome (1823-1910), correspondent for London Yearly Meeting with Australian Friends and in particular with J.F. Mather in connection with the foundation and development of The Friends' School, Hobart.

Joseph Francis Mather (1844-1925), Chairman of the Committee of Australian Friends for The Friends' School, Hobart, from 1890 to 1923.

    Complementary to Ransome's influence was the succession of Friends "travelling under concern" during the last quarter of the nineteenth century. This was a further demonstration of London Yearly Meeting's anxiety about the future of Australian Meetings. These visits, some of them for extended periods, did much to strengthen the spiritual life of the Australian Meetings, to increase their confidence, and to make them more willing to play an active role in the community. The encouragement given by the presence of English Friends revived amongst Australian members a sense of belonging to London Yearly Meeting. They had yet to gain sufficient confidence to enable them to stand on a footing of equality with the parent meeting.

    The increased importance given by English and American

Friends to visiting Australian Meetings in the last quarter of
the nineteenth century is demonstrated by comparing this
quarter with previous decades.[5]

The Friends coming out to Australia to visit and encourage
Australian Friends functioned as travelling ministers did
amongst English Meetings, where Friends with leisure offered
themselves for the service of visiting other Meetings in
England and Ireland and overseas. Until the eighties such
visits to Australia were infrequent, but with the improvement
in sea transport, steam replacing wind as the source of power,
the number of travelling Friends increased, though the length
of stay generally was shorter than that of what might be
called the classic journeys of Backhouse and Walker, Lindsey
and Mackie — and then Sharp and Neave.

American Friends also began to show an interest in Australian Friends. The first of these was Robert Douglas who was
in Australia in 1877 and 1878. His interest in coming can be
traced to his meeting with Walter Robson in America and
then later to a visit with Robson in his home in England.
Robson recorded this in his diary[6] and added that when
Douglas placed his concern before his Meeting in Richmond,
Indiana, on 25 September 1877 "he spoke of being at my
house, talking to me about Australia and how that conversation (my Tenie will remember it) settled the concern in his
mind". "Tenie" was Robson's wife, Christina, a daughter of
Dr Cox, New South Wales.

Other American Friends followed Douglas — Rufus King
and Alpheus White in 1885, Samuel Morris and Jonathan
Rhoads in 1892. All these came with travelling minutes from
their Meetings, but there was one American Friend whose
visit brought some complications. Hannah Hall came from the
group of American Friends which, having broken away from
the main body in America, was not recognized by London
Yearly Meeting. During her visit to Hobart she gained the
support of some Friends, including James Backhouse Cotton,
who then accompanied her on her self-appointed mission to
other Meetings. Finally the Hobart Meeting felt it necessary
to minute the following. "We think it right to inform Melbourne Monthly Meeting that James Backhouse Cotton is
now travelling with Hannah Hall (from America) holding

religious meetings and, as we understand, may visit Victoria. James Backhouse Cotton has not communicated with this meeting on the subject and is not liberated for this service, neither have we unity with it."[7] The other five American Friends entered upon their visits with the intention, like English Friends, of assuring Australian Friends that, though isolated, they were not forgotten.

Samuel Morris and Jonathan Rhoads visited Friends in their homes, especially in isolated localities. In a report to Meeting for Sufferings, London, they remarked:

> In all the little communities of Friends we found those who were strongly attached to the principles of Friends and endeavouring to promote wider knowledge of them. It was very encouraging also to observe in many instances that where our views had come to be understood, they met with a response from the more thoughtful class among other professing Christians, while we could but rejoice to find the good esteem in which Friends were generally held throughout the Australian colonies.[8]

They also noted a growing desire for "some closer bond of church union than at present seems practicable".

Of the English Friends Joseph Neave was perhaps the most significant, not only because he remained on the Australian scene for over forty years, travelling as a minister either on his own or accompanying another Friend, but because of the nature and quality of his service. Australian Friends had at various times voiced to London Yearly Meeting their need for Friends who could live amongst them and provide continuing pastoral care and ministry. Neave was such a Friend.

Fortunately for the future of the Sydney Meeting Neave himself, like Walker and Mackie, found a personal reason for return to Australia. Though the pull to remain in England was strong, he felt, like Walker, that there was "nothing to be feared as much as taking himself out of the Lord's hands".[9] This intuition was strengthened by his decision to marry Helen Davy, daughter of Abraham Davy. Neave had spent 1870 in New Zealand, returned to Australia in 1871 and then to England in time for London Yearly Meeting in 1872. Helen Davy followed him and they were married at Saffron Walden on 12 September 1872. They returned to Australia at the end of 1876 and settled in Sydney.

Though he was technically an English Friend travelling in the ministry, for he retained his membership of his English Monthly Meeting, Woodbridge, he was also, geographically, an Australian Friend. Reference has already been made to his first journeys in Australia. His journeys amongst Australian Friends on his return to Australia covered places as far apart as Perth and Rockhampton. The spirit in which he undertook this service is illustrated in the following extract from his report to London Yearly Meeting in 1888 after a visit to Queensland.

> It was also my privilege, whilst in Queensland, to visit among families and individuals living far away from Meeting, and from one another, and I travelled in some instances 150 miles or 200 to get to them. I once walked two days' journey from the railway to two dear Irish Friends, sleeping at night in the heart of the bush with some men who were camping out. One thing I much regret, that there are probably far more that I have never reached, and perhaps more still that I have never heard of.[10]

Sometimes his mission was solitary, sometimes in company with another Friend, as with Isaac Sharp in 1881-82, with Rufus King in 1885, and with Alfred Wright in 1891 to New Zealand and the eastern states. In 1899 when he returned his certificate to London Yearly Meeting, a certificate which had been issued in 1876, he had been nine times to Victoria, six to Queensland, four to Tasmania, three to South Australia and to New Zealand, and twice to Western Australia.

But he also brought a wider dimension to his role, for he continued to serve the world community of Friends by accepting what he felt to be a clear call to service overseas. Neave was in Hobart in 1890 at a time when Samuel Clemes, the first headmaster of The Friends' School, was taken seriously ill and was in need of nursing day and night. Neave offered to take his turn with the night nursing and it was while he was watching by Clemes' bedside that he declared he had a "divine visitation", and heard the words, "Thou must go to Russia".[11] He had no idea why or how he should fulfil this strange vision.

In 1891 however, while accompanying Alfred Wright on a visit to New Zealand, he received a letter from England telling him that a friend had died leaving him three hundred pounds. This seemed to underline his concern to go to Russia, for he now had the means to travel to London to test that concern with London Yearly Meeting. The reason too was becoming clear. Neave had heard of the sufferings of a group of Russian religious dissenters, called the Stundists, who had been exiled to Siberia for their refusal to accept the authority of the Russian Orthodox Church. London Yearly Meeting backed his concern and another Friend, John Bellows,[12] offered himself as a companion to Neave. Their incredible journey, undertaken without initial contacts inside Russia and without knowledge of the language, could be regarded either as an act of sheer madness or as a sublime leap of faith. They went, they obtained the consent of the Tsar to visit the Stundists and agreed to report back to him. So they crossed the vast tracts of desolate land to the Transcaucasus in the depths of winter, carried a message of love and hope to the exiled Stundists, and on return assured the Tsar that the Stundists were no political dissidents but suffering for their will to serve God in their own way. The journey was not without some positive effect, for soon after the two Quakers returned to England in 1893, they heard that acute persecution of the Stundists had ceased.

In 1899 Melbourne Annual Meeting recorded of Neave that "no man has laboured as long and as devotedly as he". By his travels, by his constant reporting on these to English Friends and by his active participation in the affairs of Australian Meetings, he did more, perhaps, than any other Friend, English or Australian, to carry forward the pioneering work of Backhouse and Walker.

The record of the contribution made to Australian Quakerism by English Quakers travelling in the ministry would not be complete without special reference to Isaac Sharp who, at seventy-one, spent two years in Australia, visiting isolated Friends and encouraging Friends' Meetings. Neave was his constant companion. For Sharp, as for Ulysses, it was never too late "to smite the sounding furrow". For over fifty years he carried the Quaker message around the globe. At the age of seventy-one his circuit included not only Australia, but Africa, Madagascar, California, and Mexico. At the age of eighty-four he was granted a certificate of service by London

Yearly Meeting for service in France, Syria, Constantinople, India, Japan, and America. He was taken ill at first base, Paris. "They want to bury me before I am dead," he declared to his doctor, "but I am not going to die yet." He considered it right however to get the blessing of London Yearly Meeting confirmed before proceeding further and so he returned to face the Meeting of Ministers and Overseers in London. Beginning his address with the words, "tremulous and feeble I stand before you", he pleaded his case before his peers, concluding with the following challenge:

> Among other things it has been said, "He would be a bold man who would go with me as companion.... Friends, rather than be delayed for want of a companion, I would go forth alone. The Lord who gave me a shield of faith, and not a very small one, would give me a girdle too, and place a helmet upon my head, and then would lead me forth and give me in measure to realise the words, "The Father is with me". You are about to enter the chamber of the King. May He give you a judgment there, and whatever the outcome, it is my earnest desire the decision may be to the honour of the Father and to the glory of Christ.[13]

He won the battle and, "although a pensioner of health, liable to curtailment at any moment", he continued on his journey to Vienna and Constantinople. Syria denied him entry because of an outbreak of cholera and so he substituted China via Japan, and California. He had felt a particular call to encourage the missionaries working in Chungking and so he undertook the dangerous five-weeks' upstream voyage on the Yang-tse (counting fifty wrecks on the way) and back, then home via America. But after two weeks he was off to Norway at eighty-eight, and at eighty-nine he couldn't rest until he had fulfilled the promise he made in his original certificate. So to Syria he went. At ninety he was at rest, having "girdled the earth in the service of love".

If Quakers in Australia were given to canonization, Neave and Sharp would rate a nomination alongside Backhouse and Walker, Lindsey and Mackie. This remarkable succession of Quaker travelling ministers, who felt drawn to visit their fellow-Quakers overseas, kept Quakerism afloat in the Australian colonies at a time when it could have easily gone under.

Out of the reports of these visiting Friends English Friends were able to form a much more accurate and intimate picture of the problems of Australian Friends. They came to realize the effects of isolation on their distant "brethren", not only the isolation of lonely settlement, but isolation from "the companionship of the home circle and having little religious association with our own people", as one writer expressed it in *The Friend* in 1881. "Those of us who have been in similar circumstances can feel for you when with a sense of depression coming on the mind, you may be ready to faint by the way, inclined almost to exclaim, 'No man cares for my soul'."[14] William Jones, writing about his visit to Australia in *The Friend*, urged English Friends to send copies of *The Friend* to isolated Friends in the colonies. He quoted one letter which he had received.

> Only those who experience it can realise what it is to be cut off from all connection with the Society we held dear in our lifetime. We have mixed with nearly all Christian denominations and are tired out with all. We long and wonder will we ever be again joined to Friends in the worship of Him who is seeking those who worship Him in Spirit and in Truth: the longer I live the more my soul longs for it. *The Friend* you send us seems to be the only connecting link left between us and the Society we feel ourselves bound to with ties that cannot be broken.[15]

Returning Friends also endeavoured to impress on members of their Meetings some concept of what "distance" meant on the Australian scale and therefore how difficult it was for Australian Friends to gather in a central place for a Yearly Meeting as Friends did in London.

To bring home this fact of distance one Friend, using London to John o' Groats as a unit of distance, showed graphically on a map of Australia that if a Yearly Meeting were held in Melbourne, Rockhampton members would have to travel three units, Brisbane two, Adelaide and Sydney one each. Another Friend also tried to convince the London Yearly Meeting of 1896 of this fact of distance. "Taking London" he said, "to represent Adelaide, Geneva might stand for Melbourne, Berlin for Sydney, Stockholm for Brisbane, St. Petersburg for Rockhampton."[16]

In 1892 Sayce and Wright returned from Australia with the strong feeling that in order to keep in touch with Friends in the colonies frequent visits should be made. They said it was the responsibility of London as the parent Yearly Meeting to look after Friends in Australia.

One of the most perceptive visitors was Henrietta Brown, who spent a considerable time amongst Australian Friends at the turn of the century. She saw clearly the difficulties early Quaker settlers had to contend with. "Some had come in search of health; many because they had been unsuccessful at home; others in middle life because there were better prospects for their children. . . . With such a scattered population it was not possible to win converts to our belief."[17] She understood therefore why, with the lack of Friends of leisure and experience "to vitalize Meetings and shepherd the flock", so many, not strong adherents in the first place, had joined with other Christian communities or in indifference had done nothing to hand on Quakerism to their children.

Neave, like Henrietta Brown, saw that some of the difficulties the Society of Friends had to contend with stemmed from the circumstances in which the first Friend migrants found themselves — both the circumstances surrounding their decision to migrate and the circumstances in which they felt themselves trapped in the country of adoption. "Most had come with a desire to improve their outward circumstances and some to get gold. Far the greater number were sadly disappointed and this caused a spiritual restlessness and unsettlement that was not helpful to the spiritual life."[18] Life in the new lands, Neave agreed, was good, free and independent, but indifference to authority and self-assertiveness were characteristics that were injurious to the general good.

That these visits by members of London Yearly Meeting and American Friends were appreciated is clear. William Sayce, who was a visiting Friend in 1891, was convinced that, though they had been at great expense to London Yearly Meeting, they had been most worthwhile. Without them he was sure that many more would have drifted from the Society. They had done much to bind the separate Meetings together and to promote what he called "aggressive" action by Meetings. By this he meant outgoing activities such as the establishment of the Friends' School in Hobart and of the Adult School in Sydney. He also underlined the difficulties of Australian Friends, who, because of lack of numbers, did not enjoy the frequent social contacts and spiritual stimulus provided by Quarterly and Yearly Meetings.

By the mid-eighteen-nineties there was a growing sensitivity in London Yearly Meeting to the needs of members in the Australian colonies. This groundswell of perception came to a head at the Yearly Meeting in London in 1898. The Continental Committee had initiated discussion by calling attention to the fact that it was some time since London Yearly Meeting had sent out any Friends to Australia. Between the prodding reminder and the eventual Minute came a long and thorough review of the situation of the Australian Meetings and of London Yearly Meeting's responsibility to help them. The Minute read: "Should the way open in the Lord's ordering for a prolonged visit to our friends in Australasia on the part of well-concerned friends, it would rejoice our hearts".[19] The editorial in *The Friend* immediately following this Yearly Meeting called the discussion "one of the most heart-stirring episodes during the whole of the sittings and showed the business-like capacity of English Friends to deal with practical subjects".[20] Diagnosis and remedy were both offered.

Diagnosis was directed to the state of Australian society as well as to the condition of the Society of Friends in Australia. J. B. Hodgkin, who visited Australia with his half-brother, William, in 1867, said that what struck him most was its godlessness. He added that he did not mean "open, flagrant sin, though there was plenty of that, but the whole of life moved on as if there were no God and no eternity".[21] Equating godlessness with heathenism, Hodgkin advocated a Friends' mission to help Australian Friends fight the particular Australian brand of heathenism.

The diagnosis of the condition of Australian Friends noted the isolation, the absence of religious fellowship, the depressed spirit of many who were sorry they had ever left England, and the lack of Friends with the leisure and the experience to "shepherd" the weakling flock.

As for the remedy, William Sayce believed that London Yearly Meeting should send Friends, not for a visit of a few weeks or months, but perhaps for periods of some years.

Friends in Australia, he said, were so involved in the business of making a living that there were few able to "nurse" other members of the Society. One notable exception was Neave.[22]

William Jones agreed that there was a need for Friends to be able to go without the restraints imposed by time — someone around whom Friends could rally, added Ransome. From such statements as these came the final Minute which asked the Continental Committee to confer with the Home Mission Committee concerning the possibility of Australian Friends being helped by the Friends Foreign Mission Association. "Some Friends", Thomas Pumphrey suggested, "who were not physically suited to service in India might be fitted for another in Australia, if they felt a call thither."[23]

The question remained, however, whether the patient would accept the diagnosis or the remedy. There had been signs of growing self-confidence and of the patient sitting up and attempting an independent self-diagnosis. Before the evidence for this is considered, it is interesting to note the reaction of some Australian Friends to the diagnosis and remedy decided twelve thousand miles away in the absence of the patient. Two who reacted strongly against the London Minute were J. F. Mather and Samuel Clemes. They questioned the value of a succession of visits by English Friends, coming in for a few weeks and then moving on, without being able to give more than cursory help. In this they agreed in part with the diagnosis. The remedy however they saw in London Yearly Meeting providing financial backing for concerned Australian Friends to carry out their own inter-visitation. This, in itself, was a welcome indication of the emergence of an Australian "do-it-ourselves" attitude.[24] It could be seen even as a healthy reaction against "imperial" patronage, or as the somewhat petulant outburst of an adolescent who is now sensitive to decisions being made about his future without his being consulted.

The role of London Yearly Meeting during the last quarter of the nineteenth century had been rather that of an anxious parent, deeply concerned about the health and future of a distant offspring. Yet, behind the anxiety lay a continuing desire for that offspring to give some signs of a willingness to take responsibility for its own future. For this reason it did not cease to hope that Australian Meetings would agree to unite and form their own Yearly Meeting. There were beginning to be some encouraging signs.

Growing Points for the Development of an Australian Identity

The Australian deputation of 1875, while it made clear its support for the formation as soon as possible of an Australian Yearly Meeting, gave its top priority to the establishment of a Friends' School in one of the colonies.

William Beck,[25] a member of the Australian deputation, had been critical of the faint-heartedness of Australian Friends in surrendering too easily to the difficulties of establishing a school. London Yearly Meeting was willing to let the possibility lie open in accordance with the deputation's recommendation that a school should be set up in Melbourne. Yearly Meeting went so far as to canvas English Meetings for a suitable Friend who might feel called to undertake service as headmaster in the spirit of a missionary. Melbourne Friends soft-pedalled the idea of a school, because of lack of unity amongst members, now that a state school system appeared to be offering suitable, though secular, education. It was felt that the home, not the school, should be responsible for religious education.

And then the initiative came from another Meeting, Hobart. The main mover in this was Joseph Benson Mather, a son of Robert Mather and one of the first "convinced" Friends to join the Hobart Meeting. J. B. Mather was well-known in Hobart for his interest in education. He began a night school for boys in Hobart and he taught there twice a week. He was a keen supporter of the Ragged School and was appointed by the government to be Honorary Secretary of the Boys' Training School at the Cascades. Mather had been very disturbed by the government's proposal for a Militia Bill,[26] which would have involved the training of all schoolboys over the age of twelve as cadets, and he had headed a deputation to the Minister for Defence to state Friends' total opposition to such a move. Added to this fear of schools coming under the influence of the military authorites was the increasing concern of Friends at the effects of a purely secular education on their children. They wanted neither sectarian nor secular education but a non-sectarian religious component such as had been promoted by the British and Foreign Schools' Society in what were known as the Lancastrian schools.[27] The Hobart Town High School, of which G. W. Walker had been one of the founders in 1850, had been run firmly on non-sectarian principles, but in 1885 it was taken over by the Anglican Christ College. Those parents who were opposed to the increase of influence of the established Church were likely to be interested in an alternative school run on non-sectarian principles.

Friends had already become known in Hobart for their interest in education. Attempts to set up a school had been short-lived, but they served to demonstrate that a school designed only for the children of Friends was not a viable proposition, because of the limited number of Friends' children. Thus the idea of a school organized by Friends for the education of their children but open to children of non-Friends sympathetic to Friends' aims of education gradually came to be seen as the only way to ensure viability.

When therefore the request came to London Yearly Meeting from a Hobart Committee for help in setting up a school, the factors which swung the decision of London Yearly Meeting in favour of a school in Hobart were: first, the evidence of strength of purpose in the Hobart Committee and the willingness of the Committee to guarantee meeting a significant proportion of the costs; and second, the support given to the new project by a group of Australian Friends who happened to be in London in 1886 at the time when decisions were to be made by London Yearly Meeting. The interesting point here is that four members of this group were Victorian Friends. The Continental Committee sought their advice about the change of location of the school from Melbourne to Hobart. John Horsfall, Clerk of Melbourne Monthly Meeting, William Benson, son-in-law of J. B. Mather, Edward Sayce, who had been the leading figure in previous negotiations for a school in Melbourne, and Octavius Beale, son of Margaret Beale who had conducted one of the schools

N. H. Propsting

Robert Mather

Henry Propsting

Thomas B. Mather

Joseph Benson Mather (Chairman)

J. Francis Mather (Secretary)

William May

William Benson

John Pierce

The first Committee of The Friends' School, Hobart, 1886.

in Hobart before settling in Melbourne, all agreed that if Hobart was willing to accept responsibility, a school in Hobart should be supported. This disinterested opinion given by Melbourne Friends did much to reassure Hobart members who recognized that Melbourne was the more central site for a school to serve all Australian Meetings. The reason for the selection of Hobart was not only the reasons given above. John Horsfall saw that there was another important reason. His view was that Hobart was now the right location because of the number of families "well-disposed towards our religious community".[28]

The favourable disposition of the Hobart community to the Society of Friends and the immediate support given to the school must be credited to the influence of Backhouse and Walker who had made a profound impression in Tasmania. The continuing public confidence was due to the Backhouse and Walker tradition exemplified in Tasmanian Friends, such as J. B. Mather and his son, J. Francis Mather, Francis Cotton, and Henry Propsting. The Australian Deputation visiting Hobart sensed the respect and influence these men had in the Tasmanian community.

The support of the non-Friend community was remarkably demonstrated in the first year of the school's existence by the growth in numbers from thirty-three at the commencement of the year to seventy-five at its close. A further example was the practical financial help given by the Baptist Church. When the School quickly outgrew its initial premises in Warwick Street and was seeking more adequate accommodation, the Baptist Church offered a loan of £4,000 to enable the School to move to more spacious premises in Commercial Road, North Hobart in 1889.

The School also was a significant indicator of a growing confidence amongst a group of Australian Friends. This in turn generated an influx of support from English Friends, both in money and in personal involvement. Thus a partnership in education was established which was to last until 1923 when control of the School was handed over to an Australian Committee of Friends. Until then, while London insisted that control was really vested in Hobart, the School technically was the responsibility of London Yearly Meeting.

The story of this partnership is told in some detail in *The Rose and the Waratah*.²⁹ What is important in the context of the development of Australian Quakerism is to analyze what contribution the School made to this development, at least up to the time of the establishment of an Australian General Meeting in 1902.

The School generated amongst English Friends a much greater awareness of Australian Friends and a determination to see that this visible evidence of a Quaker presence in Australia was given their full support. At each Yearly Meeting the annual report and accounts of the School were not only tabled but drew forth comments and offers of practical support. The Yearly Meeting of 1891 is a typical example.

When the report of the school's progress was presented, Edwin Ransome, who was the clerk of the committee responsible for contact with the school, spoke in glowing terms of the success of the school and of the work of the Hobart Committee, on which had now devolved the heavy responsibility of "carrying on this School for the good of Friends in the Southern Hemisphere".³⁰ Then he called upon Friends to show "metallic" sympathy by raising two

"Hobartville", 23 Commercial Road, North Hobart, site of The Friends' School in 1889, when it was transferred from Warwick Street, where it had opened in January 1887.

Samuel Clemes, first headmaster of The Friends' School, Hobart, 1887-1900.

thousand pounds to pay off a bank overdraft and to finance further necessary accommodation. He also appealed for English Friends to take over the £4,000 mortgage which the Baptist Church had made available. He hoped that English Friends would charge a lower rate of interest and thus reduce the School's annual expenditure. The School, he now assured them, was a safe investment. Ransome's appeal was answered immediately from the floor when John Hodgkin offered to take over the mortgage. Other speakers underlined the view that the School was the means whereby the Society of Friends had a recognized presence, which until then it had lacked, in the colonies. "Friends are not even known in some places, and the influence of their principles is not felt. The School, by bringing Friends together, tends to bind and strengthen our Society and will help it take its right place in the Commonwealth."[31]

There were also articles in *The British Friend* confirming the rightness of the decision by London Yearly Meeting to support the School. One article was a reprint of a report from the *Hobart Mercury* testifying to the success of the School, as judged by a non-Friend observer. What apparently appealed had been the situation of the new premises in Commercial Road, the spacious classrooms, the concern for the health of the boarders, the modern methods of teaching, progressive ideas on curriculum, in particular the stress on scientific and technical education[32] and the then dangerously modern practice of co-education. A *Mercury* reporter was clearly intent on assuring those who regarded co-education as a dangerous experiment that the School had taken every precaution: "Access may be had to the ground by two separate entrances, one on the west and one on the east side: and as the boys and girls enter by different roads and have separate playgrounds, any fears that prejudiced parents may have against a mixed school are entirely removed".[33]

The first headmaster, Samuel Clemes, was well in advance of contemporaries in his ideas on education. He insisted that public examinations were not to dominate methods or curriculum, that each student should strive, not to be *the* best in competition with other members of the class, but to *make the best use* of the abilities he had been blessed with.

> If we consider the main purpose of education to be a cramming into the mind of a child of a certain number of facts, which facts are to be elicited by appropriate questioning periodically then we shall consider these results all important, and count that those who came out top in each list are the successful ones, and those near the bottom will be reckoned as failures. But if we consider education rather as a training in the best possible use of the faculties with

which our Heavenly Father has gifted us, and training in the use of self-education, if we recognize that schooldays are only part of education, then we shall form a very different estimate. We shall not attempt a comparison as between our own children and others so much, as we shall be anxious that they shall, each according to his measure, be doing honest work, and learning about everything to glorify God by the diligent and prayerful use of the means He has placed at their disposal.[34]

Clemes was outspoken — and therefore attracted the headlines of the media of the day — on the false lure of prizes and marks, on the bad effects of homework on health, on the claims of the sciences for a place in a curriculum too long dominated by the classics, on the growing need to educate for leisure, and on the importance of the neglected areas of physical and technical education.

The success of the School in establishing a reputation as an educational institution, as well as a specifically Friends' School, did much to strengthen the confidence of Friends, who began to feel for the first time that they had some tangible contribution to make to the community. This note of confidence can be sensed, for example, in statements on school progress and policy made by the chairman of the School Committee, J. Francis Mather. He held strongly to the belief that the welfare of the Society of Friends would largely depend on the success of the School, but he also had a very clear vision of the School as the main channel by which Friends could make their influence felt in the community.

> Judging from the progress of this school, and what is said of it by people in Australasia, the extension of such a system of education will be gladly welcomed because people appear to be recognizing that institutions in which the Friend cult has free course will supply what the Australian Commonwealth is needing; for thoughtful people everywhere are increasingly feeling the need of something more in school education than the training of the intellect. There seems to be demanded not only the building of moral character, but also the laying of the foundation of that inwardness and spirituality of religion, that steadiness of judgment, that true republican feeling which abolishes class feeling and exclusiveness, that refined simplicity of life, and that right estimate of the value of time which has characterized the typical Friends.[35]

English Friends, who came out to Australia after the

School had been established, expressed great enthusiasm for the School and were impressed both by its standing in the community and by its value to the Society of Friends. Alfred Wright, one of the members of the 1875 deputation, who returned to Australia in 1890 for a second visit, recorded his observations on the value of the School to the Society. "But the great improvement I found was in the new 'High School' for children of Friends in Australasia and which I believe was doing more for the permanent help of the Society of Friends in the colonies than anything else that could have been instituted."[36] Edwin Ransome published in *The Friend* a letter he had received from Carl Schardt who had recently visited Tasmania. Ransome felt that this Friend's views were particularly worth publicizing amongst Friends because Schardt was himself a former educator and because he represented a leading Frankfurt newspaper and could therefore be regarded as an independent observer.

> As a centre and rallying point for the Society of Friends in Australasia, the school at Hobart is of greater importance still. Our meetings out here are so widely scattered, the means of intercourse so few, the disintegrating influences at work, even in this colony, are so powerful, that a school of this kind would have to be founded if it did not exist, in order to keep the Society together. Here our young Friends from all the Australasian colonies may meet now in their schooldays, and for months together, during the age when friendships are formed for life. . . I confess that my own views about the school have been considerably modified during our stay here. I could now see with my own eyes what kind of work was carried on, and that the school not only met a local want, but filled an important place in the Society at large.[37]

Frederick Mackie, who with his wife Rachel set up a school in Hobart in 1856, had already seen the school as a possible means of serving the needs of Friends in other Australian Meetings as well as in Hobart. "I had rather hoped", he wrote to James Backhouse "to have had children from the other colonies, but the expense of transit is . . . sufficient to prevent what I should like to see accomplished, an efficient educational establishment for Friends, where the children of the differing colonies might meet. However this may be, I am quite satisfied in making this humble attempt."[38]

The School clearly appeared to satisfy Friends that it provided a focus for Australian Friends and a potential means of arresting the drift of the young away from the Society. These two problems of isolation and drift had been the main topics of discussion when the four visiting Friends from Victoria met with English Friends in the new Westminster Meeting House on 2 October 1885. At this meeting William Benson had made two very pertinent observations, the first concerning the isolation of Friends' Meetings from each other, and second, the drift of their young people away from the Society because of the lack of a central educational establishment which could hold them together and train them in Friends' principles.[39]

Friends now for the first time had a centre. Though the proportion of Friends' children to non-Friends in the day school was at no time greater than ten per cent, the proportion of Friends' boarders for the years 1887–1900 was much higher at sixty per cent. These came from all the States, except Western Australia, and from New Zealand. By the end of the nineteenth century any earlier misgivings about the School being too distant from Friends' Meetings in other States seem to have been dissipated. The School increasingly became accepted as "our" school, that is, as belonging to Australian and not merely to Hobart Friends. Though located in Hobart, it was seen as an Australian Friends' School.

This concept of the School as an Australian Friends' School was further underlined by the constitution of the School Committee, which was revised in 1903, following the first Australian General Meeting in 1902, to include members from Sydney, Melbourne, and Adelaide as well as Hobart. London Yearly Meeting still retained a presence by appointing the School's trustees, of whom ten were English Friends. This partnership with London Yearly Meeting as the benign landlord and Australian General Meeting as tenants responsible through a Committee of Management for the running of the School, remained until 1923 when the trust deeds and control of the School were vested in the Australian General Meeting.

The School was the most positive public witness of Friends

to emerge in Australia in the nineteenth century. Through Samuel Clemes' enlightened and progressive leadership Friends were credited with considerable influence on education as innovators. They were also recognized as having made of their school a community in which a new spirit of co-operation between staff and students was evident. But the School was also seen as firmly linked with Friends' testimonies and it was therefore vulnerable to public opinion, should the School be too much in advance of generally accepted community attitudes.

The first example of this came with the Boer War at the end of the nineteenth century, when Friends felt that their Peace Testimony led them to try to counteract the public war fever surrounding the participation of Australian soldiers in the War. For this reason the School took no part in collecting contributions to the Patriotic Fund and when a public holiday was declared to celebrate the relief of Mafeking, the School refused to recognize it and continued normal work. Two teachers, members of the Society of Friends, when they found that the school flag had been flown to mark the relief of Ladysmith, promptly hauled it down. A report of this action reached Friends in England and led to the following comment:

> What a risk in excited times like those for a school containing over eighty per cent of non-Friends! What a lesson for those children some thirty years hence when they think over the days when they were not allowed to cheer in class for such a cause! Will they not say to themselves, how strongly those old Friends must have been opposed to war, if they could deliberately risk the popularity of the school for such a cause? May those who have the care of this school always be as valiant in the cause of Peace.[40]

An English Friend visiting the School in 1900 wrote to Ransome to tell him that the School had attracted unfavourable publicity because of such incidents. Its refusal to admit military authorities into the School grounds to run a cadet corps probably cost it some enrolments. Mather however saw the Peace Testimony as more than a negative opposition to war. He believed that the School had a responsibility to promote the principles of justice and brotherhood which would ultimately prevail and take away the occasion of war.

If, instead of forcing upon children a form of teaching which, speaking louder than words, implants in them the spirit of militarism, a great endeavour were made to instil the principles of justice and brotherhood, there would be a growing disposition to resort to arbitration as a means of settlement, and labour troubles would find a better method of adjustment than the present industrial warfare which entails so much waste and personal suffering.[41]

The Friends' School contributed significantly to the development of an Australian identity for Friends. The concern arose originally out of an awareness that the future of the Society in Australia was at stake. Education was seen as a means to survival. The School however became more than a means to survival. In one sense it rescued Friends from a preoccupation with survival and became a major channel for the expression of Quaker values and principles in the Australian community.

The Australian Friend, designated a "Religious, Literary and Miscellaneous Journal", appeared for the first time on 8 July 1887 as a quarterly, priced at nine pence a copy. It was no accident that the birthplace was Hobart, nor the year of birth the same as that of the School. Some of the most active and forward-looking Friends were behind the establishment both of the School and of the journal. Friends such as J. F. Mather, William Benson, and William May represented a new generation of Friends who believed deeply that Quakerism had a valuable contribution to make to Australian society and that the establishment of a School and a periodical Friends' paper were essential if that contribution was to be made.

William Benson, the first editor, came out to Australia in 1866 as a young man for health reasons with two other Friends, Charles and John Holdsworth. Neither of the Holdsworths remained in Australia. Charles returned to England and later succeeded Edwin Ransome as correspondent with J. F. Mather for affairs of The Friends' School in Hobart. John Holdsworth settled in New Zealand. Benson married Elizabeth Mather, daughter of J. B. Mather, in 1885 and settled in Hobart. His immediate interests became the newly established School and *The Australian Friend*. In 1890, for business reasons, he transferred to Melbourne and then in

1903 to Sydney. He filled the position of Clerk of both these Meetings and was Clerk of the first General Conference of Australian Friends held in Melbourne in 1888. He may with justice be regarded as one of the "founding fathers" of Australian Quakerism. William Benson saw the main function of the journal as preparing the ground for an Australian Annual Meeting of Friends.

> Union is strength, and if in ever so small a degree this little paper can take the place of the binding tie which knits together the weak and separate sticks into one firm bundle, it will have found a sphere of usefulness which will more than justify the attempt. One element to close union is lacking to Friends in these Colonies, namely, the general gathering of representatives from each Meeting in one Annual Assemblage. The value of such a gathering is incalculable — it is at once executive and legislative — it reviews the past and takes counsel for the future. It is the mouthpiece of the church to declare its judgment in all matters affecting public welfare, and it is the Court of Appeal before which all internal affairs are considered, and divergent views or practices brought into harmony.
>
> Only those who have been present at sittings of the London Yearly Meeting can fully appreciate its value or realize its controlling and strengthening power, which extends across the globe even to ourselves. A time will doubtless come for our Australian Meetings to unite periodically in such a gathering though at present it is thought impracticable. But perhaps this little paper may do somewhat toward removing the difficulties that now stand in the way, if by offering to all who desire it an opportunity of addressing their fellow members throughout the colonies, and by keeping all more fully informed than they now are as to what is doing amongst their distant brethren, it stimulates a keener interest in the welfare and proceedings of our Society, and lessens the sense of isolation in each Meeting.[42]

Benson believed that members should be kept informed of what was happening in Meetings in Australia and overseas, but he also wanted to cover the work of other Christian bodies. It is significant too that he was anxious to feature articles on the history of each Australian Meeting, thus helping to nurture a sense of an Australian Quaker identity. Although the editorship was in Hobart, correspondents were appointed in each Meeting.

Successive editors — William Benson, William May, J. Francis Mather — met with the usual problem of editors. At times, in spite of having correspondents in the other states, they despaired of getting contributions and began to question whether Australian Friends really took the journal seriously. Ten years after its establishment there were some Friends who advocated abandonment of the venture. Sydney Monthly Meeting expressed the view that the *Australian Friend* only "very inadequately and at great expense fulfils the object with which it was originated and that that object might be better served by a periodical communication from each of the London *Friends*".[43]

In reacting to this Minute the editor, with commendable restraint forbore to point out the retrograde nature of such a suggestion, which would mean that Australian Meetings would again have to depend on a publication twelve thousand miles and several months distant to gain news of other Meetings. Instead, he reminded his readers that *The Australian Friend* had been meant to fill partly the lack of a "superior" Meeting which could bring Meetings together. The cost of the journal was, he pointed out, much less than the cost of bringing distant Friends to a central place of meeting. It would appear then that in 1889 the prospect of establishing an Annual Meeting, whether Yearly or Quarterly, was as remote as ever and that the editor regarded *The Australian Friend* as a substitute for the foreseeable future.

The paucity of corporate Quaker concerns in the early history of Friends in Australia has been noted. The last quarter of the nineteenth century gave promise of a more outward-looking Society.

In Melbourne Sarah J. Swinborn, in the Elizabeth Fry tradition, visited hulks housing female prisoners, conducted services in Melbourne's gaol, and visited most of Victoria's prisons. She worked particularly amongst Melbourne's prostitutes and on 20 January 1885, with the help of her husband and other Friends, established the Elizabeth Fry Retreat in a six-roomed house in South Yarra.[44] Though the Melbourne Meeting did not accept full responsibility for the Retreat, members of the Meeting provided essential support. On Sarah Swinborn's death in 1902 her daughters, Fanny and Sarah Dell Swinborn, carried on the work begun by their mother.

Sarah and James Swinborn also started a Sunday School for poor children in old Hornibrook Ragged School in Commercial Road, South Yarra. This produced a curious reaction from the Catholic parish priest, who "excommunicated" Swinborn to prevent Catholic children from attending.

In Sydney there was a determined attempt to begin an Adult School. Adult schools had been organized in England by Quakers from a desire to gather young people off the streets, teach them to read and write and introduce them to the central principles of the Christian faith. The movement spread rapidly from a beginning in Nottingham in 1810 with an adult school founded by Samuel Fox to the end of the century when it was estimated that there were at least twenty thousand enrolled in Friends' First Day Adult Schools. Birmingham was regarded as the key centre of the work, with three thousand attending the schools set up there by the numerous Friends' Meetings around Birmingham.

There were several important principles on which these schools were based. One Friend identified these as a "combination of intellectual earnestness and tolerance with evangelistic zeal".[45] Insistence on equality of status between student and teacher was regarded as basic to successful operation and this was particularly striking for that period when well-known employers like George Cadbury and Joseph Sturge were among the most devoted teachers. There was no attempt at proselytizing but there was nevertheless a not insignificant number of people who joined the Society of Friends because of association with its members in Adult Schools. As most of these would have come from the working class this entry of new members did something to provide more variety of membership in what had become a largely middle-class Society.

The Adult School, begun by Sydney Meeting in 1879, lapsed between 1882 and 1885 but had a strong revival under the leadership of William Cooper, who at the time had not joined Friends.[46] William Cooper was manager of the Cadbury organization in Australia and doubtless his interest in Adult Schools stemmed from his observation of their success in Birmingham. Reports of the success of the Adult School movement in Sydney reached London Yearly Meeting and undoubtedly convinced members that it was time to recognize Sydney Monthly Meeting as a fully responsible constituent of London Yearly Meeting.

Around this time there was also a noticeable awakening of alertness to the need for continual public witness against the growth of militarism. The passing of Defence Acts by State legislatures in the eighteen-sixties drew protest from Friends in Melbourne and in Hobart. The Melbourne Meeting in 1883 drew up a memorial to the State Legislature stating that military preparedness, as indicated by the building of forts and the training of soldiers, was a denial of Christ's message of peace and non-violence — and a great economic drain on the colony's meagre financial resources. Three years later this was followed by a protest at the establishment of rifle corps in schools and the issue of rifles to older boys.

It was at this time that the Hobart Meeting became so concerned about the promotion of the military spirit, especially in the schools, and prepared a leaflet setting out Quaker views on war for distribution amongst teachers and community leaders. J. F. Mather kept up a battery of letters to the press, protesting against what he called "compulsory militarism" in schools which undermined the democratic spirit. True democracy, he claimed, bent its energies to lessening the dangers of war by the creation and development of international law. Mather was therefore considerably heartened by the Hague Peace Conference of 1902 which, he hoped, would usher in a new era of peace by establishing the rule of international law.

The Peace Movement in Australia received great stimulus in 1888-89 by the visit of the English Friend, William Jones. It was William Jones who awakened Australian Friends to the importance of the Quaker Peace Testimony. Jones was a very active member of the Peace Movement in Great Britain. During the Franco-Prussian War he was responsible for the distribution in 1870-71 of a hundred thousand pounds worth of relief to French and German peasants and he administered a similar relief programme after what were called the "Bulgarian horrors" of 1876-77. In Australia and New Zealand Jones made Peace the main theme of his public meetings. In particular he urged the necessity for arbitration to replace war as a means of settling international disputes. The *Dunedin Star*[47] labelled him as "the first visitor prepared to advocate peace on earth". He also addressed himself to Australian phobias about Russia and China, assuring people they had nothing to fear from either country and that there was no likelihood of seeing a rush of Chinese emigration. He expressed regret at what appeared to him to be Australian persecution of Chinese already living and working in Australia.

Large public meetings were organized by Friends in each capital city. In Melbourne twelve hundred were present at a meeting in Dr Strong's "Church of Australia". In Hobart the Town Hall was made available for a public meeting without charge. It was held in the presence of the Governor, Sir Robert Hamilton, and Lady Hamilton. William and Katherine Jones dined at Government House and lunched with the Premier, P. O. Fysh. Jones wrote enthusiastically about his reception in Tasmania and attributed the warmth of that reception and the interest of his audiences to the high regard in which Friends were held in Tasmania. "There are those still living", he said, "who remember the visits of James Backhouse and G. W. Walker and his disinterested work has left an open door for others who may enter into their labours."[48] At all his meetings Jones urged those present to remain afterwards and sign what was known as the Wisbech Christian Peace Declaration, which aimed at mobilizing Christian support for the Peace Movement.

One immediate objective of the Peace Societies in each state was to secure uniform legislation concerning exemption for conscientious objectors from military service. In a report on this subject[49] it was pointed out that there appeared to be no compulsion in Victoria or New South Wales; in Queensland there were no provisions for exemption; in South Australia Quakers had to pay for a substitute to take their place or have goods distrained; and in Tasmania exemption might be granted on conscientious grounds. Quakers therefore had good reason to favour the movement for Australian Federation, for they hoped that this would bring with it uniform acceptance of the right of conscientious objectors to refuse military service.

Activity in the Peace Movement brought Friends out of their self-imposed isolation into contact with fellow peace-workers in the churches and in the general community, just as in the early part of the century English Friends found common cause with other Christians in the Anti-Slavery movement. Friends focussed their peace campaign on arousing the conscience of Christians against participation in war. They distributed leaflets such as J. J. Dymond's "Essay on War". They were active in organizing public response to an international petition which was to be addressed to the Heads of thirty-two nations, seeking government action on the substitution of arbitration for force in the settlement of disputes. The Melbourne Friend, John Horsfall, was secretary of the Peace Society which organized a big public meeting in Wesley Church, Melbourne, to arouse public interest in the petition.

One interesting application of the Peace Testimony was suggested at a Friends' Meeting in Adelaide, where the question was raised of applying the Peace Testimony at the local as well as the international level, for South Australia in mid-1892 was feeling the effects of a long strike at Broken Hill. The report of the meeting to *The Australian Friend* concluded: "It transpired that we had in the Meeting members of the Unions both of Capital and of Labour. The question was raised whether we could rightly take sides in Labour disputes, which arise from the same cause as War and indeed are a species of War."[50]

Reference has already been made to another concern, which, with education and peace, drew the separate Meetings together and paved the way for greater unity of action. This was the question of race relations and in particular the problem of Kanaka labour in Queensland, in which Neave said he saw the germ of slavery.[51] As early as 1863 Thomas Crouch, then Sheriff of Tasmania, with whom Backhouse and Walker had been so hospitably lodged thirty years earlier, wrote to Backhouse to alert him to what he saw as a revival of slavery in the South Pacific. It appears that vessels flying the Peruvian flag had visited the islands and taken away natives to work in the mines of Peru.[52] Public meetings were held in Sydney and in Hobart to frame a petition praying the governor in each state to take immediate steps to stop this practice. Crouch believed that when this traffic was made known in England it would "create a sensation of no ordinary character". "Knowing the largeness of your heart", he concluded, "I am sure you will feel grieved at these events and if opportunity offers, you will be only too glad to add the weight of your influence to assist in putting a stop thereto."[53] The visit of Neave and Robson coincided with the extension of this "slave trade" to the supply of cheap coloured labour to the sugar planters in Queensland. By the end of the nineteenth century the emphasis in the controversy had shifted from "Is it right to exploit cheap coloured labour?" to "Is it right to exclude coloured labour?" Some Friends were involved as employers of Kanakas[54] on their sugar plantations and opposed therefore the government decision to repatriate all the Kanakas to the islands, arguing that many of the Kanakas, after their original term of service had expired, were happily settled and had no future in return to the islands. Other Friends, such as Alfred Sayce, a keen socialist, expressed amazement that any Friends engaged in occupations dependent on Kanaka labour.

> I cannot conceive how any Friend can possibly engage in such a trade. . . . I have no hesitation in asserting that the Kanakas are worse treated than they would be if they were slaves for life and that they lose virtues and learn vices by their contact with the White. As an Australian worker I resent their introduction which is done solely for the sake of gain, with the deliberate intention of degrading and lowering the social status of workers. . . . There is at least one individual who protests as a Christian, as a Friend and as a worker against this veiled slave trade, which I regard as a disgrace to Australia.[55]

This letter was featured in *The Australian Friend* and the Bishop of Tasmania, the Right Reverend H.H. Montgomery, who had travelled extensively through the South Pacific for the Melanesian Mission, was invited to comment. The Bishop pointed out that a deeper question was now being asked — is it possible in these days to keep white and dark apart anywhere? Alfred Sayce saw in some Friends' opposition to legislation protecting white workers from competition with cheap coloured labour an unwillingness to "try to understand the aspirations of labour or seek to guide and help it in any way".[56]

The editor of *The Australian Friend*, however, attempted to take the discussion out of the political arena by rephrasing the issue in terms of Christian imperative. "To say inferentially that there shall be no admittance to Australia for a man who has a coloured skin is against all the traditions of Christianity, and is a repetition of that exclusiveness we condemn in other people."[57] For Friends the question was seen not as a matter of expediency but of principle — whether coloured people should be denied entry to Australia on grounds of colour alone.

The need for Australian Friends to formulate a corporate judgment on national issues of defence and racial policy was now becoming much more insistent as Australia moved towards Federation. It is therefore likely that the approach of Federation was not without influence in speeding up what had until then been tardy progress towards the formulation of an Australian Quaker view on matters of national importance, for Friends began to realize that a national Parliament would provide a forum to which they could address their views on national issues

Towards an Australian General Meeting

In spite of the growing evidence of the need for an Australian Meeting some Australian Friends spread a disappointing air of vacillation and faintheartedness. Australian Meetings, paradoxically, seemed reluctant to seek independence and slow to understand that their Australian identity would not emerge until they could free themselves from dependence upon London Yearly Meeting. One of the strongest advocates of an Australian Meeting came from the most distant outpost of Friends, from Francis Hopkins in Rockhampton. Both Francis and his wife, Felicia, who moved north to Rockhampton after their marriage in Brisbane, had a much wider vision of the Society of Friends in Australia than most of their fellow-Quakers. Both had been educated at Saffron Walden Friends' School. They shared a desire to see Friends' ways of worship and principles extended in the Australian community and would have merited the description of "aggressive Friends" in the sense that this term was used in the London Yearly Meeting of 1898. They were among the few Australian Friends who were prepared to consider ways in which Friends' methods of worship could be adapted to meet the needs of an isolated community. In acknowledging a gift of books from London Francis Hopkins wrote: "We hope that in this new country the *essentials* of Quakerism will still be upheld, whilst we know that some peculiarities which are due to English social habits, must disappear".[58]

Since there were too few Friends to form a properly accredited Monthly Meeting, the Hopkins family devised an organization of their own, which they called a "Friends' Association". The constitution was "home-made" and contained a strong evangelical emphasis, as the two following extracts will show.

> All our meetings are to be held in the fear of God, under the government of his son, Jesus Christ, as Head of the Church through the assistance and guidance of the Holy Spirit.
>
> All persons enrolled under these rules individually acknowledge the Divine Truth of the whole of the Holy Scriptures and require no doctrine or practice which is not in accordance therewith.

Membership of the Association was open to anyone over the age of sixteen who accepted this credal statement and signed a declaration of faith, a signing which was repeated annually. The Association, even if somewhat irregular, maintained correspondence with London Yearly Meeting and indeed received the Continental Committee's tacit recognition, for in 1893 when Brisbane Friends were not considered strong enough[59] to be recognized as a Monthly Meeting, Brisbane was advised to adopt a Friends' Association constitution, similar to Rockhampton's[60] and on Edwin Ransome's recommendation this was done at a meeting on 4 June 1893.[61] The Rockhampton declaration included the statement that members agreed to "abide by London Yearly Meeting in matters of faith, doctrine and church government".[62] The Continental Committee tactfully refrained from detailed criticism of the rules of the Association, apart from venturing the observation that they appeared more elaborate than was necessary. It agreed that members could be recognized and marriages celebrated.

The Hopkins were keen to promote the growth of a Friends' community. Their home was for many years the hearth of Friends' activity in Rockhampton. A Meeting House was opened on 28 November 1880 in Bridge Street. English Friends, on the advice of Isaac Sharp, contributed liberally. The Meeting House became the centre for an Infant Day School 1882-83, for weekly meetings of the Band of Hope, for two sessions of a Sunday School, mostly for children of non-Friends, and for public meetings of an evangelical nature. Later a second Meeting of Friends was set up on the south side of the river.

When a considerable number of Scandinavians emigrated to Queensland in government ships from Hamburg, Hopkins wrote in 1881 to Norwegian and Danish Friends to encourage young Scandinavian Friends to join them, "provided they were willing to abstain from alcoholic drinks". Temperance was one of the Hopkins' main concerns.

When the history of Rockhampton was written recently by Lorna McDonald, full acknowledgment was made of the contribution to the community of Rockhampton by Hopkins brothers, William and Francis, and by Felicia Hopkins. "Concern for their fellow human beings was part of the Quaker religion of the Hopkins."[63] Francis and Felicia Hopkins first conducted a boys' school in Denham Street. Then Francis became the first principal of the Pink Lily State School just outside the town, Felicia Hopkins teaching needlework. In 1874, however, they gave up teaching and opened a bookshop in William Street. William Hopkins also conducted a bookshop. He was mayor of North Rockhampton in 1883.

William and Francis were foundation members of the Y M.C.A. in 1868 in Rockhampton and in 1888 Felicia Hopkins founded a branch of the Y.W.C.A. in the town. "The Hopkins family", Lorna McDonald wrote, "did not restrict themselves in any narrow fashion to religious and moral organizations but both were active in the Separatist Movement, while Francis was prominent in the Penny Savings Bank, the Co-operative bakery and the Co-operative grocery store — all to assist the working-man and his family."[64] A residential college block of the Capricornia Institute of

Advanced Education, opened in 1976, was named Felicia Hopkins House in honour of Felicia Hopkins, "who did much to promote the literacy and social development of the Rockhampton community and the interests of women and children of central Queensland in the early years of settlement of the region".[65]

However narrow Francis Hopkins' ideas on membership and doctrine may have appeared to some Friends, he was undoubtedly one of the most clear-sighted of Australian Friends in his advocacy of an Australian Quakerism. He saw the dangers of isolation. "People separated too much", he said, "gradually become self-opinionated and the whole doctrine of church fellowship, admonition, instruction and mutual assistance is nullified."[66] The first editor of *The Australian Friend* in an article for *The Friend* gave to the Hopkins the credit for initiating the idea of an Australian Friends' journal. "It was in one of the most isolated gatherings of our little church — the Meeting at Rockhampton, Queensland — that the desire for such a publication first made itself felt and found expression."[67]

Hopkins was a most enthusiastic and vocal supporter of what he saw as the three major ways to promote an Australian Quakerism — an Australian Friends' School, an Australian Friends' journal, and an Australian Yearly Meeting. The first two objectives were realized in 1887. The third had yet to be attained.

The first Meeting to make a serious move to bring Australian Friends together in conference was Melbourne. In 1879 Tasmania and South Australia both turned down Melbourne's suggestion of a conference, Tasmania on the grounds of expense and of unreadiness for such a meeting, Adelaide because it wanted first to know what powers were envisaged for a General Meeting, if the establishment of this was to be the aim of the conference. Melbourne accepted the rejection but considered that the growth of railways connecting mainland capitals would bring the possibility of an Australian conference nearer.

Melbourne repeated the offer in 1887 for a conference in 1888 and this time the conference was held. The centenary of Australian settlement in New South Wales and the International Exhibition in Melbourne were added reasons for choosing this time and location. Attendance was encouraging. William and Katherine Jones[68] came as representatives of London Yearly Meeting and Ann and Fletcher Jackson from New Zealand. Francis Hopkins had come fourteen hundred miles from Rockhampton, six had come from Sydney, six from Hobart, and twelve from Adelaide. William Benson was appointed clerk and John Horsfall assistant-clerk.

The major item on the agenda concerned the establishment of a General Meeting with the disciplinary powers of a Quarterly Meeting. The Minute indicated that this move was still considered premature.

> During this and the preceding sitting we have considered the advisability and practicability of establishing an organized Meeting to embrace all the Meetings of Australasia, with supervisory powers. It is our judgment that the time has not yet arrived when such a gathering could effectively administer discipline. We believe, however, that Conferences similar to the present may be held from time to time with much advantage, and that they promise to lead up to that condition of more perfect organization and union so much to be desired.[69]

The presence of William Jones[70] led to a discussion of Friends' Peace action and Friends were encouraged to form local Peace Associations in each state. It was also resolved to urge other Christian churches to consider their attitude to militarism. One of the practical reasons for promoting an Australian Meeting of Friends was demonstrated in the decision to initiate a survey of the variations in state laws concerning recognition of Friends' marriage regulations,[71] affirmation replacing oaths in law courts, and conditions of exemption from military service. In reviewing what was called "Christian activity" in Friends' Meetings, there was general recognition of the fact that there seemed to be little of note to be reported as corporate action by the Meetings themselves, but that Quakers were active in their communities as individuals. This first Conference was seen as a forerunner of similar gatherings in the future, but members still deferred any decision concerning effective organizational unity.

During the last decade of the nineteenth century it became

clear that some Australian inter-Meeting organization could not long be delayed. The necessity to refer to London Yearly Meeting all procedural matters, such as the attachment of the Queensland Preparative Meetings to Sydney Monthly Meeting, seemed increasingly irksome. The lack of a higher authority to which reference could be made by Monthly Meetings in cases of differences was frustrating and there was little opportunity for the co-ordination of the work of the separate Meetings. Pragmatism began to assert itself and outweigh feelings of sentiment or excuses of weakness. There were still those who saw Australian Meetings simply as outposts of London Yearly Meeting and regarded any attempt to establish inter-communication at the Australian level as disloyalty to the parent body and there were some who felt that the Meetings were too weak to support an Australian superstructure.

Nineteen hundred and one was the year of Federation. The first issue of *The Australian Friend* for that year devoted special articles to the birth of a "Twentieth Century Nation" and correspondents from each of the Meetings wrote in praise of this "great step forward". Though there was no explicit comparison drawn, it may perhaps be inferred that those who wrote in praise of the union of the separate States of the Commonwealth saw in this an example for the separate Friends' Meetings to follow.

Melbourne again took the initiative and offered to host another Conference in 1901. Contrary to the fears of some doubters, this time there was the clear decision to move forward. The Conference recommended to Monthly Meetings that a General Meeting of the Society of Friends for Australia be set up with the same powers as an English Quarterly Meeting, except that it would meet annually, not quarterly, that representation at London Yearly Meeting be not compulsory and that no contribution should be made to London Yearly Meeting's "National Stock", from which the activities of London Yearly Meeting were financed.

General Meetings were to be held in rotation in each of the Monthly Meetings as convenient, the first to be in Sydney in 1902, but the new Meeting House in Devonshire Street was not ready in time to host the first General Meeting and so this was transferred to Melbourne.[72]

The story of the first Australian General Meeting in 1902 belongs to the twentieth century. It is sufficient to say here that Australian Friends, by deciding to gather together for their first General Meeting in 1902, had taken one important step towards the development of an Australian Quakerism. There was now available the means whereby Australian Quakers could speak as one united body. Their links with England, however, were so powerful that it was to be a further sixty years before they were able to subordinate sentiment to practical reality and form an independent Australia Yearly Meeting.

Eleven
Retrospect: 1832–1901

Two courses are open if the Quaker migrations to Australia are to be examined in comparison with other religious group migrations. The first is to place the Quaker migrations in the Australian context and to see how other Christian groups by comparison adapted to a colonial environment, what changes evolved in their church organization, what contribution they made to national development. Any attempt however to compare the history of Quakers in Australia with, for example, that of the Wesleyans or Presbyterians, has proved fruitless because of the different dimensions of these religious groups. The Quakers were relatively few in number, never more than a few hundred, and much less in terms of effective membership. Smallness of size at least brought the advantage of compactness when it came to tracing origins and to following changes of occupation, religious allegiance, and attitudes in the Australian setting. The size of other religious denominations in Australia makes such compactness of treatment difficult and hence reduces the possibility of attaching any significance to comparisons.

It is more productive therefore to seek comparisons within a Quaker, rather than an Australian context and to see, for example, what differences there were between the migrations of Quakers to America in the seventeenth century and those to Australia in the nineteenth. The differences indeed are striking and serve to highlight by contrast the characteristics of the Quaker migrations to Australia.

Quaker Migrations to America

There was the obvious historical difference between the

seventeenth and nineteenth centuries. The seventeenth was a century of religious and political turmoil. In the nineteenth century economic and social factors had a greater bearing on migration. Religious persecution was no longer one of the main reasons for seeking a new land.

The initial impulse that led Quakers to the American colonies was not however a desire to escape persecution, but a burning zeal to carry the truth, as they saw it, to the New World. It was the same missionary impulse which had driven those who were called the "Valiant Sixty" to preach without fear the message of George Fox throughout England. In 1655 two Quaker women, Ann Austin and Mary Fisher, were the vanguard of the Quaker "invasion" of the American colonies. They landed in the Barbados, where they met with a sympathetic response, but their objective was the Puritan colony of Massachusetts, where there was a persecution of Quakers as ruthless as any seen in England. A second wave of Quakers followed, four men and four women in the *Speedwell*, but these were turned back and forced to return to England. A third attempt was made in a little vessel called the *Woodhouse* in 1657, when eleven Quakers, including some from the *Speedwell*, set a course for the colonies, five landing on Long Island and six at Newport, Rhode Island. Rhode Island came to be called the "nursery of Quakerism" in the colonies, because of its predisposition to religious freedom and its sympathetic reception of Quakers and the Quaker message. An edict from early Rhode Island records indicates the prevailing attitude: "It is ordered that none be accounted as delinquent for doctrine".[1] The subsequent history of the spread of Quakerism, first in the sympathetic areas such as Rhode Island and Nantucket, then in the Quaker-founded states of West and East New Jersey and Pennsylvania, underlines the important role played by Quakers in the early history of the American colonies. The rise of Quakerism there paralleled the rise of Quakerism in England. There was the same seed bed of those disillusioned with the established church, its doctrines and its formalism, but in addition there was in the American colonies a growing body of those who had gone there to escape persecution and to seek religious freedom, only to find that the Puritans in Massachusetts, the

Catholics in Maryland, the Episcopalians in Virginia, and the Calvinists on Long Island were as intolerant of any opposition in the New World as the worst of their oppressors had been in the Old. The first Quakers who went to America were not escaping from persecution, but rather confronting the new persecutors. Though their struggle cost four hangings in Boston, whippings, ear-lancings, tongue-borings and public humiliation, they persisted and held the bridgehead which finally won Quakers the right to practise their Quaker faith without fear of reprisals.

After 1664 a new phase began — of deliberately planned Quaker migration to the colonies. The Conventicle Act of 1664 was passed by the English Parliament in an attempt to suppress all other forms of worship save that of the established Church. One response to this was that Quakers acquired properties in West and East New Jersey with the purpose, it was said, of providing a haven for persecuted Quakers. West New Jersey was sold to two Quakers, John Fenwick, yeoman, and Edward Byllynge, a London merchant, for £1,000. On the death of Sir George Carteret in 1679 his East New Jersey estate was sold and in February 1681 this estate was conveyed to William Penn and eleven other Quakers. Twelve more Quakers subsequently joined them to form a Council of Proprietors. West New Jersey became a Quaker colony, William Penn being involved in the negotiations leading up to its formation and in the drawing up of its constitution. The wider purpose of this colony is seen in William Penn's statement.

> The ninety parts remaining are exposed for sale on behalf of the creditors of Edward Byllynge. And forasmuch as several Friends are concerned as creditors as well as others, and the disposal of so great a part of this country being in our hands, we did in real tenderness and regard to Friends and especially the poor and necessitous, make Friends the first offer, that any of them, though particularly those that, being low in the world and under trials about a comfortable livelihood for themselves and families, would be desirous of dealing for any part or parcel thereof, that they might have the refusal.[2]

The climate of repression of dissenters clearly led many to look to the New World as a haven from persecution, but it is also clear that many saw this as an opportunity to practise their faith in freedom. Jones gives precedence to the latter view. "The causes of Quaker emigration to the American colonies are not so much to be sought in the desire to escape from persecution, as in the idea which took shape in the mind of William Penn, to show Quakerism at work, freed from hampering conditions. . . . The impulse to migrate came as much from within the sect itself, as from the outside pressure of circumstances."[3] For some there certainly was "the outside pressure of circumstances" and especially the pressure of economic necessity for those whom Penn had in mind when he talked of "the poor and necessitous". But there were sufficient Quakers of wealth and social standing who were not only able to purchase large estates for Quaker colonization, but who were equipped to provide leadership.

There was also evidence of firm Quaker support. At a General Meeting of Friends at Scalehouse, near Skipton, in 1658, the following minute was agreed on:

> Having heard of the great things done by the mighty power of God in many nations beyond the seas, whither he has called forth many of our dear brethren and sisters to preach the everlasting gospel . . . our bowels yearn for them and our hearts are filled with tender love to those precious ones of God who so freely have given up for the Seed's sake their friends, their near relatives, their country and worldly estates, yea and their lives also. We therefore with one consent freely and liberally offer up our earthly substance, according as God hath blessed everyone, to be speedily sent up to London as a freewill offering for the Seed's sake.[4]

Quakers in the American colonies also received great moral support from an almost continuous stream of Quakers from England, George Fox himself spending almost two years in the colonies from 1671 to 1673.

There was an increasing flow of Quaker migrants, first to West New Jersey in 1675. By 1681, 1,400 had arrived. One large group of Friends who sailed in the *Kent* for West New Jersey in 1677 so attracted the interest of King Charles II that he is said to have sailed down the Thames in the royal barge to witness their departure and give them his blessing.[5] The best known migration of all was that of William Penn to Pennsylvania. By 1682 two thousand Quakers had gone to Pennsylvania. Rufus Jones said of these: "Many of all sorts came — solid Friends who had endured the horrors of English prisons... men of education and means seeking larger estates, renters who wished to be land owners, handicraftsmen of many kinds, adventurers for gain, some fairly good and some criminal. But at first the better elements were in large preponderance and in absolute control."[6]

George R. Chapman, writing about Irish Quaker migration of 1682[7] listed the reasons as a desire for adventure, relief from persecution, prospects of better economic conditions, availability of cheap, easily obtainable land, and the assurance that they would find support in Friends' Meetings already established. Intending migrants were advised to inform their respective Meetings of intention to migrate and Meetings endeavoured to ensure that all financial and domestic commitments had been met before embarkation. The basic principle stressed was that no Friend should migrate simply to avoid persecution. Relief there might be on arrival, but escape initially from persecution was not acceptable as a reason.

Migration of Quakers to Australia

It will be seen from this brief account that the migration of Quakers to Australia bears little resemblance to the early Quaker migrations to the American colonies. The former was the migration of individual Quakers, the latter bore the stamp of Quaker migration, that is, of group and not merely individual movement. Quakerism itself had undergone vast changes in the two hundred years between the two migrations. In the mid-seventeenth century Quakerism was new, dynamic, and aggressive. An exhilaration of spirit marked these early Quakers and an indomitable endurance which enabled them to meet persecution without bitterness. The American colonies were seen as a natural extension of George Fox's vision on Pendle Hill of "a great people to be gathered". Quakers saw themselves therefore as missionaries to the New World, going in obedience to the spirit of Fox's letter written from Launceston gaol:

> Let all nations hear the word by sound or writing. Spare no place,

> spare not tongue nor pen, but be obedient to the Lord God and go through the work and be valiant for truth upon the earth; tread and trample all that is contrary under. . . . Be patterns, be examples in all countries, places, islands, nations, wherever you come, that your carriage and life may preach among all sorts of people and to them: then you will come to walk cheerfully over the world, answering that of God in every one.[8]

Such missionary spirit was evident amongst only a few of the Australian Quakers, such as Walker, Mackie, and Neave who came out initially as "travellers under concern", then married and settled in Australia. By the mid-nineteenth century Quakerism had lost its initial crusading zeal and replaced it with an emphasis which was evangelical rather than specifically Quaker.

Nor was there in Australia anything akin to the large body of American colonists who were spiritually ready to accept what the early Quakers preached. There had been no preparatory harrowing of the soil in which the Quaker seed could quickly take root. The number of adherents which increased dramatically in the early days of the American colonies was sufficient to provide a sense of identity and to establish a group confidence, and this enabled the Quakers to make a significant impact on the social and political life of the American colonies. In Australia numbers remained depressingly static, and a sense of identity as Australian Quakers was slow in forming.

Not only was there group support for migration to the American colonies but Quakers migrated in groups. They carried, as it were, their institutional shell with them and therefore had immediate group support available during the difficult first years of settlement. In Australia the only positive examples of anything like group migration were those to South Australia and to Victoria and here the grouping was basically by families rather than by membership of Quaker Meetings. In Australia members were scattered and Meetings were slow in forming so that the mutual encouragement and support available to the American Quakers on arrival was not similarly available to the Australians. It is significant too that a whole network of Monthly, Quarterly, and Yearly Meetings was quickly organized in the American colonies. As early as 1661 a Yearly Meeting was formed on Rhode Island, preceding London Yearly Meeting by several years.[9] It was 130 years after the arrival of Backhouse and Walker before a Yearly Meeting was constituted in Australia.

While American Meetings quickly established independence of action, English Friends nevertheless maintained a steady stream of travelling ministers, who provided a constant reinforcement of Quaker principles and practice. By the mid-nineteenth century London Yearly Meeting was rather more intermittent in its concern for distant members. First these were much more distant than they were in America and the time taken for travelling was that much longer. In the seventeenth century concern to promote the spread of Quakerism was insistent; by the nineteenth century the missionary zeal had weakened. Australia nevertheless was well served by a succession of very able visiting Friends prepared to make the long voyage, to undertake, often on foot, the visiting of isolated Friends and to spend, in some cases, years travelling in the ministry. They rallied in many a fresh resolve, in some a flagging interest, but their influence tended to fade as their physical presence was withdrawn. The pastoral care thus provided was a demonstration of London Yearly Meeting's concern. Without it, there is doubt whether Quakerism in Australia would have survived.

Quakers migrated to Australia not to escape persecution or to establish Quaker colonies, but to seek a better future for themselves and their families. The motivation was economic, not religious. A significant proportion of Australian Quaker migrants did not reveal any strong Quaker motivation. Joseph May wrote to James Backhouse: "It has happened that nearly all the members of our Society who have come to this colony have been of that number whose principles are not very decided and a residence here, perhaps at a distance from meetings and from the society of other members, does not help them forward, but rather leads them from the practices, if not from the principles of Friends".[10] Few Quakers sought beforehand the backing or the blessing of their Quaker Meetings. Amongst the Quaker migrants were many who could be described as disaffected, having been disowned by their Meetings in England or Ireland, and therefore not likely to be staunch supporters of Meetings in Australia. There were others who were birthright members, attached to the Society of Friends by accident of birth, rather than by conviction. Some of these were merely nominal members who tended to regard themselves as attached to the Meetings of their birth, and not to the new Meetings in the land of their adoption.

Australian Friends tended to look with envy at what they saw as the vigour of American Quakerism and the high degree of commitment to Quaker ideals. When they looked at their own Meetings, they confessed to a general reluctance to promote Quakerism. They had no William Penn, no Boston martyrs, no Philadelphia as a centre of strength. Instead of spreading the Quaker message through steadily expanding membership Australian Friends were conscious of weakness of numbers and lack of growth. The membership totals submitted annually to London Yearly Meeting confirmed that the last decade of the nineteenth century was a period of decline in numbers.

In *The Proceedings of London Yearly Meeting* for the years 1891-1901, the numbers of members of Australian Meetings showed a fall from 515 in 1891 to 506 in 1901. Australian Meetings lacked the strength and the initiative to reverse this trend. They did not have the resource of committed Quakers with the will and the time to do what travelling ministers did in English and American Meetings by visiting, encouraging, exhorting, and teaching. The travelling ministers provided the ministerial and pastoral leadership which in the orthodox churches was the responsibility of the trained and ordained clergy. In Australia there was only a handful of Quakers who could spare the time from the business of making a living to travel long distances to counsel Friends in other Meetings. As a result Meetings languished through spiritual famine.

A Question of Survival

This raises a controversial, but critical question. Would some more permanent pastoral ministry, such as that which evolved in America, have been a more appropriate response in the Australian situation? At the end of the eighteenth and beginning of the nineteenth centuries in America, fresh Quaker migrations had moved westward, and north to Canada. The Quaker historian, Rufus Jones,[11] describes how whole Meetings moved, in numbers far exceeding the earlier migrations of Friends from Great Britain to the American colonies in the seventeenth century. He estimated that by 1820 there were not less than twenty thousand Friends west of the Alleghany Mountains, a stream that continued until the Civil War. As they migrated, they formed their Yearly Meetings,[12] thus signifying the confidence to set up and maintain positions of strength. For some migrant groups the lure was the opening up of new lands and the promise of new opportunities. For some in the South it was obedience to conscience which led them to seek a new society where slavery was not tolerated.

It was in these more isolated communities of Friends that the pastoral system later evolved as a result of the evangelical religious revival which swept across the country in the latter part of the nineteenth century. Though the Quaker spiritual roots remained, the methods of worship and of organization were adapted to meet the needs of Friends in isolated communities who felt the need for something more than transitory leadership.

The same evolution can be observed in the history of Canadian Quakerism. The early Canadian Quakers represented one of the branches of the "Great Migration" which fanned out west and north from American Meetings. Canadian Meetings were established and shepherded by New York and Philadelphia Yearly Meetings, but even with this help relatively near at hand frontier living brought a sense of isolation, and isolation later, under the impact of evangelical revivalism, led members to seek a more pastoral organization. In both Canadian and American Meetings, an alternative pastoral form of Quakerism evolved alongside the traditional Quaker Meeting pattern.

The reason for this development was well put by A.G. Dorland[13] who pointed out that the success of a free, lay, unprofessional ministry, as seen in England and in the non-pastoral Meetings of the United States of America, depended largely for its effectiveness on the presence of a sufficient number of "educated as well as consecrated folk among the rank and file to produce a helpful type of leadership". One might add that leisure and a certain financial independence were also necessary qualifications. In newer countries, as in Australia, this pool of educated, committed Quakers just did not exist and as a result Meetings struggled on with an overwhelming sense of isolation and weakness.

There were indications that some Friends saw a pastoral system as a way out of their difficulties. One of the early Quakers migrating to South Australia, William Everett, left Friends to join the Baptists. His first reason for leaving the Society of Friends was that he could not find a marriage partner in the limited field of eligible Quaker women, but also he had been impressed with the Baptists, who, without any assistance from the English parent church, had built their own church at the cost of ten thousand pounds with twenty-two classrooms, "sheds for conveyances and stalls for the horses". Everett raised the question: "Is it having a minister as a centre that gives such outward signs of vitality to a congregation, whilst ours is so near unto the reverse?"[14]

Another early Quaker migrant to South Australia, George Sanders, writing to James Backhouse in 1850[15] spoke of the difficulties the little Meeting had to contend with and the need for help. Then a sentence was added, indicative both of the problem and of "the stop in the mind" which hindered a Quaker solution to the problem. "For though I hope I shall never place my trust in man nor believe that the teaching of man is necessary to salvation, I certainly believe there is often a blessing attendant upon rightly authorized communications — and we have need of every aid we can obtain."

William Beck, a member of the Australian Deputation of 1875, who had spoken then of the Sydney Meeting as "reduced to a very low spot; a set of a few old crotchety men — only, pray tell it not in Gath!" had added, as if by way of explanation, "Oh what we have lost by way of organization and an earnest seeking for some to act the part of nursing fathers and mothers".[16]

Francis Hopkins was close to advocacy of a form of pastoral ministry in 1886 when he spoke in his report on

Rockhampton Meeting of "the loss of spiritual life through absence of the felt influence of the church on its members".[17] He suggested that Friends would gain more support in Australia, where there was no established church, if Friends' ideas could be explained by what he called "a qualified expounder".

Alfred Wright, a member of the 1875 Australian Deputation who, out of a sense of concern for Australian Friends, returned for a further period of service from 1890 to 1893, expressed on at least two occasions this need for pastoral help. He found Friends in Brisbane few and "disintegrated". "When I left", he wrote,[18] "it was with little hope that the Meeting would continue unless some earnest, devoted Friend were to go and live among them and devote much time and strength in working to build it up. Certainly there was no power in itself to do this." And again, when he visited Ballarat Meeting, he foresaw that the Meeting would die out unless it had "an earnest, gifted Friend" resident in that city.[19]

One Friend, Elly Thorp, writing to Edwin Ransome in 1898[20] reported that a number of Friends had urged that Australia should come under the recently established Friends Home Mission Society and be allotted a resident missionary Friend, but she admitted that conservative Friends had held up their hands in horror at what they feared would develop into a "hireling" ministry. The editor of *The Australian Friend* some years earlier had labelled the American "pastoral" Friends as decadent, accusing them of deserting the principles of Friends to gain numbers. He then read the lesson to his Australian readers.

> Our Friends, as we still call them, are manifestly on the "down grade" and going down the incline with constantly accelerated speed. It is painful to bring forward the evidence. It is sufficient to recall the fact testified to by many witnesses that in places at least their meetings for worship have no longer any correspondence with a genuine Friends' Meeting. They have become a "service", in which worshippers look no longer directly to the Lord to feed them, but to man for a stated performance. We desire to be not wanting in Christian charity, we can believe that they are zealous, earnest, warm-hearted people; but they are abandoning us and our cause and service, and accepting an easier and more popular position. What

can have led to all this? Is it not the vain and unworthy desire by all means to increase in numbers? . . . Now what is the lesson for us in Australasia to learn? and profit by when adverting to this decadence in America? We are not tempted to stoop down and popularize by any prospect of being numerous. Let us endeavour to hold our own, and to be something genuine if we are anything at all.[21]

Yet, in spite of this inherited phobia of "hireling priest" the need for pastoral help continued to surface. Elly Thorp's letter may have been in reply to a letter of the Continental Committee, dated 27 May 1898, to "Friends at Brisbane, asking them to inform us whether they would be likely to welcome any Friends who might come and reside amongst them for a time with a view of helping their Meeting".[22] This had followed an earlier report from Brisbane that unless help was received the Meeting would "bid fair to die out".[23] Adelaide Meeting was voicing independently the same plea for pastoral help, for in the minutes of the Continental Committee meeting of 6 April 1898 it was reported that Adelaide Friends had written that "unless some Friend can be found with leisure and capacity for organizing work, there seems a probability that the energies of our younger members will be expended in other directions". Clearly, Adelaide was aware that the result of lack of pastoral help would be the loss of the Quaker youth to other churches.

The Continental Committee responded to the Adelaide letter by passing the problem on to the Home Service Committee with the suggestion that this committee might see its way "to encourage some suitable Friend by a grant in aid to reside for a time with partial secular occupation". From this it was hoped "great good might result, as there are elements there for Christian work, needing a helping hand".[24]

The state of Brisbane Meeting had brought this question of pastoral help to a head. Samuel Clemes, who had been visiting Brisbane "in the ministry", had reported to the Continental Committee that the state of Brisbane Meeting was as low as it could well be, and that the only solution seemed to lie in some one or more Friends residing there for a while, but then Samuel Clemes voiced the same stop in Friends' minds — "*not* a paid pastor", he added, underlining the negative.[25]

The vestigial abhorrence of "priests" from the seventeenth century prevented Friends at home and abroad from grappling with the difficulties that faced the isolated and discouraged members scattered throughout the widely separated Australian Meetings. Samuel Clemes saw no distinction between pastor and priest, though the need he identified was pastoral, not priestly.

The second vestigial difficulty was with the idea of payment. To the early Friends payment signified the "hireling", the professional. Ministry was seen by Friends as the direct result of communication of man with God and payment of priests as a corruption of this relationship. The Society of Friends therefore had developed as a strictly "amateur" organization; the only time the question of payment arose was when a Meeting "released" a member "under concern" to "travel in the ministry". In this case, as, for example, for Backhouse and Walker, travelling expenses were considered to be the responsibility of the Society. Friends have been reluctant, however, to concede that financial support of members released for service in the Society might be necessary, if sufficient members of independent financial means and possessing the necessary qualifications of time, experience, and ability were not available. The Continental Committee's suggestion of a grant in aid to supplement "partial secular occupation" was a hesitating halfway acknowledgment of the possibility that changing conditions might require changes in attitude.

Nothing however emerged from this probing of what was really a critical problem for the Society of Friends in the Australian context. At the turn of the century the need for committed and experienced Friends to be released for pastoral, not priestly, service to the Australian Meetings was clear. Unfortunately the initial historically-based prejudice and the subsequent American turn of events, whereby the Quaker pastor was seen by some Friends as in no way different from the hireling priest, prevented a realistic alternative being developed, whereby the Australian Meetings could have had the pastoral help of concerned Friends, released and supported initially by the Home Service Committee of London Yearly Meeting and eventually by a strengthened and more confident cluster of Australian Meetings.

The difficulties which English Quakerism had in meeting the pastoral needs of isolated Friends and groups of Friends in distant colonies suggest another critical question. Was English Quakerism of the mid-nineteenth century adaptable for export? or, more specifically, was the English Quakerism of the period 1832-61 likely to make a strong appeal to Australian colonists? It must be allowed that this was a static, not a dynamic period in English Quakerism. Australian Quakers, reared in the English tradition, attempted to stick rigidly to the rules, even when conditions made it obvious that the rules were inapplicable.

By the end of the century this was admitted. At the Annual Meeting of the Hobart Monthly Meeting in 1891, when two visiting English Friends, Alfred Wright and William J. Sayce, were both present, there was a lively discussion on the state of the Society of Friends. The fact that the application of English Quakerism to Australian conditions was being questioned at all is in itself significant. Samuel Clemes was of the opinion that the Society of Friends in Australia had leant too much upon discipline and not enough on sympathy, that is, on awareness of the real needs of people and a warm response to those needs. "The regulations concerning marriage", he said, "had checked Quakerism which was just what was wanted in the colonies."[26] Samuel Clemes was clearly of the opinion that a Quakerism, free to respond to the new set of conditions operative in the colonies, and not shackled by clinging to outworn tradition, could have made a very strong appeal to the Australian colonist. He demonstrated the truth of this theory by putting it into practice in his school. Though he admitted that his own ideas on education had been shaped by his experience in English Friends' Schools, the School in Hobart was to be no mere transplant of an English Friends' School in an Australian setting. In a statement to parents he stressed that "education suited for the condition of life in these colonies should not be modelled too closely on the lines to which we have gradually been accustomed in the older countries".[27] He therefore made it clear that conditions in the colony would modify the ideas he had brought with him. The School was to be an Australian school.

William May disclosed that, before their family left England, William Forster, a leading English Friend, had told his father, Joseph May, that it would not be possible to carry out in Australia the discipline concerning marriage. Mackie and Lindsey had conveyed the same advice in 1853 when Melbourne Monthly Meeting was struggling with the problem of whether to disown a member, Alfred Clemes, for "marrying out". These reactions of English Friends indicate that the understanding on the part of English Friends would have made itself evident if the lines of communication had not been so far stretched. Distance from home led to rigidity and formalism in the outposts and rendered almost impossible the dialogue which might have led to modification and change. Alfred Wright concluded the discussion with the statement that there had been too much discipline in the old land and regulations which did not apply in the outposts. "Quakerism", he said, "is a protest against all formality, and if we have got into formality we shall have to get out of it. Some laws are more honoured in the breach than the observance."[28]

There were some who shared Samuel Clemes' intuitive feeling that Quakerism was well suited to the needs of the Australian colonist, who was alleged to be fiercely independent of authority, whether of Church or State, a staunch egalitarian and a good "mate". One correspondent, for example, writing after London Yearly Meeting in 1899, considered Quakerism had the answer to Australia's problems. "I cannot help thinking that our free constitution and liberty for the exercise of all spiritual gifts, absence of paid ministry and simple, natural methods, should, if properly set before the colonial people suit them in every way."[29] Certainly Quakers were free of any submissive attitude to the established church — and many Australians shared this attitude. Quakers upheld the equality of all in the sight of God, whatever their class or colour — Australians were proud of their tradition of "mateship", though at the turn of the century they were not keen on the thought of extending mateship to those of a different colour. Quakers abhorred injustice, but rejected violence as a way of dealing with the unjust. Most Australians would have gone no further along this path than insisting on a "fair go".

There were Friends, like George Cadbury, who regarded the Friends' method of worship as ideally suited to the needs of people in lonely places. Somewhat naively perhaps he thought that isolation and scattering, so far from being a minus, should be regarded as a potential plus, for as Friends believed in the priesthood of all believers, each Friend, even if hundreds of miles from the nearest Meeting, carried his own priesthood with him. They had no church to build, he said, no minister to wait for. "Every Friends' family and every individual Friend, even when he may be living alone, should be a centre of earnest aggressive work ... Quakerism is especially adapted for a scattered population."[30] The Friends' Meeting for Worship was, as it were, an immediate "do-it-yourself" affair, a direct link of man with God. However attractive this may have seemed in prospect, in practice it had grave difficulties. There was a dearth of travelling ministers, who could, as in English Meetings, move around to isolated Meetings and provide and encourage vocal ministry. Meetings, conducted for too many weeks in silence and without spiritual guidance, were unlikely to endure. Many Friends, well-meaning in their efforts to maintain their Quakerism, found themselves drawn to neighbouring churches where they could enjoy the religious fellowship they needed. Hobart Friends recognized this problem by actually advising isolated Friends in 1887 that it was better for them to join with another church's activities "than sit in their own rooms isolated from the Christians around".[31] William Benson added an example of two such Friends, one of whom isolated himself, the other joined in with his neighbours and became, said Benson, "a power for good".[32]

Isolation, contrary to George Cadbury's confident assumption that it would promote self-reliant worship, proved a deadly deterrent not only to the spread of Quakerism but to its continuance even in those who came to Australia as committed members.

English Friends did not really come to grips with this problem, for at home English Meetings were physically close enough together and numerous enough to make inter-visitation and mutual encouragement relatively easy. Even though the succession of English Friends visiting Australian Friends came back sounding the same theme of the depressing effects of isolation on Australian members, any practical response to this problem was never really formulated.

Friends who had for so long seen themselves as a separate people, with their own "peculiar" testimonies, found in the Australian context the need for religious fellowship outweighing the will to maintain separateness in isolation. Among Australian Friends there was a growing willingness to seek fellowship with other religious communities. This was particularly so in social work and partly explains why there was a noticeable lack of social projects coming from Quaker Meetings. Hobart Friends made this point in a report in *The Australian Friend*. "Ever since the foundation of our religious society in Hobart Friends have been too much associated with their fellow citizens in active work of an undenominational character to undertake any strong organization of their own."[33] They saw instead that, while they maintained their own mode of worship and organization, their true service lay not in separation from their fellow-Christians, but wherever possible in unison with them. The writer, J. F. Mather, added that members of Hobart Meeting served on twelve different committees of religious, philanthropic, educational, and municipal bodies in Tasmania.

The difficulties, both internal and external, facing the transplant of English Quakerism in Australian soil were considerable. The hopes that it would make an immediate appeal to Australians were unrealized. The expectation that Friends themselves would find their simple way of worship adequate for their spiritual needs was unfulfilled, for many Friends left the Society to join other churches where they could find the fellowship they lacked in isolation. To the internal problems of leadership and fellowship must be added a third — that of the induction of succeeding generations into the ideas, principles, and practices of the Society of Friends. Again numbers are an important factor. Where Meetings are large enough there are more resources of personnel available to cater for the needs of the young. In Australia in the nineteenth century the loss to the Society of succeeding generations was devastating. Studies of individual families[34] have shown that very few children and grandchildren of the first generation of Australian Quakers remained with the Society. If one examines particularly those Friend families which appeared initially to be strongly committed to the Society, the seriousness of the situation becomes evident, for it would seem that Friends were singularly unsuccessful in promoting Quaker allegiance in their children. This may indicate either the fallacy of assuming that Quaker ideals and practices can be passed on to the next generation by example alone, or it may imply that Quakerism has a one-generation limit of allegiance, each succeeding generation having to find by its own initiative the wish to seek membership. By contrast with English Quakerism, where continuity of family membership in the nineteenth century seemed generally accepted, there was little continuity of membership in Australian Quaker families. From an examination of the 1978 list of membership for Australian Meetings an estimate, allowing for the difficulty of tracing direct descent through female lineage, would put the limits of direct descendants from the "first thousand" still in active membership at no higher and probably less than three per cent.

English Friends in the nineteenth century appeared to rely very much on birthright membership to ensure continuity. No individual decision was required of those "born into membership", because their parents registered them at birth with the appropriate Monthly Meeting. Australian Friends were very suspicious of this type of membership, for by their experience, they said, of birthright members who emigrated to Australia, a high proportion did not appear to value their membership or to show any interest in supporting Australian Meetings. They therefore favoured individual application for membership whether one's parents were members or not. Rockhampton Friends developed an alternative of "associate" membership. Felicia Hopkins was sure that this helped both children of Friends and enquirers. "It is a fact", she wrote, "that in Rockhampton Meetings, where an associate membership prevailed for some years, some solid families have joined in from outside and the young people settle to the Friends' Meetings".[35]

There was a further important difference highlighted by comparison of American and Australian Quakerism. Australian Quakerism was slow to establish an identity of its own. At first sight this might appear to be simply a question of numbers. Quakers in America were numbered by the tens of thousands, in Australia by tens. Numbers certainly generate a sense of solidarity and from this comes strength to undertake corporate concerns. Quakers in America had much more impact on national life than did Australian Quakers in the nineteenth century. Until the end of this century Australian Meetings developed in isolation from each other and were tied independently by lines direct but separate to London Yearly Meeting. Any impact therefore made in Australia in that period was primarily by Quakers acting as individuals rather than by Quaker Meetings.

In America the tradition was one of independence from London. American Meetings were free to develop their own identity and to respond to American conditions in a way which was not open to Australian Meetings.

The historian of Australian Quakerism becomes increasingly aware of the difficulties which confronted Quakers in the nineteenth century attempting to practise their faith in spite of the tyranny of distance, the waywardness of man, and the strains of wresting a living from a strange and often hostile environment.

There were times when the survival of Quakerism itself was threatened.

Yet there were signs of hope. By the turn of the century Australian Quakers had begun to establish an identity of their own. The success of their school and their journal gave confidence. The decision to unite in a General Meeting provided the means for them to make their voice heard on national issues.

While Quakerism, the institution, was slow of growth, Quakers as individuals, following the example of men like Backhouse and Walker, made a notable contribution to the Australian community by their integrity of character and their sense of social responsibility. They endeavoured to express in their lives the essence of Quakerism and thus made possible a more positive corporate Quaker witness in the twentieth century.

Appendix 1
Biographical Index of Quakers in Australia Before 1862

The full index gives information (where known) concerning children, place of origin, occupation, date and place of arrival in Australia, membership of the Society of Friends, and dates of birth and death.

The names given below are limited to those of the original migrants. For families the parents only are listed here.

Manuscript copies of this index are available in Friends' Meeting Houses in each capital city of Australia, at Friends' House Library, Euston Road, London, and Friends' Historical Library, Eustace Street, Dublin.

AL(L)COCK   Henry
ALCORN   Thomas (—1883)
ALEXANDER   Reuben F. (1832–1920)
ALLEN   Richard
ALLEN   William B. (1812–69)
  m Ruth Johnson SAYERS
ARMFIELD   George (1818–65)
  m Rachel Lane WHITE
ASHWORTH   James (—1844)
ATKINSON   Joseph (1828–   )

BAILIFF   Edward
BAKEWELL   John (1807–   )
BAKEWELL   Robert (1810–   )
BALL   Joseph R. (1822–79)
  m Louise BROWN
BARNES   John (1833–   )
BARRINGER   Joseph (1816–65)
BARRINGTON   Edward E. (1827–1904)

BARRINGTON   Frederick A. (1819–   )
BARRITT   Joseph (1816–81)
  m (1) Mary Ann HARRISON
       (2) Hannah Sophia MAY
BARROW   George (1800?–   )
BARWICK   George
BASSETT   Alfred (1828–   )
BASSETT   John S. (1824–48)
BEAKBANE   William F. (1833–83)
BEALE   Joseph (1801–57)
  m (1) Elizabeth LECKY
       (2) Margaret Grubb DAVIS
BEARDMORE   Emma (1823–1896)
BECK   Charles (1805–87)
  m Sarah ANDREWS
BECKETT   Peter
BELL   George (1805–52)
BELSHAM   Abraham
BENNETT   Gabriel
BENSON   George (1823–1905)

Biographical Index

BENSON Richard Smith (1821–)
  m Eliza J. REID
BENSON Robert R. (1830–86)
  m Isabella MANSON
BENSON William
BICKERTON James
BIDDLE Rolles (1812–43)
BIGG Jeremiah (1811–38)
BIRCHALL William H. (1817–)
  m Lucy HUTCHINSON
BIRBECK Samuel B. (1802–67)
  m Damiana VALDES
BIRRILL William W. (1830–)
BLACK Thomas H.
BLACKWELL John (1788–1876)
BLAKE Samuel (1810–)
BLAKEY John (1792–)
BOADLE William B. (1795–1865)
BOUCHER John
BOWDEN Thornton
BRADY Samuel (1804–)
BRAGG John (1827–)
LeGAY BRERETON John (1827–86)
  m Mary TONGUE
BRIEN (BRYAN) George (1824–49)
BROCKBANK Edward G. (1843–1929)
BROCKBANK John T. (1836–1914)
  m Charlotte SADDLER
BROOKER David (–1845)
BROWN Benjamin (1821–)
BROWN Edmund (1824–1911)
BROWN Jane (–1870)
BROWN Lancelot D. (1829–52)
BROWN Solomon
BROWN Thomas
BROWN Walter
BUILDER William (1830–)
BURGESS Thomas (1791–1865)
BURGESS Thomas (1830–53)

CALVERT Margaret
CAPPER Alfred (1815–61)
CHAMBERS John (1819–93)
CHERRY Henry (1824–66)
CHIPCHASE John H. (1832–1906)
  m Ann SYKES
CLARK Daniel (1814–1901)
  m (1) Elizabeth DAVIDSON
    (2) Mary DAVIDSON
CLARK James (1813–96)
CLARK Joseph (1821–1900)
CLARK Reuben B.
CLARK Samuel (1825–95)
CLEMES Alfred B. (1829–1917)
  m Mary Ann RUDDLE
CLEMES Francis D. (1830–)
CLEMES Thomas P. (1825–1903)
  m Elizabeth COULSON
CLEMESHA Samuel (1804–)
CLEMESHA Solomon C. (1824–)
  m Rachel GREEN
CLIFTON Elinor Bell (1793–1866)
COAR Jeremiah I. (1812–)
COATES Isaac (1808–)
  m (1) Margaret COCKBURN
    (2) Ann HEATH
COCK Robert
COLEMAN Arthur (1829–67)
  m Lucy DAY
COLEMAN Edward C. (1797–1849)
  m Charlotte FOWLER
COLES Mary Bevan (1798–)
COMPTON John Townsend (1814–)
COOK(E) Joseph
COOK Joseph (1812–)
COOK Samuel (1800–1866)
COOK SAMUEL
COOK William (1811–)
COON Rachel (1808–)
COOPER William (1833–1921)
  m Jane RITSON

CORDER Thomas (1812–)
CORNISH Samuel (1827–)
COTTON Francis (1801–83)
  m Anna Maria TILNEY
COULSON Eliza (c.1828–79)
COWAN Richard
COX George (1805–1880)
COX John (1804–)
CRABBE William (–1880)
CRABTREE
CRANSTONE George (1820–)
CREETH Charles H. (1835–)
CREETH Edmund G. (1829–70)
CREETH George (1833–77)
  m Hannah ANNEAR
CREETH Richard (1825–91)
  m Sarah Davis BEALE
CREETH William J. (1823–1902)
  m Margaret Grubb BEALE
CROSS Charles A. (1834–)
CROSS Frederick (1832–)
CROSS Samuel
CROUCH Sarah (1806–76)
CUDMORE Daniel M.P. (1811–91)
  m Mary NIHILL

DANGAR (née MOSCROP)
DARTON Samuel (1821–)
  m Mary Graves RICHARDSON
DAVEY George
DAVEY Joseph (1835–)
DAVEY Thomas (1834–81)
DAVIES John (1828–)
DAVY Abraham (1809–74)
  m Jane DAWSON
DAY David W.
DEANE George (1791–1857)
  m Rachel GREENWOOD
DICKENSON Charlotte (1831–)
  m Robert CHURCHUS
DICKENSON Edward (1822–98)
  m (1) Isabella –
    (2) Grace E. WRIGHT

DICKENSON James (1806–)
  m Margaret BLAKEY
DIXON Esther (–1872)
  m Robert MATHER
DIXON James (1787–1865)
DIXON John (1817–54)
DOCKRAY Thomas (1825–)
DODGSON Robert (1812–)
DOIDGE William
DORE James
DUDLEY Guilford (1814–)
  m Ellen POWER
DUFFIELD Walter (1817–82)
DUNSFORD Robert (1772–1847)
  m Sophia MULLETT

EADE Mary Gibbs
EVANS William (1820–)
EVERETT William (1788–1856)

FAYLE Anna Maria (1828–)
  m James PAULL
FAYLE Sara (1835–)
  m James SEYMOUR
FAYLE William Knott (1829–90)
FENNELL George F. (1821–51?)
FENNELL Robert (1813–77)
  m Maria MCKINNEY (née BATMAN)
FERRIS Thomas F. (1823–71)
  m Capella E. SMITH
FISHER Edward C. (1825–1908)
  m Rosa L. ROBINSON
FISHER John (1809–)
FLOWER Abraham C.
  m. Susannah M. PETTITT
FORSTER John
FORSTER Noble
FOSTER Edmund (1803–)
FOSTER John (1821–)
FOWLER Hannah Pole (1809–97)
FOX Alexander (1837–76)
  m Ellen PHILLIPS

Biographical Index 353

FOX   Henry Tregelles (1826–97)
  m Melita ABRAHAMS
FOX   John
FREEMAN   William H.
  m Emma GORHAM

GALLIENE   John (1799–1853)
GALLOWAY   John
GERRARD   Mary Ann (1813–)
GILLETT   George F. (1828–)
  m Harriet SMITH
GILPIN   James Bernard (1818–)
  m Sarah SHANNON
GODLEE   John (1815–)
GOLDNEY   ——
GORDON   Eleanor
GORHAM   William (1795–)
GRAVELY   Arthur (1814–52)
GRAVELY   Arthur (c.1803–c.1902)
GRAVES   Henry Swan (1819–)
GRAVES   William Curtis (1809–)
GRAY   George (1813–73)
GRAY   William F. (1819–)
GREEN   Joseph (1833–59)
GREEN   Mary S. (1828–90)
  m James HOPE
GREEN   Rachel (1838–78)
  m Solomon CLEMESHAW
GREEN   Thomas (1827–)
GREENWOOD   James C. (1844–)
GREENWOOD   Robert J. (1842–)
GREER   Joseph Webb
  m Susanna McDONNELL
GRUBB   Abraham (1826–65)
GRUBB   Richard D. (1820–65)
  m Margaret GRUBB

HACK   Ellen M. (1807–)
  m John KNOTT
HACK   John Barton (1805–84)
  m Bridget WATSON
HACK   Priscilla (1810–41)
  m Edward PHILCOX

HACK   Stephen (1816–94)
  m Elizabeth M. WILTON
HAGEN   Jacob (1809–70)
  m (1) Jane GREENWOOD
    (2) Mary BAKER
HALL   Hurtley (1825–67)
HALLIDAY   William J. (1812–73)
  m Sarah DRUITT
HAMILTON   Archibald
HARDING   Francis S. (1829–56)
HARDING   Frederick (1821–)
HARDING   John H. (1826–67)
HART   Elijah
HARVEY   Thomas
HATTON   Edward (1831–)
HAWLEY   Robert
HAYE   Lydia de la (1827–)
HAYES   David (–1864)
HAWKINS   Caleb (–1854)
HEAD   Benjamin (1824–)
HEAD   Joseph J. (1823–)
HEATH   Newman (1815–79)
HEATH   William H. (1813–68)
HEATON   Robert
HELTHAM   John
HENDERSON   Andrew (–1854)
  m Hannah MULCASTER
HEYWOOD   Francis (1829–)
HITCHCOCK   Robert (c.1784–1851)
HODGSON   John Baker (1817–)
HODGSON   Thomas (1822–)
HOLDSHIP   William
HOLLINGSHEAD   William F.
HOLTON   Richard (1792–)
HOPE   James (1825–92)
  m Mary Skinner GREEN
HORSFALL   John A. (1819–99)
  m Rachel GOUNDRY
HORSNAILL   Robert (1831–72)
HORTIN   William E. (1819–)
HOWIE (HOOWE)   Samuel (1830–1912)
  m Laura BEALE

HOWIE (HOOWE) William (1825–1903)
  m Anna BEALE
HOWIE (HOOWE) Elizabeth M. (1827–)
  m George MYLES
HOWISON Ebenezer (1817–54)
HOWITT Godfrey (1800–1873)
  m Phoebe BAKEWELL
HOWITT Richard (1799–)
HOWITT William (1792–1879)
  m Mary BOTHAM
HUNT Alfred (1830–)
HUNT Harriet (1805–79)
HUNT John Hawkins (1816–)
HUNT William (1809–)
HUNTLY Robert (1785–1853)
  m Isett Rachel REYNOLDS

IRWIN William
ISAAC Samuel (1832–)

JACKSON William Harvey (c.1799–1855?)
JACOB Joseph (1835–1921)
  m Louise LOWMAN
JACOB Richard (1833–1907)
JACOB Samuel (1830–71)
JEFFRIES Joel (1809–79)
JELLICOE Samuel (1833–)
JELLICOE Thomas W. (1829–65)
JESPER John (1825–)
  m Isabella COLENDER
JESPER Robert W. (1831–)
  m Catherine NEVILLE
JESPER Thomas (1839–1910)
  m Susannah BARRITT
JESSUP Alfred F. (1833–)
JOHNSON Joseph
JOHNSON Thomas
JOHNSTON Hugh (1827–)
JONES Henry (1832–97)
  m Edith E. WILSON
JONES Jonathan H. (1836–66)
JONES Joseph (1824–)
  m Priscilla GRAVES
JONES Robert
JOSLIN(G) David (1829–73)
JOYCE William
JUBB George and Catherine

KEKWICK Daniel (1788–1866)
  m Mary Ann DARTON
KELSHALL John
KENDREW Thomas J. (1828–)
KEY Catherine H. (1837–)
KEY William S.D.O.
KNIGHT Edwin (1817–)
KNIGHT Joseph (1837–)

LAMBERT James
LAMBKIN John (1794–1863)
LANDSDALE John
LAWSON John (1795–1875)
LAWSON Sarah (1821–)
  m (1) James GREGORY
    (2) Chas. G. LAWSON
LEACH Amram
LEICESTER Chamney (1823–)
  m Elizabeth ASHWORTH
LEICESTER William (1824–)
LEITH Mary Forbes (1813–)
LESTER John (1830–1906)
  m Agnes BINNEY
LESTER Robert (1832–1917)
  m Margaret RANKINE
LEVITT Charles
LEVITT John North (1823–58)
LEVITT Samuel I. (1822–93)
  m Sarah KELLAND
LIDBETTER Henry A. (1828–c.60)
LIDBETTER Thomas (1823–1908)
  m (1) Deborah WILSON
    (2) E.L. STAPLES
LIDGEY John (1834–)
  m Hannah CORNISH
LINNEY James S.
LISTER William H. (1828–59)

LLOYD John Sanderson (1831–   )
  n Charlotte E. WATSON
LOCKE William (c.1791–1866)
  m Arabella SHAW
LORD Simeon
LUCAS Charles (1793–   )
  m Deborah ABATT
LUMSDEN David
LUMSDEN Robert (1804–71)

McGOWAN James
MACKIE Frederick (1812–93)
  m Rachel MAY
McLEAY Alexander
MARRIAGE Joseph (1807–84)
  m Eliza GREENWOOD
MARRIAGE Richard (1816–   )
MARSH Thomas Gray (1821–   )
MARSHALL Lucy (1811–   )
MARSHALL Samuel (1822–   )
MASON Thomas (1818–1903)
  m Jane WILFORD
MASON Thomas (1827–69)
MATHER Robert (1782–1855)
    m (1) Ann BENSON
      (2) Esther DIXON
MATTHEWS Susan
MAW Alfred (1823–   )
MAW John (1835–89)
MAW Thomas (1843–1917)
MAY Joseph (1787–1878)
  m Hannah MORRIS
MAY Henry (1786–1846)
MERCHANT Mary E. (1812–   )
METCALF John (–1855)
METFORD Ellen E. (1816–1900)
    born RUTTER
  m (1) Seymer METFORD
      (2) John PALSER
MIDDLEBROOK Matthew
  (1816–   )
MIDDLETON John How (1823–   )
  m Esther BEARDMORE
MILLER George Benson

MITCHELL Thomas
  m Ellen DEANE
MOFFAT Eleanor
MOLD James (–1869)
  m Elizabeth HARRIS
MOORE George Augustus
MORING John (c.1814–89)
MORRIS John G. (1831–53)
MORRIS Maxwell
MOULD Charles (1809?–80?)
MOXHAM Marcus (1835–1917)
MULLEN Thomas (1804–   )

NAINBY Frederic (1808–86)
NAINBY Frederick (1837–   )
NEALE Joseph J. (1836–   )
NEALE Margaret (1812?–65)
NEAVE James R. (1828–   )
NEILD John Cash (1815–93)
  m Maria GREENWOOD
NEILD William H. (1832–   )
NEVILLE Emmaretta (1825–   )
    born ALEXANDER
NEVINS Charles (1825–   )
NEVINS Penrose (1819–78)
  m Eliza OUTWAITE
NEWMAN Henry H.
NEWSOM Robert W. (1821–67)
NEWSOM Thomas
NICHOLAS or NICHOLLIAS Wm.
  (c.1801–51)
  m Isabella RAYNER
NICHOLAS William
NICHOLSON James (–1875)
NICHOLSON John
NICHOLSON Mary
  m Thomas WEATHERHEAD
NICHOLSON Thomas (1830–53)
NICHOLSON William (–1890)
NIXON Robert Ward (1809–   )

ODDIE Ann (1812–   )
ODDIE Richard (1827–89)
OLLIER John

Appendix 1

OVERTON William (c.1812–98)
  m Elizabeth RULE
OXLEY Edward (1815–)

PACE John H. (1814–)
PAGE James (1808–)
  m Mary JARVIS
PALMER Henry (1800–1855)
PALSER John (1803–79)
  m (1) Hannah ——
    (2) Ellen E. METFORD
PARKER Thomas
PARKER William (c.1808–87)
PARKINSON Roger (1808–54)
  m Mary FENNELLY
PARKINSON Sydney (c.1745–71)
PASLEY Walter
PELL Morris Birbeck (1827–79)
  m Julia RUSDEN
PENNY John Kemp (1832–)
PENNY Richard (1817–44)
PENROSE James
PERRY John H. (1814–53)
  m Priscilla BROWETT
PHELAN Richard
PHELPS James Christy (1782–)
  m Anne LECKY
PHILLIPS Archibald
  (alias HAMILTON)
PHILLIPS Charles (1806–53)
PHILLIPS George (1820–1900)
  m Margaret MAY
PHILLIPS Henry W. (1811–98)
  m Maria MAY
PHILLIPS John
PHILLIPS John Aldam (1814–)
PHILLIPS Joseph E. (1813–1900)
PIERCE Thomas (1802–69)
  m Mary OLIVER
PIERSON Joseph (1831–1909)
  m Indiana SAYCE
PIM Joseph H. (1831–54)
POLLARD Theophilus (1795–1872)

  m (1) Ann LIDBETTER
    (2) Elizabeth F. WARREN
PRATT ——
PRINCE James (–1882)
PROPSTING Henry (1810–1901)
  m (1) Ann BEAZER
    (2) Hannah CATER
PROPSTING Richard (1819–99)
  m Elizabeth R. DAVIDSON
PRYOR Alfred (1824–)
PRYOR Frederick (1813–)

RALEIGH Joseph (1803–52)
  m Priscilla THORP
RALEIGH Rachel (1793–1860)
RALEIGH Sarah (1789–1861)
RANSOME Henry (1810–)
RANSOME James (c.1807–1875)
RASHLEIGH Francis & Priscilla
RAWLINGS Henry (1830–)
RAWSON Sarah (1820–90)
RAYNER William (1767–1850)
  m (1) Elizabeth GOLDSMITH
    (2) Susannah CHAPMAN
READ Charles (–1910)
REEVES Isaac G.
REILLY John
REILLY William
REYNOLDS Robert
REYNOLDS William S.
REYNOLDS Frederick (1833–1900)
  m Gulielma METFORD
RICHARDS David (1773–1853)
RICHARDSON John Stratton (1827–)
RICHARDSON Samuel (1821–)
RIDLER Henry Harford
RISHTON George (1818–)
RISHTON Henry (1812–)
RITCHIE Joseph (c.1804–54)
RIVERS Robert
ROBERTSON Margaret
ROBINSON Arthur (1836–)

Biographical Index 357

ROBINSON   Edward Gaynor (1830–80)
  m Elizabeth GREER
ROBINSON   John Pim Penrose (1823–   )
ROBINSON   Joseph P. (1813–48)
  m Margaret MEALE
ROBINSON   Richard J. (1828–85)
ROBINSON   William (1823–1906)
  m Emily J. DICKSON
ROBSON   William
ROSS   Ellen
ROWNTREE   Edward C. (1811–93)
  m Hannah NICHOLS
ROYCE   John
RUTTER   Elizabeth (1827–   )
RUTTER   Farley (1830–89)
RUTTER   Richard B. (1826–98)
  m Anna M. CLAPHAM
RUTTER   Samuel (1820–57)

SANDERS   Andrew (1797–1865)
  m Hannah SPENCE
SANDERS   George (1793–1864)
  m (1) Ann SMURTHTHWAITE
     (2) Sarah GOODE
SANDERS   William (1823–1900)
  m Elizabeth MAY
SANGER   Daniel (1800–1867)
SANGER   Mildred (1791–1867)
SANSOM   Edward Pearn (1803–59)
SANSOM   John (1806–   )
SAUNDERS   Arthur (1829–   )
SAUNDERS   Thomas J. (1828–56)
SAUNDERS   Thomas (1825–   )
SATTERTHWAITE   Henry
SATTERTHWAITE   Wm. (1794–1837)
SAUL   William (1822–   )
SAYCE   Edward (1813–92)
  m Deborah A. SMITH
SAYCE   Joseph (1815–76)
  m Emma HARGRAVE
SCHOLEFIELD   James (1825–58)

SHANNON   Elizabeth
SHEA   Dennis
SHEPPARD   Edward (1822–   )
SHERWIN   Catherine
SHERWIN   William (1825–87)
  m (1) Ellen O'CONNOR
     (2) Eliza HILL
SHOOBRIDGE   William (1781–1836)
  m (1) Mary JENKINS
     (2) Harriett SHAW
SHIPTON   John
SIMMS   Benjamin (1800–   )
SIMMS   Joseph (1797–1882)
SIMPSON   Emma Jane
SIMPSON   Joseph (1800–1888)
SKEWES   John (1800–1875)
SKINNER   Alfred (1808–   )
  m Maria J. BLANCH
SKINNER   Thomas (1807–79)
SKINNER   William (1803–   )
SLADE   Alfred (1838–   )
SLATER   Henry
SMART   Sir Benjamin (1824–49)
SMEAL   James (1837–   )
SMETHURST   John Furness
SMITH   Alfred (1814–   )
  m —— BOARDMAN
SMITH   Ellen (1835–   )
SMITH   Frederick (1830–   )
SMITH   Granville (1847–88)
SMITH   Henry Eckroyd (1823–89)
SMITH   Howard (1838–   )
SMITH   Humphrey (1835–   )
SMITH   Richard H. (1820–   )
SMITH   Rosamund (1836–70)
SMITH   William R.
SMITH   William (1831–c.58)
SMYTH   George
SMYTH   Samuel Hodgson (1808–   )
  m Eliza YELDHAM
SPARROW   Robert
SQUIRE   Thomas (1790–1866)

STEAD   David (1797–1886)
  m —— BELCHER
STEPHENS James (1811–   )
STEVENS Isaac (1833–53)
STEVENS Thomas (1813–   )
STEVENSON William D.
STIGLITZ Frederick L. (–1866)
  m (1) Catherine McNALLY
     (2) Hester A. BLACKER
STOCK John
STORY George F. (1800–1885)
STRANGMAN Alfred G. (1832–   )
SUMMERLAND Abraham
SWINBORN James (1827–1912)
  m Sarah SINGLETON
SYKES Thomas G. (1829–c.57)

TATHAM Edward (1805–   )
  m Dorothy MENNELL
TAWELL John (1784–1845)
  m (1) Mary ——
     (2) Sarah CUTFORTH
TAYLOR Anthony Harris (1816–70)
TAYLOR Morris (1831–   )
  m Augusta GRAVES
TAYLOR Rebecca (1813–96)
  m Wm. PEACOCK
THISTLETHWAITE Betty (1787–1868)
  born DAVISON
THISTLETHWAITE David (1821–93)
  m Ellen CLAYTON
THISTLETHWAITE Fitz
THISTLETHWAITE Henry (1814–   )
THOMAS Charles (1828–   )
THOMPSON John (1815–   )
  m Deborah WEBB
THOMPSON Thomas (1807–   )
  m Sarah KNIGHT
THOMPSON Walker (c.1797–   )

THORNE Alfred (1823–91)
THORNE Anna (1827–65)
  born POLLARD
THORNE Robert (1795–   )
THORP John (1808–   )
THORP Joshua (1796–   )
THORP Samuel (1810–68)
  m (1) Maria LONG
     (2) Anna ——
THORP Thomas (1815–88)
  m Emilia M. WILMOT
TOWNSEND John
TREE Stephen
  (alias John WILSON)
TUCKETT Alfred C. (1833–   )
TURNER Thomas (1800–1849)
  m Elizabeth Lees SWITHENBANK
TYLOR Frederick (1819–   )
TYLOR Joshua

UNTHANK Gabriel F. (1814–95)
  m Mary MERRICK

VEALE James (1801–82)
  m Elizabeth GRIFFIN
VEALE Samuel (1800–1875)
VEEVERS Henry (1827–63)
VEEVERS John (1825–94)
  m Frances A. HICKMOCK

WALKER Albert (1830–   )
WALKER Bemjamin (1831–   )
WALKER Catherine (c.1797–   )
WALKER George W. (1800–1859)
  m Sarah Benson MATHER
WALKER Joseph J. (1821–51)
WALL Mary Ann
  born CULLIFORD
WALLIS Algernon (1829–   )
WALPOLE Edward (1836–1926)
  m Charlotte MURCHISON

WALPOLE George (1797–   )
  m Ann MANTLE and/or
     Anne BROWNE
WALPOLE Henry (1833–95)
  m Deborah FAYLE
WALPOLE John J. (1825–   )
WALPOLE John T. (1826–77)
  m Sarah J. MURCHISON
WALPOLE Thomas (1830–1922)
  m Jane CALVERT
WALPOLE Thomas (1827–   )
WALPOLE William J. (1835–   )
WALTON John
WALTON Thomas (–1855)
WARNER Henry (1819–   )
WARNER Joseph J.
  m (1) Mary NEVILLE
     (2) Mary MILLER
WATSON Henry (1811–   )
WATSON Joseph (1813–   )
WATSON William (1773–1858)
  m Martha WATERHOUSE
WEBB Alfred (1834–1908)
  m Elizabeth SHACKLETON
WEBSTER John (1793–1855)
  m Rachel A. WEATHERALD
WELLS Joseph J. (1820–   )
  m Anna M. S. REYNOLDS
WELLS Thomas (1835–1911)
WERE George (1816–   )
WERE Jonathan Binns (1809–85)
  m (1) Sophia Mullett DUNSFORD
     (2) Elizabeth McARTHUR

WEST Theodore (1826–98)
  m (1) Margaret HAIGH
     (2) Mary ROULSTON
WESTON Charles H.
WESTON Henry T.
WESTWOOD Joseph J. (1828–   )
WHITE Alfred (1820–   )
WHITE Edwin
WHITE Frederick
WHITE George
WHITE George (1815–   )
WHITE James D. (1834–60)
WHITE Samuel (1824?–   )
WHITE William (1831–   )
WHITE William How (1836–60)
WHITE William J. (1821–   )
WHITE William and Jane
WHITTON Joseph
WILLIAMS Isaac
WILLIAMS Sarah
WILLIAMS Thomas (1830–   )
WILLIAMSON John and Sarah
WILLINGTON Thomas (1809–84)
WILMOT John (1805?–   )
WILSON John (1784–1846)
WINTER William
WOOD William
  m Lydia BROWN
WOODHEAD James D. (1831–63)
WORMALD Richard
WORMALD William (1829–93)

YATES George Joseph
YOUNG James

Appendix 2
Visiting Friends from Overseas
1832—1901

1832—61

1832—38	J. Backhouse and G. W. Walker
1840	G. W. Walker returns to Hobart
1852—55	R. Lindsey and F. Mackie
1855	F. Mackie returns to South Australia
1859	W. Tallach
1961	R. and S. Lindsey

1862—75

1867—72	J. J. Neave and W. Robson
1867—78	J. B. and W. Hodgkin
1875	The "Australian Deputation" of J. J. Dymond, W. Beck and A. Wright

1876—1902

1876	J. J. Neave returns to Sydney
1877—78	R. W. Douglas (U.S.A.)
1879—80	Hannah Hall (U.S.A.)
1881—82	Isaac Sharp (and J. J. Neave)
1882	Charles Robinson
1883	Antoinette Stirling
1885—86	Rufus P. King and A. White (U.S.A.)
1886	Thomas Houston — Irish Friend Evangelist
1886—87	H. Hodgkin and W. Hazell — emigration survey
1888—89	Ann and Fletcher Jackson (New Zealand)
1889	William and Katherine Jones (Peace Society)
1891	Robert Harding, William Jesper Sayce, Alfred Wright
1892	Samuel Morris and Jonathan Rhoads (U.S.A.)

1893	Carl Schardt
1896—97	Jonathan Edward Hodgkin
1897	Sarah Pumphrey and Alice Pierce
1898	Anna L. Evens (Friend missionary from Hoshangabad, India)
1900	Caroline Woodruff, Samuel and Rose Hurnard
1900—1901	Henrietta Brown and Emma Bishop
	Sarah Lury
	Edward and Dorothy Cadbury
	Lydia Whitehead

Abbreviations

A.D.B.	*Australian Dictionary of Biography*
A.O.T.	Archives of Tasmania
A.S.A.	Archives of South Australia
F.H.A.L.	Friends' House Archives, London
F.L.E.D.	Friends' Library, Eustace Street, Dublin
F.M.H.	Friends' Meeting House
G.W.W.	George Washington Walker
J.B.	James Backhouse
L.L.M.	La Trobe Library, Melbourne
M.L.	Mitchell Library, Sydney
M.M.	Monthly Meeting
O.L.	Oxley Library, Brisbane
Q.M.	Quarterly Meeting
R.A.H.S.	Royal Australian Historical Society
T.U.A.	Tasmanian University Archives
V.D.L.	Van Diemen's Land
Y.M.	Yearly Meeting

Notes to Text*

Chapter One

1. J. Nickalls, ed., *Journal of George Fox*, p. 58.
2. Henry Cadbury, in notes to the second edition of W. C. Braithwaite's *The Beginnings of Quakerism*, p. 570, claims that the use of the term "Society of Friends" can be traced back no further than 1793.
3. Nickalls, p. 11.
4. Ibid., p. 104.
5. Ibid., p. xl.
6. J. W. Rowntree, *Essays and Addresses*, p. 92.
7. Matthew 5:34.
8. Matthew 5:37.
9. M. Ignatieff, *Just Measure of Pain*, p. 150.
10. J. Backhouse, *Narrative*, app. B, p. xii.
11. "The rich and mighty of the times thought themselves degraded by the mode of address, as reducing them from a plural magnitude to a singular or individual, or simply station in life" (Clarkson, *Portraiture of Quakerism*, vol. 1, p. 301). Clarkson quoted the reaction of "the rich and mighty" as "Why, you ill-bred clown, do you thou me?"
12. Nickalls, p. 37.
13. William Howitt, in his introduction to an 1834 Tract, *Word to Dissenters*, attacked the state-supported clergy, "The returns of 1831 show that of 10,000 incumbents, only 4649 are doing duty and therefore nearly 6,000 are eating, in the very face of the British public, in contemptuous idleness, the bread set apart by the nation for the *working* clergy."
14. *The Friend*, n.s. 30 (1 September 1891):242.
15. Nickalls, p. 65.
16. Ibid., p. 520.
17. S. E. Fox, ed., *Edward Octavius Tregelles*, pp. 90-92.
18. Ignatieff, p. 59.
19. Stephen Grellet, 1773–1855, originally known by his French name, Etienne de Grellet, was educated in France, fought as a royalist, was captured, but escaped to Holland; he then emigrated to British Guiana in South America and in 1795 arrived in New York. Through contact with Friends he joined

---

* The English periodical, *The Friend*, began in 1843. A new series began in January 1861. To distinguish between the earlier and later series, references in the later series are marked (n.s.). Where dates are important to an understanding of the text, these are also given.

the Society of Friends in 1796 and during a long life of service to the Society he visited Europe on four occasions. When Grellet visited Newgate prison early in 1813 he confessed that he was "astonished beyond description at the mass of woe and misery" he beheld there. On leaving the prison he went straight to Elizabeth Fry and appealed to her for help. The result is described in his memoirs: "The appeal to such a pious and sensible mind as dear Elizabeth possesses was not in vain. She immediately sent for several pieces of flannel and had speedily collected a number of young women Friends who went to work with such diligence that on the very next day she repaired to the prison with a bundle of made-up garments for the naked children." (Seebohm, *Stephen Grellet*, vol. 1, pp. 196-97).
20. *The Friend*, n.s.36, no. 24:398.
21. It is interesting to compare Extract Nos. 559 and 560 in *Christian Faith and Practice in the experience of the Society of Friends* (London: Headley Bros., 1960) to see the difference in emphasis between the years 1751 and 1857. In 1751 the advice stresses temperance and moderation, "and as excess in drinking has been too prevalent among many of the inhabitants of these nations, we recommend to all Friends a watchful care over themselves". By 1857 the social effects of "ardent spirits" led London Yearly Meeting to record a Minute of "deep concern in view of the fearful amount of sin and misery existing in our land through the prevailing use of intoxicating liquors" and in this and subsequent statements Friends were urged to consider whether abstinence might be undertaken as an "individual duty".
22. Ibid., preface to Extracts 349–59.
23. Ibid., extract 363.
24. Though this practice of "recognizing" a spiritual hierarchy seemed alien to Quaker belief in "the priesthood of all believers", it nevertheless persisted until 1924, when London Yearly Meeting abandoned the recording of "ministers". But recording of "ministers" is still widespread in the United States of America.
25. See p. 33.
26. D. Pike, *Paradise of Dissent*, p. 21.
27. Hardwicke Act in the 26th year of George II, 1753.
28. Act of William IV 6 and 7 of 1837.
29. The term "in profession with Friends" meant in sympathy with Friends, as shown generally by attendance at Meetings for Worship.
30. *Proceedings of London Y.M.* (1859):16.
31. R. L. Brett, ed., *Barclay Fox's Journal*, p. 278.
32. W. A. C. Stewart, *Quakers and Education*, p. 67.
33. R. Jones, *Later Periods of Quakerism*, vol. 1, p. 488.
34. Ignatieff, p. 149.
35. Jones, p. 324.
36. *Epistles of London Y.M.* (1836):272.
37. Jones, p. 499.
38. From Elizabeth Fry's Memoirs, reprinted from *The Philadelphia Friend* as a supplement to *The British Friend*, 28 February 1849, p. 3.
39. Godfrey Howitt was one of the first doctors to set up in practice in the new settlement at Port Phillip. He sailed in September 1839 with his wife and five children and a brother, Richard. His more famous brother, William, came twelve years later with his two sons, Alfred and Charles, to see for himself the life of a gold-digger. His two years in Australia provided him with rich material for his book, *Land, Labour and Gold*, published in London in 1855.

40. M. Howitt, *Mary Howitt*, vol. 1, p. 260.
41. Ibid., p. 263.
42. Ibid., vol. 2, p. 43.
43. *Journal of the Friends' Historical Society* 2:71.
44. J.S. Rowntree, *Quakerism, Past and Present*, p. 130.
45. J.J. Fox, *Enquiry*, p. 7.
46. E.P. Thompson, *English working-class*, p. 30.
47. Ibid., p. 793.
48. *Quakeriana* 3, no. 1.
49. W. Robson, Journal, Microfilm 206, F.H.A.L.

Chapter Two

1. Rowntree added, "From the youthful age of many of the scholars in 1843, a considerable addition must be made to this number for those who may be expected to migrate. It is known that one-third of the sons of Friends pass through Ackworth School. It is probable that a larger proportion of Ackworth scholars emigrated than of any other section of the Society; but from the date we have given, we think it will readily be admitted that, in estimating the whole number of members who during the present century have emigrated from England and Wales at seven hundred, we have not exceeded the actual number, but are probably below the reality" (J.S. Rowntree, *Quakerism, Past and Present*, p. 86).
2. The records of the London and Middlesex Meetings are housed at the Friends' House Library, Euston Road, London; the records of Ireland Meetings at Eustace Street, Dublin, and in Belfast. Most of the other Meetings have lodged their records with County Record Offices or with University archives.
3. J.S. Rowntree, *Friends' Register*, p. 20.
4. A leaflet, *Genealogical Materials*, supplied to readers at Friends' House Library, London, explains: "In 1840, when the registers were surrendered, digests were prepared. These digest registers contain all the information available in the originals, except witnesses to marriages. There were in 1840 twenty-six quarterly meetings, for each of which three digests (births, marriages, burials) were prepared. The arrangement is not strictly alphabetical, but roughly chronological within each letter of the alphabet. In some cases there are supplementary registers for material surrendered after 1840. A separate series of digests covers the period from 1837 to the mid-twentieth century."
5. A total of over two hundred sources has been listed in *Quakers in Australia before 1862 – a Biographical Index*. Manuscript copies of this Index have been lodged with Regional Meetings of the Society of Friends in all Australian capital cities and with Friends' House Library, London and with the Friends' Historical Library, Eustace Street, Dublin.
6. W. Howitt, *Land, Labour and Gold*, vol. 1, pp. 357-58.
7. See table 7.
8. This figure covers the 153 total from table 3 together with the post-1861 numbers of 30 disowned and 22 disassociated.
9. These samples are taken from the membership statistics for 1800–1851 given in the *Journal of the Friends' Historical Society* 52, no. 2:98.
10. See table 6.

11. See pp. 11-16.
12. From membership statistics 1800—1851 in *Journal of the Friends' Historical Society* 52, no. 2:98-99.
13. W. Robson, Diary, microfilm 206, p. 86, F.H.A.L.
14. "White" was the self-assigned name given to a group of Quakers (never more it is thought than thirty or forty) who in the eighteen-forties claimed to receive direct revelations through the Holy Spirit, but they refused to submit what were often extravagant claims of revelation to the testing judgment of a Quaker Meeting. Joshua Jacob was the leader of the group. "White" was taken as the symbol of purity and so they dressed in white. They labelled those who disagreed with them "Black Quakers". Isabel Grubb called the White Quakers "an extreme perversion of Quietism" (Grubb, *Quakers in Ireland*, p. 129).
15. The difference between the totals of 983 in table 7 and 1213 in table 2 is accounted for by the inclusion in table 2 of all those born after the arrival of their parents in the colonies.
16. M. Nichols, ed., *Traveller under Concern*, pp. 269-70.
17. E. Isichei, *Victorian Quakers*, p. 170.
18. Isichei, pp. 288-89.
19. This figure is obtained by subtracting from the total of adult members migrating from the United Kingdom, viz. 707 in table 2, the total of Irish migrants, 121, from table 8, and a proportion of the children born before 1846 — say a hundred, giving a remainder of 486.
20. Vann, *English Quakerism 1655—1755*, p. 57.
21. Ibid., p. 70.
22. Harrison, *Early Victorians*, p. 48.
23. Table 9, class one, col. 2(e).
24. Table 9, col. 4(f).
25. Isichei, p. 177.
26. It must be noted however that information on schooling came only from the well-known, established Quaker Schools given in the table. It is likely that a considerable additional number attended smaller schools, organized by individual Friends Meetings or by individual Friends privately, for in 1837 there were alleged to be at least sixty-seven schools labelled "Friends" schools — see p.
27. J.S. Rowntree, *Quakerism, Past and Present*, p. 101.
28. Croydon had its beginning in 1702 as St James' workhouse in Clerkenwell, a combined old people's refuge and boarding-school for young children. The two functions were separated in 1786, the children being moved to Islington. In 1825 there was a further move to Croydon and in 1875 to Saffron Walden, where it has remained to the present day.
29. From *Inspection of Friends' Boarding Schools by the Board of Education*, 1905, quoted in Stewart, *Quakers and Education*, p. 70.
30. In *The Friend*, 1, no. 8 (August 1843):194, it was reported that of the ninety-three leavers in the period 1834 to 1842 forty had been successfully placed in employment with Friends or with "those attached to Friends' principles".
31. Ibid., 4, no. 42 (June 1846):114.
32. Rowntree, *Past and Present*, p. 101.
33. Ackworth old scholars were sufficiently strong in the colonies by the eighteen-seventies for them to press for the establishment of a Friends' School in Melbourne, which, it was hoped, would be an "Ackworth of the South" (see Oats, *Rose and Waratah*, pp. 45-49).

Chapter Three

1. From G.K. Clark, *Making of Victorian England*, p. 66.
2. E.P. Thompson, *English working-class*, p. 269.
3. Mayhew, *London Labour and London Poor*, vol. 2, p. 338. Mayhew cited the example of tailoring. In 1849, of 23,517 London tailors, 2,748 were independent master-tailors, 3,000 society men in "honorable" trade, 18,000 in "dishonorable", that is, employed in factories making goods for shoddy markets.
4. Briggs, *Age of Improvement*, pp. 211 and 295:
   1824—25 the first "cyclical boom"
   1832—36 good harvests, plentiful employment, peak employment in railway construction
   1837 serious recession, particularly affecting merchants who had bought goods when prices were high
   1840 light recovery
   1841 recession
   1842 "no gloomier year in the whole nineteenth century", prolonged business difficulties, bread dear
   1845 railway boom
   1845 October — boom "busted"
   1847 crisis — shortage of cotton affected Lancashire cotton mills
   1850 weight of crisis lifted.
5. J.F.C. Harrison, *The Early Victorians*, p. 74.
6. See table 7, page 39.
7. In *London Friends' Meetings* (1869):90.
8. Minutes of Leeds M.M., 19 June 1846, 15 September 1848, 2 February 1849.
9. *The Friend* 1, no. 1 (14 January 1843):14.
10. Ibid., 3, no. 28 (April 1845):85.
11. Ibid., 5, no. 53 (May 1847):91.
12. Ibid., 5, no. 60 (December 1847):229.
13. *Journal of Economic History* 13 (1953).
14. Committees of Friends were set up in the areas worst hit by the failure of the potato crops. Navy vessels were hired to transport food to Irish ports and Friends supervised centres for the distribution of relief.
15. C. Woodham-Smith, *The Great Hunger*.
16. See pp. 39, 40.
17. Beale, ed., *Earth Between Them*, pp. 25-26.
18. Port. 43.24 MS in possession of the Friends' Historical Library, Eustace St, Dublin.
19. A. Webb, unpublished diary, vol. 1, p. 191, F.L.E.D.
20. Ibid. Whether Webb regarded Australian Friends, as well as Irish Friends, as influenced by "the good society" is open to conjecture.
21. William May, to his sister, Rachel Mackie, 17 September 1889, unpublished letters of William May.
22. MS. 9863 2(a) 23 May 1852, La Trobe Library, Melbourne.
23. Gen. Despatches 1828, no. 21. Pardon dated 27 April 1828, M.L.
24. G. Rudé, *Protest and Punishment*, p. 144.
25. CON 37/1692, A.O.T.
26. J. Fry, *Alphabetical Extract*, pp. 76-77.
27. W.P. Thistlethwaite, *Yorkshire Quarterly Meeting*, p. 160.
28. Vol. 1, no. 3:94-95.

29. Ibid., p. 128.
30. *Perth Gazette*, 27 July 1833, 10 August 1833, 12 September 1833, 19 September 1822.
31. G.W. Walker, Journal, B 719, 26 December 1837, p. 37, M.L.
32. There was a succession of Friends' periodicals in the eighteenth century, particularly in the thirties, all reflecting the interest in philanthropy, migration, and protection of the rights of native peoples. *The Lindfield Reporter* was a revival of *The Philanthropic Magazine*, first published in 1811 by William Allen. *The Irish Friend* was begun as an alternative to *The British Friend* and in turn gave way to *The Friend* in January 1843. These two Friends' periodicals continued to be published in parallel throughout the nineteenth century.
33. *The Lindfield Reporter* 1, no. 8 (August 1835):127.
34. *The Irish Friend*, 1, no. 6 (April 1838):45.
35. Ibid., p. 42.
36. Minute of London Y.M. from *Proceedings of London Y.M.* 25:236-37.
37. *The Irish Friend* 3, no. 3 (March 1840):23.
38. Port. 8/3, dated 6 August 1841, F.H.A.L.
39. *The Irish Friend*, 1 June 1839.
40. J. Backhouse, *Narrative*, pp. 559-60.
41. Ibid., p. 159.
42. Ibid., p. 451.
43. The Continental Committee was the outcome of measures taken by the Meeting for Sufferings to maintain contact with and give encouragement to groups of Friends as they sprang up on the Continent of Europe. In the mid-nineteenth century it accepted responsibility for Friends in Australia and New Zealand. Following the establishment of an Australian General Meeting in 1902, Meeting for Sufferings appointed a separate Committee to correspond with the new General Meeting and give advice or assistance as requested. (Minute 10 of Meeting for Sufferings, 2 October 1903) The first meeting of the Australian Committee, or Committee for Australian Affairs, was held on 6 November 1903. When New Zealand was added to the committee's responsibilities in 1906, the name was changed to the Australasian Committee, its first meeting under its change of name being on 4 May 1906. The Continental Committee, which continued to correspond with European Friends was disbanded in 1920.
44. Minutes of the Continental Committee, p. 94, F.H.A.L.
45. Minutes of Lancaster Quarterly Meeting, 20 January 1853.
46. MS. 2A, XL nos. 46-50, Lancaster Meeting House.
47. The Continental Committee also took responsibility for making detailed arrangements for such travelling ministers as Lindsey and Mackie, for communication with them and for control of expenditure.
48. From *Ackworth O.S. Reports*, London 1906.
49. *The British Friend*, July 1854, p. 170.
50. Nichols, ed., *Traveller Under Concern*, pp. 195-96.
51. *Journal of the Friends' Historical Association* 19 (1922):53.
52. Ibid., p. 55.
53. Quaker firms, such as Benson and Co. and the Thompsons, owned a number of trans-Atlantic packet lines, carrying both mails and passengers. Since it was the practice to mount cannon on board merchant ships to ward off intruders in the shipping lanes, Quaker firms found it necessary to reassure passengers by providing dummy guns of wood, which came to be known as "Quaker

cannon" (see under James Beale in the D.Q.B. and Barry, *Steam Navigation*, pp. 22-37).
54. *The British Friend*, June 1849, p. 146.

Chapter four

1. See pp. 108-9. Parkinson died of fever on 26 January 1771 in Batavia on the return voyage.
2. Biographical Catalogue, London. London Friends' Institute, 1888.
3. See p. 11.
4. S. Backhouse, *Memoir*, p. 13.
5. See pp. 13-14.
6. The gross expenditure by Backhouse and Walker for the period August 1831 to February 1841 was £3,426.12.6½. This covered
books and printing	£419.16.8
horses, wagons, etc. (after re-sale)	287. 8 .9
passage monies by sea	611.13.6
Misc. expenses Hobart Meeting	13. 1.0
personal expenses — board, land travel, forage, hire of horses, coach fares	2094.12.7½

    (from J. Backhouse, *Diary*, B 732, pp. 107-8, M.L.)
7. J. Backhouse, *Diary*, vol. 19, pp. 113-14, B 782, M.L.
8. *The Friend*, n.s. 9 (4 June 1869):147.
9. J. Backhouse, Letters, Case 19, p. 1, F.H.A.L.
10. J. Backhouse, *Narrative*, pp. 2-3.
11. Arthur to Viscount Howick, 14 August 1832, G 33/10, p. 634, A.O.T.
12. Arthur had already been faced with a similar problem during his period as superintendent and commandant at Belize in the West Indies, when the Secretary of State, Earl Bathurst, decided to settle pensioners of the 5th West India regiment there with grants of land — see Shaw, *Sir George Arthur*, pp. 28-29.
13. J. Backhouse, *Narrative*, p. 309.
14. Ibid., p. 401.
15. Walker, Journal, B 710, 7 February 1833, p. 77.
16. Ibid., B 714, 18 September 1835, pp. 107-8.
17. Dr John Service, 1832-1894, came as a minister from Glasgow, first to Victoria, and then in January 1866 as Presbyterian minister at St John's Church, Hobart. He returned to Glasgow in 1870. He was granted a doctorate of divinity by the University of Glasgow in recognition of his publications.
18. Japp, ed., *Master Missionaries*, p. 186.
19. For the full description of this entry to Macquarie Harbour see Backhouse, pp. 44-45.
20. Ibid., pp. 18-19.
21. G. W. Walker, Journal, B 708, 22 February 1832, pp. 210-14.
22. Ibid., p. 215.
23. Arthur to Howick, 14 August 1832, GO 33/10, p. 633, A.O.T.
24. CSO 1/807/17244, 22 May 1835, A.O.T.
25. Lady Franklin, Journal, Folder 13, p. 27, A.O.T.
26. Ibid., pp. 28-29.
27. Ibid., pp. 73-75.
28. Ibid., pp. 76-85.

29. Ibid., pp. 90-91.
30. K. Barne, *Elizabeth Fry*.
31. J. Backhouse, Letter Book, no. 1, p. 15, 17 February 1832, MS. vol. S 48, F.H.A.L.
32. J.F.H.S., vol. 26, pp. 22-23.
33. E.g. Query no. 5: "How many women have learned to read since they left England and have they generally been regular and attentive at their hours for instruction?" (Ibid., pp. 22-23).
34. Ibid., p. 24.
35. Walker, Journal, B 711, 16 October 1833, p. 125.
36. Backhouse, *Narrative*, pp. 419-20.
37. Walker, Journal, B 717, 17 September 1836, p. 19.
38. Backhouse, *Narrative*, p. 476.
39. Ibid., p. 50.
40. Ibid., p. 279.
41. Ibid., p. 280.
42. Walker, Journal, B 713, 29 April 1835, p. 109.
43. Backhouse, *Narrative*, app. F, p. xlvii.
44. Ibid., pp. liv-lv.
45. A. G. L. Shaw, *Sir George Arthur*, p. 81 and n. 45.
46. Backhouse, *Narrative*, app. F, p. xlix.
47. Walker, Journal, B 718, 23 April 1837, pp. 17-18.
48. J. V. Barry, *Alexander Maconochie*, pp. 77-78.
49. See p. 100.
50. Letters dated 29 April, 10 August, 5 September 1837, quoted in full in Barry, pp. 256-58.
51. A. H. Japp ed., *Master Missionaries*, pp. 217-18.
52. Backhouse, Letter Book, no. 2, pp. 89-101, 29 August 1837.
53. This confirms the point made by Shaw (p. 87) that flogging was more common in New South Wales under "lenient" Bourke than in Van Diemen's Land under "hard" Arthur.
54. Walker, Journal, B 708, 12 February 1832, pp. 188-89.
55. Ibid., B 709, 3 November 1832, pp. 171-72.
56. See V. R. Ellis, *Trucanini: Queen or Traitor*, pp. 38-40, 43.
57. Ibid., p. 64.
58. Walker, Journal, B 709, 9 October 1832, p. 128.
59. Backhouse, *Narrative*, introd. p. xvii.
60. Ibid., pp. 78-79.
61. Walker, Journal, B 709, 9 October 1832, pp. 123-24.
62. Plomley also records this story (*Friendly Mission*, p. 804).
63. Backhouse, *Narrative*, p. 147.
64. Ibid., p. 147.
65. Smith, *Spectre of Truganini*, p. 21, quoting Darwin, C. *Descent of Man* (London: Murray, 1887), p. 83.
66. Backhouse, *Narrative*, pp. 173-74.
67. Walker, Journal, B 709, 16 October 1832, pp. 148-49.
68. B. Smith, *Spectre of Truganini*, p. 26.
69. S. Parkinson, *Journal*, p. 15.
70. Ibid., introd., p. vii.
71. Lady Franklin, Journal, Folder 13, p. 119, A.O.T.
72. Backhouse to Bourke, J. Backhouse, Letter Book, 25 April 1837, no. 2, p. 80.
73. Walker, Journal, B 714, 11 July 1835, p. 49.

74. For Backhouse's use of this term see J. Backhouse, *Narrative*, introd. p. xvii.
75. Ibid., p. 503.
76. Walker, Journal, B 719, 12 December 1837, pp. 26-27.
77. Ibid., p. 27.
78. Backhouse, *Narrative*, pp. 518-19.
79. Ibid., p. 517.
80. GRG 2/6/1, 5 October 1838, Archives of S. Australia.
81. Walker, Journal, B 719, 1 December 1837, p. 14.
82. Louis Guistiniani, the "controversial missionary" (Stannage, *Western Australia*, p. 522) sent out by the London Missionary Society, Dublin, arrived in Western Australia in 1836. In 1837 he was the first European to defend an Aborigine in court. For this he felt himself humiliated by the judge and opposed by his Church. He therefore left Western Australia to return home in 1838.
83. Backhouse to Buxton, Backhouse, J., Letter Book, no. 4, p. 123, 16 March 1838. MS. vol. S 69, F.H.A.L.
84. Backhouse, *Narrative*, pp. 87-88.
85. Ibid., p. 326.
86. Ibid., p. 224.
87. Ibid., pp. 356-77.
88. Ibid., pp. 500-501.
89. Ibid., pp. 509-21.
90. Ibid., p. 527.
91. W. H. Harvey, the Quaker botanist whom Backhouse met at Capetown on his way home to England, named a new genus of Zygophyllae "Backhousia Australis" — *The Friend*, n.s. 9 (4 June 1869):147.
92. Backhouse, *Narrative*, p. 15.
93. *The Tasmanian*, 7 November 1834.
94. Backhouse, *Narrative*, p. 472.
95. Walker, Journal, B 717, 5 April 1837, p. 125.
96. Backhouse, Letters, 22 September 1837, Case 72, F.H.A.L.
97. The first edition of *Extracts*, printed by W. Eade, at the Schools of Industry, Lindfield, appeared in 1834. In his *Letters*, on which the Extracts were based, Backhouse wrote on 13 June 1837: "I read the *Extracts* from my journal printed in England, having borrowed a copy of Lady Franklin (the only one I know of in the colony)." This must have been the first edition, for the second edition was not printed until 1837.
98. Walker, Journal, B 718, 29 October 1837, p. 115.
99. Lady Franklin to G. W. Walker, 25 October 1843, T.U.A.
100. Daniel Wheeler (1771—1840) and his son, Charles, spent four years in the South Pacific in the *Henry Freeling*, chartered by London Yearly Meeting for their voyage. Daniel Wheeler had spent several years of his life previously in Russia as agricultural adviser to Czar Alexander I. Lady Franklin wrote to her sister, Lady Mary Simpkinson, about the Wheelers: "I begged them to call on you. They are great favourites of mine, particularly the old man whose placid countenance and demeanour I'm sure will delight you." (Lady Franklin to Lady Mary Simpkinson, MS. 248/174/1-23, A.O.T.)
101. Walker, Journal, B 716, 27 April 1836, p. 43.
102. Backhouse, Letters, Case 19, F.H.A.L.
103. Foster Fyans (1790-1870), army captain from Dublin, was posted to Norfolk Island in 1833 as captain of the guard for two years, then commandant at Moreton Bay until he settled at Port Phillip in 1837 (*A.D.B.*, vol. 1, pp. 422-24).

Notes to pages 125-39

104. Fyans, "Reminiscences, 1810" Unpublished MS. c.1843. MS, 6939-40, vol. 2, p. 683. La Trobe Collection, State Library of Victoria.
105. Lady Franklin to Lady Simpkinson, 9 December 1837, MS. 248/174/1-23, A.O.T.
106. West, *History of Tasmania*, p. 425.
107. Japp, *Master Missionaries*, p. 194.

Chapter Five

1. G.W. Walker, Journal, B 708, 5 March 1832, p. 235, M.L.
2. Letter from G.W. Walker, Richardson MSS, Box R, F.H.A.L.
3. Reel M 698, p. 293, 29 March 1833, A.O.T.
4. J. Backhouse, *Narrative*, p. 16.
5. This book was presented to The Friends' School, Hobart, by the granddaughter of T. J. and S. Crouch.
6. Minutes of Albans M.M., Record Office, Cambridge, England.
7. See pp. 233-34.
8. "His friends feel careful about him, but not in a position to help him." Backhouse to Walker, 21 November 1843, W9/1/1(1), T.U.A.
9. John Fisher to Reuben Fisher, 30 January 1844, F1, T.U.A.
10. John Fisher to Henry Morris, Cork, 11 November 1849, F1, T.U.A.
11. Minutes of Hobart M.M., 6 February 1836.
12. Anna Maria Cotton was a member in Hobart ten years before she gained readmission to Devonshire House M.M., see pp. 153, 156.
13. Launceston M.M. kept separate minutes in the period 4 January 1844 to 30 July 1851 — see S 1/13, T.U.A. The holding of meetings alternately in Launceston and Kelvedon meant that much of the business was adjourned from one meeting to the next, because difficulties of transport made travelling from one location to the other the exception rather than the rule. Meetings at Kelvedon therefore were attended only by the Cotton family and Dr Story. Disownments, resignations, and removals reduced membership in Launceston to two and it was clear by 1851 that a separate meeting in Launceston was no longer viable. Kelvedon then rejoined Hobart.
14. Minutes of Hobart M.M., 6 January 1859.
15. For a description of Australind as it was in 1855 when Frederick Mackie and Robert Lindsey visited the Cliftons, see Nichols, ed., *Traveller Under Concern*, pp. 269-72. Mackie described the reasons for the failure of the Australind experiment. The Cliftons' house was the sole reminder of the town that was to be. Mackie said that the influence of Elinor Clifton spread far beyond her own family.
16. Minutes of Hobart M.M., 6 December 1844.
17. Though some Friends in Victoria settled in Western Australia later in the nineteenth century, there was no organization of a Meeting of Friends until after the visit of the South Australian Friends, Edwin Ashby and Frederick Coleman, in the nineteen-thirties.
18. Letter dated 6 December 1858, Port. 8/32, F.H.A.L.
19. Edwin Ransome was for many years the Clerk of the Continental Committee of London Yearly Meeting. This Committee was responsible for maintaining contact with distant Meetings by correspondence.
20. E. R. Ransome to S. Morris, 28 April 1893, MS. Box 27/2, F.H.A.L.
21. Quakers used the term "labour", suggestive of wrestling with the spirit

perhaps, to describe the act of ministering in Meeting for Worship (Walker, Journal, 10 March 1833).
22. See p. 131.
23. Minutes of Hobart M.M., 3 February 1836.
24. CON 31/11, A.O.T.
25. Minutes of Hobart M.M., 12 December 1833.
26. For the significance of this term, see p. 13.
27. *The Irish Friend* 1, no. 8 (1838):59.
28. Boyes, G.W.T., Diary, 18-19 January 1842, T.U.A.
29. J. Backhouse, Letter dated 22 July 1837, F.H.A.L.
30. *Hobart Town Courier*, 20 October 1837.
31. Minutes of Launceston M.M., 11 March 1847.
32. Ibid., 1 April 1847.
33. Neave, Journal, 4 January 1868, p. 153, M.L.
34. Walter Robson's Diary — in the possession of Anne Bauld, Doncaster, Victoria.
35. Proceedings of London & Middlesex Gaol Delivery, Case 1329, 5 July 1830.
36. H.H. Ridler joined the Society of Friends on 2 July 1835. He must surely hold the record for the number of resignations and readmissions. He resigned four times and his resignation was finally accepted on 3 December 1846. This record attests the patience of the Hobart M.M. His application for readmission generally seemed to coincide with imminent departure on business trips to England.
37. *The British Friend*, 39, no. 8 (August 1881):203.
38. *Hobart Town Courier*, 22 June 1858.
39. Minutes of Hobart M.M., 6 June 1844.
40. See pp. 15-17.
41. Minutes of Hobart M.M., 3 March 1859.
42. Ibid., 3 June 1874.
43. F. Cotton to J.B. Mather, 28 February 1846.
44. During that time he was chairman of two committees, Waterworks and Lighting.
45. Minutes of Hobart Town Corporation, 3 January 1860.
46. F.H.A.L.
47. Reel 6, M 698, p. 246, A.O.T.
48. CON 14/3, A.O.T.
49. Walker, Journal, B 711, 12 July 1833, p. 43.
50. Ibid., B 715, 4 December 1835, p. 68.
51. Minutes of V.D.L. Y.M., 4 December 1835.
52. Walker, Journal, B 708, 5 March 1832, p. 235.
53. Minutes of Hobart M.M., 7 February 1839.
54. The early register of members of Sydney Meeting has been lost. Walker noted in his Journal, 23 November 1840, T.U.A., that J.B. Mather had brought back news from his visit to Sydney, that Jane Davy had joined Friends and that Abraham Davy was doing well in business — and presumably had rejoined Friends.
55. J.B. Mather, Diary, 15 April 1840, M 19/100, T.U.A.
56. M. Nichols, ed., *Traveller Under Concern*, pp. 128 and 235-36.
57. This diary has been lodged with the Mitchell Library, Sydney, and is as yet uncatalogued.
58. Macarthur Papers, A 2937, vol. 41, p. 272, M.L.
59. Ibid., A 2939, vol. 43, pp. 51-52, M.L.
60. Backhouse, *Narrative*, p. 240.

61. Ibid., app. 0, pp. cxxiv and cxxvi.
62. The marriage of William Rayner (junior) and Isabella Nicholias was the first Quaker marriage in Van Diemen's Land.
63. Walker, Letters, 28 May 1835, W 9/1/1.3(1), T.U.A.
64. The Minutes of Southwark M.M. 20 March 1821 record that Francis Cotton was disowned for being married "by a priest to a member of another Meeting". Cotton declined to say when or where the the marriage had taken place, "although he expressed some regret that circumstances had induced him to break the rules of the Society". At the same time as Southwark Meeting was engaged in disowning him, members of the Devonshire House M.M. were visiting Anna Maria concerning what they termed "reproachful conduct" before marriage. This may have been the reason why Cotton advanced the date of marriage and did not seek the usual pre-marriage clearance with his own Meeting (Minutes of Devonshire House M.M., 8 May, 5 June, 4 September 1821).
65. Backhouse, *Narrative*, p. 184.
66. Backhouse, Letters, Reel M 698, p. 312, A.O.T.
67. Minutes of Southwark M.M., 16 September 1834.
68. Minutes of Devonshire House M.M., 9 June 1853.
69. J. Backhouse, Journal, B 731, 10/31, M.L.
70. This was because Cotton beat Meredith over tenders for supply of meat to the Rocky Hills settlement — 2¼d to Meredith's 2½d.
71. N. Hewitt, *Friends in Tasmania*, p. 11.
72. *The British Friend*, July 1851, p. 159.
73. Ibid., p. 159.
74. Cotton designed the plans for the Council Chambers in Swansea.
75. See p. 101.
76. Maconochie to Walker, 7 December 1838, W 9/1/1(1), T.U.A.
77. Cotton to Walker, quoted in Hewitt, p. 22.
78. Cotton to Walker, 2 April 1856.
79. Walker, Letter W. 9/1/1.4(1), T.U.A.
80. Backhouse, *Narrative*, app. B, p. xiv.
81. About fifty were interred in this burial-ground. In 1926 the ground was no longer in use for this purpose, a Friends' section having been reserved at Cornelian Bay cemetery. Friends therefore leased the ground to the Hobart City Council so that half of it could be used as a children's playground. In 1937 the Meeting agreed to transfer the whole area for use as a playground on the condition that the headstones were arranged along the boundary wall. At first known as "Friends' Park", the name was changed to "Children's Playground" by agreement with Hobart M.M. on 26 September 1941 to give the City Council legal control over persons using the ground.
82. Ann Mather's daughter, Sarah Benson Walker, the wife of G. W. Walker, writing in 1882 to her brother, J.B. Mather, was answering his request for information about family history and in particular his desire to know whether there were any knights in that history. Robert Mather's father was a blacksmith and farmer from Lauder in Berwickshire. Ann Mather's mother was Agnes Hamilton, daughter of a Scottish shepherd. "The only knights thou canst speak of or remember", wrote Sarah Walker, "is a knight of the loom and a knight of the sledge-hammer . . . so I think, weighing things in the right balance, we have descended from a *good stock*." From a letter dated 31 July 1882, in possession of Edith Brice, Brisbane.
83. Robert Barclay's *Apology for the True Christian Divinity in the same is held forth and preached by the people in scorn called Quakers* was published in

Latin in 1676 and in English in 1678. This book was for many years the standard theological statement of Quakerism.
84. Mather Letters, 20 April 1832, R 7/50, T.U.A.
85. Backhouse, *Narrative*, p. 63.
86. Mather could not produce evidence of written authority for rendering this service, but he had copies of written requests from those who sought his help. Thus:

24 December 1834	"Would you oblige me by crossing my boat over the Muddy Plains Neck?" J.E. Calder
27 January 1834, 16 December 1835, 7 October 1835	"Be so good as to cross the boat attached to this station, being on Government duty." — 2nd Lieut. M. Macgregor, the 21st Fusiliers.
17 November 1834	from the Colonial Secretary for crossing Backhouse and Walker en route to Port Arthur.
3 December 1834	from the Port Officer for a crew of six en route to Port Arthur.

Government Despatch boats used the service two or three times a week (R 7/51(a), T.U.A.).
87. Walker, Journal, B 715, 28 December 1835, pp. 97-98.
88. Walker to Bell, undated, W 9/1/1.2, T.U.A.
89. Walker to A. M. Cotton, W 9/1/1.3(2), T.U.A.
90. Ibid.
91. Walker, Letters, 9 December 1846, W 9/1/1.4(2), T.U.A.
92. Walker was treasurer of the Total Abstinence Society; but in June 1846 he gave up all connection with this group because he objected to the morals of some of its members and he also objected to the use of music at its meetings. (Letters, 6 June 1846, W 9/1/1.4(2)) Two weeks later the name of George Walker, Esquire, appeared on an advertisement for a new Temperance Society. In spite of being upset by the use of the unauthorized title of "esquire", he continued to throw his weight behind this new committee.
93. Walker, Letters, 3 January 1845, W 9/1/1.4(2), T.U.A.
94. Walker to Bennington, 17 June 1845, W 9/1/1, T.U.A.
95. These nine names can be seen on a bronze plaque fixed to the west wall of the main meeting-room in what today is known as Domain House, Hobart. This room was the library during the period when the buildings of the Hobart Town High School were used for the University of Tasmania.
96. For a more detailed account of Walker's interest in education, see Oats, *Rose and the Waratah*, pp. 9-17.
97. Walker, Letters, 9 July 1847, W 9/1/1.4(2), T.U.A.
98. W. Denison, *Varieties of vice-regal life*, vol. 1, p. 82.

Chapter Six

1. *The Friend*, n.s. 34 (13 April 1894):231.
2. From Daniel Wheeler's Journal, quoted in *The Friend*, n.s. 34 (13 April 1894):231.
3. C. H. Bertie, *Story of Castle Hill*, A 4101, p. 4, M.L.
4. Piper Papers, A 256, p. 546, M.L.
5. G. W. Walker, Journal, B 714, 9 June 1835, p. 27.
6. Ibid., B 716, 26 June 1836, p. 84.
7. M. Nichols, ed., *Traveller under Concern*, p. 136.
8. See pp. 148-49.

9. The following transactions are recorded in *The Australian*:
    26 January 1827   Buy parts of Orphan Grant Land, George Street, Sydney
    30 September 1831   Land grant in St Andrews
    20 May 1831   )
    14 October 1831   )   Land grants in Sydney
    4 May 1832   )
    16 March 1832   Land grant at St Lawrence
    25 July 1834   Buys land at Morpeth
    16 February 1836   Buys premises of T. H. James, George Street, for £5,500
    1835   Grant of 2 ac. 1 rd, 20 perches, site of present 10 Ferry St, Hunter's Hill, sold on 23 February 1838 before Tawell's return to England (information supplied by present owners, Professor and Mrs J. F. D. Wood).
10. Petition mitigating sentences, 1818, N–Y, p. 265, C 5 Pet. 11, 4/1856, M.L.
11. Bigge Report, app., p. 4543, BT Box 23, M.L.
12. J. Backhouse, *Narrative*, pp. 352-53.
13. Henson, G., *History of John Tawell, with his life, trial, confession and execution*, Northampton, 1845, Tract Vol. 377/26, F.H.A.L.
14. Petition mitigating sentences, 1818, N–Y, p. 265, C 5, Pet. 11, 4/1856, M.L.
15. According to the Sydney Grammar archivist, the date of foundation was 1857, but it was preceded by what was known as Sydney College in the 1830s. In the S.G. file at the Mitchell Library there is on 1 January 1824 record of Master John Tawell being 3rd class scholar at SGS, and on 1 July award of 1st Silver Medal to him at the half-yearly exam. of SGS. For the same dates Master William Tawell was enrolled as 2nd class scholar and gained a prize for the half-yearly exam. in Virgil and Caesar.
16. MS. Q 991/N, vol. 19, pp. 30-33, M.L.
17. *Truth*, 29 January 1911. Q 991/N, vol. 19, pp. 30-33, M.L.
18. *Journal of the Royal Australian Historical Society* 18:35.
19. Tawell was a regular and generous subscriber to the Benevolent Society, and he appeared on the list of subscribers to the Roman Catholic Chapel 1824–25, to the Wesleyan Missionary Society and to the School of Industry. In 1825 he became a governor of the proposed Public Free Grammar School (SG, September 1829); in 1826 he became a trustee of the P.F.G.S.; on 13 May he was present at a meeting of the proprietors of the Bank of N.S.W. and on 8 July at a Meeting of the Chamber of Commerce (SG/ML).
20. *Journal of the R.A.H.S.* 18:35.
21. Walker, Journal, B 713, 22 December 1834, p. 26.
22. Backhouse, *Narrative*, p. 235.
23. Walker, Journal, B 714, 12 June 1835, p. 30.
24. M. Nichols, *Traveller*, p. 138.
25. J. Backhouse, Diary, B 731, 8/113, M.L.
26. J. Backhouse, Letters, 17 September 1834, Case 19, F.H.A.L.
27. Walker to Wilmot, 1 March 1837, W 9/1/1.3(2), T.U.A.
28. *Journal of R.A.H.S.* (26 May 1925) vol. 11, pt. 4, p. 226.
29. J. Backhouse, Letters, 31 October 1835, MS. Case 72, no. 66, F.H.A.L.
30. Walker, Journal, B 715, 1 November 1835, p. 45.
31. MS. Port 17/115, F.H.A.L.
32. Minutes of Meeting for Sufferings, 3 April 1840, vol. 45, pp. 22-23.
33. MS. Q 991/N, vol. 19, pp. 30-33, M.L.
34. MS. Box 18/4, F.H.A.L.
35. For some years the building appears to have been used by the Baptists. It was known as The Tabernacle when Lindsey and Mackie ruefully inspected it in 1854. In July 1859 a section of the Jewish community used it as a synagogue and in 1862 it was sold to two members of the Jewish congregation.

Until 1878 it was in use as one of Sydney's two synagogues. In 1878 it was bought by a Mrs Burdekin who lived next door and the building was then demolished for development (*Truth*, vol. 106, pp. 14-15, Q 991.1/N, M.L.).
36. Minutes of Devonshire House M.M., 18:26, 31, 33.
37. *Journal of R.A.H.S.* 13:201-2.
38. Tract, vol. 377/26, p. 26, F.H.A.L.
39. Copy of letter, Tawell to H. C. Backhouse, 25 March 1845, Gibson MSS., 4/135, F.H.A.L.
40. Tract, vol. 377/26, p. 37, F.H.A.L.
41. *Journal of R.A.H.S.* 18:31, 35.
42. J. Backhouse, Letter Book, no. 5, MS. vol. 58, F.H.A.L.
43. J. Backhouse to Walker, 28 November 1844, W 9/1/1(1), T.U.A.
44. Ibid., 23 January 1845.
45. Ibid., 11 April 1845.
46. Ibid., 8 July 1845.
47. Hannah Chapman Backhouse and her son-in-law, John Hodgkin, visited Tawell in Aylesbury gaol on 14-15 March. Hannah Backhouse wanted to pay another visit — in spite of some warnings from Friends who discouraged her from going again to see "that wretched murderer". Two other Friends, John and Martha Yardley, also visited him.
48. Tract vol. 377/26, 1845, p. 48, F.H.A.L.
49. *The British Friend*, 3 (March 1845):41.
50. Tallach, *Spitalfield Philanthropist*, p. 102.
51. Nichols, *Traveller*, p. 134.
52. For comments on this constitution issue see *The Australian Encyclopedia* 4 (1958):380.
53. W. Robson, Diary, 2 April 1968, vol. 1, p. 135, Microfilm 206, F.H.A.L.
54. Minutes of V.D.L. Y.M., 21 November 1836.
55. Minutes of Longford (England) M.M., 12 February 1846.
56. J. B. Mather, Diary, 1 March 1840, M 19/100, T.U.A.
57. Minutes of Witney M.M., 14 November 1853.
58. Ibid., 11 December 1854.
59. D. Adams, ed., *Letters of Rachel Henning*, p. 26.
60. W. Robson, Diary, 15 April 1868, Microfilm 206, p. 161, F.H.A.L.
61. *The Friend*, n.s. 17 (1 January 1877):9.
62. See p. 134.
63. These dates are determined by reference to Minutes of Hobart Monthly Meeting, viz.

    5 October 1837   J.B. and R.A. Mather appointed as agents of James Backhouse in Hobart
    2 April 1838   R. A. Mather and Abraham Davy report from Sydney that Tawell has left for England
    4 January 1844   R. A. Mather's name reappears on the list of those present at Hobart M.M.
64. See pp. 149-50.
65. Nichols, ed., p. 133.
66. This site is now covered by the suburban platforms of Sydney's central railway. The area was generally known as the "Sandhills" — from Evans, *History of the Sydney Meeting*, pp. 19-22.
67. Nichols, ed., p. 238.
68. J. B. Mather, Diary, 2 February 1840, M 19/100, T.U.A.
69. Ibid., 16 February 1840.
70. Backhouse, *Narrative*, pp. 293-94.

Chapter Seven

1. Nichols, ed., *Traveller under Concern*, p. 232, entry for 28 June 1854.
2. J. Backhouse, *Narrative*, p. 514.
3. Hack to Watson, 17 December 1837, Hack-Watson Papers, 1488/5, A.S.A.
4. Hack, Diary, MSS. 394 M, A.S.A.
5. Quoted by Miss Halse in a paper, "Days of our Fathers", MS. Box 1.9, A.S.A.
6. Walker, Journal, B 719, 28 November 1837, p. 9.
7. Hack-Watson Papers, 1488/6, A.S.A.
8. Ibid., 1488/9.
9. On 23 September 1857 Stephen Hack led an expedition from Port Lincoln to explore the Gawler Ranges and John McDouall Stuart made use of his maps on his exploration of Central Australia.
10. Hack referred to a store "as grand as Cappers in Gracechurch Street". Hack-Watson Papers, 1488/46, A.S.A.
11. Barritt to his parents, 20 May 1840, 1274/2, A.S.A.
12. Henry Watson to his brother, 14 March 1839, 1488/36, A.S.A.
13. Hack-Watson Papers, 1488/41, A.S.A.
14. Ibid., Hack to his mother, 1488/14, A.S.A.
15. Hack to Margaret Darton, 31 August 1844, 1488/17, A.S.A.
16. Letters of Margaret May, 1363 M, A.S.A.
17. Ibid.
18. Hack-Watson Papers, 17 December 1841, 1488/53, A.S.A.
19. Minutes of Lewes and Chichester M.M., 20 March 1846.
20. Hack-Watson Papers, 19 July 1840, 1488/46, A.S.A.
21. Ibid., 17 December 1841, 1488/53, A.S.A.
22. Hindmarsh to Malcolm, 22 June 1838, A 1197, A.S.A.
23. Hack-Watson Papers, 12 June 1842, 1488/55, A.S.A.
24. Circular to Quarterly Meetings, copy in A.S.A., dated 10 January 1840.
25. MS. Port. 8.87, F.H.A.L.
26. Ed. May to Forster, 21 December 1863, Port. 8, F.H.A.L.
27. Hack-Watson Papers, 1488/44, A.S.A.
28. Josiah Forster to Hack, MS. Port. 8.88, F.H.A.L.
29. Letter in Adelaide Meeting's historical records box, 17 July 1844.
30. Darton to Forster, 22 September 1842, MS. Port. 8.84, F.H.A.L.
31. MS. Port. 8.65, 15 February 1843, F.H.A.L.
32. MS. Port. 8.74, F.H.A.L.
33. Minutes of the Continental Committee, 31 October 1842, F.H.A.L.
34. Adelaide Meeting historical records, unsigned letter, 23 March 1846.
35. *The Australian Friend*, 21 December 1891, pp. 64-65.
36. Hack-Watson Papers, 15 December 1839, 1488/42, A.S.A.
37. See p. 58.
38. May to Forster, MS. Port. 8.48, F.H.A.L.
39. W. L. May, unpublished letters, Tasmania, 1922.
40. William May to Rachel Mackie, unpublished letter, 17 September 1889.
41. "Fairfield" was burnt down on 28 January 1905 and was the subject of a nostalgic article on "Old Times in Mount Barker" in the South Australian *Register*, 11 February 1905.
42. Letter of Maria May to her aunt, 29 December 1839.
43. Minutes of Adelaide Two Months' Meeting, 5 September 1843, SRG 103/1/1, A.S.A.
44. Ibid., 4 March 1849.

45. *The Australian Friend*, 21 December 1891, p. 66.
46. Minutes of the Two Months' Meeting, 6 November 1853, SRG 103/1/1, A.S.A.
47. Oats, *The Rose and Waratah*, pp. 40-42.
48. M. Nichols, ed., *Traveller under Concern*, p. 207.
49. Ibid., p. 212.
50. Ibid., p. 222.
51. Minutes of Two Months' Meeting, 5 November 1854, SRG 103/1/1, A.S.A.
52. Neave, Journal, MSS. 3842, 17/18, p. 27, M.L.
53. Nichols, *Traveller*, p. 230.
54. SRG 103/1/1, 4 March 1856, A.S.A.
55. SRG 103/11, 2 November 1856, A.S.A.
56. Thus George Sanders, a South Australian Friend, complained to Backhouse in a letter dated 14 November 1851 that English Friends should not allow Friends like R.H., aged, lame and weak, to emigrate and be a charge on South Australian Friends (J. Backhouse, Letters, Case 19, F.H.A.L.).
57. SRG 103/1/1, 6 March 1859, A.S.A.
58. See p. 196.
59. Epistle of Meeting for Sufferings to South Australian Friends "who have already gone or who are about to go" (MS. Port. 8.3, 5 October 1838, F.H.A.L.).
60. George Fox to the Commonwealth Commissioners, 1651 (Nickalls, *Journal of George Fox*, p. 65).
61. *The Australian Friend*, 25 June 1891, p. 16.
62. Ibid., p. 14.
63. Record of the judge's notes at the trial, MS. 1165, A.S.A.
64. Margaret May, Diary, 1363 M, p. 303, A.S.A.
65. Hagen grew some of South Australia's first wines on Hack's Echunga estate.
66. Hack to T.G. Darton, 31 August 1844, Hack-Watson Papers, 1488/17, A.S.A.
67. *A.D.B.* vol. 1, pp. 498-99.
68. Walker to Richardson, 29 July 1839, Box R 415, Richardson MSS., F.H.A.L.
69. Pike, *Paradise of Dissent*, p. 263.
70. May — private correspondence.

Chapter Eight

1. See table 7, p. 39.
2. See p. 46.
3. J. Backhouse, Letters, 13 November 1837, Case 72, F.H.A.L.
4. Owen, *Chronicles of early Melbourne*, vol. 2, p. 567.
5. See pp. 129-30.
6. Stead to Robson, 9 October 1839, Microfilm H 15969, L.L.M.
7. Minutes of Pontefract M.M., 18 July 1853, Ackworth School.
8. MS 9863, Box 1521/1, L.L.M.
9. *Proceedings of London Y.M.* (1893):136.
10. Minutes of Cheshire M.M., 4 January 1844.
11. Melbourne followed the advice of Hobart, which had organized an Annual Meeting to bring scattered Friends together. This Meeting was first called a Yearly Meeting, but later the name was changed to Annual Meeting because Melbourne Friends had expressed some sensitivity on the former nomen-

clature, which seemed to them to make Melbourne Meeting answerable to a Yearly Meeting in Hobart. The first Annual Meeting in Melbourne was held on 9 December 1867.
12. See p. 44.
13. Minutes of Nottingham M.M., 26 February 1857.
14. W. Howitt, *Land, Labour and Gold*, vol. 1, p. 57.
15. The eastern end of Collins Street was known at one time as "Howitt's Corner" (Owen, vol. 2, p. 325).
16. Minutes of Melbourne M.M., 2 March 1862, MS. 9863, Box 1521/3, L.L.M.
17. Letter dated 29 February 1840, Box 647/3, L.L.M.
18. *A.D.B.*, vol. 2, p. 589.
19. *Melbourne 1903*, vol. 1, p. 348.
20. *A.D.B.*, vol. 2, p. 589.
21. Minutes of Gracechurch M.M., 9 November 1842.
22. M. Nichols, ed., *Traveller under Concern*, pp. 249-50.
23. MS. 9863, Box 1521/2, L.L.M.
24. MS. 9863, L.L.M.
25. Minutes of Dublin M.M., November 1842.
26. Jane White, from Cork M.M., was said to have settled with her family on the Logan River, Moreton Bay, as early as 1838.
27. Beale, ed., *Earth between them*, p. 95.
28. Trinity College, Dublin, was opened to Quakers in 1793. In England however universities were closed to dissenters until 1871. Barrington gained his B.A. degree in 1847, his M.A. in 1850, and his M.B. in 1870.
29. Beale, p. 77.
30. Ibid., p. 52.
31. Ibid., p. 78.
32. Ibid., p. 83. In n. 5 on p. 119 of *The earth between them* the editor says that the reason a subscription was not accepted from Beale himself was that Friends, seeing him in financial straits, would not allow him to contribute. The reason, however, may have been rather in his not being a recognized member, having been disowned by his Mountmellick Meeting. There is a note in a minute of a later meeting in Melbourne that in soliciting donations to the Meeting House fund they agreed "not to accept pecuniary aid from those not in profession with us" (Minutes of Melbourne M.M., 15 March 1854, MS. 9863, Box 1521/2, L.L.M.). There was evidence, too, that they had returned donations given by non-members in 1853. A George Mackay, L.L.D., gave five guineas, but this donation was returned to him. It says much for Joseph Beale's generosity that he accepted his ineligibility to make a direct donation and so placed it in the names of his two sons, Joseph and Francis, who had retained membership.
33. Locke had emigrated with his wife and children as early as 1833 to Sydney and then in early 1840 to Melbourne.
34. Locke and Raleigh had been disowned before coming to Australia and Thorp had resigned his membership in Hardshaw East M.M. at the time of the Crewdson controversy. This doctrinal dispute, though for a time threatening to cause a serious division of Friends in England as a similar dispute had in America, did not spread far beyond the Liverpool area.
35. Private Papers, Port. 43/2, Friends' Library, Eustace St., Dublin.
36. See pp. 55-57.
37. "The "Friend Minister" was either Lindsey or Mackie. Webb was apparently confused by his meeting with them, rather than helped to face what was a real "Crise de conscience".

38. Nichols, *Traveller*, p. 251.
39. Ibid., p. 251.
40. Ibid., p. 255.
41. W. Howitt, *Land, Labour and Gold*, vol. 1, p. 36.
42. Ibid., p. 36.
43. Ibid., p. 288.
44. *The Friend* 13:154.
45. Nichols, *Traveller*, pp. 253-54.
46. Minutes of Melbourne M.M., 2 May 1855, MS. 9863, Box 1521/2, L.L.M.
47. Extract from Lindsey's Journal, as quoted in the Minutes of East Division Cornwall M.M., 3 July 1855.
48. MS. 22/1, on Microfilm M 705, A.O.T.
49. *The Friend*, n.s. 33 (8 December 1893):792.
50. Minutes of Melbourne M.M., 28 July 1858, MS. 9863, Box 1521/3, L.L.M.
51. Ibid., 8 December 1858.
52. Minutes of the Continental Committee, as reported in *Proceedings of London Y.M.* (1859):38.
53. Ibid., p. 60.
54. Ibid.
55. *The Friend*, February 1857, p. 33.
56. *The Friend*, October 1857, pp. 186-87.
57. William Tallach (1831-1908), taught at Croydon and Ackworth Friends' Schools, travelled extensively in Malta, Egypt, Australia, the Pacific Islands, Mexico, and America. In 1866 he became secretary of the Howard Association for Penal Reform.
58. *The British Friend*, 1 May 1860, p. 166.
59. MS. S 1/2/1, T.U.A.

Chapter Nine

1. Ireland Yearly Meeting followed the lead of London Y.M.
2. From an Epistle of the Two Months' Meeting of Friends in South Australia to Hobart Annual Meeting 1885.
3. In 1872 London Y.M. decided that written answers should be required for only two queries — those which asked whether the meetings for worship and meetings for discipline had been held regularly. Even these requirements were dropped in 1905.
4. In notes on Ballarat members, the Australian Deputation traced William Tunks' interest in Friends to his contact with a well-known English Quaker, Robert Tindale, to whom he was apprenticed as a seaman — "From Robert Tindale's integrity and scrupulosity in the smallest matters dates his (Tunks') first attraction towards Friends" (Australian Deputation Notes, MS. Box 16 (5), F.H.A.L.).
5. *The Friend*, n.s. 8 (4 June 1868):162.
6. Minutes of Melbourne M.M., MS. 9863, 1521/4, L.L.M.
7. *Proceedings of London Y.M.* (1839):36.
8. Correspondence of Melbourne M.M., MS. 9863, Box 1527, L.L.M.
9. Australian Correspondence, MS. Box 16, F.H.A.L.
10. Microfilm M 705, A.O.T.
11. MS. Box 16(5), F.H.A.L.
12. Joseph Jones was a member of Hardshaw East M.M., who had been disowned

for "marrying out", but had been reinstated on appeal to London Y.M. He was a partner with Clemesha in a coffee and spice store in Ballarat. He entered Parliament and became Minister of Works. He was a brother of William Jones (see pp. 320-21).
13. MS. Box 16 (5), F.H.A.L.
14. *The British Friend*, 33, no. 4 (April 1875):74.
15. From a paper, "Revival in Adelaide", by Charles Stevenson, p. 1.
16. M. Sykes, *Quakers in India*, p. 48.
17. *The British Friend*, 3 March 1863, p. 26.
18. *The Friend*, n.s. 3 (September 1863):33.
19. The Sydney Friend, William Cooper, visited the Calcutta group in 1889 while on a visit to India representing the firm of Cadbury.
20. Minutes of the Meeting for Sufferings, 7 November 1862.
21. The Meeting for Sufferings advanced £200 for the Calcutta visit. Edward May submitted the following statement of expenditure:

Passages to India	£60. 0.0
Sundry trav. expenses	7. 3.5
Board in Calcutta	21. 2.1
Passages to Melbourne	70. 0.0
Melbourne — Adelaide	12.12.0
Sundry trav. expenses	2. 6.2
Exchange	2. 9.7
	£175.13.3
Balance	£24. 6.9

(From MS. Port. 8.46, 22 May 1863, F.H.A.L.)
22. Ibid.
23. MS. Port. 8.12, F.H.A.L.
24. William Bell Allen was a pioneer of the Protectionist movement — see *A.D.B.*, vol. 3, pp. 25-26. The older son, William Johnston, was also a protectionist, but Alfred opposed his brother in Parliament.
25. *The British Friend*, 31, no. 1 (January 1873):5.
26. MS. Q 246 A, M.L.
27. MS. Box 27 (4), 27 November 1867, F.H.A.L.
28. MS. vol. S 292, F.H.A.L.
29. William Rokes to Joseph Crosfield, 9 July 1869, MS. Box 18/4, F.H.A.L.
30. MS. Box 16 (5), F.H.A.L.
31. Green, ed., *Journal of Joseph James Neave*, p. 45.
32. See pp. 190, 296.
33. Uncatalogued, August 1981, M.L.
34. Ibid.
35. For a full description of the events leading to the closure see Neave's journal, entries for 26 and 28 February 1868, M.L.
36. Ibid.
37. *The British Friend*, 9 March 1869, p. 54.
38. From a letter dated 14 October 1868, quoted in *The Friend*, n.s. 9 (March 1869):55.
39. Minutes of Melbourne M.M., 21 January 1869.
40. MS. Box 8.38, F.H.A.L.
41. MS. Box 18/4, 1 January 1869, F.H.A.L.
42. W. Robson, Diary, 12 December 1868, Microfilm No. 206, F.H.A.L.
43. Bronner, *Walter Robson*, introduction.
44. Neave, Journal, p. 96, M.L.
45. Ibid., p. 123.
46. Ibid., p. 123.

47. Ibid., p. 119.
48. *The Friend*, n.s. 4 (1 August 1864):193.
49. Ibid., n.s. 3 (1 October 1863):245.
50. *The British Friend* 22, no. 8 (August 1864):198.
51. *The Friend*, n.s. 21 (1 April 1881):100.
52. "Wind-blown grasses caress the now abandoned sugar mill's source of power, the wheel of a horse-turned whim, with sockets for four shafts." (*The Queenslander*, 2 December 1871. See also *The Register*, 21 March 1913.)
53. *The Friend*, n.s. 31 (1 September 1891):245.
54. *The Australian Friend*, 1 September 1891, p. 245.
55. *The British Friend*, 2 November 1868.
56. Ibid., p. 281.
57. W. Robson, Diary, 2 November 1861, Microfilm 206, F.H.A.L.
58. Ibid., 9 December 1868.
59. Letter, dated 17 December 1868, MS. Box 18/4, F.H.A.L.
60. Robson, Diary, vol. 2, p. 248, Microfilm 206, F.H.A.L.
61. Neave to Crosfield, 30 November 1871, MS. Box 18(4), F.H.A.L.
62. MS. Box 16(4), F.H.A.L.
63. *Friends Quarterly Examiner* 12:153.
64. MS. Box 16(4), F.H.A.L.
65. *The Friend*, n.s. 15 (7 June 1875):142.
66. Ibid. (2 August 1875):218-19.
67. Neave, Journal, p. 50, M.L.
68. Minutes of Melbourne M.M., 5 March 1868.
69. For details, see Oats, *The Rose and the Waratah*, pp. 45-46.
70. *The Friend*, n.s. 10 (1 November 1870):265.
71. A few Friends felt able to send their children to attend Friends' Schools in England. James Backhouse Walker, son of G. W. Walker, was a boarder at Bootham (see Oats, pp. 29-36). The two Horsfall daughters were at Ackworth. Other families also sent children — the Birchalls one, the Barritts two, the Leicesters two. Edward and Deborah Sayce went back to England during the period of schooling at Ackworth for their two oldest children, Joseph John Wells for his two sons' education and Lucy Coleman for her three sons and a daughter at Croydon and Ackworth.
72. Beck to Ransome, 19 November 1874, MS. Box 16, F.H.A.L.
73. MS. Box 16(4), F.H.A.L.

Chapter Ten

1. Ransome to J.L., 1 August 1899, MS. Box 18(5), F.H.A.L.
2. 22 September 1892, MS. Box 18(4).
3. See Oats, p. 51.
4. Ransome to J. B. Mather, 7 January 1888, MS. Box 22(2), F.H.A.L.
5. See appendix 2.
6. Bronner, ed., *Walter Robson*, p. 67.
7. Minutes of Hobart M.M., Min. 7, April 1884.
8. MS. Box 27/2, 1 December 1893, F.H.A.L.
9. MS. Box 18(4), F.H.A.L.
10. *The Friend*, n.s. 28 (9 June 1888):157.
11. Green, *Journal of Joseph James Neave*, p. 105.
12. John Bellows offered himself as companion as a result of a chance postscript

in a letter from Ransome, thanking him for the donation of some geological specimens to The Friends' School, Hobart. The postscript reported the Meeting that morning which had approved Neave's plans.

13. Budge, *Isaac Sharp*, p. 182.
14. *The Friend*, n.s. 21, no. 247 (1881):120.
15. Ibid., 36, no. 14 (1896):221.
16. *Proceedings of London Y.M.* (1896):81.
17. *Friends' Quarterly Examiner* 37:497.
18. Green, p. 97.
19. *Proceedings of London Y.M.* (1898):38.
20. *The Friend*, n.s. 38 (1 July 1898):413.
21. Ibid. (3 June 1898):349.
22. Financial support for his travelling in the ministry came from his Woodbridge M.M., from London Y.M., from a small legacy from a relative, and from his wife's family. Jane Davy's father, Abraham Davy, had been a convict who by his industry made possible the freeing of Neave for travelling in the ministry.
23. *The Friend*, n.s. 38 (3 June 1898):350.
24. But this had one ironic result. Samuel Clemes saw himself as one who, with English Friends' help, could be freed for service amongst Australian Meetings. It was his absence on such service to Brisbane and Rockhampton that was one of the factors which contributed to his resignation from the headmastership of The Friends' School in 1900. For a full discussion of this see Oats, *The Rose and the Waratah*, pp. 113-14, and for background, chapter six, "The Anatomy of a Crisis", pp. 106-28.
25. See pp. 286, 290.
26. J. B. Mather to Ransome, 24 July 1885, MS. Box 22/1, F.H.A.L.
27. Oats, pp. 6-14.
28. *The Hobart Mercury*, 7 January 1933, A.O.T.
29. Oats, 1979.
30. *The Friend*, n.s. 31 (9 June 1891):153.
31. Ibid., 154.
32. Oats, pp. 69-71.
33. *The Hobart Mercury*, 8 July 1888, p. 84.
34. Oats, p. 82.
35. J. F. Mather to Ransome, 23 June 1902, F 4/6, F.H.A.L.
36. A. Wright, "Stones of Memorial", vol. 3, p. 25, MS. vol. series 349, F.H.A.L.
37. *The Friend*, n.s. 33 (28 April 1893):262.
38. Mackie to Backhouse, 15 June 1857, Case 19, p. 40, F.H.A.L.
39. *The Friend*, n.s. 25 (2 November 1885):228-29.
40. Ibid. (16 May 1902):316.
41. *The Australian Friend*, 20 August 1906.
42. Ibid., the first editorial, 8 July 1887, pp. 1-2.
43. Minutes of Sydney M.M., September 1898, MS. 3842, 7 (18), M.L. *Friends* refer to *The British Friend* and *The Friend*. The Sydney Minute Book dates back to the 8th month 1887. In the beginning of the book there is a certificate signed by the first clerk of the newly recognized Meeting, J. J. Neave: "I hereby certify that many of the Minutes of Sydney Meeting of Friends in use prior to the date set forth on the opposite page, i.e. 8th mo. 1887, were destroyed about the year 1886 or 1887 and that to the best of my knowledge and belief no copies of these minutes were ever taken." The earlier minutes were destroyed, it appears, deliberately by a member or members of the Sydney Meeting who did not wish minutes prejudicial to their supposed

interests to be preserved. As a result an historian's task in tracing the history of the Sydney Meeting before 1887 is not an easy one.
44. "A substantial brick building with an individual room for 22 inmates was opened in 1914. The work continued unobtrusively for teenage mothers, alcoholics and women ex-prisoners. The Retreat was finally handed over to the Melbourne City Mission free of debt and renamed 'Swinborn Lodge'." (Stevenson, *With unhurried pace*, p. 21)
45. J. W. Rowntree, ed., *Present Day Papers*, vol. 2, p. 18.
46. Within three years of 1885 William Cooper had joined Friends and succeeded Neave as Clerk of Sydney Meeting.
47. *The Dunedin Star*, 26 January 1889.
48. *The Friend*, n.s. 29 (1 April 1889):90.
49. Minutes of Melbourne M.M., Book 5, 7 January 1889.
50. *The Australian Friend*, 26 September 1892, p. 128.
51. See p. 285.
52. This Peruvian "slave" trade was at its height in the years 1862-64, when an Irish adventurer, J.C. Byrne, had a licence from Peru to introduce "colonists" from the Pacific Islands. The story is told in H. E. Maude's *Slavers in Paradise*.
53. This letter was published in *The Friend* and *The British Friend* of 1 September 1863.
54. See pp. 283-84.
55. *The Australian Friend*, 15 April 1899, p. 608.
56. Ibid., 23 October 1899, p. 647.
57. Ibid., 21 December 1901, p. 66.
58. MS. OM 74-62, 20 May 1881, O.L.
59. Wright to Ransome, 10 February 1893: "They must learn to walk before going on stilts" (MS Box 18(5), F.H.A.L.).
60. Brisbane appeared to go one step further in its rules by including provision for disownment either "for manifestly unchristian and unrighteous life" or for persisting after warning in "speaking or supplicating unacceptably in monthly meeting".
61. MS. OM 74-62, 20 May 1881, O.L.
62. Ibid.
63. McDonald, *Rockhampton, A History of City and District*, p. 365.
64. Ibid., p. 397.
65. *The Morning Bulletin*, Rockhampton, 20 March 1978.
66. Francis Hopkins to Sydney Friends, 16 January 1887, MS. OM 74-62, O.L.
67. *The Friend*, n.s. 27 (1 October 1887):275.
68. See pp. 320-21.
69. *The Australian Friend*, 8 December 1888, p. 119.
70. See p. 321.
71. There were considerable variations in the Marriage Acts in the colonies. In Victoria, South Australia and Tasmania there were no restrictions placed upon solemnization of marriages in the Friends' Meeting House. In New South Wales both parties had to be members of the Society of Friends and there was no provision for recognition of a Registrar to witness marriages legally without acting in a priestly capacity. South Australia was recognized as having the desired marriage regulations.
72. Sydney Friends had been given notice that the site of their Meeting House would be required for the building of the new Sydney Railway station. The old Meeting House was last used in July 1901. While a new site was being chosen, meetings were held in the People's Hall, Sussex Street, through the

courtesy of the Sydney City Mission. The new Meeting House in Devonshire Street was not ready in time to host the first General Meeting and this was transferred to Melbourne. The Meeting House in Devonshire Street was opened on 8 August 1903.

Chapter Eleven

1. Rhode Island Records, 1, p. 118.
2. Jones, *Quakers in the American Colonies*, p. 366.
3. Ibid., p. 357.
4. Port. 16/1, F.H.A.L.
5. Vipont, *Story of Quakerism*, p. 116.
6. Jones, p. 421.
7. Chapman, *Ballyhagen and Richhill Meetings*, p. 32.
8. J. Nickalls, ed., *Journal of George Fox*, p. 263.
9. Records of London Yearly Meeting date back to 1672 when a General Meeting was held to discuss the affairs of the Society. A similar meeting had been convened in 1668 and this was probably the first of such meetings to be convened in the metropolis, an epistle being issued, signed by George Fox. In 1672 the resolution was made to meet once a year "for the better ordering, managing and regulation of the public affairs of Friends, relating to the Truth and the service thereof" (Epistle from the Yearly Meeting of Friends, London [1818], p. 2).
10. J. Backhouse, Letters, 6 November 1850, Case 19, F.H.A.L.
11. Jones, chapter eleven.
12. Yearly Meetings were established in Ohio in 1813, Indiana 1821, Western Indiana 1858, Iowa 1863, Canada 1867, Kansas 1872, Wilmington 1891, Oregon 1893, California 1893.
13. Dorland, *History of the Society of Friends*, p. 261.
14. MS. Box 16/5, F.H.A.L.
15. Backhouse, Letters, 14 November 1850, Case 19, p. 38, F.H.A.L.
16. MS. Box 16/4, F.H.A.L.
17. OM 74-62, 6 April 1886, O.L.
18. A. Wright, "Stones of Memorial", MS. S 349, p. 39, F.H.A.L.
19. Ibid., p. 55.
20. MS. Box 18/3, 6 August 1898, F.H.A.L.
21. *The Australian Friend*, 29 June 1892, p. 99.
22. Minutes of the Continental Committee, 30 June 1898, F.H.A.L.
23. Ibid., 31 March 1898, F.H.A.L.
24. Ibid., 4 May 1899.
25. This letter of Clemes was reported in the Minutes of the Continental Committee, 4 January 1900.
26. *The Australian Friend*, 25 June 1891, p. 6.
27. *The Mercury*, Hobart, 22 June 1893.
28. Cf. p. 344.
29. *The Friend*, n.s. 35 (24 November 1895):773.
30. Ibid. (3 June 1896):351.
31. Reported in *The Friend* 27, no. 322 (1887):214-15.
32. Ibid.
33. *The Australian Friend*, 14 July 1898, p. 553.
34. See appendix 1.
35. *The Australian Friend*, 15 October 1898, p. 564.

Bibliography

Books

Adams, D., ed. *The Letters of Rachel Henning.* London: Penguin, 1969.
Aldridge, A. *Man of reason: Life of Thomas Paine.* London: Cresset, 1960.
Armfield, J. G. *A Complete list of scholars educated at Croydon School 1825–1879.* London: Croydon School, 1882.
Australian Dictionary of Biography. Melbourne: Melbourne University Press, 1968.
Australian Encyclopedia. Sydney: Angus and Robertson, 1957.
Backhouse, J. *Extracts of the Letters of James Backhouse.* Lindfield: Printed by W. Eade, at the School of Industry, 1834.
———. *A Narrative of a Visit to the Australian Colonies.* London: Hamilton, Adams, 1843.
Backhouse, J. and Tylor, C. *The Life and Labours of George Washington Walker.* London: A. W. Bennet, 1862.
Backhouse, S. *Memoir of James Backhouse.* York: William Sessions, 1870.
Barne, K. *Elizabeth Fry.* London: Penguin, 1950.
Barrett, J. *That better country.* Melbourne: Melbourne University Press, 1966.
Barry, J. V. *Alexander Maconochie of Norfolk Island.* Melbourne: Oxford University Press, 1958.
Barry, W. J. *The history of Port of Cork Steam Navigation.* Cork: Guy & Co., 1919.
Beale, E. ed. *The earth between them.* Sydney: Wentworth Press, 1975.
Beck, W. and Hall, T. *London Friends' Meetings.* London: F. B. Kitto, 1869.
Bibliography of Ackworth School. Manchester, 1889.
Billot, C. P. *John Batman.* Melbourne: Hyland House, 1979.
Biographical Catalogue. London: Friends' Institute, 1888.
Bolam, D. W. *Unbroken community: the story of the Friends' School, Saffron Walden, 1703–1952.* Cambridge: Friends' School, 1952.

Braithwaite, J. B. *Memoirs of J. J. Gurney.* 2 vols. London: Norwich, Fletcher and Alexander, 1855.
Braithwaite, W. C. *The Beginnings of Quakerism.* Cambridge: Cambridge University Press, 1955.
Brayshaw, A. N. *The Quakers: their history and message.* London: Allen & Unwin, 1927.
Brett, R. L. ed. *Barclay Fox's Journal.* London: Bell & Hyman, 1979.
Briggs, A. *The Age of Improvement (1783–1867).* London: Longman, 1959.
———. *Victorian People.* London: Pelican, 1965.
Bronner, E. B. *The other branch.* London: Friends' Historical Society, 1975.
———. ed. *Walter Robson: An English view of American Quakerism.* Philadelphia: American Philosophical Society, 1970.
Brown, J. C. *Poverty is not a crime.* Hobart: Tasmanian Historical Research Association, 1972.
Brownhill, W. R. *The history of Geelong and Corio Bay.* Melbourne: Anchor, 1955.
Budge, F. A. *Isaac Sharp, an apostle of the Nineteenth Century.* London: Headley Bros., 1898.
The Centenary of Australian Quakerism 1832–1932. Hobart: Society of Friends, 1933.
Chapman, G. R. *The history of Ballyhagan and Richhill Meetings.* Dungannon: n.p. 1979.
Christian Faith and Practice in the experience of the Society of Friends. London: Headley Bros., 1961.
Clark, G. K. *The making of Victorian England.* London: Methuen, 1963.
Clarkson, T. *A portraiture of Quakerism.* 3 vols. London: Longman, Hurst, Rees and Orme, 1807.
Clifton, R. B. *Old Australind recalled.* Perth: Australind 150th Committee, 1979.
Cole, A. The social origin of early Friends. In *Journal of the Friends' Historical Society* 48 (1957).
Darwin, C. *The descent of man.* London: Murray, 1887.
Denison, W. *The Varieties of vice-regal life.* London: Longmans & Green, 1870.
Doncaster, Phebe. *John Stephenson Rowntree: his life and work.* London: Headley Bros., 1908.
Dorland, A. G. *The history of the Society of Friends (Quakers).* Toronto: Macmillan of Canada, 1927.
Drake, T. E. *Patterns of influence in Anglo-American Quakerism.* London: Friends' Historical Society, 1958.
Elliott, E. T. *Quakers on the American Frontier.* Richmond (Indiana, U.S.A.): The Friends' United Press, 1969.

Ellis, V. R. *Trucanini: Queen or Traitor?* Canberra: Australian Institute of Aboriginal Studies, 1981.
Evans, V. *History of the Sydney Meeting.* Sydney: Sydney Regional Meeting of the Society of Friends, 1981.
Fawell, R. and West, M. *The Story of New Zealand Quakerism, 1842–1972.* Auckland: Yearly Meeting of the Religious Society of Friends, 1973.
Finn, E. *The chronicles of early Melbourne.* 2 vols. Melbourne: Fergusson & Mitchell, 1888.
Fox, J. J. *An enquiry into the causes of decline of the Society of Friends.* London: A. W. Bennett, 1859.
Fox, S. E. ed. *Edward Octavius Tregelles.* London: Hodder & Stoughton, 1892.
Fry, J. *An Alphabetical Extract of all the Annual Printed Epistles from London Y.M. 1682–1762.* London: Luke Hinde, 1766.
Fry, J. S. *To Friends, wherever found in Australia.* London: London Y.M., 1874.
Garden, D. S. *Albany: A Panorama of the Sound from 1827.* West Melbourne: Nelson, 1977.
Goldney, F. H. *The Quaker Meeting House, North Adelaide.* Adelaide: Pioneers' Association of S. Australia, 1968.
Goodbody, O. C. *Guide to Irish Quaker Records, 1654–1860.* Dublin: Irish Manuscripts Commission, 1967.
Goodbody, O. C. and Carroll, J. F. eds. *Extracts from the letters of John Grubb to Joseph Grubb.* Dublin: 1966.
Green, J. J. ed. *Leaves from the Journal of Joseph James Neave.* London: Headley Bros., 1910.
Greenwood, J. O. *Quaker Encounters.* 3 vols. York: Ebor Press, 1978.
Grubb, I. *Quakers in Ireland.* London: Swarthmore Press, 1927.
Hall, T. and Beck, W. *London Friends' Meetings.* London: F. B. Kitto, 1869.
Harrison, J. F. C. *The early Victorians, 1832–1851.* St Albans: Panther, 1973.
Hazell, W. and Hodgkin, H. *The Australasian Colonies: Emigration and Colonization.* London: Edward Stanford, 1887.
Heard, D. ed. *Journal of Charles O'Hara Booth.* Hobart: Tasmanian Historical Research Association, 1981.
Hewitt, N. *Friends in Tasmania.* Hobart: Hobart Regional Meeting of the Society of Friends, 1981.
Hicks, N. *This sin and scandal.* Canberra: Australian National University Press, 1978.
A History of Great Ayton School. London: Ayton School, 1891.
A History of Wigton School, 1815–1915. Wigton: Wigton Old Scholars' Association, 1916.

The Hobart Savings Bank 1845—1945. Hobart: The Savings Bank of Tasmania, 1945.
Hodgkin, H. T. *Friends beyond the seas.* London: Headley Bros., 1916.
Hodgson, J. S. *Ackworth School Records 1779—1894.* Ackworth: Ackworth School, 1895.
———. *A history of Penketh School, 1834—1907.* London: Headley Bros., 1907.
Howitt, Margaret, ed. *Mary Howitt: An autobiography.* 2 vols. London: Isbister, 1889.
Howitt, R. *Impressions of Australia.* London: Longman, Brown, Green and Longmans, 1845.
Howitt, W. *Land, Labour and Gold* or *Two years in Victoria.* 2 vols. London: Longman, Brown, Green and Longmans, 1855.
Ignatieff, M. *A just measure of pain.* London: Macmillan, 1978.
Insell, T. *John Cadbury, 1801—1889.* Birmingham: Cadbury, 1979.
Isichei, E. *Victorian Quakers.* Oxford: Oxford University Press, 1970.
Japp, A. H. ed. *Master Missionaries.* London: Marshall and Japp, 1880.
Jones, R. *The Quakers in the American Colonies.* London: Macmillan, 1923.
———. *The later periods of Quakerism.* 2 vols. London: Macmillan, 1921.
Kaye, W. J. *The history of Rawden School.* Batley: Rawden School, 1882.
Kiek, E. S. *The life and reminiscences of Joseph Coles Kirby.* London: Independent Press, 1927.
Knight, J. ed. *N. Bartley: Australian Pioneers and Reminiscences.* Brisbane: Gordon & Gotch, 1896.
Lea-Scarlett, E. *Roots and branches.* Sydney: Collins, 1979.
Lee, A. *Laurels and rosemary, the life of William and Mary Howitt.* London: Oxford University Press, 1955.
Lerner, L. ed. *The Victorians.* London: Methuen, 1978.
Lindsey, R. *The travels of Robert and Sarah Lindsey.* Edited by his daughter. London: Samuel Harns, 1886.
Lloyd, A. *Quaker social history, 1669—1738.* London: Longmans, Green, 1950.
Lloyd, H. *The Quaker Lloyds in the Industrial Revolution.* London: Hutchinson, 1975.
McDonald, L. *Rockhampton, a History of City and District.* St Lucia: University of Queensland Press, 1981.
Martin, R. C. *The Adult School Movement.* London: National Adult School Union, 1924.
Maude, M. E. *Slavers in Paradise.* Canberra: Australian National University Press, 1981.
Mayhew, H. *London Labour and the London Poor.* 8 vols. London: Griffin, 1861.

Morphett, G. C. *John Barton Hack, a Quaker pioneer.* Adelaide: Pioneers Association of South Australia, 1943.
Myers, A. C. *The immigration of Irish Quakers into Pennsylvania.* Swarthmore (Pa): 1902.
Nadel, G. *Australia's colonial culture.* Cambridge, Mass.: Harvard University Press, 1957.
Newman, G. *Quaker Profiles.* 8 vols. London: Bannisdale Press, 1946.
Newman, D. *A Procession of Friends.* New York: Doubleday, 1972.
Newman, E. W. ed. *Sidcot School Register, 1808–1912.* Birmingham: Sidcot School, 1919.
Nichols, M. ed. *Traveller under concern.* The Quaker journals of Frederick Mackie on his tour of the Australasian colonies, 1852–1855. Hobart: University of Tasmania, 1973.
Nickalls, J. ed. *The Journal of George Fox.* London: London Y.M. of the Society of Friends, 1975.
Oats, W. N. *The Rose and the Waratah.* Hobart: Blubberhead Press, 1979.
O'Farrell, P. *The Catholic Church in Australia.* Melbourne: Nelson, 1968.
One hundred years of Mountmellick School. Dublin: Richard D. Webb & Son, 1886.
Oxford Dictionary of the Christian Church. London: Oxford University Press, 1974.
Owen, ("Garryowen") *Chronicles of early Melbourne.* 2 vols. Melbourne: Fergusson, Mitchell, 1888.
Parkinson, S. *Journal of a voyage to the South Seas.* Facsimile edition. Adelaide: Libraries Board of South Australia, 1972.
Pike, D. *Paradise of Dissent.* London: Longmans, Green, 1957.
Plomley, N. J. B. *Friendly Mission.* Hobart: Tasmanian Historical Research Association, 1966.
Pollard, W., Frith, F., and Turner, N. *A reasonable faith.* rev. ed. London: Macmillan & Co., 1886.
Raistrick, A. *Quakers in science and industry.* London: Bannisdale Press, 1950.
Reed, D. W. *Friends' School, Wigton, 1815–1953.* Wigton: Wigton Old Scholars Association, 1954.
Robinson, W. ed. *Friends of half a century.* London: E. Hicks, 1891.
Roe, M. *Quest for authority in Eastern Australia 1835–1851.* Melbourne: Melbourne University Press in association with the Australian National University, 1965.
Rowntree, J. S. *Friends' Register of Births, Deaths and Marriages, 1650–1900.* Leominster: Orphans' Printing Press, 1902.
———. *Quakerism, past and present.* London: Smith, Elder, 1859.
Rowntree, J. W. *Essays and Addresses.* London: Headley Bros, 1905.

———.ed. *Present Day Papers.* York: Society of Friends, 1898.
Rudé, G. *Protest and punishment.* Oxford: Clarendon Press, 1978.
Seebohm, B. *Memoirs of the life and gospel labours of Stephen Grellett.* London: A. W. Bennett, 1862.
Shaw, A. G. L. *Sir George Arthur.* Melbourne: Melbourne University Press, 1980.
Smith, B. *The Spectre of Truganini.* 1980 Boyer Lecture. Sydney: Australian Broadcasting Commission, 1980.
Stannage, C. T. ed. *A new history of W. Australia.* Nedlands, W.A.: University of Western Australia Press, 1981.
Stevenson, C. *With unhurried pace.* Melbourne: The Religious Society of Friends (Quakers) in Australia, 1973.
Stewart, W. A. C. *Quakers and Education.* London: Epworth Press, 1953.
Sutherland, A. *Victoria and its metropolis.* Melbourne: McCarron, Bird, 1888.
Sykes, M. *Quakers in India.* London: Allen & Unwin, 1980.
Tallach, W. *Peter Bedford, The Spitalfields philanthropist.* London: S. W. Partridge, 1865.
Therry, R. M. *Reminiscences of thirty years' residence in New South Wales and Victoria.* Facsimile edition. Sydney: Sydney University Press, 1974.
Thistlethwaite, W. P. *Yorkshire Quarterly Meeting 1665—1966.* Harrogate: n.p. 1969.
Thompson, E. P. *The making of the English working-class.* Harmondsworth, Middlesex: Penguin Books, 1968.
Thomson, D. *England in the Nineteenth Century.* Harmondsworth, Middlesex: Penguin Books, 1966.
Tobias, J. J. *Crime and industrial society.* Harmondsworth, Middlesex: Penguin Books, 1972.
Tolles, F. B. ed. *The Journal of John Woolman and A plea for the poor. The John Greenleaf Whittier text.* New York: Corinth Books, 1961.
Vann, R. T. *The social development of English Quakerism 1655—1755.* Cambridge, Mass.: Harvard University Press, 1969.
Vipont, E. *The Story of Quakerism.* London: Bannisdale Press, 1954.
Walker, J. B. *Early Tasmania.* Hobart: Government Printer, 1950.
Walker, M. H. *Come wind, come weather.* Melbourne: Melbourne University Press, 1971.
Walker. P. B. *All that we inherit.* Hobart: J. Walch, 1968.
West, J. *The history of Tasmania.* Edited by A. G. L. Shaw. Sydney: Royal Australian Historical Society, Angus & Robertson, 1971.
West, M. and Fawell, R. *The Story of New Zealand Quakerism 1842—1972.* Auckland: Society of Friends, New Zealand, 1973.

Westwood, J. J. *The journal of J. J. Westwood.* Melbourne: Clarson, Shallard, 1865.
Wheeler, D. Jnr. *Memoirs of Daniel Wheeler.* London: Harvey and Darton, 1842.
Whitney, J. *Elizabeth Fry.* London: Guild Books, 1937.
Williams, I. A. *The firm of Cadbury 1831—1931.* London: Constable & Co., 1931.
Woodham-Smith, C. *The Great Hunger: Ireland 1845—49.* London: Hamish Hamilton, 1962.
Worsdell, E. *The Gospel of Divine Help.* 2nd ed. London: Samuel Harris, 1888.
Young, G. M. *Victorian England: Portrait of an Age.* London: Oxford University Press, 1936.

Genealogies

Australian Society of Genealogists, History House, 8 Young Street, Sydney, for records of settlers and prisoners arriving in Australia.

Barrington, A. *The Barringtons — a family history.* Dublin: 1917.
Beakbane, R. *Beakbane of Lancaster.* Kidderminster, U.K.: 1977.
Beck, W. *Family fragments, respecting the ancestry, acquaintance and marriage of Richard Low Beck and Rachel Lucas.* Privately printed by John Bellows. Gloucester: 1897.
Benson, R. S. *Photographic pedigree of descendants of Isaac and Rachel Wilson, 1740.* Middlesborough: 1912.
Forster, J. *The Pedigree of the Forsters of Cold Hesledon.* Sutherland: 1862.
Foster, J. *Descendants of John Backhouse, Yeoman.* London: 1894.
Foster, S. B. *The pedigree of Wilson of High Wray and the families connected with them.* London: 1890.
Grubb, G. W. *The Grubbs of Tipperary, Ireland.* 1972 (F.H.A.L.).
Jesper, W. A. *Short History of the Jesper family.* York: 1916.
Penney, N. *My ancestors.* Private circulation, 1920 (F.H.A.L.).
Smith, H. E. *Annals of Smith of Cantley, Balby and Doncaster, County York.* F.H.A.L.
Steel, D. J. *Sources for nonconformist genealogy and family history.* London: Society of Genealogists, 1973.
Thistlethwaite, B. *The Thistlethwaite family.* London: 1910.

Journals and Pamphlets

Annual Monitor. Published annually. Record of deaths of members of the Society of Friends.
The early history of the convict, John Tawell. Published undated, unauthored. 5D14, Bevan Naith Library, Woodbrooke College Birmingham.
Friends' Quarterly Examiner. London.
Journal of Economic History. New York.
Journal of the Friends' Historical Society. London.
Journal of the Royal Australian Historical Society. Sydney.
Proceedings of London Yearly Meeting. London.
The Australian Friend. Published bi-monthly, commencing 1887.
The British Friend. London.
The Friend. Published weekly, commencing 1843. London.
The Irish Friend. 1837–43.
The Lindfield Reporter. 1835–36 and 1842.
The Philanthropist. 1811–18.

Manuscripts

Manuscript material is classified according to location.

County Record Offices and Libraries
where Minute Books and Registers of following English Friends' Monthly Meetings are located.

Albans M.M. at C.R.O., Shire Hall, Castle Hill, Cambridge.
Balby M.M. at Sheffield Central Library.
Banbury M.M. at Oxfordshire C.R.O.
Brighouse M.M. at the Brotherton Library, University of Leeds.
Bristol and Frenchay M.M. (to 1933) at Bristol Archives Office, Council House, Bristol.
Cambridge Monthly Meeting at C.R.O., Shire Hall, Castle Hill, Cambridge.
Cheshire M.M. at Cheshire R.O., the Castle, Chester.
Colchester and Coggeshall M.M. at University of Essex, Colchester.
Cornwall M.M. at C.R.O., County Hall, Truro.
East Devon M.M. at Devon R.O., Castle Street, Exeter.
Edinburgh M.M. at R.O., Edinburgh.
Gloucester M.M. at Gloucestershire R.O., Gloucester.
Hardshaw East M.M. at Manchester Central Library, St Peter's Square, Manchester.

Hertford and Hitchin M.M. at Hertfordshire R.O., Hertford.
Leicester M.M. at Department of Archives, Leicester Museum, Leicester.
Lewes and Chichester M.M. at East Sussex R.O., Lewes.
Lincolnshire M.M. at Lincolnshire Archives Office, the Castle, Lincoln.
    H. W. Brace, *Index of Quaker names*, also located here.
Northampton M.M. at C.R.O., the Abbey, Northampton.
Nottingham M.M. at Notts R.O., County House, High Pavement, Nottingham.
Pardshaw M.M. at C.R.O., the Castle, Carlisle.
Pontefract M.M. at Ackworth School, Ackworth.
Preston and Marsden M.M. at Lancashire R.O., Bow Lane, Preston.
Witham M.M., pre-1850, at Essex R.O., County Hall, Chelmsford.
Witney M.M. at Oxfordshire R.O., County Hall, Oxford.
Woodbridge M.M. at Ipswich and E. Suffolk R.O., Ipswich.

Friends' Meeting Houses
where Minute Books and Registers of the following English Friends' Monthly Meetings are located.

Hardshaw East M.M. Some records at F.M.H., Manchester.
Hardshaw West M.M. at F.M.H., Liverpool.
Newcastle M.M. at F.M.H., Newcastle-upon-Tyne.
Swarthmore, M.M. at F.M.H., Cartmel.
Thaxted M.M. at F.M.H., Saffron Walden.
Warwickshire North M.M. at F.M.H., Bull Street, Birmingham.
Witham M.M., post-1850, at F.M.H., Chelmsford.
York M.M. at F.M.H., York.

Friends' House Archives, London

The Library at Friends' House, Euston Road, London, contains much of the official records and private correspondence between English and Australian Friends in the nineteenth century. Most of this material was microfilmed for the Australian Joint Copying Project (see Phyllis Mander-Jones, ed., *Manuscripts in the British Isles, relating to Australia, New Zealand and the Pacific* [Canberra: 1972], 314-20).

There are fifteen reels of microfilm, copies of which are available in the Archives of each State Library in Australia. The catalogue numbers for reels 1 to 15 are M693-707. Manuscript material at F.H.A.L. is listed as
   (1)   on micro-film
   (2)   *not* on micro-film.

Bibliography

(1) on micro-film

Film No.	Catalogue No.	F.H.A.L. Ref.	Description
1	M693	MS.Vols. 25 26(to 1908)	Mins. of London Y.M. 1834–56. Reports of Continental Ctee. Reports of Meeting for Sufferings *Note*: from 1857 Minutes of London Y.M. were printed as "Proceedings"
2	M694	MS.Vols.43-55	Mins. of Meeting for Sufferings, 1823–1916, relating to Australia.
3	M695	MS.Vol.55(cont.) MS.Vol.56 MS.Vols.65-70	Ditto Ditto Epistles of London Y.M. Minutes of Continental Ctee. 1817–1905, indexed.
4	M696	Portfolios 8, 17, 18, 19, 25, 28, 30, 40, 42	Miscellaneous correspondence with Australian Meetings.
5	M697	MS.Vol.S48 (J. Backhouse Collection)	J. Backhouse Letter-Book 1 1831–35.
6	M698	MS.Vol.57 MS.Vol.S69 MS.Vol.58 Temp.Box 61/1 MS.Vol. S 355 Case 101	J.B. Letter-Book 2 (1835-67) J.B. Letter-Book 4 (1837-41) J.B. Letter-Book 5 (1841-68) J.B. Journal letter transcripts 1831-33, 2 vols. J.B. Account Book and correspondence.
7	M699	Robert Lindsey MSS. (MS.S240)	Journal of Lindsey's visit Australia 1852–55.
8	M700	ditto MS.Boxes 1/9, 2/4, 5/13, 5/23, 13/1	ditto Miscellaneous — Australian Meetings.
9	M701	MS.Box 16	Miscellaneous, including some letters of Edwin Ransome and reports of Australian Deputation of 1875.
11	M703	MS.Box 18/5 and 18/6	Correspondence with Australian Meetings.
13	M705	MS.Box 27(1) to (4)	Matters concerning Australian Meetings.

		MS.Box 27 (20)	List of migrant members drawn up by Cont. Ctee.
		MS.Box 27(92)	List of members in Australia, 1874–75.
		MS.Vol.Series S	William Benson, Journals
		S 286-92	1866–88, 7 vols.
		S 347	Alfred Wright, "Stones of Memorial", Vol. 1.
14	M706	S 347 (cont.)	Vol. 1 (contd.)
		S 349	Vol. 3, record of 2nd visit to Australia, 1890–92.
		Isaac Sharp MSS.	Diaries of visit to Australia and New Zealand, 1880–82.
15	M707	ditto	contd.
		Letter Box R 2/4	List of members drawn up by Lindsey and Mackie during visit to Australia 1852–55.
	206	Robson MSS. (MS 429)	Walter Robson, "Diary of Visit to Australia" (1867-70) 2 vols.

(2) *not* on micro-film

Dictionary of Quaker Biography
Digest of births after 1837
Quarterly Meeting records of births, marriages and deaths to 1837
Minutes of the following Monthly Meetings:
                    Devonshire House
                    Gracechurch Street
                    Kingston
                    Longford
                    Peel
                    Southwark
                    Tottenham
                    Westminster

Port 17/115   John Tawell, Letter to Devonshire House M.M.
Gibson Mss. 4/135   Letters including one re John Tawell
MS. Vol. 58   James Backhouse to John Tawell
Tract Vol. 377/26   G. Henson, *History of John Tawell, with his life, trial, confession and execution.* Northampton: 1845.
Case 19   Letters of James Backhouse, including one from Captain Charles Sturt to J.B.
Case 172   Letters of James Backhouse
Vol. B 60   Address to colonists of Australind, W. Australia, 1840

Vol. 458/7   Appeal from Sydney Friends, 1869
Port. 8/57 to 8/80   Lists of members compiled by J. B. Hack for S. Australia Meeting before 1848

The Friends' Library, Eustace Street, Dublin

Minutes of Irish M.M.s and register of members of Ireland Y.M.
Port. 43/2   Private papers
Port. 43/24   Diary of Alfred Webb

The Mitchell Library, Sydney

B708-718   MSS. of G.W. Walker, "Journal of Visit to Australia and South Africa 1831—1841".
B730-732   MSS. of J. Backhouse, "Journal of Visit to Australia and South Africa 1831—1841".
MS. B 729   J. Backhouse, "Recollections of past life".
MS. 3842   1 (18)   Letters — Sydney Monthly Meeting
             17 (18)   Journal of J. J. Neave, 1867-68 and 1870.
                       Journal of Helen Davy, 1869-76
A 2939, Vol. 43   Macarthur Papers.
Box 3 (18)   Record book of Sydney Monthly Meeting, being mainly correspondence, 1897-1912.
Box 7 (18)   Minutes of Sydney Monthly Meeting, 1887-1909.
Box 10 (18)   Records of Ministry and Oversight Committee 1889—1922.
Box 13x (18)   Register of births, marriages and deaths.

The La Trobe Collection State Library of Victoria

MS. 9863	Box 1521 (1) to (4)	Minute Books of Melbourne Monthly Meeting to 1869 (Books 1 to 3) [post-1869 Minutes (Books 4-7) at F.M.H., 631 Orrong Road, Toorak, Victoria]
MS. 9863	Box 1526	Correspondence with Melbourne M.M.
”	Box 1528 (1)	Record of members of Melbourne M.M. around 1857.
”	Box 1528 (2)	Undated alphabetical list of members.
”	Box 1528 (3)	Marriage register of Melbourne M.M. List of Friends in Victoria, compiled by Lindsey and Mackie, 1854-55. List of members of Eng. M.M. in Victoria "to about 1860". Ireland Y.M. list of members resident in Australia in 1852. List of

members of Melbourne M.M. who signed petition to London Y.M. seeking help with building of a Meeting-House.
MS. 6939-40   Foster Fyans, "Unpublished Reminiscences".
   (by permission of State Library of Victoria)
MS. Box 647/3   Letters, J. Were to his brother
Microfilm H 15969   Letters, Stead to Robson

The Oxley Library, Brisbane

MS. OM 74-62/4   Correspondence of Francis Hopkins, Rockhampton

Archives of South Australia

SRG 103/1/1-4	List of members compiled by J. B. Hack. List of S.A. Friends, 1853, as prepared for S.A. 2 Months' Meeting, 6 November 1853. Minutes of 2 Months' Meeting, Adelaide. List of members in S. Australia, 1854.
SRG 103/3	Register of members of Adelaide 2 Months' Meeting.
1363M	Letters of the May family (*Note*: further letters in possession of descendants).
1488/1-46	Hack-Watson correspondence.
MS. Box 1.9	Miss Halse; *Days of our fathers*.
A1197	Government despatches.
GRG 2/6/1	Stephen to Lord Glenelg.

Tasmanian University Archives

1. *Records of the Society of Friends* on indefinite loan to T.U.A. from the Hobart Regional Meeting of the Society of Friends.
   Access: permission (in writing) required from the Clerk of Hobart Regional Meeting.
   S 1/11   Minutes of Hobart Monthly Meeting 1833-1950 (6 vols.) in vol. 1, rear, following registers are kept: marriage, 1834-87; births, 1834-Jan. 1886; deaths, 1834-Jan. 1888; List of members, 1833-69.
   S 1/12   Duplicates of above for use at Kelvedon, when Monthly Meetings were held in alternate month: with Hobart 1833-43; with Launceston 1844-51. 2 vols.
   S 1/13   Minutes of Launceston M.M. 1844-51.
   S 1/14   Minutes of Annual Meetings 1834-1902 (2 vols.). Vol. 2 (rear) contains list of members 1834-95.

2. F 4/1-5 Correspondence of J.B. and J.F. Mather with Edwin Ransome and Charles Holdsworth, particularly with reference to the Friends' School, Hobart (access: by authority of Board of Governors only).
   F 4/67 J.B. Mather, "Account of the rise of the Society of Friends in Tasmania", Typed MS., Hobart, 1883.
3. *The Walker Papers*
   Access: at the discretion of the archivist:
   W 9/1/1 Correspondence of G.W. Walker
   W 9/1/1/4 Letter Books of G.W. Walker, 1831-44, 4 vols.
4. M 19/100 Diary of J.B. Mather
   R/7 Letters of J.B. Mather.
   F 1 Letters of John Fisher.

Archives Office of Tasmania

M 693-707	Microfilm records of England-Australia correspondence and MSS. — see above under F.H.A.L.
CON series	Convict records
G 33/10	Arthur to Howick correspondence
MS. 248/174/1-23	Letters of Lady Franklin
Folder 13	Journal of Lady Franklin

Index

Aborigines, 65, 102-15, 226-27
   Aborigines' land rights, 110-14
   Aborigines Protection League, 11, 114
Adult Schools, Friends', 293, 302, 319-20
Alcoholism, 35, 57-58, 224
Alexander, Reuben Fisher, 243, 245
Allen, Alfred, 269-75, 277, 283, 293, 382 n24
Allen, Ruth, 269
Allen, William, 19, 368 n32
Allen, William Bell, 269, 382 n24
Allen, William Johnston, 269, 382 n24
American Quakers in Australia, 296-97
American Quaker migrations, 58, 61, 331-35, 339
Anti-Slavery Movement, 18, 284, 287, 322
Appleton, Cornelius, 275, 276
Apprenticeship, 14, 47
Armfield, George, 14-15
Arthur, Lt Gov. George, 84, 88-90, 92, 97, 100, 102, 104, 109, 110, 116, 120-22, 149, 162, 163, 369 n12
Ashby, Edwin, 372 n17
Ashton, Rita, 172
Austin, Ann, 332
Australian Deputation (of London Y.M.), 238, 264, 283, 285-90, 291, 305, 308, 313, 340, 341, 381 n4
Australian Friends' Meetings
   General Meeting, 259, 309, 314, 327-30, 349
   New South Wales, 75, 170-94
      Pitt Street group, 272, 274, 281, 283
      Sydney, 134, 150, 170-73,
      178-82, 186-94, 269-75, 276, 277, 293, 318, 319, 320, 340, 373 n54, 384 n43, 385 n72
   Queensland, 278-85, 298
      Brisbane, 279-81, 341, 342
      Mooloolah group, 281, 283, 383 n52
      Rockhampton, 281-82, 324-26, 341, 348
   South Australia, 62-64, 66, 75, 204-31, 264-68, 322, 342
      Adelaide, 77, 206-13, 216, 218, 230
      Mount Barker, 204, 215, 216, 230
   Van Diemen's Land (after 1853 Tasmania), 75, 77, 127-69
      Hobart, 127-37, 158, 182, 191, 192, 218, 220, 260, 269, 296-97, 344, 347
      Kelvedon, 132, 157, 372 n13
      Launceston, 132, 142-43, 372 n13
      Yearly Meeting, 132, 134, 136, 143, 150, 156, 182, 192, 193, 260
   Victoria, 71, 75, 232-34
      Melbourne, 234-40, 248-52, 260, 261, 262, 276, 288-90, 292-93, 379 n11
      Ballarat, 247, 262-64, 341, 381 n4
   Western Australia, 62, 64, 134-37, 372 n17
      Yearly Meeting, 288, 291, 305, 318, 324, 337
Australind, 40, 134–36, 372 n15

Backhouse, Hannah, 183, 377 n47

Backhouse, James, 11, 19, 27, 35, 60, 62, 63, 64, 66, 75, 77, 78-126, 192, 194, 207, 221, 226, 227, 233, 234, 257, 265, 270, 286, 291, 296, 299, 300, 308, 313, 321, 322, 337, 340, 343, 349, 369 n6, 371 n91 and n97
  Aborigines, 102-15
  Aborigines, Tasmanian, 104-8, 115
  Arthur, Lt Gov., 120-22
  convicts, 137-53
  Cotton, Francis, 153-60
  Franklin, Sir John, 122
  Fry, Elizabeth, 11, 79, 81, 91-93
  Macquarie Harbour, 87, 90, 95
  Moreton Bay, 117, 124
  NSW, 122-24
  Norfolk Island, 95-97
  objectives of visit to Australian colonies, 82-83
  partnership with Walker, G.W., 78-79, 81-82
  penal reform, 87-102
  Port Arthur, 90-91
  Port Phillip, 118, 233
  settlers, 86-87
  South Australia, 118, 195-97
  Sydney Meeting, 170-73, 177-81, 188-94
  Tawell, John, 173, 177-81, 184, 185-86
  Temperance, 115-17, 375 n92
  transportation, 99-100, 158
  Van Diemen's Land, 119-22, 127-37
  Western Australia, 118
  Wesleyans, 161-64
Bakewell, John, 235, 236
Bakewell, Robert, 235
Banks, Sir Joseph, 75
Baptist Church, Hobart, 308, 310
Barclay, Robert, 134, 162, 270, 271, 374 n83
Barclays (Bank), 7, 43
Barrington, Edward, 241-42, 380 n28
Barritt, Joseph, 201, 216, 218, 228, 231, 383 n71
Barrymore, E., 279
Batman, John, 106, 110, 118, 233, 234
Beaconites, 38
Beale, Francis, 242

Beale, Joseph, 54-55, 241-43, 380 n32
Beale, Joseph, Jun., 242
Beale, Margaret, 55, 241, 306
Beale, Octavius, 306
Beck, William, 51, 286, 290, 305, 340
Bedford, Peter, 19, 83, 141
Belcher, Dr, 234
Bell, Daniel, 134
Bell, George, 165
Bellows, John, 299, 383 n12
Bennet, Gabriel, 177, 178
Bennington, George, 164
Benson, Ann. See Mather, Ann
Benson, Joseph, 162
Benson, William, 271, 306, 314, 316-17, 328, 346
Bevan, William, 187
Bewley, Samuel, 81
Biddle, Rolles, 30, 227
Bigg(e), Jeremiah, 180
Birchall, Lucy, 239, 383 n71
Birchall, William Harding, 239
Boer War, 315
Booth, Charles O'Hara, 91
Bourke, Gov., 63, 89, 95, 109, 122, 124, 151
Boyes, G.W.T., 140-41
Bragg, Charles, 164
Bragg, Hadwen, 81
Bragg, Margaret, 81, 163
Bragg, Mary, 81
Braithwaite, J.B., 276
Bright, John, 57
British and Foreign School System, 151, 306
Bronner, Edwin, 277
Brooks, William, 284, 285
Broughton, Archdeacon, 123
Brown, Amelia, 177, 178
Brown, Henrietta, 302
Brown, Thomas, 177
Bryant and May, 43
Burra, South Australia, 202, 222
Buxton, Hannah, 18
Buxton, Sir T. Fowell, 18, 102, 109, 111, 112, 114, 115
Byllynge, Edward, 333
Byrne, J.C., 385 n52

Cadbury, 43
Cadbury, George, 319, 346
Cadbury, John, 66

Index

Calcutta Quakers, 266-68, 382 n19 and n21
Calder, J.E., 375 n86
Camm, John, 44
Campbelltown (NSW) gaol, 94
Canadian Quakers, 339-40
Capper, Alfred, 200, 378 n10
Carteret, Sir George, 333
Castle Hill Rebellion, 171-72
Chapman, George R., 335
Charles the Second, 334
Chartists, 56, 60
Chelsea pensioners, 83-85
Clarkson, Thomas, 8, 18
Clemes, Alfred, 248, 249-50, 345
Clemes, Samuel, 294, 298, 304, 311-12, 315, 342, 343, 344, 345, 384 n24
Clemesha, Solomon, 263, 382 n12
Clifton, Elinor, 40, 134-37, 372 n15
Clifton, Marshall, 40, 136
Clint, R., 64
Cock, R., 113-14, 228
Coleman, Edward, 218, 229, 231
Coleman, Frederick, 372 n17
Coleman, Lucy, 383 n71
Coleman, Sarah, 268
Conventicle Act, 333
Convicts, Quaker, 46, 59-60
Cooper, William, 319, 382 n19, 385 n46
Corporation Act of 1861, 52
Cotton, Anna Maria, 153, 156, 158, 165, 372 n12, 374 n64
Cotton, Francis, 119, 147, 149, 153-60, 181, 192, 220, 224, 265, 269, 273-74, 308, 374 n64 and n70
Cotton, Francis, Jun., 157
Cotton, James Backhouse, 296, 297
Cottrell, A., 106
Cowper, Charles (Hon.), 284
Cox, Christina. See Robson, Christina
Cox, George, Dr, 190, 296
Creeth, William James, 239
Crewdson, Isaac, 19, 38, 39, 243, 380 n 34
Cross, Samuel, 177, 178
Crouch, Sarah, 128, 129
Crouch, Thomas, 128, 129, 322, 323
Cunningham, James, 168
Curr, Edward, 120
Cutforth, Eliza, 182, 185

Darbys of Ironbridge, 43

Darton, Samuel, 193, 207, 208, 209, 210, 224, 263
Darton, Thomas Gates, 200, 207, 209, 210
Darwin, Charles, 106
Davy, Abraham, 134, 148-52, 172, 190, 192, 193, 270, 297, 384 n22
Davy, Helen. See Neave, Helen
Davy, Jane (Dawson), 149, 150
Deane, George, 200, 203, 229
Denison, Lady, 168
Denison, Sir William, 187
Dixon, Joseph, 283, 284
Dorland, A.G., 339
Douglas, Robert, 296
Dunsford, Frederick, 237
Dunsford, Robert, 235, 237
Dymond, J.J., 264, 286, 287, 290, 322

Eagle Farm, 117
Edwards, Richard (alias). See Flower, Abraham
Elizabeth Fry Retreat, 318, 385 n44
Evangelicals, 17, 18-20, 83, 121
Everett, William, 340

"Fairfield", Mount Barker, 215-17, 378 n41
Famine in Ireland, 53, 54, 367 n14
Federation of Australia, 321, 324, 329
Fennell, George Frederick, 241
Fennell, Robert, 241
Fenwick, John, 333
Fisher, Abraham, 131
Fisher, John, 130-31
Fisher, Mary, 332
Fisher, Reuben, 131
Flinders Island, 104, 107-8
Flounders Institute, 263
Flower, Abraham, 139-45, 149
Forster, Josiah, 207, 208, 209, 210, 214, 266, 268
Forster, Robert, 207
Forster, William, 19, 345
Foss, Ambrose, 176
Fox, Barclay, 16-17
Fox, George, 3, 4, 5, 8, 9, 15, 18, 24, 29, 65, 334, 335-36
Fox, Henry Tregelles, 71
Fox, J.J., 23
Fox, Samuel, 319
Franklin, Lady Jane, 91, 109, 122, 125, 371 n97 and n100

Franklin, Sir John, 101, 102, 118, 122
Friends' burial grounds, 31-32, 161
   Adelaide, 212
   Hobart, 161, 374 n81
   Melbourne, 235
   Sydney, 192
Friends' Meeting Houses
   Adelaide, 204, 206-13
   Australind, 135, 136
   Ballarat, 262, 263-64, 288
   Brisbane, 279-81
   Hobart, 133-34
   Melbourne, 241, 248, 249, 250-51, 288, 380 n32
   Mount Barker, 216
   Rockhampton, 281, 326
   Sydney, 179-82, 184, 186, 193, 274, 329, 376 n35, 385 n72
Friends' Periodicals, 368 n32
   Annual Monitor, 28
   Australian Friend, 155, 316-18, 327
   British Friend, 68, 70, 119, 157, 368 n32
   Irish Friend, 63, 64, 65, 66, 114, 140, 368 n32
   Lindfield Reporter, 63, 368 n32
   Philanthropic Magazine, 368 n32
   Quakeriana, 24, 25
   The Friend, 368 n32
Friends' Peace Testimony, 9, 226, 246, 315-16, 320, 322
Friends' Relief Committee, 53
Friends' Schools, 10
   Ackworth, 28, 46, 47, 48, 60, 68, 69, 191, 235, 278, 287, 290, 365 n1, 366 n33, 381 n57, 383 n71
   Ayton, 17, 46, 47, 221
   Bootham, 46, 47, 383 n71
   Brookfield, 47
   Croydon, 46, 47, 48, 278, 366 n28, 381 n57, 383 n71
   Grove House, 46
   Hobart, 293-95, 302, 305-16, 344
   Lisburn, 46
   Melbourne, 248, 288-90, 305
   Mountmellick, 46
   Newtown, 46, 243
   Penketh, 17, 46, 47
   Rawdon, 17, 46, 47
   Saffron Walden, 278, 324
   Sibford, 17, 46, 47
   Sidcot, 46, 47

   Wigton, 46, 47
   York Girls', 46, 47
Friends, Society of, 3
   Birthright Membership, 258, 348
   "Concerns", 13-14
   Disownment, 6, 15, 33-34
      for insolvency, 6-7, 37, 52, 54, 203, 240
      for "marrying out", 15-17, 20, 22, 35-37, 146, 158-60, 223, 249-50
   "Dress and Address", 7-8, 22
   Education, 10
   equality, 7
   honesty in business, 6-7
   the Inward Light, 4, 5, 25
   marriage, 15-16, 385 n71
   meeting for worship, 12
   membership, 12
   militarism, 305, 320, 321
   ministry, 13-14, 246-47, 364 n24
   Monthly Meetings, 12-15
   oath-swearing, 6, 158
   Pastoral Ministry, 338-43
   Preparative Meetings, 12-13
   penal reform, 10-11
   Queries, 261, 381 n3
   Quarterly Meetings, 13
   "Quietism", 17-18
   "Radicalism", 21, 24-25, 57
   Records, 29-30
   simplicity, 7
   State Aid to education, 289
   Temperance, 11, 62, 98-99, 115-17, 166, 196, 326, 364 n21, 375 n92
   tithes, 9, 51
   "travelling in the ministry", 13-14, 338, 343, 346
   Yearly Meeting, 13. See also London Yearly Meeting
Fry, Elizabeth, 11, 18, 19, 20, 79, 81, 91-93, 102, 134, 136, 318
Fyans, Capt. Foster, 124-25, 233, 371 n103
Fysh, P.O., 321

Gardiner, John, 233
Gardiner, Mary, 233
Gawler, Governor, 202
Glenelg, Lord, 111, 113
Goderich, Lord, 83, 85
Godlee, John, 203
Gold-diggers, 46, 58-59, 245

Index   405

Gold-fields, 220, 232-33, 245-46
Gougar, Robert, 197
Great Seal Case, 187-88
Green, Mary Skinner, 249
Green, Rachel, 263
Grellett, Stephen, 11, 24, 79, 363 n19
Grey, Governor, 230
Grubb, Abraham, 241
Grubb, Isabel, 366 n14
Grubb, Richard Davis, 241
Grubb, Sarah Lynes, 21
Guistiniani, Dr, 114-15, 371 n82
Gurney, Joseph John, 20, 222
Gurney, Samuel, 83, 136, 207, 210, 211

Hack, Bridget, 195, 222
Hack, John Barton, 195-213, 214, 216, 222, 226, 228, 229, 230, 234
Hack, Margaret, 202
Hack, Mary, 207
Hack, Stephen, 200, 203, 205, 207, 230, 378 n9
Hagen, Jacob, 200, 202, 203, 209-10, 211, 227, 228-29, 230, 379 n65
Hall, Hannah, 296
Hamilton, Sir Robert, 321
Harrison, J.F.C., 45, 51
Harrison, Mary Ann, 216
Hart, John, 228
Hart, Sarah, 182, 183
Harvey, Thomas, 172
Harvey, William H., 82, 244, 371 n91
Henning, Rachel, 190
High School, Hobart Town, 168, 306, 375 n95
Hindmarsh, Capt. John, 113, 118, 197, 199, 205, 230
Hodgkin, John, 311
Hodgkin, J.B., 303
Hodgkin, William, 303
Holdship, William, 131, 139
Holdsworth, Charles, 316
Holdsworth, John, 316
Hood, Arthur, 283
Hope, James, 238, 249
Hopkins, Anne, 278
Hopkins, Felicia (Smith), 278, 281, 282, 324-27, 348
Hopkins, Francis, 278, 281, 282, 324-27, 328, 340-41
Hopkins, Rachel, 278, 279

Hopkins, William, 278, 326
Horsfall, John, 306, 308, 322, 328, 383 n71
Horsfall, Rachel, 288
Horton, Rev. William, 162
Howard, John, 10
Howitt, Godfrey, 235, 236, 237, 364 n39
Howitt, Mary, 20-21
Howitt, Margaret, 20
Howitt, William, 20-21, 32, 236, 245-46, 364 n39
Hunter, Joseph, 174
Huntly, Robert, 188-89
Huntly, Robert, Jun., 189

Ignatieff, M., 6, 10, 18
Indian National Congress, 57
Ireland Yearly Meeting, Society of Friends, 13, 27, 28
  Cork M.M., 40
  Dublin M.M., 40, 56, 240
  Grange and Richhill, M.M., 40
  Lisburn M.M., 40, 270
  Mountmellick M.M., 40
Irish Quakers, 54, 55, 59, 240-44, 335
Isichei, E., 41, 43, 45

Jackson, Ann, 328
Jackson, Fletcher, 328
Jackson, William Harvey, 239
Jacob, Joshua, 366 n14
Janson, William, 174
Jones, Joseph, 381 n12
Jones, Katherine, 321, 328
Jones, Rufus, 17, 18, 20, 334, 339
Jones, William, 301, 304, 320-21, 328
Jose, Arthur, 177, 184-85
Joslyn, David, 223-24
Joyce, William, 172

Kanakas, 283-85, 322-24, 385 n52
Kapunda, 202, 222
Keane, Mary, 177, 178
Kekwick, William Darton, 230
Kelvedon, 119, 154-60
King, Rufus, 293, 296, 298
Knott, Ellen Maria, 200

Lambert, James, 262
Lang, Dr, 71, 123
Lancastrian schools, 306
Langhorne, George, 233

Lauderdale, 162
Levitt, Charles, 239
Levitt, Samuel, 273
Lindsey, Robert, 19, 27, 28, 32, 48, 68, 192-93, 194, 220-23, 245-47, 248, 253, 254, 291, 296, 300, 345, 372 n15, 380 n37
Lindsey, Sarah, 221
Lloyds, 7, 43
Locke, Annabella, 240
Locke, William, 240, 243, 380 n33 and n34
London Yearly Meeting, Society of Friends, 7, 14, 16, 17, 19, 21, 22, 23, 26, 27, 32, 36, 38, 46, 48, 61, 64, 65, 66, 67, 71, 77, 78, 81, 82, 132, 146, 170, 207, 218, 225, 238, 248, 251, 252, 254, 257, 258, 259, 260, 261, 262, 264, 266, 268, 272, 274, 280, 285, 286, 287, 290, 291, 292, 293, 295, 296, 298, 299, 300, 302, 303, 304, 305, 306, 308, 311, 314, 317, 319, 320, 324, 325, 328, 329, 338, 343, 345, 349, 386 n9
Continental Committee of London Y.M., 28, 67, 181, 211, 252, 291, 292, 293, 303, 304, 306, 325, 342, 343, 368 n43, 372 n19. See also Meetings for Sufferings
Monthly Meetings of London Y.M.
Albans, 129
Barnsley, 234
Brighouse, 34, 36, 40, 52
Bristol, 36, 40
Cheshire, 234
Devonshire House, 18, 36, 40, 129, 153, 156, 173, 174, 182, 184, 185
Devon West, 40, 237, 238
Frenchay, 34, 36, 40
Hardshaw East, 19, 38, 40, 47, 243, 380 n34, 381 n12
Hardshaw West, 40, 47, 68
Hertford and Hitchin, 40, 200
Kingston, 134, 136
Lancaster, 67, 68
Lewes and Chichester, 40, 203
Longford, 188
Newcastle, 40, 60, 191
Nottingham, 40, 178, 235, 236
Pontefract, 34, 36, 263
Poole, 40, 227

Preston, 239
Southwark, 14, 40, 52, 153, 156, 200, 228, 374 n64
Thaxted, 71
Warwickshire North, 40
Witham, 40, 200, 201, 223, 224
Witney, 40, 189
Woodbridge, 298, 384 n22
York, 34, 36
Lutheran refugees, 63-64

Macarthur, William, 123, 151
McDonald, Lorna, 326
McGowan, James, 216
McGregor, Lt M., 375 n86
Mackie, Frederick, 19, 27, 28, 30, 32, 33, 43, 48, 68, 69, 137, 186, 192-93, 194, 220-23, 224, 236, 239, 245-48, 253, 254, 265-68, 273, 291, 296, 297, 300, 313, 336, 345, 372 n15, 380 n37
Mackie, Rachel, 58, 221, 313
McLeay, Alexander, 123, 180
Maconochie, Capt., 101-2, 158
Macquarie Harbour, 90, 95
Malcolm, Sir Pulteney, 205
Marsden, Rev. Samuel, 123, 172
Martyn, Dr, 88
Mason, Thomas, 218, 219, 223
Mather, Ann (Benson), 162, 163, 374 n82
Mather, Elizabeth, 316
Mather, Joseph Benson, 134, 136, 147, 149, 150, 151, 162, 181, 189, 192, 193, 194, 265, 269, 294, 306, 308, 374 n82
Mather, Joseph Francis, 293, 294, 295, 304, 308, 312, 316, 317, 320, 347
Mather, Robert, 162-64, 229, 374 n82, 375 n86
Mather, Robert Andrew, 134, 149, 150, 162, 166, 191-92
Mather, Sarah Benson. See Walker, Sarah Benson
May, Edward, 208, 230, 265-68, 382 n21
May, Frederick, 216
May, Hannah, 58, 214, 217
May, Henry, 58, 214
May, Joseph, 58, 200, 206, 208, 214-16, 217, 222, 229, 231, 235, 337, 345

Index   407

May, Margaret, 203, 228
May, Maria, 215, 216
May, Rachel. See Mackie, Rachel
May, William, 58, 212, 215, 219-20, 226-27, 230, 316, 317, 345
May, W. Lewis, 215
Meeting for Sufferings, 65, 133, 134, 143, 164, 181, 204, 207, 210, 211, 212, 213, 220, 225, 239, 248, 268, 287, 289, 297, 368 n43
Mitchell, Marshall, 283
Montgomery, Rt. Rev. H.H., 323
Moreton Bay, 117
Morphett, 205
Morris, Samuel, 138, 296, 297
Mould, Charles, 249

Neave, Edward, 272
Neave, Eliza, 272
Neave, Helen (Davy), 151, 297
Neave, Joseph James, 19, 144, 152, 188, 190, 191, 224, 263, 272-78, 284, 285, 286, 289, 296, 297-99, 300, 302, 304, 322, 323, 336, 384 n22 and n43, 385 n46
Nichollias, Isabella, 374 n62
Nield (or Neild), John Cash, 191
Norfolk Island, 95-97
Norton, James, 181, 187
Norton, William, 272

Occupational Survey of Quaker migrants, 41-46, 51
Orange Tree Conspiracy, 60
d'Ortez, Mariano, 266, 267
d'Ortez, Cecilia, 266
Overton, William, 248, 249

Paine, Thomas, 24-25
Palser, John, 190-91
Parkinson, Joel, 75
Parkinson, Sydney, 75, 76, 108-9, 369 n1
Peace Movement, 230, 287, 320-22, 328
Pease family, 43
Penn, William, 4, 11, 24, 65, 70, 110, 114, 128, 333, 334, 338
Phelps, Joseph, 241
Philcox, Priscilla, 200, 203
Phillips, Henry, 209-10, 211
Phillips, John, 262
Pike, Prof. Douglas, 230
Pim, James, 241

Pim, James Robertson, 70
Pollard, Ann, 129, 192
Port Arthur, 90, 91
Port Phillip, 110, 118, 233
Propsting, Hannah, 145, 146
Propsting, Henry, 142, 145-48, 149, 152, 160, 269, 308
Pumphrey, Thomas, 304

"Quaker", origin of name, 3, 8, 11, 12
Quakers Hill, 172

Raleigh, Joseph, 238, 243, 380 n34
Raleigh, Rachel, 238
Raleigh, Sarah, 238, 248
Ransome, Edwin R., 138-39, 286, 292-95, 304, 309, 310, 315, 316, 325, 341, 372 n19
Rayner, William, 149, 152, 374 n62
Rechabites, 142, 143
Reibe, Gustaphus, 283
Rhoads, Jonathan, 296, 297
Rhode Island, 332, 337
Richards, David, 172, 173, 192
Richardson, George, 229
Richardson, James, 70
Ridler, H.H., 145, 146, 149, 373 n36
Ritchie, Joseph, 60
Robinson, George Augustus, 102-3, 106
Robinson, William, 239, 240, 242, 248
Robson, Christina (Cox), 272, 296
Robson, Isaac, 234
Robson, Walter, 25, 37, 144, 188, 190, 263, 272-78, 284, 285, 286, 296, 323
Rowntree firm, 43
Rowntree, Edward, 152
Rowntree, John Stephenson, 21-22 25, 28, 47, 48, 365 n1
Rowntree, John Wilhelm, 5
Russell, Henry (Dublin Friend), 240
Russell, Henry (Irish entertainer), 56

Sanders, George, 197, 222, 226, 229, 231, 340
Sanders, Jane, 196, 197, 226
Sanderson, John, 83
Savery, Henry, 99
Savings Bank, Hobart Town, 166-67
Sayce, Alfred, 323

408   Index

Sayce, Deborah, 234, 238, 242, 383 n71
Sayce, Edward, 59, 234, 238, 239, 242, 248, 273, 306, 383 n71
Sayce, George, 59
Sayce, Joseph, 239
Sayce, William Jesper, 155, 170, 283, 301, 302, 303, 304, 344
Schardt, Carl, 313
Schofield, Rev. W., 140
"Seekers", 4
Service, Dr John, 87, 90, 125, 369 n17
Sharp, Isaac, 19, 145, 293, 296, 298, 299-300
Sherwin, Isaac, 145
Shillitoe, Thomas, 81
Ships
   Albemarle, 172
   Avon, 69
   Beagle, 106
   Elizabeth, 88
   Endeavour, 108
   Eudora, 118
   Heroine, 162
   Henry Freeling, 122, 177
   Isabella, 117, 199
   Kent, 334
   Larkins, 148
   Lord Sidmouth, 176
   Norval, 234
   Parkfield, 136
   Ragasthon, 207
   Rattler, 70
   Samoa, 285
   Science, 82, 83-85, 98, 115
   Shamrock, 155
   Sirius, 70
   Speedwell, 332
   Sultana, 278
   Swan, 144
   Swarthmore, 68, 69, 70
   William Metcalfe, 237
   Woodhouse, 332
Shoobridge, William, 161
Simpkinson, Lady Mary, 371 n100
Simpson, James, 233
Slater, Henry, 263
Smart, Benjamin ("Sir"), 30
Smith, Bernard, 106, 108, 109
Smith, Felicia. *See* Hopkins, Felicia
Smith, Granville, 278
Smith, Howard, 278
Smith, Lyra, 278

Smith, Rosamond, 278, 279
Smith, William, 239
Spitalfield weavers, 19
Spode, Joshua, 162
Squire, Thomas, 129, 149
Stacey, George, 207, 211
Stead, David, 129, 233-34
Stephen, G.M., 113-14, 228
Stirling, Captain, 62
Story, Dr George, 134, 153, 155, 156, 157, 218, 219, 223, 250, 265, 269
Story, Joseph, Jun., 181
Strong, Samuel, 239
Stuart, John McDouall, 230
Stubbs, Charles, 227
Stundists, 299
Sturge, Joseph, 319
Sturt, Capt. Charles, 123-24
Swinborn, Dell, 318
Swinborn, Fanny, 318
Swinborn, James, 319
Swinborn, Sarah J., 318, 319
Sykes, Marjorie, 266, 267

Tallach, William, 186, 253-54, 381 n57
Tatham, Edward, 52
Tawell, Isabella, 186
Tawell, John, 163, 173-88, 192, 194, 204, 270, 376 n9, n15, n19, n35, 377 n47
Tawell, John Jun., 79, 376 n15
Tawell, Mary, 174, 177-78
Tawell, William, 187, 376 n15
Telegraph, first use of by Scotland Yard, 183
Temperance. *See* Friends, Society of
Test Act, 52
Therry, Sir Roger, 177
Thompson, Deborah, 243
Thompson, E.P., 24, 50
Thompson, John, 243
Thompson, Robert, 61-62
Thorp, Elly, 341, 342
Thorp and Co., 243, 380 n34
Threlkeld, L.E., 123
Tilney, Anna Maria. *See* Cotton, Anna Maria
Tindale, Robert, 381 n4
Toleration Act, 61
Torrens, Colonel, 197
Tregellis, Edwin, 10
Trimmer, Edmund, 211
Truc(g)anini, 103, 106

Index 409

Tunks, William, 262, 381 n4
Turner, George, 187

Unthank, Gabriel Fisher, 30, 243, 245

Vann, R.T., 44-45
Van Diemen's Land Co., 103, 119, 120
Veevers, John, 239

Wakefield, Edward (father of E.G.), 134
Wakefield, Edward Gibbon, 111, 134. 195, 197
Walker, George Washington, 19, 27, 35, 62, 75, 77, 78-126, 192, 194, 197, 221, 226, 229, 233, 257, 265, 269, 270, 291, 296, 297, 299, 300, 306, 308, 321, 322, 336, 337, 343, 349
  Aborigines, 102-15
  Aborigines, Tasmanian, 104-8,
  Arthur, Lt Gov., 120-22
  convicts, 137-53
  Cotton, Francis, 153-60
  drapery business of, 164–66
  Franklin, Sir John, 122
  Franklin, Lady Jane, 122
  Hobart Town High School, 168
  Macquarie Harbour, 87, 90, 95
  Moreton Bay, 117, 124
  NSW, 122-24
  Norfolk Island, 95-97
  objectives of visit to Australian colonies, 82-83
  partnership with Backhouse, 78-79, 81-82
  penal reform, 87-102
  philanthropist, 168-69
  Port Arthur, 90-91
  Port Phillip, 118, 233
  return to Hobart from Africa, 164
  Savings Bank, 166-67
  settlers, 86-87
  South Australia, 118, 195-97
  Sydney Meeting, 170-73, 177-81, 188-94

Tawell, John, 173, 177-81, 184, 185
Temperance, 115-17, 375 n92
transportation, 99-100, 158
Van Diemen's Land, 118–22, 127-37
Western Australia, 118
Wesleyans, 161-64
Walker, James Backhouse, 383 n71
Walker, Sarah Benson (Mather), 162, 164, 374 n82
Wallis, Algernon, 262
Wallis, Marriage, 262
Walpole, George, 59-60
Walpole, Thomas, 56, 243
Watson, Charlotte, 200, 201
Watson, Henry, 196, 199, 200, 201, 203, 205, 206, 208, 214
Watson, Martha, 200
Watson, Thomas, 200
Watson, William, 200, 222
Webb, Alfred, 55-57, 243-44
Wells, Joseph John, 383 n71
Were, Jonathan Binns, 237-38
Were, Jonathan Henry, 237
Were, Sophia Louisa, 237–38
Wesley, John, 162
Wesleyans, 137, 161-64
West, John, 125
West, Theodore, 250, 280
Wheeler, Charles and Daniel, 122, 125, 170-71, 177, 188, 371 n100
White, Alpheus, 296
White, Jane, 380 n26
"White" Quakers, 38, 366 n14
Wilberforce, William, 18, 102
Williamson, Sarah, 264
Willington, Thomas, 152, 223
Wisbeck Peace Declaration, 321
Woodham-Smith, Cecil, 54
Woolman, John, 103-4
Wright, Alfred, 283, 286, 298, 301-2, 313, 341, 344, 345

Yates, George, 143